**W9-CYS-003**

# Copyright Acknowledgments

Grateful acknowledgment is made to the following sources for permission to reprint material copyrighted or controlled by them:

"Genius at Work: How to Argue," by Diane Cyr, reprinted from *US Airways Attache*, Jan. 1998.

"Nobody Means More to Me Than You and the Future Life of Willie Jordan," by June Jordan, reprinted from *On Call*, 1995.

"Shakespeare in the Bush," by Laura Bohannan, reprinted from *Natural History*, August–September 1966.

"Class Action," by Dave Barry, reprinted from the *Washington Post Magazine*, 1995, Tribune Media Services.

"Legalizing Prostitution: An Act of Compassion for Both Genders," by Sabrina Ford Hall, reprinted from *Honolulu Star-Bulletin*, Tuesday, November 27, 2001, Oahu Publications.

"The Secret Plagiarists," by Marion Meade, reprinted from *Brill's Content*, March 2000, Brill Media Ventures, LLP.

"High-Tech Corner Cutting," by Daniel S. Greenberg, reprinted from the *Washington Post*, January 20, 1999.

"What You Don't Know Will Hurt You," by Edward G. Berlinski, reprinted from the *Washington Post*, March 1, 1999.

"Women to Watch . . . And Watch Out For," by Marilyn Krasner, Megan Rudeseill, Shirley Lin and Irin Carmon, reprinted from *Ms. Magazine*, June/July 2001.

"Helen Zia: Voice and Visibility," by Lynn Lu, reprinted from *Ms. Magazine*, April/May 2000.

"A 'Friends'-Shaped Hole," by Carina Chocano, reprinted by permission from *Salon.com*.

"Classical Romance from Awadagin Pratt," by T. Brooks Shepard, reprinted from *American Visions*, February/March 1998.

"Stephen King's Redemption," by Paul F. M. Zahl, reprinted from *Christianity Today*, March 6, 2000.

# Contents

# UNIT TWO: THE ENCOMIUM

# UNIT THREE: RHETORICAL ANALYSIS

# UNIT FOUR: MAPPING THE DEBATE

# UNIT FIVE: DEFINITION

# UNIT SIX: THE AFFIRMATIVE ARGUMENT

## UNIT SEVEN: PUTTING IT ALL TOGETHER

# An Introduction to Perspectives

Your perspective is a position from which you see and interpret everything around you. Each of the writers in this book comes to the issue he or she discusses from a different perspective, whether it be one of race, class or gender, or some other unique personal experience and background. The way in which a writer presents her argument depends to a large extent upon her perspective, both in what she has to say about a subject and how she says it. For example, on the subject of the high prices of gasoline, the perspective of a writer drawing on her own experience and knowledge from working with an environmental group will probably be much different from that of an oil company research engineer. One perspective is not necessarily better or more correct than the other; however, depending on the writer's intended audience, one might be more persuasive than the other.

As a reader, you too will see each essay from a different perspective. The values and ideas you bring to a piece of writing strongly affect the reaction you will have to it. Whether you will agree with the writer, what will appear to you as logically sound, what you will consider to be an inappropriate appeal to your emotions—all of these are to some degree determined by your preconceived outlook on the subject. As you respond to these issues in your own writing, you will find many ways to articulate your personal perspective. Indeed, depending on your rhetorical situation, you may adopt any one of a number of voices or approaches. It is this multiplicity of perspectives that makes rhetoric so interesting. There are endless ways of looking at issues; ideas you once thought of as incontrovertible you realize are highly debatable to others. Learning to recognize and respond to these potential controversies is an important part of your education.

This book is designed both to provide you with examples of writing from different points of view and to introduce you to the kinds of writing you will be doing in English 101. The book is divided into seven units. The first unit, "What Is Rhetoric?" introduces you to rhetoric and some of the many different ways it is used, from informal conversations to formal proceedings like courtroom trials. This unit also introduces you to the concept of academic writing and the expectations your professors will have concerning your original work and your documentation of others' work.

Unit Two offers several examples of encomia: arguments in praise of someone or something. The writers of these essays, encouraging us to see the object from a different viewpoint, sometimes choose unlikely subjects of praise and use unlikely topics of praise to interest their intended readers. Unit Three, "Rhetorical Analysis," contains many selections that lend themselves to careful analysis of the writers' uses of the rhetorical appeals, i.e., the ways in which writers make their arguments more persuasive to their intended audiences. As you will see, even arguments in favor of the same position can vary greatly in how they are presented. Unit Four, "Mapping the Debate," provides you with examples of articles that survey the debates surrounding some current controversies. Its second section contains an in-depth look at the debate surrounding media violence, giving you a chance to trace a single issue and identify different key positions in it. Unit Five, "Definition," explains why it is important to define a term clearly before moving on to other arguments about it. In this unit you will find single essays and pairs of essays that define the same word in different ways. Unit Six introduces you to the concept of the affirmative argument and to writing for a sympathetic audience. In addition to providing examples of strong affirmative arguments, some of the essays in this unit provide examples of parody and uses of the figures of speech. Finally, Unit Seven consists of student essays that are the end results of the writers' extended work on a single topic. These longer argumentative essays are well researched and documented, a fitting capstone for the work these writers have dedicated to their issues.

Several of the units contain examples of writing by your fellow students at the University of Maryland. Think of these essays not as templates for you to imitate slavishly, but as examples of what is possible with the types of writing you will encounter this semester.

While the primary purpose of this book is to provide readings to complement the rhetorical skills and strategies introduced in the *Introduction to Academic Writing*, we also invite you to engage with the subjects and argue with the writers. We encourage you to adopt new perspectives as you look critically at the issues the writers raise and explore the controversies further, whether in English 101 or elsewhere.

**Elisa Warford**
**Editor of 2nd Edition**

## Acknowledgments

The 3rd edition of *Perspectives* owes much to the editors of the previous two editions—literally so, for over half the content of the second edition has been retained. That edition was compiled by Sonya Brown, Mark Childs, Nancy Dickson, Erin Kelly, and Tricia Slusser, under the editorship of Elisa Warford, building on the solid foundation established by the first editorial board: Nancy Dickson, Patricia Lissner, Matthew Elliott, Dina Longhitano, and Tricia Slusser, under the leadership of general editor Adrianne diMarco. The editorial team for the current edition is Nora Bellows, Ryan Claycomb, Linda Coleman, Erin Kelly, and Erin Sadlack. We are grateful to the many English 101 teachers who have provided ideas and have proposed essays for inclusion, and to the English 101 students who are generously allowing us to use their work. Special thanks to Tom Engram, the Freshman Writing Program's office manager, who has kept everything running smoothly, and to Dave Fleming of Pearson Custom Publishing.

# UNIT ONE

## Introduction to Rhetoric

# INTRODUCTION

If you hear the word *rhetoric* in conversation or read it in a news article, you are likely to find the term used negatively. Typically, a speech by a politician, a written statement by an activist organization, or an editorial in a newspaper will be denounced as "mere rhetoric" by those who disagree with its argument. The term rhetoric, in such instances, is used to mean empty language, a bunch of words that sound good but have no real meaning.

Not everyone defines rhetoric in this negative way. From Aristotle in the fourth century BCE to the college professors in the present, scholars have studied rhetoric as the art of speaking and writing well. At its most basic, the term rhetoric applies to any form of communication that seeks to persuade. Some speeches or articles may fail to persuade you, and therefore seem like "mere rhetoric" or empty language. But a speech by a politician that convinces you to vote for her, an advertisement on television that inspires you to buy a product, and even a note from a friend that motivates you to go out to a party are also examples of rhetoric: language that effectively persuades you to take a certain action.

Clearly, when you write you want your work to be an example of the latter kind of rhetoric. This unit of *Perspectives* introduces you to some elements of rhetoric associated with persuasive communication. Readings in the first section, "What is Rhetoric?", introduce some expectations for different types of communication ranging from casual conversations to legal briefs to journalistic writing. As you encounter these readings, reflect on what it means to persuade someone. This question is raised by the very first article in this reader, as the author explores whether it is sufficient for a writer to force or trick an audience into going along with an argument, or whether it is better to convince them that a certain point of view is correct.

Since rhetoric attempts to persuade, it is not surprising that the means of persuasion will vary depending upon the audience an author or speaker seeks to sway. For example, an administrator might be persuaded that the University of Maryland needs to double student fees if he or she is told that the increase will balance the university budget and fund some new programs. However, in order for you to be convinced, you might need to hear that the fee increase will fund a program to give every incoming undergraduate a laptop computer and will pay for the construction of a new parking garage for students. What should be clear from this example is that not all communication can effectively persuade every person. For this reason, before you set out to persuade an audience, you need to determine exactly who your audience is and what they will find most persuasive. The readings in the second section of this unit, "Audience," allow you to examine how authors create an argument convincing to a specific group of readers and thus can provide useful models as you construct your own persuasive rhetoric.

While looking at a variety of readings—articles for magazines, pieces for academic journals, newspaper editorials, and even letters—teaches you a great deal about rhetoric in general, the work you produce as a college student will be a specific type of rhetoric: academic writing. Throughout the semester, your English 101 class will discuss the expectations readers have for academic writing. Readings in the third section of this unit, "Researching and Using Sources," introduce some of these expectations as they argue about a basic element of academic writing, the use of outside sources. When you read these articles and those in other sections of this book, think about how you can make the academic writing you produce as a college student into examples of effective persuasive rhetoric.

**Erin Kelly**

# I

# *What Is Rhetoric?*

## GENIUS AT WORK: HOW TO ARGUE

Diane Cyr

*In this article, which first appeared in the in-flight magazine US Air-ways Attaché, Diane Cyr profiles prominent attorney Alan Dershowitz. According to Cyr, Dershowitz makes effective arguments in court because he follows a particular set of guidelines. As you read, notice the strategies that, according to Dershowitz, help an individual to persuade others. Dershowitz's record as a successful attorney suggests that his strategies work well when he presents arguments to judges and juries. You might think about whether these same strategies would be equally effective in other situations to persuade other types of audiences. In particular, consider how following Dershowitz's advice would make your academic writing more persuasive. Consider also whether (and how) these techniques could harm your effectiveness.*

On the one hand, lawyer, professor, and professional provocateur Alan Dershowitz likes to find bones to pick. He has defended Claus von Bulow, Mike Tyson, O. J., and flag-burning. He has given his books such titles as *Contrary to Popular Opinion, Chutzpah,* and *Taking Liberties.* He does sound-byte battle with just about anyone on cable, network, or syndication.

On the other hand, his favorite joke goes like this: This man orders a bowl of soup at the same deli from the same waiter every day. One day the soup comes and the man doesn't eat it. So the waiter comes by and says, "You don't like the soup? Maybe it's too hot? Maybe it's too cold? What's the matter with it?"

The man looks at him and says, "Why don't you taste it?"

"All right, I'll taste it," says the waiter. Pause. "There's no spoon!"

"Aha!" says the man.

"AHA! AHA!" says Dershowitz, cracking up. Because his point is this: In-your-face opinions are one thing. In-your-face arguments are another. The best arguments aren't won by bullies who make you scream "Uncle!" They're won by the guys who make you go "Aha!"—who lead you subtly down the garden path of your own undoing.

In this, Dershowitz has had much practice. In 35 years of law (he's 59), he has consulted on or argued approximately 250 cases. He argues before judges, trial juries, grand juries, television audiences, classrooms, and assorted paying listeners and readers. He also argues with just about anyone, from his Harvard criminal-law students (student: "The police invited them to headquarters . . ." Dershowitz: "They invited? What, like a little engraved card?") to crackpot Holocaust revisionists.

Throughout, he argues that argument—whether with one's spouse, boss, or chief justice—is best achieved "with a scalpel, not a hatchet." In other words, if you want to get your way, first you have to get your opponent invested in *wanting* things your way. Like the man in the deli, you have to go for the "Aha!"

The bad news: This methodology ain't easy. The good news: It's got a terrific track record.

"Look, this is not my invention," Dershowitz says of his argument style. "Socrates invented it. Rabbi Hillel invented it in the Talmud. It's a technique as old as recorded history, and the best philosophers, the best arguers, have always been those who led their students to come to their [own] conclusions." Take Jesus. "Did he say 'Don't cast the first stone?' He said, cast it! 'Let he who is without sin cast the first stone.' Socratic teaching at its best."

Of course, emulating Dershowitz is likely more doable (if less noble) than emulating Jesus or Hillel. For those who choose to wield the scalpel in their encounters with the Other, consider the following:

## 1. Don't fight just to win.

If you're arguing simply to best your opponent, you just might do it. But it won't make anyone happy. The object, remember, is to get the person on your side. "Why should anybody else want you to win?" Dershowitz reasons. "You have to have a motive beyond winning." So if you're fighting with your boss about more vacation time, or with your spouse about whose family to visit for Christmas, fight for the larger picture: the health of the relationship, or the ability to do a better job at work.

"Advocacy is not overpowering your opponent," says Dershowitz. "It's *persuading* your opponent that your ideas are his." Hence:

## 2. Know your opponent.

Injustice, ill will, shoddy treatment, and plain idiocy are all perfectly clear from one's own side. The harder part is placing yourself in the purported idiots' shoes to determine what accounts for their point of view. "You have to think like they do," he says. "You have to put yourself in their position." Which further means:

### 3. Don't assume the opponent's an idiot.

Go in swinging, and your opponents will swing back. Go in humble, shaking hands and making eye contact, and your opponent just might soften to hear your side. "Don't believe you're going to make yourself seem smarter than they are, or better then they are," says Dershowitz. "Assume they're smarter than you are, they're righter than you are, they believe in their position as much as you do or more, they're as nice as you are."

And by the way: Mean it. "Never underestimate your opponent," Dershowitz says. "I learned that from a friend of mine, a lawyer from Atlanta. She spoke with some kind of rural Alabama accent, and people thought they could run all over her. And she was one of the most brilliant lawyers and the best poker players I ever met."

### 4. Do your homework.

It's one thing to tell your boss that Project X is stupid. It's another to line up pages of market research, focus-group studies, customer call reports, budget projections, and profitability estimates. It's even better to bring it up in the context of the boss's top ten Favorite Things about Project X—and then show why Project Y (your baby) just might be what your boss really wanted all along.

Doing homework is more than merely lining up evidence for your side. It is also key to defusing intimidation. It's letting your opponent know that, yes, while she might be brighter, tougher, or better-paid than you, she can't slip you up on the facts.

"I work my head off in preparation," says Dershowitz. "I have to know more than anyone in the room. I have to know the record cold. Know all the cases. Once I know everything, then I feel comfortable shifting to the psychological strategies of winning."

### 5. Then make your case.

The first serve in tennis tends to set the rhythm of the game. Same in arguing: Keep the serve, and you can keep things in your court.

The way to do it is to pick the framework for the argument. You want to go bowling with your buddies on Monday nights? Then set out a road-map you know your spouse will follow. Talk about your need for quality time with him, your crabbiness after a long day at work, your mutual need to make more time for fun. "Start the logical argument," says Dershowitz, "and let the other person be able to finish it for you. If you can frame the question knowing what the answer is going to lead to, then you don't have to hammer away."

Warning: Make your case real, or else prepare yourself for major resentment (perhaps accompanied by flying dishes) over your passive-aggressive shenanigans. "You must truly believe it," says Dershowitz. "It can't be an act. People see through acting."

### 6. Listen.

"This is key, key, key," says Dershowitz, who won't let his law students take notes for the first two weeks of class. Listening not only establishes respect for your opponent's point of view, it also clues you to information for your own case. Since people love the sounds of their own arguments, "take advantage of the last thing said," he says. "I always start my argument, in almost every case, with 'My opponent said . . .' And I turn their argument into my argument."

## 7. Avoid the following:

- EGO, the desire to be right at any cost (usually your own);
- EMOTION, the desire to engage in fights with bank tellers or rotten drivers, or to call your opponent a big, fat jerk; and
- ELOQUENCE, the desire to bowl over the opponent with craft and vocabulary (see "ego"). Advice: Stories and analogy work best. When defending, for instance, flag-burning (controversial), Dershowitz compared it to dumping tea in Boston Harbor (noncontroversial). "Let your opponent make the leap," he says.

## 8. And when you win, don't hog the credit.

If you've done a great job on your argument, your opponent just might end up thinking he has won—which is fine, if you've gotten your way. After all, the true object isn't winning, but getting on the same side. Once you're there, who cares who gets the credit?

Besides, credit usually backfires. "Claiming credit is a way of distancing people from your point of view," Dershowitz says. "I learned this early on when I clerked for a justice of the Supreme Court. When I would shove my ideas down his throat, he would always say to me, 'I'm the Justice, you're the law clerk.' So I learned the technique of subtly conveying information. In the end, it works. People will notice that when you're there, more is done."

In other words, strong arguments, by extrapolation, can actually lead to a chain reaction of "Ahas!" Rather than buckle under the sledge-hammer of your self-righteousness, your opponents and observers might simply observe, by your humble example, that yes, thank you, you were right all along.

Of course, that's assuming you're facing reasonable opponents. Mention one particular TV host to Dershowitz, for instance, and he grimaces. "I can't argue with someone like him," he says. "He's smug, he's self-righteous, he thinks he knows it all." Then he grins, momentarily emulating the dozens of Dershowitz faces on the book jackets stacked on the shelves behind his desk. "He could benefit," he says, "from coming to a class on the philosophy of law."

# NOBODY MEAN MORE TO ME THAN YOU[1] AND THE FUTURE LIFE OF WILLIE JORDAN

June Jordan

*This article by professor, poet, essayist, and playwright June Jordan orig-inally appeared in* On Call, *a collection of her political essays. Jordan's subject here is the power of language, both Standard English and Black English. Within the essay, she narrates events from a course she taught on the subject of Black English, placing those events in relation to the killing by police of Reggie Jordan, her student Willie Jordan's brother. Be sure to notice the many types of writing mentioned and quoted: novels, lists of rules, letters, and even a student paper. Think about how all of the writers mentioned in the essay (from June Jordan herself to Alice Walker, Willie Jordan, and other students) make choices about whether to write in Standard English or Black English depending on the audi-ence and purpose of their writings. Like the students in June Jordan's class, you probably use different voices to speak or write in different sit-uations; for example, you have probably written papers for high school and college classes that follow the rules of Standard English more close-ly than does your speech during conversations with your friends. What conditions cause you to make changes to your language?*

Black English is not exactly a linguistic buffalo; as children, most of the thirty-five million Afro-Americans living here depend on this language for our discovery of the world. But then we approach our maturity inside a larger social body that will not support our efforts to become anything other than the clones of those who are neither our mothers nor our fathers. We begin to grow up in a house where every true mirror shows us the face of somebody who does not belong there, whose walk and whose talk will never look or sound "right," because that house was meant to shelter a family that is alien and hostile to us. As we learn our way around this environment, either we hide our original word habits, or we completely surrender our own voice, hoping to please those who will never respect anyone different from themselves: Black English is not exactly a linguistic buffalo, but we should understand its status as an endangered species, as a perishing, irreplaceable system of community intelligence, or we should expect its extinction, and, along with that, the extinguishing of much that constitutes our own proud, and singular, identity.

What we casually call "English," less and less defers to England and its "gentlemen." "English" is no longer a specific matter of geography or an element of class privilege; more than thirty-three countries use this tool as a means of "intranational communi-cation."[2] Countries as disparate as Zimbabwe and Malaysia, or Israel and Uganda, use it as their non-native currency of convenience. Obviously, this tool, this "English," can-not function inside thirty-three discrete societies on the basis of rules and values absolutely determined somewhere else, in a thirty-fourth other country, for example.

In addition to that staggering congeries of non-native users of English, there are five countries, or 333,746,000 people, for whom this thing called "English" serves as a native tongue.[2] Approximately 10 percent of these native speakers of "English" are Afro-American citizens of the U.S.A. I cite these numbers and varieties of human beings dependent on "English" in order, quickly, to suggest how strange and how tenuous is any concept of "Standard English." Obviously, numerous forms of English now operate inside a natural, an uncontrollable, continuum of development. I would suppose "the standard" for English in Malaysia is not the same as "the standard" in Zimbabwe. I know that standard forms of English for Black people in this country do not copy that of Whites. And, in fact, the structural differences between these two kinds of English have intensified, becoming more Black, or less White, despite the expected homogenizing effects of television[3] and other mass media.

Nonetheless, White standards of English persist, supreme and unquestioned, in these United States. Despite our multi-lingual population, and despite the deepening Black and White cleavage within that conglomerate, White standards control our official and popular judgements of verbal proficiency and correct, or incorrect, language skills, including speech. In contrast to India, where at least fourteen languages co-exist as legitimate Indian languages, in contrast to Nicaragua, where all citizens are legally entitled to formal school instruction in their regional or tribal languages, compulsory education in America compels accommodation to exclusively White forms of "English." White English, in America, is "Standard English."

This story begins two years ago. I was teaching a new course, "In Search of the Invisible Black Woman," and my rather large class seemed evenly divided among young Black women and men. Five or six White students also sat in attendance. With unexpected speed and enthusiasm we had moved through historical narration of the 19th century to literature by and about Black women, in the 20th. I then assigned the first forty pages of Alice Walker's *The Color Purple*, and I came, eagerly, to class that morning:

"So!" I exclaimed, aloud. "What did you think? How did you like it?"

The students studied their hands, or the floor. There was no response. The tense, resistant feeling in the room fairly astounded me.

At last, one student, a young woman still not meeting my eyes, muttered something in my direction:

"What did you say?" I prompted her.

"Why she have them talk so funny. It don't sound right."

"You mean the language?"

Another student lifted his head: "It don't look right, neither. I couldn't hardly read it."

At this, several students dumped on the book. Just about unanimously, their criticisms targeted the language. I listened to what they wanted to say and silently marvelled at the similarities between their casual speech patterns and Alice Walker's written version of Black English.

But I decided against pointing to these identical traits of syntax. I wanted not to make them self-conscious about their own spoken language—not while they clearly felt it was "wrong." Instead I decided to swallow my astonishment. Here was a negative Black reaction to a prize-winning accomplishment of Black literature that White readers across the country had selected as a best seller. Black rejection was aimed at the one irreducibly Black element of Walker's work: the language—Celie's Black English. I wrote the opening lines of *The Color Purple* on the blackboard and asked the students to help me translate these sentences into Standard English:

*You better not never tell nobody but God. It'd kill your mommy.*

Dear God,
　　I am fourteen years old. I have always been a good girl. Maybe you can give me a sign letting me know what is happening to me.
　　Last spring after Little Lucious come I heard them fussing. He was pulling on her arm. She say it too soon, Fonso. I ain't well. Finally he leave her alone. A week go by, he pulling on her arm again. She say, Naw, I ain't gonna. Can't you see I'm already half dead, an all of the children.[4]

Our process of translation exploded with hilarity and even hysterical, shocked laughter: The Black writer, Alice Walker, knew what she was doing! If rudimentary criteria for good fiction include the manipulation of language so that the syntax and diction of sentences will tell you the identity of speakers, the probable age and sex and class of speakers, and even the locale—urban/rural/southern/western—then Walker had written, perfectly. This is the translation in Standard English that our class produced:

*Absolutely, one should never confide in anybody besides God. Your secrets could prove devastating to your mother.*

Dear God,
　　I am fourteen years old. I have always been good. But now, could you help me to understand what is happening to me?
　　Last spring, after my little brother, Lucious, was born, I heard my parents fighting. My father kept pulling at my mother's arm. But she told him, "it's too soon for sex, Alfonso. I am still not feeling well." Finally, my father left her alone. A week went by, and then he began bothering my mother, again: Pulling her arm. She told him, "No, I won't! Can't you see I'm already exhausted from all of these children?"

(Our favorite line was "It's too soon for sex, Alfonso.")

Once we could stop laughing, once we could stop our exponentially wild improvisations on the theme of Translated Black English, the students pushed to explain their own negative first reactions to their spoken language on the printed page. I thought it was probably akin to the shock of seeing yourself in a photograph for the first time. Most of the students had never before seen a written facsimile of the way they talk. None of the students had ever learned how to read and write their own verbal system of communication: Black English. Alternatively, this fact began to baffle or else bemuse and then infuriate my students. Why not? Was it too late? Could they learn how to do it, now? And, ultimately, the final test question, the one testing my sincerity: Could I teach them? Because I had never taught anyone Black English and, as far as I knew, no one, anywhere in the United States, had ever offered such a course, the best I could say was "I'll try."

\*   \*   \*

He looked like a wrestler.

He sat dead center in the packed room and, every time our eyes met, he quickly nodded his head as though anxious to reassure, and encourage me.

Short, with strikingly broad shoulders and long arms, he spoke with a surprisingly high, soft voice that matched the soft bright movement of his eyes. His name was Willie Jordan. He would have seemed even more unlikely in the context of Contemporary Women's Poetry, except that ten or twelve other Black men were taking the course, as well. Still, Willie was conspicuous. His extreme fitness, the muscular density of his presence underscored the riveted, gentle attention that he gave to anything anyone said. Generally, he did not join the loud and rowdy dialogue flying back and forth, but there could be no doubt about his interest in our discussions. And, when he stood to present an argument he'd prepared, overnight, that nervous smile of his vanished and an irregular stammering replaced it, as he spoke with visceral sincerity, word by word.

That was how I met Willie Jordan. It was in between "In Search of the Invisible Black Women" and "The Art of Black English." I was waiting for departmental approval and I supposed that Willie might be, so to speak, killing time until he, too, could study Black English. But Willie really did want to explore contemporary women's poetry and, to that end, volunteered for extra research and never missed a class.

Towards the end of that semester, Willie approached me for an independent study project on South Africa. It would commence the next semester. I thought Willie's writing needed the kind of improvement only intense practice will yield. I knew his intelligence was outstanding. But he'd wholeheartedly opted for "Standard English" at a rather late age, and the results were stilted and frequently polysyllabic, simply for the sake of having more syllables. Willie's unnatural formality of language seemed to me consistent with the formality of his research into South African apartheid. As he projected his studies, he would have little time, indeed, for newspapers. Instead, more than 90 percent of his research would mean saturation in strictly historical, if not archival, material. I was certainly interested. It would be tricky to guide him into a more confident and spontaneous relationship both with language and apartheid. It was going to be wonderful to see what happened when he could catch up with himself, entirely, and talk back to the world.

September, 1984: Breezy fall weather and much excitement! My class, "The Art of Black English," was full to the limit of the fire laws. And in Independent Study, Willie Jordan showed up weekly, fifteen minutes early for each of our sessions. I was pretty happy to be teaching, altogether!

I remember an early class when a young brother, replete with his ever-present porkpie hat, raised his hand and then told us that most of what he'd heard was "all right" except it was "too clean." "The brothers on the street," he continued, "they mix it up more. Like 'fuck' and 'motherfuck.' Or like 'shit.'" He waited. I waited. Then all of us laughed a good while, and we got into a brawl about "correct" and "realistic" Black English that led to Rule 1.

**Rule 1: *Black English is about a whole lot more than mothafuckin.***

As a criterion, we decided, "realistic" could take you anywhere you want to go. Artful places. Angry places. Eloquent and sweetalkin places. Polemical places. Church. And the local Bar & Grill. We were checking out a language, not a mood or a scene or one guy's forgettable mouthing off.

It was hard. For most of the students, learning Black English required a fallback to patterns and rhythms of speech that many of their parents had beaten out of them. I mean *beaten*. And, in a majority of cases, correct Black English could be achieved only by striving for *incorrect* Standard English, something they were still pushing at, quite uncertainly. This state of affairs led to Rule 2.

**Rule 2:** *If it's wrong in Standard English it's probably right in Black English, or, at least, you're hot.*

It was hard. Roommates and family members ridiculed their studies, or remained incredulous, "You *studying* that shit? At school?" But we were beginning to feel the companionship of pioneers. And we decided that we needed another rule that would establish each one of us as equally important to our success. This was Rule 3.

**Rule 3:** *If it don't sound like something that come out somebody mouth then it don't sound right. If it don't sound right then it ain't hardly right. Period.*

This rule produced two weeks of compositions in which the students agonizingly tried to spell the sound of the Black English sentence they wanted to convey. But Black English is, preeminently, an oral/spoken means of communication. *And spelling don't talk*. So we needed Rule 4.

**Rule 4:** *Forget about the spelling. Let the syntax carry you.*

Once we arrived at Rule 4 we started to fly, because syntax, the structure of an idea, leads you to the worldview of the speaker and reveals her values. The syntax of a sentence equals the structure of your consciousness. If we insisted that the language of Black English adheres to a distinctive Black syntax, then we were postulating a profound difference between White and Black people, *per se*. Was it a difference to prize or to obliterate?

There are three qualities of Black English—the presence of life, voice, and clarity—that intensify to a distinctive Black value system that we became excited about and self-consciously tried to maintain.

1. Black English has been produced by a pre-technocratic, if not anti-technological, culture. More, our culture has been constantly threatened by annihilation or, at least, the swallowed blurring of assimilation. Therefore, our language is a system constructed by people constantly needing to insist that we exist, that we are present. Our language devolves from a culture that abhors all abstraction, or anything tending to obscure or delete the fact of the human being who is here and now/the truth of the person who is speaking or listening. Consequently, *there is no passive voice construction possible in Black English*. For example, you cannot say, "Black English is being eliminated." You must say, instead, "White people eliminating Black English." The assumption of the presence of life governs all of Black English. Therefore, overwhelmingly, *all action takes place in the language of the present indicative*. And every sentence

assumes the living and active participation of at least two human beings, the speaker and the listener.

2. A primary consequence of the person-centered values of Black English is the delivery of voice. If you speak, or write Black English, your ideas will necessarily possess that otherwise elusive attribute, *voice*.

3. One main benefit following from the person-centered values of Black English is that of *clarity*. If your idea, your sentence, assumes the presence of at least two living and active people, you will make it understandable, because the motivation behind every sentence is the wish to say something real to somebody real.

As the weeks piled up, translation from Standard English into Black English or vice versa occupied a hefty part of our course work.

Standard English (hereafter S.E.): "In considering the idea of studying Black English those questioned suggested—"

(What's the subject? Where's the person? Is anybody alive in here, in that idea?)

Black English (hereafter B.E.): "I been asking people what you think about somebody studying Black English and they answer me like this."

But there were interesting limits. You cannot "translate" instances of Standard English preoccupied with abstraction or with nothing/nobody evidently alive, into Black English. That would warp the language into uses antithetical to the guiding perspective of its community of users. Rather you must first change those Standard English sentences, themselves, into ideas consistent with the person-centered assumptions of Black English.

## Guidelines for Black English

1. Minimal number of words for every idea: This is the source for the aphoristic and/or poetic force of the language; eliminate every possible word.

2. Clarity: If the sentence is not clear it's not Black English.

3. Eliminate use of the verb *to be* whenever possible. This leads to the deployment of more descriptive and, therefore, more precise verbs.

4. Use *be* or *been* only when you want to describe a chronic, ongoing state of things.

   He *be* at the office, by 9. (He is always at the office by 9.)

   He *been* with her since forever.

5. Zero copula: Always eliminate the verb *to be* whenever it would combine with another verb, in Standard English.

   S.E.: She is going out with him.

   B.E.: She going out with him.

6. Eliminate *do* as in:

   S.E.: What do you think? What do you want?

   B.E.: What you think? What you want?

Rules number 3, 4, 5, and 6 provide for the use of the minimal number of verbs per idea and, therefore, greater accuracy in the choice of verb.

7.  In general, if you wish to say something really positive, try to formulate the idea using emphatic negative structure.

    S.E.: He's fabulous.

    B.E.: He bad.

8.  Use double or triple negatives for dramatic emphasis.

    S.E.: Tina Turner sings out of this world.

    B.E.: Ain nobody sing like Tina.

9.  Never use the *ed* suffix to indicate the past tense of a verb.

    S.E.: She closed the door.

    B.E.: She close the door. Or, she have close the door.

10. Regardless of intentional verb time, only use the third person singular, present indicative, for use of the verb *to have*, as an auxiliary.

    S.E.: He had his wallet then he lost it.

    B.E.: He have him wallet then he lose it.

    S.E.: We had seen that movie.

    B.E.: We seen that movie. Or, we have see that movie.

11. Observe a minimal inflection of verbs. Particularly, never change from the first person singular forms to the third person singular.

    S.E.: Present Tense Forms: He goes to the store.

    B.E.: He go to the store.

    S.E.: Past Tense Forms: He went to the store.

    B.E.: He go to the store. Or, he gone to the store. Or, he been to the store.

12. The possessive case scarcely ever appears in Black English. Never use an apostrophe ('s) construction. If you wander into a possessive case component of an idea, then keep logically consistent: *ours, his, theirs, mines.* But, most likely, if you bump into such a component, you have wandered outside the underlying worldview of Black English.

    S.E.: He will take their car tomorrow.

    B.E.: He taking they car tomorrow.

13. Plurality: Logical consistency, continued: If the modifier indicates plurality then the noun remains in the singular case.

    S.E.: He ate twelve doughnuts.

    B.E.: He eat twelve doughnut.

    S.E.: She has many books.

    B.E.: She have many book.

14. Listen for, or invent, special Black English forms of the past tense, such as: "He losted it. That what she felted." If they are clear and readily understood, then use them.

15. Do not hesitate to play with words, sometimes inventing them: e.g. "astropotomous" means huge like a hippo plus astronomical and, therefore, signifies real big.

16. In Black English, unless you keenly want to underscore the past tense nature of an action, stay in the present tense and rely on the overall context of your ideas for the conveyance of time and sequence.

17. Never use the suffix -*ly* form of an adverb in Black English.

    S.E.: The rain came down rather quickly.

    B.E. The rain come down pretty quick.

18. Never use the indefinite article *an* in Black English.

    S.E.: He wanted to ride an elephant.

    B.E.: He wanted to ride him a elephant.

19. Invariant syntax: in correct Black English it is possible to formulate an imperative, an interrogative, and a simple declarative idea with the same syntax:

    B.E.: You going to the store?

    You going to the store.

    You going to the store!

Where was Willie Jordan? We'd reached the mid-term of the semester. Students had formulated Black English guidelines, by consensus, and they were now writing with remarkable beauty, purpose, and enjoyment:

> I ain hardly speakin for everybody but myself so understan that.
> —*Kim Parks*

## Samples from student writings:

> Janie have a great big ole hole inside her. Tea Cake the only thing that fit that hole. . . .

> That pear tree beautiful to Janie, especial when bees fiddlin with the blossomin pear there growin large and lovely. But personal speakin, the love she get from starin at that tree ain the love what starin back at her in them relationship. (Monica Morris)

> Love a big theme in, *They Eye Was Watching God*. Love show people new corners inside theyself. It pull out good stuff and stuff back bad stuff . . . Joe worship the doing uh his own hand and need other people to worship him too. But he ain't think about Janie that she a person and ought to live like anybody common do. Queen life not for Janie. (Monica Morris)

> In both life and writin, Black womens have varietous experience of love that be cold like a iceberg or fiery like a inferno. Passion got for the other partner involve, man

or women, seem as shallow, ankle-deep water or the most profoundest abyss. (Constance Evans)

Family love another bond that ain't never break under no pressure. (Constance Evans)

You know it really cold/When the friend you/Always get out the fire/Act like they don't know you/When you in the beat. (Constance Evans)

Big classroom discussion bout love at this time. I never take no class where us have any long arguin for and against for two or three day. New to me and great. I find the class time talkin a million time more interestin than detail bout the book. (Kathy Esseks)

As these examples suggest, Black English no longer limited the students, in any way. In fact, one of them, Philip Garfield, would shortly "translate" a pivotal scene from Ibsen's *A Doll House*, as his final term paper.

*Nora:* I didn't gived no shit. I thinked you a asshole back then, too, you make it so hard for me save mines husband life.

*Krogstad:* Girl, it clear you ain't any idea what you done. You done exact what I once done, and I losed my reputation over it.

*Nora:* You asks me believe you once act brave save you wife life?

*Krogstad:* Law care less why you done it.

*Nora:* Law must suck.

*Krogstad:* Suck or no, if I wants, judge screw you wid dis paper.

*Nora:* No way, man. (Philip Garfield)

But where was Willie? Compulsively punctual, and always thoroughly prepared with neat typed compositions, he had disappeared. He failed to show up for our regularly scheduled conference, and I received neither a note nor a phone call of explanation. A whole week went by. I wondered if Willie had finally been captured by the extremely current happenings in South Africa: passage of a new constitution that did not enfranchise the Black majority and militant Black South African reaction to that affront. I wondered if he'd been hurt somewhere. I wondered if the serious workload of weekly readings and writings had overwhelmed him and changed his mind about independent study. Where was Willie Jordan?

One week after the first conference that Willie missed, he called: "Hello, Professor Jordan? This is Willie. I'm sorry I wasn't there last week. But something has come up and I'm pretty upset. I'm sorry but I really can't deal right now."

I asked Willie to drop by my office and just let me see that he was okay. He agreed to do that. When I saw him I knew something hideous had happened. Something had hurt him and scared him to the marrow. He was all agitated and stammering and terse and incoherent. At last, his sadly jumbled account let me surmise, as follows: Brooklyn police had murdered his unarmed, twenty-five-year-old brother, Reggie Jordan. Neither Willie nor his elderly parents knew what to do about it. Nobody from the press was interested. His folks had no money. Police ran his family around and around, to no point. And Reggie was really dead. And Willie wanted to fight, but he felt helpless.

⋆   ⋆   ⋆

With Willie's permission I began to try to secure legal counsel for the Jordan family. Unfortunately, Black victims of police violence are truly numerous, while the resources available to prosecute their killers are truly scarce. A friend of mine at the Center for Constitutional Rights estimated that just the preparatory costs for bringing the cops into court normally approaches $180,000. Unless the execution of Reggie Jordan became a major community cause for organizing and protest, his murder would simply become a statistical item.

Again, with Willie's permission, I contacted every newspaper and media person I could think of. But the Bastone feature article in *The Village Voice* was the only result from that canvassing.

Again, with Willie's permission, I presented the case to my class in Black English. We had talked about the politics of language. We had talked about love and sex and child abuse and men and women. But the murder of Reggie Jordan broke like a hurricane across the room.

There are few "issues" as endemic to Black life as police violence. Most of the students knew and respected and liked Jordan. Many of them came from the very neighborhood where the murder had occurred. All of the students had known somebody close to them who had been killed by police, or had known frightening moments of gratuitous confrontation with the cops. They wanted to do everything at once to avenge death. Number One: They decided to compose a personal statement of condolence to Willie Jordan and his family, written in Black English. Number Two: They decided to compose individual messages to the police, in Black English. These should be prefaced by an explanatory paragraph composed by the entire group. Number Three: These individual messages, with their lead paragraph, should be sent to *Newsday*.

The morning after we agreed on these objectives, one of the young women students appeared with an unidentified visitor, who sat through the class, smiling in a peculiar, comfortable way.

Now we had to make more tactical decisions. Because we wanted the messages published, and because we thought it imperative that our outrage be known by the police, the tactical question was this: Should the opening, group paragraph be written in Black English or Standard English?

I have seldom been privy to a discussion with so much heart at the dead beat of it. I will never forget the eloquence, the sudden haltings of speech, the fierce struggle against tears, the furious throwaway, and useless explosions that this question elicited.

That one question contained several others, each of them extraordinarily painful to even contemplate. How best to serve the memory of Reggie Jordan? Should we use the language of the killer—Standard English—in order to make our ideas acceptable to those controlling the killers? But wouldn't what we had to say be rejected, summarily, if we said it in our own language, the language of the victim, Reggie Jordan? But if we sought to express ourselves by abandoning our language wouldn't that mean our suicide on top of Reggie's murder? But if we expressed ourselves in our own language wouldn't that be suicidal to the wish to communicate with those who, evidently, did not give a damn about us/Reggie/police violence in the Black community?

At the end of one of the longest, most difficult hours of my own life, the students voted, unanimously, to preface their individual messages with a paragraph composed in the language of Reggie Jordan. "*At least we don't give up nothing else. At least we stick to the truth: Be who we been. And stay all the way with Reggie.*"

It was heartbreaking to proceed, from that point. Everyone in the room realized that our decision in favor of Black English had doomed our writings, even as the distinctive reality of our Black lives always has doomed our efforts to "be who we been" in this country.

I went to the black board and took down this paragraph dictated by the class:

YOU COPS!

WE THE BROTHER AND SISTER OF WILLIE JORDAN, A FELLOW STONY BROOK STUDENT WHO THE BROTHER OF THE DEAD REGGIE JORDAN. REGGIE, LIKE MANY BROTHER AND SISTER, HE A VICTIM OF BRUTAL RACIST POLICE, OCTOBER 25, 1984. US APPALL, FED UP, BECAUSE THAT ANOTHER SENSELESS DEATH WHAT OCCUR IN OUR COMMUNITY. THIS WHAT WE FEEL, THIS, FROM OUR HEART, FOR WE AIN'T STAYIN' SILENT NO MORE.

With the completion of this introduction, nobody said anything. I asked for comments. At this invitation, the unidentified visitor, a young Black man, ceaselessly smiling, raised his hand. He was, it so happens, a rookie cop. He had just joined the force in September and he said, he thought he should clarify a few things. So he came forward and sprawled easily into a posture of barroom, or fire-side, nostalgia:

"See," Officer Charles enlightened us, "Most times when you out on the street and something come down you do one of two things. Over-react or under-react. Now, if you under-react then you can get yourself kilt. And if you over-react then maybe you kill somebody. Fortunately it's about nine times out of ten and you will over-react. So the brother got kilt. And I'm sorry about that, believe me. But what you have to understand is what kilt him: Over-reaction. That's all. Now you talk about Black people and White police but see, now, I'm a cop myself. And (big smile) I'm Black. And just a couple months ago I was on the other side. But it's the same for me. You a cop, you the ultimate authority: the Ultimate Authority. And you on the street, most of the time you can only do one of the two things: over-react or under-react. That's all it is with the brother. Over-reaction. Didn't have nothing to do with race."

That morning Officer Charles had the good fortune to escape without being boiled alive. But barely. And I remember the pride of his smile when I read about the fate of Black policemen and other collaborators, in South Africa. I remember him, and I remember the shock and palpable feeling of shame that filled the room. It was as though that foolish, and deadly, young man had just relieved himself of his foolish, and deadly, explanation, face to face with the grief of Reggie Jordan's father and Reggie Jordan's mother. Class ended quietly. I copied the paragraph from the blackboard, collected the individual messages and left to type them up.

*Newsday* rejected the piece.

*The Village Voice* could not find room in their "Letters" section to print the individual messages from the students to the police.

None of the TV news reporters picked up the story.

Nobody raised $180,000 to prosecute the murder of Reggie Jordan.

Reggie Jordan is really dead.

I asked Willie Jordan to write an essay pulling together everything important to him from that semester. He was still deeply beside himself with frustration and amazement and loss. This is what he wrote, unedited, and in its entirety:

> Throughout the course of this semester I have been researching the effects of oppression and exploitation along racial lines in South Africa and its neighboring countries. I have become aware of South African police brutalization of native Africans beyond the extent of the law, even though the laws themselves are catalyst affliction upon Black men, women and children. Many Africans die each year as a result of the deliberate use of police force to protect the white power structure.
>
> Social control agents in South Africa, such as policemen, are also used to force compliance among citizens through both overt and covert tactics. It is not uncommon to find bold-faced coercion and cold-blooded killings of Blacks by South African police for undetermined and/or inadequate reasons. Perhaps the truth is that the only reasons for this heinous treatment of Blacks rests in racial differences. We should also understand that what is conveyed through the media is not always accurate and may sometimes be construed as the tip of the iceberg at best.
>
> I recently received a painful reminder that racism, poverty, and the abuse of power are global problems which are by no means unique to South Africa. On October 25, 1984 at approximately 3:00 p.m. my brother, Mr. Reginald Jordan, was shot and killed by two New York City policemen from the 75th precinct in the East New York section of Brooklyn. His life ended at the age of twenty-five. Even up to this current point in time the Police Department has failed to provide my family, which consists of five brothers, eight sisters, and two parents, with a plausible reason for Reggie's death. Out of the many stories that were given to my family by the Police Department, not one of them seems to hold water. In fact, I honestly believe that the Police Department's assessment of my brother's murder is nothing short of ABSOLUTE BULLSHIT, and thus far no evidence had been produced to alter perception of the situation.
>
> Furthermore, I believe that one of three cases may have occurred in this incident. First, Reggie's death may have been the desired outcome of the police officer's action, in which case the killing was premeditated. Or, it was a case of mistaken identity, which clarifies the fact that the two officers who killed my brother and their commanding parties are all grossly incompetent. Or both of the above cases are correct, i.e., Reggie's murderers intended to kill him and the Police Department behaved insubordinately.
>
> Part of the argument of the officers who shot Reggie was that he had attacked one of them and took his gun. This was their major claim. They also said that only one of them had actually shot Reggie. The facts, however, speak for themselves. According to the Death Certificate and autopsy report, Reggie was shot eight times from point-blank range. The Doctor who performed the autopsy told me himself that two bullets entered the side of my brother's head, four bullets were sprayed into his back, and two bullets struck him in the back of his legs. It is obvious that unnecessary force was used by the police and that it is extremely difficult to shoot someone in his back when he is attacking or approaching you.
>
> After experiencing a situation like this and researching South Africa I believe that to a large degree, justice may only exist as rhetoric. I find it difficult to talk of true

justice when the oppression of my people both at home and abroad attests to the fact that inequality and injustice are serious problems whereby Blacks and Third World people are perpetually short-changed by society. Something has to be done about the way in which this world is set up. Although it is a difficult task, we do have the power to make a change.

—WILLIE J. JORDAN, JR.
*EGL 487, SECTION 58, NOVEMBER 14, 1984*

## Notes

1. Black English aphorisms crafted by Monica Morris, a junior at S.U.N.Y., Stony Brook, October, 1984.

2. *English Is Spreading, But What Is English?* A presentation by Professor S. N. Sridhar, Department of Linguistics, S.U.N.Y., Stony Brook, April 9, 1985: Dean's Convocation Among the Disciplines.

3. *New York Times*, March 15, 1985, Section One, p. 14: Report on Study by Linguists at the University of Pennsylvania.

4. Alice Walker. *The Color Purple* (New York: Harcourt Brace Jovanovich, 1982), p. 11.

# II

## Audience

### ST. CRISPIN'S DAY SPEECH FROM *HENRY V*

William Shakespeare

> *Taken from Shakespeare's play* Henry V, *this speech shows the English King Henry V's reply when one of his military commanders wishes for more men to take into an imminent battle against the French. Henry addresses the English noblemen, archers, and foot soldiers who make up his audience in an attempt to motivate the vastly outnumbered English forces. As you read, notice how he attempts to appeal to all of these different types of listeners.*

What's he that wishes so?
My cousin Westmoreland? No, my fair cousin:
If we are mark'd to die, we are enow
To do our country loss; and if to live,
The fewer men, the greater share of honour.
God's will! I pray thee, wish not one man more.
By Jove, I am not covetous for gold,
Nor care I who doth feed upon my cost;
It yearns me not if men my garments wear;
Such outward things dwell not in my desires:
But if it be a sin to covet honour,
I am the most offending soul alive.
No, faith, my coz, wish not a man from England:
God's peace! I would not lose so great an honour
As one man more, methinks, would share from me

For the best hope I have. O, do not wish one more!
Rather proclaim it, Westmoreland, through my host,
That he which hath no stomach to this fight,
Let him depart; his passport shall be made
And crowns for convoy put into his purse:
We would not die in that man's company
That fears his fellowship to die with us.
This day is called the feast of Crispian:
He that outlives this day, and comes safe home,
Will stand a tip-toe when the day is named,
And rouse him at the name of Crispian.
He that shall live this day, and see old age,
Will yearly on the vigil feast his neighbours,
And say 'To-morrow is Saint Crispian:'
Then will he strip his sleeve and show his scars.
And say 'These wounds I had on Crispin's day.'
Old men forget: yet all shall be forgot,
But he'll remember with advantages
What feats he did that day: then shall our names,
Familiar in his mouth as household words,
Harry the king, Bedford and Exeter,
Warwick and Talbot, Salisbury and Gloucester,
Be in their flowing cups freshly remember'd.
This story shall the good man teach his son;
And Crispin Crispian shall ne'er go by,
From this day to the ending of the world,
But we in it shall be remembered;
We few, we happy few, we band of brothers;
For he to-day that sheds his blood with me
Shall be my brother; be he ne'er so vile,
This day shall gentle his condition:
And gentlemen in England now a-bed
Shall think themselves accursed they were not here,
And hold their manhoods cheap whiles any speaks
That fought with us upon Saint Crispin's day (4.3.18–67).

# SHAKESPEARE IN THE BUSH

Laura Bohannan

> *In this article from a 1966 issue of the magazine* Natural History, *cultural anthropologist Laura Bohannan attempts to tell the plot of Shakespeare's play* Hamlet *to members of the West African Tiv tribe. She quickly discovers that in order for an audience to understand a story in the same way, they must share common knowledge and beliefs. As you read, consider what knowledge and assumptions you have that you might find difficult to explain to an audience that does not share your background.*

Just before I left Oxford for the Tiv in West Africa, conversation turned to the season at Stratford. "You Americans," said a friend, "often have difficulty with Shakespeare. He was, after all, a very English poet, and one can easily misinterpret the universal by misunderstanding the particular."

I protested that human nature is pretty much the same the whole world over; at least the general plot and motivation of the greater tragedies would always be clear—everywhere—although some details of custom might have to be explained and difficulties of translation might produce other slight changes. To end an argument we could not conclude, my friend gave me a copy of *Hamlet* to study in the African bush: it would, he hoped, lift my mind above its primitive surroundings, and possibly I might, by prolonged meditation, achieve the grace of correct interpretation.

It was my second field trip to that African tribe, and I thought myself ready to live in one of its remote sections—an area difficult to cross even on foot. I eventually settled on the hillock of a very knowledgeable old man, the head of a homestead of some hundred and forty people, all of whom were either his close relatives or their wives and children. Like the other elders of the vicinity, the old man spent most of his time performing ceremonies seldom seen these days in the more accessible parts of the tribe. I was delighted. Soon there would be three months of enforced isolation and leisure, between the harvest that takes place just before the rising of the swamps and the clearing of new farms when the water goes down. Then, I thought, they would have even more time to perform ceremonies and explain them to me.

I was quite mistaken. Most of the ceremonies demanded the presence of elders from several homesteads. As the swamps rose, the old men found it too difficult to walk from one homestead to the next, and the ceremonies gradually ceased. As the swamps rose even higher, all activities but one came to an end. The women brewed beer from maize and millet. Men, women, and children sat on their hillocks and drank it.

People began to drink at dawn. By midmorning the whole homestead was singing, dancing, and drumming. When it rained, people had to sit inside their huts: there they drank and sang or they drank and told stories. In any case, by noon or before, I either had to join the party or retire to my own hut and my books. "One does not discuss serious matters when there is beer. Come, drink with us." Since I lacked their capacity for the thick native beer, I spent more and more time with *Hamlet*. Before the end of the second month, grace descended on me. I was quite sure that *Hamlet* had only one possible interpretation, and that one universally obvious.

Early every morning, in the hope of having some serious talk before the beer party, I used to call on the old man at his reception hut—a circle of posts supporting a thatched roof above a low mud wall to keep out wind and rain. One day I crawled through the low doorway and found most of the men of the homestead sitting huddled in their ragged cloths on stools, low plank beds, and reclining chairs, warming themselves against the chill of the rain around a smoky fire. In the center were three pots of beer. The party had started.

The old man greeted me cordially. "Sit down and drink." I accepted a large calabash full of beer, poured some into a small drinking gourd, and tossed it down. Then I poured some more into the same gourd for the man second in seniority to my host before I handed my calabash over to a young man for further distribution. Important people shouldn't ladle beer themselves.

"It is better like this," the old man said, looking at me approvingly and plucking at the thatch that had caught in my hair. "You should sit and drink with us more often. Your servants tell me that when you are not with us, you sit inside your hut looking at a paper."

The old man was acquainted with four kinds of "papers": tax receipts, bride price receipts, court free receipts, and letters. The messenger who brought him letters from the chief used them mainly as a badge of office, for he always knew what was in them and told the old man. Personal letters for the few who had relatives in the government or mission stations were kept until someone went to a large market where there was a letter writer and reader. Since my arrival, letters were brought to me to be read. A few men also brought me bride price receipts, privately, with requests to change the figures to a higher sum. I found moral arguments were of no avail, since in-laws are fair game, and the technical hazards of forgery difficult to explain to an illiterate people. I did not wish them to think me silly enough to look at any such papers for days on end, and I hastily explained that my "paper" was one of the "things of long ago" of my country.

"Ah," said the old man. "Tell us."

I protested that I was not a storyteller. Storytelling is a skilled art among them; their standards are high, and the audiences critical—and vocal in their criticism. I protested in vain. This morning they wanted to hear a story while they drank. They threatened to tell me no more stories until I told them one of mine. Finally, the old man promised that no one would criticize my style "for we know you are struggling with our language." "But," put in one of the elders, "you must explain what we do not understand, as we do when we tell you our stories." Realizing that here was my chance to prove *Hamlet* universally intelligible, I agreed.

The old man handed me some more beer to help me on with my storytelling. Men filled their long wooden pipes and knocked coals from the fire to place in the pipe bowls; then, puffing contentedly, they sat back to listen. I began in the proper style, "Not yesterday, not yesterday, but long ago, a thing occurred. One night three men were keeping watch outside the homestead of the great chief, when suddenly they saw the former chief approach them."

"Why was he no longer their chief?"

"He was dead," I explained. "That is why they were troubled and afraid when they saw him."

"Impossible," began one of the elders, handing his pipe on to his neighbor, who interrupted, "Of course it wasn't the dead chief. It was an omen sent by a witch. Go on."

Slightly shaken, I continued. "One of these three was a man who knew things"— the closest translation for scholar, but unfortunately it also meant witch. The second elder looked triumphantly at the first. "So he spoke to the dead chief saying, 'Tell us what we must do so you may rest in your grave,' but the dead chief did not answer. He vanished, and they could see him no more. Then the man who knew things—his name was Horatio—said this event was the affair of the dead chief's son, Hamlet."

There was a general shaking of heads round the circle. "Had the dead chief no living brothers? Or was this son the chief?"

"No," I replied. "That is, he had one living brother who became the chief when the elder brother died."

The old men muttered: such omens were matters for chiefs and elders, not for youngsters; no good could come of going behind a chief's back; clearly Horatio was not a man who knew things.

"Yes, he was," I insisted, shooing a chicken away from my beer. "In our country the son is next to the father. The dead chief's younger brother had become the great chief. He had also married his elder brother's widow only about a month after the funeral."

"He did well," the old man beamed and announced to the others, "I told you that if we knew more about Europeans, we would find they really were very like us. In our country also," he added to me, "the younger brother marries the elder brother's widow and becomes the father of his children. Now, if your uncle, who married your widowed mother, is your father's full brother, then he will be a real father to you. Did Hamlet's father and uncle have one mother?"

His question barely penetrated my mind; I was too upset and thrown too far off balance by having one of the most important elements of *Hamlet* knocked straight out of the picture. Rather uncertainly I said that I thought they had the same mother, but I wasn't sure—the story didn't say. The old man told me severely that these genealogical details made all the difference and that when I got home I must ask the elders about it. He shouted out the door to one of his younger wives to bring his goatskin bag.

Determined to save what I could of the mother motif, I took a deep breath and began again. "The son Hamlet was very sad because his mother had married again so quickly. There was no need for her to do so, and it is our custom for a widow not to go to her next husband until she has mourned for two years."

"Two years is too long," objected the wife, who had appeared with the old man's battered goatskin bag. "Who will hoe your farms for you while you have no husband?"

"Hamlet," I retorted without thinking, "was old enough to hoe his mother's farms himself. There was no need for her to remarry." No one looked convinced. I gave up. "His mother and the great chief told Hamlet not to be sad, for the great chief himself would be a father to Hamlet. Furthermore, Hamlet would be the next chief: therefore he must stay to learn the things of a chief. Hamlet agreed to remain, and all the rest went off to drink beer."

While I paused, perplexed at how to render Hamlet's disgusted soliloquy to an audience convinced that Claudius and Gertrude had behaved in the best possible manner, one of the younger men asked me who had married the other wives of the dead chief.

"He had no other wives," I told him.

"But a chief must have many wives! How else can he brew beer and prepare food for all his guests?"

I said firmly that in our country even chiefs had only one wife, that they had servants to do their work, and that they paid them from tax money.

It was better, they returned, for a chief to have many wives and sons who would help him hoe his farms and feed his people; then everyone loved the chief who gave much and took nothing—taxes were a bad thing.

I agreed with the last comment, but for the rest fell back on their favorite way of fobbing off my questions: "That is the way it is done, so that is how we do it."

I decided to skip the soliloquy. Even if Claudius was here thought quite right to marry his brother's widow, there remained the poison motif, and I knew they would disapprove of fratricide. More hopefully I resumed, "That night Hamlet kept watch with the three who had seen his dead father. The dead chief again appeared, and although the others were afraid, Hamlet followed his dead father off to one side. When they were alone, Hamlet's dead father spoke."

"Omens can't talk!" The old man was emphatic.

"Hamlet's dead father wasn't an omen. Seeing him might have been an omen, but he was not." My audience looked as confused as I sounded. "It *was* Hamlet's dead father. It was a thing we call a 'ghost.'" I had to use the English word, for unlike many of the neighboring tribes, these people didn't believe in the survival after death of any individuating part of the personality.

"What is a 'ghost?' An omen?"

"No, a 'ghost' is someone who is dead but who walks around and can talk, and people can hear and see him but not touch him."

They objected. "One can touch zombis."

"No, no! It was not a dead body the witches had animated to sacrifice and eat. No one else made Hamlet's dead father walk. He did it himself."

"Dead men can't walk," protested my audience as one man.

I was quite willing to compromise. "A 'ghost' is the dead man's shadow."

But again they objected. "Dead men cast no shadows."

"They do in my country," I snapped.

The old man quelled the babble of disbelief that arose immediately and told me with that insincere, but courteous, agreement one extends to the fancies of the young, ignorant, and superstitious, "No doubt in your country the dead can also walk without being zombis." From the depths of his bag he produced a withered fragment of kola nut, bit off one end to show it wasn't poisoned, and handed me the rest as a peace offering.

"Anyhow," I resumed, "Hamlet's dead father said that his own brother, the one who became chief, had poisoned him. He wanted Hamlet to avenge him. Hamlet believed this in his heart, for he did not like his father's brother." I took another swallow of beer. "In the country of the great chief, living in the same homestead, for it was a very large one, was an important elder who was often with the chief to advise and help him. His name was Polonius. Hamlet was courting his daughter, but her father and her brother . . . [I cast hastily about for some tribal analogy] warned her not to let Hamlet visit her when she was alone on her farm, for he would be a great chief and so could not marry her."

"Why not?" asked the wife, who had settled down on the edge of the old man's chair. He frowned at her for asking stupid questions and growled, "They lived in the same homestead."

"That was not the reason," I informed them. "Polonius was a stranger who lived in the homestead because he helped the chief, not because he was a relative."

"Then why couldn't Hamlet marry her?"

"He could have," I explained, "but Polonius didn't think he would. After all, Hamlet was a man of great importance who ought to marry a chief's daughter, for in his country a man could have only one wife. Polonius was afraid that if Hamlet made love to his daughter, then no one else would give a high price for her."

"That might be true," remarked one of the shrewder elders, "but a chief's son would give his mistress's father enough presents and patronage to more than make up the difference. Polonius sounds like a fool to me."

"Many people think he was," I agreed. "Meanwhile Polonius sent his son Laertes off to Paris to learn the things of that country, for it was the homestead of a very great chief indeed. Because he was afraid that Laertes might waste a lot of money on beer and women and gambling, or get into trouble by fighting, he sent one of his servants to Paris secretly, to spy out what Laertes was doing. One day Hamlet came upon Polonius's daughter Ophelia. He behaved so oddly he frightened her. Indeed"—I was fumbling for words to express the dubious quality of Hamlet's madness—"the chief and many others had also noticed that when Hamlet talked one could understand the words but not what they meant. Many people thought that he had become mad." My audience suddenly became much more attentive. "The great chief wanted to know what was wrong with Hamlet, so he sent for two of Hamlet's age mates [school friends would have taken long explanation] to talk to Hamlet and find out what troubled his heart. Hamlet, seeing that they had been bribed by the chief to betray him, told them nothing. Polonius, however, insisted that Hamlet was mad because he had been forbidden to see Ophelia, whom he loved."

"Why," inquired a bewildered voice, "should anyone bewitch Hamlet on that account?"

"Bewitch him?"

"Yes, only witchcraft can make anyone mad, unless, of course, one sees the beings that lurk in the forest."

I stopped being a storyteller, took out my notebook and demanded to be told more about these two causes of madness. Even while they spoke and I jotted notes, I tried to calculate the effect of this new factor on the plot. Hamlet had not been exposed to the beings that lurk in the forest. Only his relatives in the male line could bewitch him. Barring relatives not mentioned by Shakespeare, it had to be Claudius who was attempting to harm him. And, of course, it was.

For the moment I staved off questions by saying that the great chief also refused to believe that Hamlet was mad for the love of Ophelia and nothing else. "He was sure that something much more important was troubling Hamlet's heart."

"Now Hamlet's age mates," I continued, "had brought with them a famous story-teller. Hamlet decided to have this man tell the chief and all his homestead a story about a man who had poisoned his brother because he desired his brother's wife and wished to be chief himself. Hamlet was sure the great chief could not hear the story without making a sign if he was indeed guilty, and then he would discover whether his dead father had told him the truth."

The old man interrupted, with deep cunning, "Why should a father lie to his son?" he asked.

I hedged: "Hamlet wasn't sure that it really was his dead father." It was impossible to say anything, in that language, about devil-inspired visions.

"You mean," he said, "it actually was an omen, and he knew witches sometimes send false ones. Hamlet was a fool not to go to one skilled in reading omens and divining the truth in the first place. A man-who-sees-the-truth could have told him how his father died, if he really had been poisoned, and if there was witchcraft in it; then Hamlet could have called the elders to settle the matter."

The shrewd elder ventured to disagree. "Because his father's brother was a great chief, one-who-sees-the-truth might therefore have been afraid to tell it. I think it was for that reason that a friend of Hamlet's father—a witch and an elder—sent an omen so his friend's son would know. Was the omen true?"

"Yes," I said, abandoning ghosts and the devil; a witch-sent omen it would have to be. "It was true, for when the storyteller was telling his tale before all the homestead, the great chief rose in fear. Afraid that Hamlet knew his secret he planned to have him killed."

The stage set of the next bit presented some difficulties of translation. I began cautiously. "The great chief told Hamlet's mother to find out from her son what he knew. But because a woman's children are always first in her heart, he had the important elder Polonius hide behind a cloth that hung against the wall of Hamlet's mother's sleeping hut. Hamlet started to scold his mother for what she had done."

There was a shocked murmur from everyone. A man should never scold his mother.

"She called out in fear, and Polonius moved behind the cloth. Shouting, 'A rat!' Hamlet took his machete and slashed through the cloth." I paused for dramatic effect. "He had killed Polonius!"

The old men looked at each other in supreme disgust. "That Polonius truly was a fool and a man who knew nothing! What child would not know enough to shout, 'It's me!'" With a pang, I remembered that these people are ardent hunters, always armed with bow, arrow, and machete; at the first rustle in the grass an arrow is aimed and ready, and the hunter shouts "Game!" If no human voice answers immediately, the arrow speeds on its way. Like a good hunter Hamlet had shouted, "A rat!"

I rushed in to save Polonius's reputation. "Polonius did speak. Hamlet heard him. But he thought it was the chief and wished to kill him to avenge his father. He had meant to kill him earlier that evening. . . ." I broke down, unable to describe to these pagans, who had no belief in individual afterlife, the difference between dying at one's prayers and dying "unhousell'd, disappointed, unaneled."

This time I had shocked my audience seriously. "For a man to raise his hand against his father's brother and the one who has become his father—that is a terrible thing. The elders ought to let such a man be bewitched."

I nibbled at my kola nut in some perplexity, then pointed out that after all the man had killed Hamlet's father.

"No," pronounced the old man, speaking less to me than to the young men sitting behind the elders. "If your father's brother has killed your father, you must appeal to your father's age mates; *they* may avenge him. No man may use violence against his senior relatives." Another thought struck him. "But if his father's brother had indeed been wicked enough to bewitch Hamlet and make him mad that would be a good story indeed, for it would be his fault that Hamlet, being mad, no longer had any sense and thus was ready to kill his father's brother."

There was a murmur of applause. *Hamlet* was again a good story to them, but it no longer seemed quite the same story to me. As I thought over the coming complications of plot and motive, I lost courage and decided to skim over dangerous ground quickly.

"The great chief," I went on, "was not sorry that Hamlet had killed Polonius. It gave him a reason to send Hamlet away, with his two treacherous age mates, with letters to a chief of a far country, saying that Hamlet should be killed. But Hamlet changed the writing on their papers, so that the chief killed his age mates instead." I encountered a reproachful glare from one of the men whom I had told undetectable forgery was not merely immoral but beyond human skill. I looked the other way.

"Before Hamlet could return, Laertes came back for his father's funeral. The great chief told him Hamlet had killed Polonius. Laertes swore to kill Hamlet because of this, and because his sister Ophelia, hearing her father had been killed by the man she loved, went mad and drowned in the river."

"Have you already forgotten what we told you?" The old man was reproachful. "One cannot take vengeance on a madman; Hamlet killed Polonius in his madness. As for the girl, she not only went mad, she was drowned. Only witches can make people drown. Water itself can't hurt anything. It is merely something one drinks and bathes in."

I began to get cross. "If you don't like the story, I'll stop."

The old man made soothing noises and himself poured me some more beer. "You tell the story well, and we are listening. But it is clear that the elders of your country have never told you what the story really means. No, don't interrupt! We believe you when you say your marriage customs are different, or your clothes and weapons. But people are the same everywhere; therefore, there are always witches and it is we, the elders, who know how witches work. We told you it was the great chief who wished to kill Hamlet, and now your own words have proved us right. Who were Ophelia's male relatives?"

"There were only her father and her brother." Hamlet was clearly out of my hands.

"There must have been many more; this also you must ask of your elders when you get back to your country. From what you tell us, since Polonius was dead, it must have been Laertes who killed Ophelia, although I do not see the reason for it."

We had emptied one pot of beer, and the old men argued the point with slightly tipsy interest. Finally one of them demanded of me, "What did the servant of Polonius say on his return?"

With difficulty I recollected Reynaldo and his mission. "I don't think he did return before Polonius was killed."

"Listen," said the elder, "and I will tell you how it was and how your story will go, then you may tell me if I am right. Polonius knew his son would get into trouble, and so he did. He had many fines to pay for fighting, and debts from gambling. But he had only two ways of getting money quickly. One was to marry off his sister at once, but it is difficult to find a man who will marry a woman desired by the son of a chief. For if the chief's heir commits adultery with your wife, what can you do? Only a fool calls a case against a man who will someday be his judge. Therefore Laertes had to take the second way: he killed his sister by witchcraft, drowning her so he could secretly sell her body to the witches."

I raised an objection. "They found her body and buried it. Indeed Laertes jumped into the grave to see his sister once more—so, you see, the body was truly there. Hamlet, who had just come back, jumped in after him."

"What did I tell you?" The elder appealed to the others. "Laertes was up to no good with his sister's body. Hamlet prevented him, because the chief's heir, like a chief, does not wish any other man to grow rich and powerful. Laertes would be angry, because he would have killed his sister without benefit to himself. In our country he would try to kill Hamlet for that reason. Is this not what happened?"

"More or less," I admitted. "When the great chief found Hamlet was still alive, he encouraged Laertes to try to kill Hamlet and arranged a fight with machetes between them. In the fight both the young men were wounded to death. Hamlet's mother drank the poisoned beer that the chief meant for Hamlet in case he won the fight. When he saw his mother die of poison, Hamlet, dying, managed to kill his father's brother with his machete."

"You see, I was right!" exclaimed the elder.

"That was a very good story," added the old man, "and you told it with very few mistakes. There was just one more error, at the very end. The poison Hamlet's mother drank was obviously meant for the survivor of the fight, whichever it was. If Laertes had won, the great chief would have poisoned him, for no one would know that he arranged Hamlet's death. Then, too, he need not fear Laertes' witchcraft; it takes a strong heart to kill one's only sister by witchcraft.

"Sometime," concluded the old man, gathering his ragged toga about him, "you must tell us some more stories of your country. We, who are elders, will instruct you in their true meaning, so that when you return to your own land your elders will see that you have not been sitting in the bush, but among those who know things and who have taught you wisdom."

# NYU APPLICATION ESSAY

## Hugh Gallagher

*The following text circulated widely on the Internet labeled as "an actual essay written by a college applicant. The author, Hugh Gallagher, is reputed to attend NYU." As you read, consider Gallagher's audience for this essay. What reaction do you imagine a college admission board would have to such an essay? Also, think about the ways in which Gallagher shows awareness of his audience's expectations for this kind of essay. Which of these expectations does he meet and which does he violate?*

**3a.** ESSAY: in order for the admission staff of our college to get to know you, the applicant, better, we ask that you answer the following questions: are there any significant experiences you have had, or accomplishments you have realized, that have helped to define you as a person?

I am a dynamic figure, often seen scaling walls and crushing ice. I have been known to remodel train stations on my lunch break, making them more efficient in the area of heat retention. I translate ethnic slurs for Cuban refugees, I write award-winning operas, I manage time efficiently. Occasionally, I tread water for three days in a row. I woo women with my sensuous and godlike trombone playing, I pilot bicycles up severe inclines with unflagging speed, and I cook Thirty-Minute Brownies in twenty minutes. I am an expert in stucco, a veteran in love, and an outlaw in Peru. Using only a hoe and a large glass of water, I once single-handedly defended a small village in the Amazon Basin from a horde of ferocious army ants. I play bluegrass cello, I was once scouted by the Mets, I am the subject of numerous documentaries. When I'm bored, I build large suspension bridges in my yard. I enjoy urban hang gliding. On Wednesdays, after school, I repair electrical appliances free of charge. I am an abstract artist, a concrete analyst, and a ruthless bookie. Critics worldwide swoon over my original line of corduroy eveningwear. I don't perspire. I am a private citizen, yet I receive fan mail. I have been caller number nine and have won the weekend passes. Last summer, I toured New Jersey with a traveling centrifugal-force demonstration. I bat .400. My deft floral arrangements have earned me fame in the international botany circles. Children trust me. I can hurl tennis rackets at small moving objects with deadly accuracy. I once read *Paradise Lost*, *Moby Dick*, and *David Copperfield* in one day and still had time to refurbish an entire dining room that evening. I know the exact location of every food item in the supermarket. I have performed several covert operations for the CIA, I sleep once a week; when I do sleep, I sleep in a chair. While on vacation in Canada, I successfully negotiated with a group of terrorists who had seized a small bakery. The laws of physics do not apply to me. I balance, I weave, I dodge, I frolic, and my bills are paid. On weekends, to let off steam, I participate in full-contact Origami. Years ago, I discovered the meaning of life, but forgot to write it down. I have made extraordinary four course meals using only a mouli and a toaster oven. I breed prizewinning clams. I have won bullfights in San Juan, cliff-diving competitions in Sri Lanka, and spelling bees at the Kremlin. I have played Hamlet, I have performed open-heart surgery, and I have spoken with Elvis. But I have not yet gone to college.

Not a bad essay, I would say, as one who has done almost none of these things.

# CLASS ACTION

Dave Barry

> *What follows appears to be a commencement address written to the class of 1995, and it follows many of the conventions for such a piece. In actuality, this is an article written by Dave Barry, a writer for* The Miami Herald, *whose syndicated column appears weekly in newspapers throughout the U.S. including* The Washington Post *and* The Baltimore Sun. *Although Barry's columns are humorous, his work often touches on contemporary social and political issues. Barry won the Pulitzer Prize for commentary in 1988. At the beginning of the article it seems that the audience is the graduating class of 1995. But is it really? His stated thesis, "A lot has changed since 1965," might be appropriate for an audience of high school seniors, but as you read it will become apparent that Barry's actual thesis is quite different. Think about the intended audience for this article, and, more importantly, think about what evidence you can find as to the nature of that audience.*

## Commencement Address to the High School Class of 1995

I am especially pleased to be addressing you, the Class of 1995, because it just so happens that I graduated from Pleasantville (N.Y.) High School in 1965, which is exactly 30 million years ago.

A lot has changed since 1965, young people. For example, in those days, most schools did not have modern technology such as the Xerox brand copier machine. When teachers wanted to give us a test, they'd run it off on a "mimeograph" machine, which was a device originally developed by spies for the purpose of smearing ink so thoroughly that enemy code-breakers would never figure out what the original words were. The teachers would hand us students a piece of paper with questions that consisted mostly of purple smears, with an occasional word sprinkled in, like this:

"1. Assuming that (smear) and (smear) (smear) Renaissance (smear), helium (smear) Treaty of (smear) (smear) (smear) cosine. Cite three examples."

We'd ponder the question, then generally write down: "The Tigris and Euphrates rivers." Surprisingly often this turned out to be the correct answer, even in algebra.

Also, back in those days some schools still had real desks, solid wooden structures roomy enough to house Third World families and covered with the initials of students dating back to the original 12 disciples. Students traditionally carved these initials with a device called a "compass," which every student was required, for some mysterious scholastic reason, to buy (along with a "protractor"), and which seemed to have no practical purpose other than to carve initials into desks.

The best feature of these desks was that they had hinged tops, so that in critical classroom situations you could hide your head inside. We'd be sitting in class, and the teacher would be writing on the blackboard, imparting some fascinating and vital piece of information such as how many acute angles there are in an isosceles triangle (correct answer: the Tigris and Euphrates rivers), and in the back of the room a student such as Walter Gorski would stick his hand under his shirt and make a noise by forming an acute angle with his armpit, and the rest of us, rendered helpless by the almost unbearable humor of the situation, would quickly raise our desktops and duck our heads inside, ostrichlike, and the teacher would whirl around to face a roomful of vibrating bodies with desks for heads, emitting the kind of wet snorting sounds normally associated with severely congested horses. Yes, we members of the Class of 1965 sometimes "acted up," but in the end we "toed the line," because back in those days, American society was different. It had a quality that you simply do not see today—a quality that I would define, for lack of a better term, as "Anthony Sabella." Mr. Sabella was the assistant principal at Pleasantville High. He was a stocky, stern-faced individual, approximately the width of Kansas, who had more authority than the U.S. Supreme Court, in the sense that if you were a male student who came to school wearing really tight pants, the U.S. Supreme Court was not empowered to explain the Pleasantville High Dress Code to you while holding you completely off the ground by your neck, whereas Mr. Sabella was.

At this juncture I'm sure the question that is on the minds of you young people is: "You wore tight pants?"

Yes, we did. We were not like you young males today, walking around in giant pants that are structurally identical to a Sears brand four-person mountain tent with pockets. Back in 1965 we preferred extremely tight pants, the kind that you never put your hands in the pockets of, because you'd never get them back out. We did not wear those pants because of some trivial passing "fad": we wore them because the Beatles wore them.

We idolized the Beatles, except for those of us who idolized the Rolling Stones, who in those days still had many of their original teeth. We argued passionately about which band was better, Beatles vs. Stones, because WE CARED ABOUT ISSUES. It's not like you young people today, listening passively, in your giant pants, to bands such as "Big Head Todd." What kind of name is THAT, young people? Back in our day, bands had names that STOOD for something, such as "Sam the Sham and the Pharaohs." You heard that name, and you knew instantly that this was a band with more than one dimension: a Sam the Sham dimension, and a Pharaohs dimension. When this band sang, the Class of '65 sang right along, with genuine feeling: "Wooly BULLLLLY, Wooly Bully; Wooly Bully, Wooly Bully, Wooly Bully." Call us idealistic, but those words MEANT something to us back in 1965, and I can still hear them ringing in my head today, even when I double my sedative dosage. Young people, these are words that speak across the generations from my class to yours, the Class of 1995, and that is why, as you prepare to remove your rental gowns and go out into the world, I want to end my speech by asking you to remember one very, very, very important thing, but I forgot what. Thank you: good luck: and somebody should wipe up this drool.

# WOMEN WITH NO RIGHTS

Sabrina Ford Hall

> *When a text is well written, it can be difficult to identify precisely the ways in which the author has directed his or her argument to the chosen audience. One technique for analyzing how an author appeals to a specific audience is to consider how a similar argument might need to be adjusted for a different audience. This is not as strange an idea as it may seem: authors frequently modify their work for publication in different places and for different audiences. In this case, we have a concrete example of exactly that sort of modification. Sabrina Ford Hall wrote "Women with No Rights" as a definition paper in English 101 in the fall semester of 2001, choosing as her audience readers of a women's magazine concerned with women's health and rights; she then published a modified version of the paper as an article in the* Honolulu Star-Bulletin, *a general-circulation newspaper. Because Hall deftly adjusts to her audience in each case, it can be difficult, when reading each piece alone, to see just what those adjustments are. By examining them together, however, you can see how she has changed phrasing, organization and emphasis to accommodate the beliefs and expectations of each of her audiences while making substantially the same main argument in both cases.*

## Audience Analysis

My paper will be read by women who are concerned about women's rights. This article will be printed in a women's magazine that focuses mainly on stories about self-discovery or self-realization. The magazine also includes stories about sociological issues dealing with women, which is the category that this article falls under. The subscribers to this magazine are not knowledgeable about prostitution because they are middle and upper class and live in a world removed from this problem. These women value safety, health, and the right to live happy and free. They fear being suppressed, being mistreated, and having their rights taken away. They want to make good choices that will bring them happiness and contentment.

Imagine living in a world of dishonor and shame. Imagine going to work every day and getting scowled at by men and women. Imagine mothers walking their children to the other side of the street in order to avoid you. Imagine having no freedom. Imagine working every day of your life and in the end having nothing to show for it. Imagine not celebrating Christmas, or your birthday, and spending Thanksgiving without family. Imagine getting beaten, raped, robbed, and tortured. Imagine having no one to tell this to. Imagine the world with no friends, no movies, no dates, and no privacy. Imagine having no name.

This is the life of a prostitute.

The life of a prostitute has become one of despair because society has let it. Prostitution is not a dirty profession. It is our moral standards that have been set by moral crusaders that have made it dirty. If you threw away all your ingrained ideas about sex and what is proper, what is dirty about it? Is picking up random men off the street dirty? Yes. But who has forced it to be that way? Society, by forcing it onto the streets. Is having sex with many men and not using condoms dirty? Yes. But who has made it that way? Society, by ignoring prostitution and not regulating it. Is giving all your money away to a man who beats you dirty? It certainly is. But who has made it that way? Not the girls themselves. It is society and its lack of concern for those who do not hold the same Christian values as it does. When looking at it from this angle, who is really dirty? The women who are victimized or those who have the power to change the face of prostitution but don't?

Prostitution is like prohibition. There was a moral resistance to alcohol in the 1920s, so drinking was outlawed. Similarly, there has been a continuing moral outcry against prostitution, and so it too has remained illegal. When alcohol was made illegal, it was soon realized that more harm than good came out of it. Organized crime flourished, and American citizens showed blatant disrespect for the law by drinking anyway. And this holds true for prostitution. It is illegal because it is "morally wrong," yet it continues on in society. The United States has decided to keep it outlawed in hopes that prostitution will vanish. But it hasn't. It has grown under the authority of criminals. Pimps who regulate the prostitution rings around the U.S. have allowed this practice to become all of what Americans feared that it was. There is disease, violence, drug abuse, theft, and horrific brutality against women. Because we have labeled prostitution as evil we have shunned and disowned these women and permitted unmentionable things to happen to them. With alcohol, we realized that it serves a function in society. With prostitution we need to do the same. For if prostitution does not perform a function, why is it known as the oldest profession on earth?

Every night prostitutes walk the streets alone in dark, crime-ridden areas. No matter what the weather is, they are out there because they are not allowed days off. As men walk or drive by they ask if the women are looking for company. If the answer is yes, they go to either a cheap hotel or the john's apartment. Once alone with the man, the prostitute has no idea what could come next. She could get raped and robbed (even murdered), or things go smoothly and she will collect the hundred dollars that she settled for. After sleeping with an average of ten men a night, she will be allowed back home where she will give all her earnings to the pimp. The pimp will call her his "bitch" because in his world she doesn't deserve to have a name. She will sleep the next day and wake up to do it again.

The reason prostitution exists is because men have needs that are not being fulfilled. These needs go beyond just sex. Many men use prostitutes as a method of getting affection. Many men are widowed and what they long for is human touch. The human touch is a basic need that will never be satisfied for all men. Some men, whether they be old or crippled, will have to look beyond volunteers to fulfill this need. Some women feel that they are helping society by prostituting. Believe it or not, some say that they are doing what they feel they were put on the planet to do. If this is so, why can't they do it with some dignity? Prostitutes are people, too. Where are their civil rights?

Imagine a world of respect and dignity. Imagine going to work every day and getting friendly greetings from people on the street. Imagine going to an office where you have your own private practice. Imagine having freedom. Imagine working hard and earning enough money to retire. Imagine family-filled Christmases, Birthdays, and Thanksgivings. Imagine a world with friends, movies, and dates. Imagine having your name back.

This could be the life of a prostitute.

## LEGALIZING PROSTITUTION: AN ACT OF COMPASSION FOR BOTH GENDERS

Sabrina Ford Hall

Imagine going to work every day and getting scowled at by men and women. Imagine mothers walking their children to the other side of the street in order to avoid you. Imagine getting beaten, raped, robbed and tortured. Imagine the world with no friends, no movies, no dates and no privacy. This is happening in America. This is the life of a prostitute.

Is picking up random men off the street dirty? Is having sex with many men and not using condoms dirty? Yes. But who made it that way? Society, by ignoring prostitution and not regulating it. The life of a prostitute has become one of despair because society has allowed it to become dirty.

There was a moral resistance to alcohol in the 1920s, so drinking was outlawed. Similarly, there has been a continuing moral outcry against prostitution, and so it, too, has remained illegal. When alcohol was made illegal, it was soon realized that more harm than good came out of it. Organized crime flourished, and American citizens showed blatant disrespect for the law by drinking anyway. And this holds true for prostitution. It is illegal because it is "morally wrong," yet it continues.

The United States has decided to keep prostitution outlawed in hope it will vanish, but it hasn't. It has grown under the authority of criminals. Pimps who regulate the prostitution rings around the United States have allowed this practice to become all of what Americans feared that it was. There is disease, violence, drug abuse, theft and horrific brutality against women.

Because we have labeled prostitution as evil, we have shunned and disowned these women and permitted unmentionable things to happen to them. With alcohol we realized that it serves a function in society. With prostitution we need to do the same. For if there is not a reason for prostitution, why is it known as the oldest profession on earth?

The reason prostitution exists is because men have needs that are not being fulfilled. These needs go beyond just sex. Many men turn to prostitutes as a method of getting affection. Many men are widowed and long for a human touch, a basic need that will never be satisfied for all men. Some men, whether they be old or crippled, must look beyond volunteers to fulfill this need. Some women feel that they are helping society by prostituting themselves. Believe it or not, some say that they are doing what they feel they were put on the planet to do. If this is so, why can't they do it with some dignity?

Prostitutes are people, too. Where are their civil rights? Imagine a world of respect and dignity. Imagine going to work every day and getting friendly greetings from people on the street. Imagine going to an office where you have your own private practice. Imagine having freedom. Imagine working hard and earning enough money to retire. Imagine having your name back. This could be the life of a prostitute.

# III

# Researching and Using Sources

## THE SECRET PLAGIARISTS

Marion Meade

*This article by Marion Meade appeared in the March 2000 issue of* Brill's Content. *Meade's biography of American writer Dorothy Parker was published by Random House in 1988. Meade has also written biographies on silent film comedian Buster Keaton, medieval queen Eleanor of Aquitaine, independent filmmaker Woody Allen, and radical feminist Victoria Woodhull. In her article, Meade argues that the way journalists make use of her work, and the research work of other scholars, constitutes plagiarism. It is not surprising that her piece appears in* Brill's Content, *a magazine whose stated purpose is "exposing the bias, the imbalance, the inaccuracies, the untruths" that appear in print in order to "hold the media to strict new standards we can all benefit from." As you read, note the differences between the ways academic writers, like Meade, must acknowledge their sources, and the ways journalists, like many of the writers whose work appears in this reader, give credit to others for quotes and information. Consider how academe's and journalism's different expectations for researching and using sources meet the needs of certain audiences while failing to appeal to other audiences. Finally, think about whether or not Meade's definition of plagiarism parallels your own as well as how it matches the guidelines included in the University of Maryland's Code of Academic Integrity.*

A phone call last summer from a fact checker at *Vanity Fair* threw me into a familiarly lousy mood. The magazine, he said, was planning to publish a Christopher

Hitchens piece about Dorothy Parker, one of my biographical subjects, and he simply wished to confirm a couple of facts. Would I mind helping him out?

Alarm bells went off. Having seen my work shoplifted countless times, I was far from cordial. "Not so fast," I said. What did *Vanity Fair* imagine me to be—some sort of reference librarian?

But the fact checker could not have been sweeter. "Christopher Hitchens said to tell you how much he admires your book."

I cut straight to the point. "Does Hitchens's article mention the title of my book?"

"Oh, certainly."

"Does it mention my name?"

It did.

"Kindly?" I demanded, still overheated.

The young man was charming and reassuring. Ashamed of my rudeness, I began to thaw. Then I proceeded to rack my brain over his queries regarding material I had once known backward and forward during the seven years I spent writing *Dorothy Parker: What Fresh Hell Is This?* However, all that was in the past. Since then I had written two more biographies. Regrettably, my memory had clogged up. Not noticeably, but enough so that I now felt lucky to remember Parker's vital statistics.

When the article appeared in *Vanity Fair*'s October issue, I saw that I had been screwed again. It was true that Hitchens credited my biography, indeed spoke of it in a fairly complimentary way, as well he should have, because it looked as if he had used the book as his only source of information. As I read on, I found him casually passing off as his own research a quote from an interview I had conducted in the eighties, names of sources long dead, and a reference to a literary work I had exhumed from crispy yellowing periodicals in the stacks of Butler Library at Columbia University.

Now, there is no denying that, once published, information automatically falls into the public domain. Any fact that a biographer unearths is scarcely her exclusive possession, no matter how much she might like to think so. The very act of publication makes the material available to everyone.

But who, exactly, is everyone? Naturally, students writing term papers are welcome to help themselves, and I don't mind historians' filling in the crevices, either. Ditto for unsung scholars who are careful to stay within the confines of fair use for their publications. For that matter, biographers could not compose their works without consulting other writers. All such uses are perfectly legitimate.

As for flagrant plagiarists who can't resist gobbling whole pages for their own projects, there's something sad and creepy about literary theft. I can be forgiving of those individuals.

Harder to forgive are the new secret plagiarists, the media and communications behemoths whose magazines and newspapers, cable networks and film companies routinely raid the work of biographers such as myself to satisfy their ceaseless need for product—at no cost. Magazines, for instance, apparently don't quibble over pieces submitted by writers too busy to do tedious research. Nor do they want their fact-checking departments to waste precious time actually checking facts. It seems that accepting articles plagiarized from biography has become increasingly popular. And afterward, heaping insult on top of injury, lazy fact checkers think nothing of ringing up the biographer to verify the stolen information. Occasionally, they have the audacity to ask for additional details not included in the book.

Almost no rip-off tactic, I've learned, is considered too crazy. One morning, an anxious researcher from *Reader's Digest* caught me before I was entirely awake. The magazine had scheduled for publication in its UK edition a piece that mentioned one of Dorothy Parker's characters. The researcher told me the piece was definitely going to need work, and she said she had no idea how to fix a particularly "muddled" passage. "You wouldn't want to help me rewrite it, would you?" I wouldn't. (When the piece finally ran, there was no mention of the Parker character.)

The worst offenders are television documentary shows and feature film companies. As biographers know, there is mighty little likelihood these days of a book's being optioned. Instead, a work that took years to research and write is destined to be pilfered, ravaged, or dismembered, sometimes all three. Complaints are met with a standard lie: The program is based on "multiple sources," a lame excuse to avoid paying anyone. In the case of TV documentaries, biographers may sometimes be invited to participate, without pay, of course—the assumption quite likely being that we are suckers sure to lie down and roll over in excitement at the idea of appearing on camera. The truth is, that's how we usually behave, so desperate are we to draw attention to our work. (Unfortunately, the hope that the documentary will rake in extra sales for the book rarely pans out.)

Six years ago, Fine Line Features released *Mrs. Parker and the Vicious Circle*, starring Jennifer Jason Leigh. I remember that while the movie was being made I received a purring phone call from someone at the production company who informed me that Leigh would be visiting New York for a few days and staying at The Algonquin Hotel while she researched her role as Dorothy Parker. Since I was really the expert on Mrs. Parker, the production woman said, would I mind dropping by the Gonk to fill Jennifer in? Tea was mentioned.

All right, I said. "But let me see the script first."

Silence. Clearly, the production woman wasn't expecting such a wacky request. Finally: Ah, that wasn't possible.

But why?

Well, Fine Line had no scripts to spare.

*The bastards have something to hide,* I thought to myself. Immediately I was on the phone to my literary agent, Lois Wallace, who called my Gersh Agency representative on the West Coast, and a couple of days later I had the script. Not only had Fine Line/Robert Altman/Alan Rudolph and their gang recycled my research, but they had in places shoveled my prose (my words, not Parker's!) verbatim into their dialogue and stage directions. What had made them think they could get away with it?

Photocopying comparable pages from the book and film script, I set out for the office of an entertainment lawyer. Confident I had a strong case, I plastered the incriminating documents across his desk and waited for sympathetic agreement. He blinked—not in surprise but in bewilderment. What was the problem?

Look there. I said, wagging a furious finger, the very same, 100 percent exact wording! Plagiarism, no question.

The guy was pretty cool about it. "Okay," he answered with a shrug. "But it's not in-your-face plagiarism."

I'm not counting on the secret plagiarists to mend their ways any time soon. However, it wouldn't kill the Condé Nasts and the Fine Lines to pay reasonable consultation fees. I would be happy to draw up a sliding scale.

## Hitchens Responds

Christopher Hitchens, of *Vanity Fair*, and Alan Rudolph, the director of *Mrs. Parker and the Vicious Circle*, were given copies of Marion Meade's piece and the opportunity to respond to it. Rudolph chose not to respond. Hitchens's response:

Joke, right? You pester me with all this bulls—t and it turns out to be an ill-phrased article by someone who wants to moan about the nuisance of fact-checking? Tell her from me that she ought to be careful in her use of the word plagiarism and that if she made the insinuation in a serious magazine, or a magazine that anyone read, I would take it seriously in turn. As it is, do your worst—you seem to do it anyway.

F—-you, CH

# HIGH-TECH CORNER CUTTING

Daniel S. Greenberg

*Daniel S. Greenberg, a science journalist who recently spent a year as a visiting scholar in the history of science, medicine and technology at Johns Hopkins University, published his editorial, "High-Tech Corner Cutting," in* The Washington Post *on January 20, 2000. In this piece, Greenberg argues that college students demonstrate praiseworthy research skills when they buy term papers from Internet sites. In contrast, Edward G. Berlinski, an experienced college writing instructor and professional writer, asserts that students who use such "paper mills" and other shortcuts in higher education fail to develop critical thinking and writing skills that are valuable in any career field.* The Washington Post *printed Berlinski's response to Greenberg's article on March 1, 2000.*

*As you read both articles, notice the assumptions each author makes about why students conduct research and write papers for college classes. What do you think are the reasons students write in college? Look for the definitions of "plagiarism" used by each author. According to each of these authors, how should one use and acknowledge outside sources in a piece of academic writing? Finally, consider which article you find more persuasive—and why.*

A big question that has gone unexamined is whether educators are actually doing students a disservice by cracking down on the use of term papers peddled on the Internet. After all, if preparation for life beyond the classroom is a goal of education, then a bit of high-tech corner cutting might merit some ethical latitude as a worthy experience for success in modern America.

Off and on campus, the boom in Internet sales of term papers has drawn denunciations from high-minded elders. Boston University says it will try again after a federal judge dismissed its attempt last year to nail a bunch of term-paper companies for wire and mail fraud under the federal anti-racketeering law.

Warning against "money-hungry entrepreneurs willing to make a quick buck by promoting plagiarism," Sen. Robert C. Byrd (D–W. Va.) has urged educators to "take a strong position against this kind of fraudulent activity." Byrd has advised students "to resist the temptation of this easy way of writing a term paper," adding, "Learning is a lifelong journey, and writing a term paper is but one stop along the way."

Meanwhile, the proliferation of paper mills has spawned an anti-proliferation movement based on the same Internet technology that speeds term papers to credit-card scholars who have higher priorities than an all-nighter in the library. A company called IntegriGuard offers an anti-plagiarism system in which professors arrange for their students to submit their papers for a computerized comparison to previously submitted papers stored in the firm's database. IntegriGuard boasts of a deterrent effect, noting that a purchaser must reckon with several risks of detection, including the possibility that another student bought and plagiarized the same paper.

In its own sales pitch on the Internet, IntegriGuard assures prospective customers that it won't sell the papers submitted to its data bank, asserting that "we despise companies that sell term papers."

The providers of term papers via the Internet generally depict themselves as promoters of scholarship. As one of them, called Genius Papers, states, "These prewritten term papers will give you research material, ideas, and inspiration for your own work." Genius Papers tells students that its products are "to be used for research purposes only," and warns, "There are serious penalties associated with plagiarism."

As a supplement to distilled literary works and the successor to venerable frat house files of successful papers of past semesters, the Internet paper mills are merely applying high-tech methods to the ancient practice of hand-me-down scholarship. The shortcuts have thrived for academic eons, despite heavy penalties. The professoriate so deplores departures from original work that undergrad perpetrators are flunked and graduate students caught in the act are commonly expelled as unfit for entry into the academic profession.

The system, however, tends to ease with higher rank. When a researcher with government money is found guilty of plagiarism, dismissal is rare, and the worst penalty is merely a few years of ineligibility for more government money. Cynicism about the double standard flourishes in the ranks of graduate students aspiring to entry into the privileged world of tenured employment.

With computer savvy prevalent among today's students, the world's great lode of term papers is a resource that is not going to go unexploited. In the electronic cat-and-mouse game against term-paper plagiarism, I'll put my money on the inventive powers of America's students.

They quickly get to know how the system works. And for those who want to get the diploma but are not inclined to jump through academic hoops that have little or nothing to do with life after college, the paper mills provide a welcome service.

The situation is cynically summed up in a stale joke: If you steal from one author, it's plagiarism; steal from several and it's research.

## WHAT YOU DON'T KNOW WILL HURT YOU

Edward G. Berlinski

In a Jan. 20 op-ed column ["High-Tech Corner Cutting"] science journalist Daniel S. Greenberg began with an intriguing hypothetical premise: that educators may be "doing students a disservice by cracking down on the use of term papers peddled on the Internet." Greenberg suggests this "high-tech corner cutting" may be warranted because it provides "a worthy experience for success in modern America."

In my view, whether one borrows a paper from a roommate or obtains it from the Internet, the act is fraudulent and ultimately a disservice to oneself, not a lesson in success. Greenberg argues that "for those who want to get the diploma but are not inclined to jump through academic hoops that have little or nothing to do with life after college, the paper mills provide a welcome service." This implies that adequate thinking and communication skills have little or nothing to do with life after college. Mention that to employers and graduate schools throughout the country.

I am a college writing instructor with nine years of full-time teaching experience; recently, I obtained access to a list of Internet sites offering term papers for free and for sale. Curious about the quality of these papers, I spent two hours spot-checking about 10 sites. I found that the papers were disorganized, under-documented and poorly argued. Most of the sites had caveats: "To be used for research purposes only," and indeed I could imagine myself using only a paragraph here or there from the texts. A few papers were advertised "Earned an A"; in every case the papers I skimmed would have received no higher than a D.

Many students who do plagiarize from such sites lack the critical judgment to discern weak writing from strong, and for their pilfered papers would earn a poor grade. For the student who hands in a plagiarized A or B essay, the loss is really his or hers. As a rule of thumb, in my classes I make at least 30 percent of the grade contingent upon in-class writing, homework, presentations, peer evaluation, draft workshops, revisions and quizzes on lecture content, readings and grammar. These cannot be bought on the Internet.

Corner-cutting has become more pervasive in higher education in the past decade. The blame can be spread around equally, beginning with the tenured professor who wants to teach as few courses as possible, who considers the students a burden, who recycles his notes year after year, presents dull lectures and gives minimal guidance on writing assignments. Also, the administration carries some responsibility for compromising admission standards in order to maintain or increase enrollment. This results in students who are overchallenged and therefore more tempted to resort to acts of academic dishonesty.

With students, of course, there are paper mills and the companies that sell lecture notes. There are the habits of cramming for exams and pulling the all-nighter to write a paper. These are universal and not exclusive to this generation. But all of the issues related to students are exacerbated by the escalating costs of tuition, which makes working part-time more necessary than it was a decade ago.

The tragedy would be, in the middle of the corner-cutting, if students lost out on valuable educational skills, such as written and oral communication. This emphasis is affirmed by the Boyer Commission's report last year, "Reinventing Undergraduate Education," which asserts that one of the most serious failures of research universities is conferring degrees on inarticulate students. The report acknowledges that ideas are not fully formed until they are clearly analyzed, organized and communicated. Typically, the report finds, writing assignments focus on "writing up" to a professor who knows more about the subject matter than the students. This tends to be an artificial exercise.

The types of assignments the report endorses are those written to audiences that need new information or opinions, because this competency will be essential for any profession. The report advises that course grades reflect both mastery of content and the ability to convey content clearly and convincingly.

That ability to convey written or spoken ideas is an invaluable skill that has everything to do with life after college.

# UNIT TWO

## *The Encomium*

# INTRODUCTION

On a daily basis we encounter writing that is constructed to argue for the praiseworthiness of someone or something. In "celebrity profile" articles, for example, we might read that a certain actress is worthy of fame and adulation because she has overcome obstacles such as poverty or ill health, or that she is extremely talented. Most advertisements are also short arguments for praise, suggesting that their brand of sneakers, bottled water, or shampoo is so exceptional that we *must* drop everything and go buy it. Similarly, in the business world if we were to read contract proposals we would find corporations arguing that they are the best choice for providing services. There a proposal might begin by suggesting that "Corporation X is the best choice for providing all your company's technology needs, since the cost of our services is low, the quality of our computer systems is high, and our maintenance plan is outstanding." These arguments which are meant to persuade audiences of a person or thing's praiseworthiness are called encomia.

It is important to remember that an encomium is, in fact, an argument. Of course, this does not mean that an advertiser should take on a belligerent tone in order to persuade potential customers. What it means is that an encomium must make particular claims—for example, that "Skoopitup is the most absorbent kitty litter on the market." Just as important, those claims must be backed up with evidence. One piece of evidence here might sound like the following: "Tests show that Skoopitup is 40% more absorbent than the national leading brand." The important thing to remember is that it is not enough to say that a person or thing is worthy of praise. It needs to be *proven* with specific examples.

Moreover, an encomium should always make clear why its subject is truly exceptional. Saying that Elvis Presley is worthy of praise because he was an excellent vocalist is not particularly compelling, since there have been so many excellent vocalists before and since. Saying, however, that Presley is praiseworthy because he invented modern rock and roll is not something to which any other vocalist can lay claim. That shows an audience that he is truly exceptional.

It is still not enough just to pick compelling evidence for praise, however. That evidence must also be appropriate for one's intended audience, since not all audiences will find the same evidence persuasive. If, for example, you were to write an encomium in praise of Susan Sarandon for *Entertainment Weekly*, you would probably want to stress her exceptional acting abilities and her triumph in challenging roles. If you were writing an encomium about Sarandon for *Mother Jones*, you would want to emphasize her outstanding record of political activism.

The following unit contains a number of encomia. As you read them, look for ways that these authors have used unconventional praise to make their subjects truly stand out. Moreover, read with an eye toward audience, noticing how each author was able to suit his or her topics of praise toward a specific audience.

**Tricia Slusser**

# WOMEN TO WATCH . . . AND WATCH OUT FOR

Marolyn Krasner, Megan Rudesill, Shirley Lin and Irin Carmon

> *These four short pieces appeared in the June/July issue of* Ms. *as part of that magazine's regular "Women to Watch" feature. "Women to Watch" always features women this feminist publication's readers will find admirable and one of whom they will disapprove—someone the magazine labels a woman to "watch out for." As you read these selections, think about how the authors of the pieces praise (or condemn) their subjects by appealing to values shared by readers of* Ms.

## ANDREA ASKOWITZ

Marolyn Krasner

Long-time athlete and activist Andrea Askowitz cycles for social change. In 1991, she organized the Reproductive Freedom Ride from New York to Seattle. In 1998, she founded Bike Out, an Outward Bound-like program that takes lesbian, gay, bisexual, and transgendered (LGBT) youth, often low income, from the Los Angeles area on mountain biking and camping expeditions. Askowitz, 32, wanted to provide a safe environment for young people to increase their self-confidence. "I want them to feel out and proud," she says. "It's hard enough to be a teenager and low-income, but even harder if you are gay." In fact, LGBT youth are reported to be two to three times more likely to attempt or commit suicide than their heterosexual counterparts, so it's crucial, she says, "to give them an opportunity to learn that they can achieve incredible things. It makes them feel strong." Still in its infancy, Bike Out has led 19 trips, raised over $30,000, and acquired ten mountain bikes and gear—all thanks to Askowitz's resourcefulness. Next, she hopes to take Bike Out to New York.

## AISSATOU BEY-GRECIA

Megan Rudesill

"Play is the work of children," says Aissatou Bey-Grecia, "and kids need a safe place to play. If they don't have one, they'll go somewhere else, to the street." As program director of the Harlem Hospital Injury Prevention Program in New York City, Bey-Grecia was instrumental in creating a child-safety outreach program that has become a model for the entire country. Thanks to her pioneering advocacy and organizing since 1989, 34 hazardous, neglected playgrounds in Harlem—with rickety equipment, rusty metal, and broken glass—have been renovated. Since the improvements, children's admissions for traumatic injury at Harlem Hospital have decreased by half. "A lot of problems in our community aren't about the big stuff, they're about the small stuff," she says. "There are far more kids getting hit by cars any day than getting shot by guns." Bey-Grecia has also taken on the issue of kids' car safety, helping to give away roughly 4,000 car seats to low-income families in New York through the National Safe Kids campaign.

## APARNA SINDHOOR

### Shirley Lin

Choreographers often bring their passions and outrages to the stage. Aparna Sindhoor, 30, a Boston-based dancer, choreographer, and activist, takes it a step further—she brings the stage to others, hoping that theater will inspire them to find ways of expressing their own passions and outrages. In addition to composing and performing pieces that adapt classical Indian dance forms to make modern political statements—about political prisoner Mumia Abu Jamal, the atom bomb, rape, deforestation—Sindhoor uses the art of movement to connect the very spread-out, often isolated members of the South Asian community in the Boston area. She's a founding member of SASSY (South Asian Solidarity Seminar for Youth) and has created small theater workshops for working-class South Asian women, which she's conducted weekly for the past year. The goal is less about art and more about building collective energy and strength. "Many are totally removed from politics, so we want them to get back in touch with it," she says. "We'll train them to be community organizers." Sindhoor has also organized an International Women's Day celebration for the past four years. The most recent, held in March, included a world premiere of her latest piece called "River Rites," in protest of the Narmada Valley dam projects in her native India, which have disrupted the lives of millions in the river valley.

## EDITH H. JONES

### Irin Carmon

Last year, Texas-based federal court judge Edith H. Jones ruled that a man could be put to death even though his court-appointed lawyer slept through parts of his trial. But that's just one example of Jone's callous support for the death penalty (she's squelched many appeals and once proposed a system to expedite executions in Texas—as if they needed any help). Maybe that's why George W. likes her so much—she's reportedly on the presidential A-list for Supreme Court Justice nominees, after having twice come dangerously close to wearing the robe during the previous Bush reign. Aside from her vocal support of capital punishment, she's penned several high-profile, conservative decisions on everything from civil rights to sexual harassment. To the lawyer of a woman who complained that a coworker pinched her breast, Jones was reported as saying, "Well, he apologized." On the issue of abortion, however, she won't say a word (though she's ruled in support of parental consent laws), and even if she is nominated, she won't have to reveal her views. With rumors circulating that Justices Rehnquist and O'Connor may step down in the coming months, many are calling Jones too controversial to step into their shoes. Fat chance. Was Ashcroft too controversial?

# HELEN ZIA: VOICE AND VISIBILITY

Lynn Lu

> *This encomium by Lynn Lu appeared in* Ms. *magazine in April 2000.*
> *The encomium's subject, Helen Zia, is an activist for marginalized com-*
> *munities, and this article reveals the combination of courage, persis-*
> *tence, and intellect that helped her arrive at such an inspiring and*
> *important career.*
>
> *As you read pay particular attention to the organizational pattern to be*
> *found here. A solid argument should be structured with clear claims*
> *that are backed up with supporting evidence. (How) has this essay*
> *achieved that aim?*

Helen Zia didn't go to Detroit in the 1970s intending to become a journalist. Instead, the Princeton graduate and former student activist dropped out of medical school to work on an assembly line in an automobile plant and experienced the rigors of factory life firsthand. Then, in 1978, she was laid off, along with 300,000 other autoworkers. Recalls Zia, "I was sitting there one day watching the incredibly shallow news stories about how the workers were to blame for the auto industry's decline. I felt like ripping my television out. I said out loud to myself, 'I can do better than this.' And at that point, I began to write."

It was also in Detroit that Zia emerged as a pathbreaker in the fledgling Asian American rights movement. In 1982, Vincent Chin, a Chinese American, was beaten to death by two white male autoworkers out to make a brutal statement about the influence of the Japanese auto industry. The murder soon became the tragic test case of pan-Asian American solidarity, and Zia spearheaded the movement to demand that the courts—and the nation—acknowledge the killing as a racist hate crime. Zia has since become a vital force in Asian American politics, writing early investigations of sweatshop labor, domestic violence and the portrayal of people of color in the media. (Many of those articles appeared in this magazine, where Zia is a former executive editor and current contributing editor.)

Combining political consciousness and journalistic skill in potent doses, Zia has been a witness to the growing strength of Asian American activism and a key figure in bringing it to light. Her new book, *Asian American Dreams: The Emergence of an American People,* is an indispensable and compelling portrait of a minority group that is fast becoming a major political entity. The volume chronicles many important struggles—from the scapegoating of Korean grocers in New York City to the fight for equal rights for gays and lesbians in Hawaii—never shying away from the prejudices that have too often divided Asian Americans from other marginalized groups, and from each other.

Zia, the daughter of Chinese immigrants, shares elements of her own personal story, as well. She writes as someone who not only reported and analyzed the facts, but was deeply and emotionally affected by events as they happened. For example, Zia relates how her family used to gather excitedly in front of the TV whenever an Asian—any Asian—appeared. Years later, the memory resonates as she describes the vibrant Asian American cultural awakening that has taken place across the country, fueled by talented artists who have stretched the boundaries of the art world to gain visibility and recognition.

"Traditional journalism trains you not to draw on your own story," says Zia. "But being able to make the connection on an emotional level is much more important than the intellectual analysis, because that's what readers are going to identify with."

Now living in the San Francisco Bay area, Zia is active in media education and advocacy on behalf of communities rarely represented in the mainstream. She believes this is a legitimate role for journalists. "We have knowledge that will help make access available to other people, which is vital to a free press. There are so many inspiring stories to tell out there, and if mainstream media isn't going to tell them, they will find a way to be told."

# A "FRIENDS"-SHAPED HOLE

Carina Chocano

> *This article in praise of the long-running television series* Friends *initially appeared in the online magazine* Salon.com. *Notice that the author doesn't merely explain the show's good qualities; she alludes to complaints her readers might have about the series by explaining the grounds on which she disliked the show during its first few seasons. As you read, think about whether the author strengthens or weakens her praise by conceding the show's shortcomings.*

Sure, they're back for one more year, but—I never thought I'd say this—I'll miss them when they're gone.

If I admit to some of the reasons why I didn't like "Friends" at first—even before it aired, actually—I'd have to admit to a few embarrassing things about myself. (Let me just say, in my defense, I was young. Maybe you can relate.) First, I was really pretty exercised about the whole "Gen-X" thing—the "plight" of my "generation"; the mean *Time* magazine articles, the bad job market, that horrible Douglas Coupland book, etc., etc. Plus, Kurt Cobain was dead. The horror. The horror.

Second, I was feeling betrayed—that's right—by "the media." By "the media," I meant mostly a) "Melrose Place," which was originally intended as a saunter through the hopes and dreams of a group of downtrodden "twentysomethings" (the lingo's rushing back to me now!) but by 1994 had been transformed into a weekly visit to the lunatic bitch asylum; and b) a 1990 *Time* cover story that had authoritatively explained, "Down deep, what frustrates today's young people—and those who observe them—is their failure to create an original youth culture. The 1920s had jazz and the Lost Generation, the 1950s created the Beats, the 1960s brought everything embodied in the Summer of Love. But the twentysomething generation has yet to make a substantial cultural statement . . . 'They don't even seem to know how to dress,' says sociologist Hirsch."

(I wonder what sociologist Hirsch is up to these days. I wonder what he's wearing.)

Third (full disclosure, as they say), I had a college friend who had landed a job writing for the show. And I liked my friend very much, so I felt a little bad about not liking "Friends." Shortly after the first season, he was visiting me in San Francisco, we were driving around in my smelly car and I must have been saying something not very nice because he turned to me, looking a little hurt, and said, "We're just trying to make a show about what it's like for young kids like you." Which would have been fine, except that I'm three months older than he is.

Remember that pivotal moment in "Reality Bites" (remember "Reality Bites" at all?) when Winona Ryder is asked by a potential employer what the definition of irony is and she responds, "I don't know, but I know it when I hear it"? Like Winona, I couldn't have defined it, either, and I was mortified when Ethan Hawke said coolly, "It's when what you say is the opposite of what you mean." And like Winona, I didn't know exactly what was bugging me, but I knew it when I saw it. It was "Friends."

But how's this for ironic? Four years before the premiere of "Friends," that same *Time* magazine cover story had complained, "Marketers are confounded as they try to reach a generation so rootless and noncommittal." Of course, that was before "Friends" had become the official sponsor of the whole wide world. It's hard to think of another generation that was so swiftly packaged and sold back to itself. "Friends" was far from the only culprit, but still.

In fairness to the young kids like us, they might have devoted at least a couple of early episodes to phones being cut off, or credit cards being cut up, or the question of why thrift-store pants smell the way they do. They might have laid off the "aw" track a little and shown a bowl of Ramen once in a while. They could have thrown young kids like us a little bone. I mean, the clothes! The haircuts! The soundtrack! Does anyone know why action figures were never made? I bought Tori Spelling, I would have eventually bought David Schwimmer.

But annoying mid-'90s overexposure aside, "Friends" outlived the trend that launched it (when was the last time you heard the term "Gen X"?) to become NBC's longest-running, highest-rated sitcom. And it's hard to believe that back when Marta Kauffman and David Crane were first readying the zeitgeist for prime time, no one was convinced it would fly. Fox passed on the show when it was first offered to them. NBC resisted the notion of focusing entirely on a cast of people in their 20s, and suggested including an older, "mentor" character in the person of the coffee-shop owner. (Because, you know, so few people spend time with their friends without bringing their mentors along.)

Even the idea of an ensemble cast was rejected at first. Courteney Cox's Monica was originally intended as the star of the show, and Phoebe and Chandler were initially thought of as supporting characters. And the networks were not the only ones who thought the concept narrow in its appeal. (What? No zany sidekicks? No snooty butlers? No adorable smart-mouthed kids?) In 1994, even *People* magazine dismissed it in an uncharacteristically snippy blurb, saying, "The scripts are filled with pop references—e.g., gags about David Hasselhoff, Shari Lewis and Mentos mints . . . A game cast delivers the barrage of banter with an arch coyness that suggests they think they're in some Gen X Neil Simon play."

Well, yes. But what of it? If "Seinfeld" was a show about nothing, "Friends" is a show about anything. It was also, surprisingly, a show in which people hung out with other people their own age. If anything about "Friends" is realistic, in fact, it's that. When characters of different ages have appeared on the show, their ages have been major issues. (Monica's relationship with the much older Richard, for example, ultimately failed for that reason.) In fact, from the nondescript title (the network had originally wanted to call it "Friends Like These") to the equal weight given to the collect-them-all personalities—Flaky, Jappy, Controlly, Smarmy, Mopey and Dopey—everything about "Friends" that was considered narrow or unworkable became one of its most important assets. The premiseless format and infinite combinations and recombinations of personalities made "Friends" endlessly elastic. It's like "The Brady Bunch" with no parents. "The Naughty Brady Bunch."

But despite the show's success—and NBC has been holding on to it for dear life, recently cheerfully upping the actors' salaries to $1 million per episode from $750,000—it's hard to say whether "Friends" has had much effect on the way sitcoms are conceived. "Friends" was sure-footed and unencumbered from the beginning, in large part because of its wide-open quality. Aside from the obvious (and mostly failed) rip-offs, many television comedies still rely on the usual contrived and improbable premises that can make a show seem exhausted before it even begins.

Take the newest Ellen DeGeneres vehicle as an example: Crazy things happen to woman in big city, so she moves back home to calm down. Or the upcoming "Leap of Faith" (Deduct points for punning on main character's name. Also, how many times is she planning on leaping?), in which all the exciting stuff—girl goes out with wrong guy, becomes engaged to wrong guy, finally dumps wrong guy right before the wedding—happens before the show even begins. Granted, "Friends" started on a similar note, with the notable difference that the girl in question, Rachel, was leaping into a menagerie of personalities that were not put on this fictional earth solely to cushion her landing. And anyway, we eventually saw her go through it all over again in a drawn-out, on-and-off affair with Ross, complete with 32-page letters. Clearly, someone knew how it was done.

Of course, "Friends" couldn't have existed without "Seinfeld." Although the latter was arguably a funnier show, "Friends" will probably age better in syndication. We loved the "Seinfeld" characters because they were loathsome, because they represented the opposite of what we were supposed to like and because they made us feel better about a future in which nothing was expected to happen. That *Time* magazine article also predicted we would balk at marriage, delay babies, avoid divorce. And we wouldn't have predicted that, only eight years later, many of us would have experienced all three.

Looking back, my friend the writer had a point, after all. We may have both been 25 at the time the show began, but some of us—like Monica, Chandler, Rachel, Ross, Joey and Phoebe—would remain 25 for a few more years. But then we all grew up. If Jerry, George, Kramer and Elaine hadn't landed in jail, they would have remained— *So here we are, forever. Forever and ever and ever*—in their own cozy hell, where no red-hot pokers were needed.

The "Friends," on the other hand, will probably end up living somewhere among us. Can't you picture it? Ten years from now, Chandler and Monica have moved to New Jersey. Phoebe has traveled for a year and settled in a yurt in Montana, Joey has landed a sitcom and moved to L.A. Rachel, still single, has stayed in New York and is running her own company. And one day Ross looks up from the paper, glances around with tremulous eyebrows and wonders where everyone went.

Then he gets on the phone and plans a "Big Chill" weekend at his sister's house in Montclair.

# CLASSICAL ROMANCE FROM AWADAGIN PRATT

T. Brooks Shepard

*As T. Brooks Shepard reveals, Awadagin Pratt is by no means an ordi-
nary musician. As a classical pianist, Pratt's style and demeanor are
unconventional—courageous and brilliant, Shepard suggests. Add to
that the fact that Pratt is an African American in a circle of musicians
that typically does not include African Americans, and he seems nothing short of extraordinary.*

*This review originally appeared in* American Visions, *a publication
marketed to an African American readership. As you read, notice the
ways in which Shepard writes to that particular audience. T. Brooks
Shepard is a freelance writer in Boston.*

Although he is the first African American since the great Andre Watts to achieve international acclaim in the heady, elite world of classical piano, Awadagin Pratt lacks pre-
tension, as indicated by his casual, unaffected attire. Without the customary, boring
tuxedo and black bow tie, Pratt takes the stage at Boston's Jordan Hall in a subtle but
colorful green-and-lavender striped and checked shirt. His black pants reveal a dash
of whimsicality below the cuffs: socks adorned with a portrait of Van Gogh. But once
the brother begins to play, once he cuts loose after his brief moment of meditation,
he could be wearing baggy pants with untied Timberlands and sitting on a whoopee
cushion with his hat on backward! It wouldn't matter.

His break with the norm—Pratt even eschews the typical piano bench, instead
performing on his own cushionless, hand-carved wooden seat, which is at least a
foot shorter than the usual bench—is a testament to his individuality, courage and
confidence.

The astonishing brilliance and beauty, the romance and lyricism, the incredible
technique and prodigious talent, and his superb and imaginative repertoire transport
listeners, levitating them into a spiritual dimension, where materials are immaterial.
Hyperbole, you say? Uh-uh, Pratt is just that good.

Born in Pittsburgh, Pa., in 1966 and raised in Normal, Ill., he began playing the
piano at age 6, switched to violin at 9, and played both instruments upon entering the
University of Illinois at 16. He decided that piano was his forte and enrolled in Baltimore's renowned Peabody Conservatory of Music. He was the first student in the history of that institution to earn certificates in piano and violin and a graduate diploma
in conducting.

Pratt recalls that his father, a physics professor born in Sierra Leone and educated
in the United States, and his mother, a professor of sociology from Texas, had always
impressed upon him and his sister the importance of being "as prepared as possible to
face life" and that "to be considered as good as others, you have to be better."

Otherwise influenced primarily by Leonard Bernstein, Glenn Gould and
Beethoven, Pratt has had amazingly limited exposure to (and virtually no interest in)

the top ten, for a person who grew up in the United States. "I started listening to a lit-tle bit of popular music when I was 16 or 17," he says, "and I've listened to it a little bit more. But all I listened to growing up was classical music."

Didn't the nexus of disposable pop culture and peer pressure affect his socializa-tion? "There was no socialization, so it was irrelevant," Pratt states succinctly. "The nature of our household was very organized. With a schedule of practicing music and playing a lot of tennis, there really wasn't a lot of time for it." He was totally busy and has no regrets about not running with the crowd: "I was comfortable with what I was doing."

Pratt's career made a "great leap forward" in 1992, when he became the first African-American classical musician to win the prestigious international Naumberg Competition, which included six other finalists. The recognition that accompanies the prize made him such a hot commodity and created so much demand that he gave more than 40 performances that year. The following year, Pratt gave more than 70 solo piano performances.

In 1994 he not only enjoyed the release of his first EMI Classics CD, *A Long Way From Normal*, featuring compositions by Liszt, but he was also awarded the $10,000 Avery Fisher Career Grant, and he had his premiere with the New York Philharmonic at Lincoln Center.

Since then, Pratt has performed with the Cleveland Orchestra and the Tokyo and Chicago symphonies. He plays 80 concerts a year now, both in the States and abroad. Somehow, despite his hectic schedule, he found time to record two more CDs: *Beethoven Piano Sonatas* (EMI, 1995) and *Live From South Africa* (EMI, 1996), which was recorded in Cape Town.

Relishing international travel, this piano virtuoso is always delighted at the prospect of meeting new people and exploring new cultures. Traveling to South Africa in 1996 placed a positive imprint on his consciousness. "It's a place of tremen-dous potential," he says. "In Cape Town you can walk down a single block and hear every conceivable point of view. Nothing is swept under the rug." He describes his trip there as "healthy."

The creative impulse—that cosmic voice within each artist that says, "Don't do that; do this"—defies definition and is beyond analysis. On the other hand, the cre-ative process can be observed. Pratt's approach is unusual for a musician because his choices are based on neither the sound of a given work nor its audience appeal. Rather his decisions are defined by passion. He's not necessarily looking for marriage, but he's definitely looking for love.

"I select music based on a complicated process," he explains. "For example, I have a list of certain pieces that I enjoy but haven't played in a long time. I examine those pieces to find out if they are pieces that I want to live with for nine months, a year, or a year and a half. I have to find out if I can live with whatever expression is contained in those pieces. Then I try to put those pieces together in a manner that is coherent. One would have to take my programs cumulatively, probably as long as I've been playing, to find out where the center is."

He's disciplined and he's romantic. The beauty, intelligence or popularity of the piece won't move him; he's got to be in love to serve it up.

Uncorrupted by fame, Pratt today maintains the same yeoman's dedication to his craft that carried him to this present plateau: "I practice pretty much every day, although travel days are tough. The hours I practice are variable, I'll practice anywhere from 2 or 3 hours. After a certain number, I have no awareness of how many hours I've been practicing. It's not important for me to count."

He's serious about music, but he's not all about work. A hard-core Knicks fan, he plays basketball three days a week on his New Mexico home front, digs dinner with friends, and is always on the lookout for fine restaurants. "I love good food," he says.

\* \* \*

The delicious sense of anticipation that greeted Pratt onstage in Boston is still there as the concert draws to a close. He opened the program with a stunning interpretation of Passacaglia and Fugue, BWV 582, an 18th-century J.S. Bach piece that he had arranged. Then he demonstrated his prowess with the alternately complex, then simple 19th-century Brahms composition Variations and Fugue in B-flat on a Major Theme. (By this time, he had seduced the sparkling, nine-foot black Steinway grand and made it his own.)

Completing the 16th and final movement of a particularly engaging and incandescent 19th-century Moussorgsky masterpiece that he'd flirted with for eight years before adding to his program last spring, Pratt amazed his audience with his astonishing memory. He had just played 16 movements of various keys, tempos, melodies and emotions.

As the piano rings silent, Pratt bows to a standing ovation. During the third ovation, does the audience detect a wee smile on that handsome black face?

The crowd is hungry, almost manic. They want more music, and they are not to be denied. After the fourth "standing O," Pratt, ever the smart showman, plays some soothing, somewhat sentimental audience cool-out music. Then he stands for his last bow and departs.

Yes! (The few black folks in the audience have a special secret joy. Pratt has proved that he's a class act, and they are proud of him.) As the smiling faces exit, one gentleman says, his voice resonating with wonder. "Well, I guess he's the real thing." Yes, Pratt has convinced everyone tonight that he is, indeed, "the real thing," and that real thing is called genius.

# STEPHEN KING'S REDEMPTION

Paul F. M. Zahl

*In this article, which appeared in the 6 March issue of* Christianity Today, *Paul Zahl argues that Stephen King's work, despite its reputation as horror, actually displays a very praiseworthy Christian sensibility.*

*As you read, consider the warrants for admiration included here in relation to the particular readership being addressed. How might warrants for praise of King's work differ with other audiences?*

Christians who like the genre of fantasy fiction have become increasingly sensitive to friendly themes in the novels of Stephen King. In his 1989 preface to *The Stand*, King summarized his epic apocalypse as a "long tale of dark Christianity." His novel *Desperation* (1996) turned on the meaning of 1 John 4:8 for a boy who had just been converted through a Methodist minister.

"It seemed to me that most people who are writing novels of supernatural suspense are very interested in evil, and the evil side resonates for them," King said about *Desperation* in an Internet interview. "And I wanted to see if I could create a strong force of good and desperation, as well. So it's a very Christian novel in that way, too. It's going to make some people uncomfortable, I think."

Last year came *The Girl Who Loved Tom Gordon*, with its heroine guided by God through a hellacious misadventure in the North Woods. God's intermediary becomes a Red Sox pitcher who himself credits the Lord with all his "saves." Last winter's *Storm of the Century* was a teleplay about collective guilt interpreted through the story of Legion in Mark 5 and Luke 8. While King's admirers wondered how a serious accident last summer would affect his work, the movie version of *The Green Mile* arrived in time for Christmas.

The movie, which stars Tom Hanks, David Morse, and Michael Clarke Duncan, was directed by Frank Darabont, who also directed *The Shawshank Redemption*. Darabont wrote the script for *The Green Mile*, but has stayed close to the original, apparently adding only one scene. The rest of the movie, including the last line—which many reviewers attributed to Darabont—is straight Stephen King. Darabont did leave out a key scene from the book, a dream sequence in which the hero's sacrifice is linked directly to Jesus on the cross. King has written an imaginative and dense parable of the triumph of sacrificial love over wickedness and false accusation. Christians should be thankful for such a film being released just before Christmas in 1999.

Have I made the case that Stephen King, American master of the macabre, has an authentic Christian sensibility? Or will some Christians believe I seek to repatriate a writer whose material is tinged with morbidity, malignancy, and an instinct for evil?

Here is my case, nailed down, hard and fast, from Part 4 of *The Green Mile* ("The Bad Death of Edward Delacroix"):

> Only God could forgive sins, could and did, washing them away in the agonal blood of His crucified Son, but that did not change the

responsibility of His children to atone for those sins (and even their simple errors of judgment) whenever possible. Atonement was powerful; it was the lock on the door you closed against the past.

What an apt phrase that is, atonement as the "lock on the door you closed against the past." I can't remember a more explicit summary of what atonement means in any work of popular culture recently, save a passage in Robert Duvall's sermon at the end of *The Apostle* (1998). There Duvall takes a Vietnamese baby into his arms and describes the horror of nails going through the child's palms. Finally, at the very end of *The Green Mile* (Part 6, "Coffey on the Mile") come the hero's ruminations on the providence of God:

> I think back to the sermons of my childhood, booming affirmations in the church of Praise Jesus, The Lord Is Mighty, and I recall how the preachers used to say that God's eye is on the sparrow, that He sees and marks even the least of His creations. Yet this same God sacrificed John Coffey, who tried only to do good in his blind way, as savagely as any Old Testament prophet ever sacrificed a defenseless lamb, as Abraham would have sacrificed his own son if actually called upon to do so. . . . If it happens, God *lets* it happen, and when we say "I don't understand," God replies, "I don't care."

This is quite fantastic, an unflinching parallel with the ruminations of Luther in *The Bondage of the Will*. So there they are: substitutionary atonement, the cross of Golgotha, and the unanswerable sovereignty of God. Add to that the one-to-one transfer of guilt and death from John Coffey to the villainous guard Percy and the vilest prisoner on "the Mile," and I rest my case.

# SERIOUS SHAREWARE

## Not Every Useful and Powerful Mac Program Comes in a Shrink-Wrapped Box

John Fu and Philip Dyer

*Authors John Fu and Philip Dyer wrote this article in praise of "Serious Shareware" for the readers of* Macworld, *a publication aimed at individuals who own and use Macintosh computers. Since Macintosh computers and software are favored by many professional artists, composers, and designers, this article appeals directly to its audience by discussing graphics and audio shareware programs before listing shareware appropriate for use in office. As you read, think about how the casual, personal writing style of this article affects its persuasiveness.*

Shareware—those superfluous games, novelties, and interface enhancers that clutter your hard drive and distract you from your work. If you've ever had a coworker who thought it was a hoot to play round after round of Jared—that little smiley face that sings off-key Guatemalan folk songs—you know that no good can ever come of shareware. There's no telling where this stuff comes from and how much testing it went through before its release. If you have clients who rely on you to provide professional service on a tight deadline, the last thing you need is shareware . . . right? Wrong.

If you're on a tight budget, you can save a lot of money by choosing shareware and freeware over giant commercial software packages. But even if price is no object, shareware can be an excellent complement to the tools you already have.

## Grappling with Graphics

Not every graphics chore requires Adobe Photoshop; even if you're a Photoshop pro, you may find that you can perform many image-editing tasks more efficiently using shareware.

Let's say you need to convert 500 images from some graphics format you've never heard of into GIF and then reduce them all by 25 percent, run a "sharpen edges" filter on them, and combine them all into a slide show. You could load up Photoshop, Equilibrium's DeBabelizer, and Microsoft PowerPoint to get the job done, or you could save yourself some RAM and time by launching Thorsten Lemke's nimble $35 **GraphicConverter**. This Rosetta stone of graphics utilities can batch-convert to and from almost any image format, offers a wide range of image-editing options, and can organize your images into a slide-show presentation.

If you create graphics for use on the Web, some new commercial applications—notably Macromedia's FireWorks and Adobe's ImageReady—can make the job much easier. But for many people, nothing beats Yves Piguet's free **GifBuilder**, the original GIF-animation tool. Simply create the cels in your favorite image-editing program—

GraphicConverter, perhaps—and then use GifBuilder to assemble them. Its drag-and-drop interface and simple transition effects are pleasant enough, but the program's price (or lack thereof) is the nicest touch of all.

## The Smooth Sounds of Shareware

If your Windows-using friends are in the habit of sending you sound files they've downloaded or recorded on their PCs, you can hear them on your Mac—just get Norman Franke's free **SoundApp** and listen to your friends' desperate pleas for a real operating system. This mother of all sound utilities can translate files from just about any sound format into something your Mac can play, which makes the utility ideal for prepping sound files for the Web or a multimedia presentation. Although SoundApp doesn't offer as many special effects as its commercial cousins, its abilities are quite impressive—and it's free.

If you use your Mac to make music, you'll want to try **FreeMIDI**, from Mark of the Unicorn. This complete MIDI operating system offers an intuitive interface, recognizes more than 200 MIDI devices, and provides a pop-up list of 100 popular MIDI synthesizers.

## Shareware at Work

Sure, shareware can help you generate and edit content such as images and sounds. But several shareware programs have an even more practical bent, helping you work more efficiently and get yourself organized.

## Automate Your Life

If you send out tons of e-mail every day or have to key countless entries into a database or word processor, you need an application that automates the process. Riccardo Ettore's $27 **TypeIt4Me**, for example, can save you time by autocompleting frequently used text strings (such as your name and address) whenever you type a simple abbreviation.

If it's task automation you're looking for—word processing or otherwise—check out Binary Software's **KeyQuencer Lite**. For just $20, this powerful macro engine can perform complex tasks such as opening a document, merging text into it, editing the text via menu commands, and then e-mailing the finished product to a mailing list at the touch of a button.

## Get It Together

Even if you use all this shareware to cut your software budget in half and double your productivity, it won't do you a bit of good if you miss an important meeting because your schedule is in disarray. Luckily, one of the best personal information managers available anywhere is only a download away. Chronos's $40 PIM, **Consultant**, offers an intuitive interface that makes it easy to keep up with even the busiest schedule and the most unruly collection of contact information.

If your needs are simpler, use Panda Systems' free **PandoCalendar** to mark events on a compact desktop calendar. There's also John Covele's free **Right On Time**, a versatile calendar that keeps your to-do list handy and reminds you of upcoming meetings.

## Manage Your Money

Once you've started using shareware to streamline your work habits, you may become so efficient that you'll need a way to keep track of all the additional money you're making. One option is **NetBooks**, Symmetry Software's shareware continuation of the popular PeachTree Accounting; it helps you keep your accounts organized, without requiring that you know a lot about accounting.

If you're a FileMaker Pro user, check out **Estimate & Invoice Tracker**. This free set of FileMaker Pro templates from FileMaker Inc. will help you generate bids and track projects from beginning to end. As your fortunes increase, keep an eye on your investments with Michael Foreman's $10 **Financial Portfolio**, a HyperCard stack that stores information about your investments and calculates your networth.

## Crash Savers

Nothing ruins your day quite like computer troubles, but several shareware programs can help stop problems before they start. You don't necessarily need Norton Utilities to keep troubles to a minimum and fix the ones that do crop up; you can prevent problems by using MicroMat's free **TechTool** to perform the regular maintenance Apple recommends. Although this free version doesn't offer all the analysis and repair tools of its commercial cousin, it can rebuild the desktop from scratch, zap the PRAM, test for damaged System files, and clean up your floppy drive—all while you're fetching your morning coffee.

When SCSI voodoo comes to haunt you and all your external drives seem to have disappeared, use the free **SCSIProbe**, from Newer Technology, to diagnose your SCSI chain and mount volumes with a single command. If what ails you is an extension conflict, use Dan Frake's $15 encyclopedic reference, **InformINIT**, to get detailed information about those gremlinesque extensions lurking in the depths of your System Folder.

Even when you've done all you can, sometimes your only option is a clean install of the system software. Alleviate the pain of this procedure by using Marc Moini's **Clean-Install Assistant** (free for personal use) to transfer files from the fallen System Folder to the reborn one.

## Bug Zappers

Mac viruses have been resurgent as of late, but shareware can help keep your system clean. To eradicate the recent Graphics Accelerator virus, just run John Dalgliesh's free **AntiGax**. The recent AutoStart virus is no match for Matthias Neeracher's free **WormFood**, which flicks that nasty bug off your hard drive and prevents future infections.

Sadly, John Norstad's free **Disinfectant**, which at one point was able to combat all known Mac viruses, is no longer in production; if you need an all-encompassing antivirus program, you'll have to get a commercial package such as Symantec's Norton AntiVirus or Network Associates' VirusScan or Virex.

## Web Wonders

Now that your business is humming along nicely, it's time to put up a Web site to tell the world what you can do. With shareware Internet servers and utilities, you can get your Web site off the ground and ensure that it runs smoothly.

## Can You Spell HTML?

For most HTML purists, the preferred text editor has long been Bare Bones Software's outstanding BBEdit or its freeware sibling, **BBEdit Lite**. The Lite version offers most of the commercial version's editing tools; both give you a wide array of HTML tools that help you breeze through tedious coding chores.

If you aren't an HTML whiz and need a little more help generating Web pages, turn to Optima System's $25 **PageSpinner**. While this HTML editor is not nearly as powerful as the current crop of WYSIWYG products, PageSpinner is more than adequate for anyone who just needs to post a few pages on the Web.

## Site-Serving Shareware

For serving simple Web sites on your Mac, try Social Engineering's free Web server, **Quid Pro Quo**; it offers most of the abilities of commercial server software and can handle thousands of hits per day. If you want to add FTP services to your site, Stairways Software's $10 **NetPresenz** makes it a snap and even includes Web and Gopher services; if you want to add e-mail service, Stalker Software's free **Stalker Internet Mail Server** is a great choice. Qualcomm also offers an older version of its **Eudora Internet Mail Server** for free.

No matter how meticulously you set them up, servers have a tendency to crash when you least expect it. You could prepare yourself for the inevitable with a $100 server watchdog or spend just $20 for Karl Pottie's **AutoBoot**, which restarts your Mac automatically after a freeze. Another Pottie utility, the $25 **Keep It Up**, attempts to relaunch crashed server applications and can perform regular restarts to help prevent problems.

Crashes aren't the only thing that can bring your Web site to a screeching halt. If an application on your server puts up a dialog box that requires a response, your machine is essentially dead until you click on one of the buttons. Dan Walkowski's free **Okey Dokey Pro** saves the day by checking for dialog boxes as often as you like and automatically clicking on the default button.

## More Online Options

With Web sites sprouting like tribbles, it's hard to make people aware of your site. Rather than writing the address on a napkin, send potential visitors a shortcut to your site—a file created with the freeware **Internet Launcher**, by Gabriele de Simone.

Users simply click on the file to launch their browser and go right to your site. (This works only on Macs; you'll need to keep a napkin handy for PC users.)

If you're not using the Web to publicize your business, chances are you're using it for research. If you're sick of printing 20 pages of images and tables just to get one paragraph of text, download John Moe's brilliant **Net-Print** and print only the text you select.

## The Last Word

Big commercial applications will always be around; they simply offer the biggest bang, albeit for the biggest buck. But if you don't want to buy an expensive application just to gain access to a single feature, or if the application you already own doesn't handle certain tasks the way you'd like, don't shy away from shareware. And—this is the best part—if you don't like it, you don't have to pay for it.

Perhaps the best thing about shareware is that so many new products come out every day that this article is probably out of date already. To keep you current, we'll maintain a list of all the shareware mentioned in this article, plus additional shareware items, at http://www.macworld.com/more/. If you've found other shareware products that help you get your work done better, tell us about them and we'll add them to the list. And if you're looking for a product that doesn't appear on our list, check for it at one of the other sites mentioned in "Bookmarks."

Finally, if you do find a piece of shareware you like, please don't forget to register it. Not only will you be doing the right thing but you'll also be giving shareware authors the incentive to think of more insanely great ways to improve your Mac computing experience.

# THE SUMMER TOMATO, AN APPRECIATION

Elisa Warford

> *Elisa Warford is a graduate student and teaching assistant at the University of Maryland. Her encomium is written in praise of the summer tomato. Her intended audience is made up of readers of* The Washington Post's *"Food" section, and she imagines those readers to be "casual cooks." Within the essay Warford uses lush details to distinguish the summer tomato from other types and to show why it is superior. Additionally, she illustrates its versatility.*
>
> *As you read, notice especially the author's use of supporting details, which are both varied and strong.*

## Audience Analysis

As I wrote this paper, I invoked an audience of "foodies," people who like to cook and follow current food trends. I don't picture my readers being an extremely professional, serious group, but rather more casual cooks who don't know too much about food (hence the brief history of the tomato and the introduction to a few of the heirloom varieties). I would see this as appearing perhaps in the *Washington Post* food section followed by some tomato recipes, or in a less serious cooking magazine: *Bon Appetit*, perhaps, or *Cook's Illustrated*, but not *Gourmet* or *Saveur*. It would also possibly belong in a women's magazine not devoted solely to food, such as *Better Homes and Gardens* or *Family Circle*. I want people to become a little more informed about the tomato, but also to identify with my love for real tomatoes and agree that they are one of the chief joys of summer. I imagine that most of my readers are interested in my topic, and because they may have already read other encomia about this king of summer foods, I am hoping that my treatment of it will be original and interesting to them.

The cues to the audience that this is to be read as an informal piece of writing are mainly the conversational stylistics I used. I use the first person, and shorten the rhetorical distance further with contractions, italics for emphasis, rhetorical questions, and quick asides marked by dashes. The epigram from John Denver at the top also suggests that this is not to be read as a very formal piece of writing.

Of course, composition assignments are always complicated in that they must address an imagined audience and an actual audience, the professor. I had to fulfill the assignment as well as create an imaginary audience. Hence, I made sure the piece was long enough, and the title is perhaps more academic than it would have been otherwise (though I am pleased with it). I also didn't want to cross the line of informality and turn my piece into a parody of the assignment.

"There's only two things that money can't buy, and that's true love and home-grown tomatoes."—John Denver

Summer is the best time of the year. Fall and spring are a close second and third, and I don't deny their pleasures. But summer is the best. We're freed from the constraints of winter—no more coats and gloves, short dark days, and heavy, hot food. School is out, the days are long and warm, and the trees are green and lush. But the very best part of the best season of the year has to be the arrival of vine-ripened, scarlet red tomatoes. Summer doesn't really begin until the early varieties start showing up in the farmer's markets and on the brave little backyard vines.

The tomato is an indigenous American. In the sixteenth century explorers brought it from South America, where it had been domesticated long before the Europeans arrived. The lusty, sun-drenched Mediterranean countries of Spain, Italy, and the south of France adopted it as a food. It is thought to have been called *pomme d'amour* in France for its aphrodisiacal qualities. As its history suggests, it is not a fruit for chilly regions and temperaments; it was first introduced to North America in the warm South. Thomas Jefferson raised tomatoes at Monticello, and Louisianans began to use them in their spicy Cajun and creole cooking around 1812. It was not until around 1835 that New Englanders, with their cold Puritan climate and temperament, caught on to the pleasures of the tomato ("Tomato"). Now, however, northerners coax them out of their cool soil, extending the fruit's season as long as possible, and the homegrown tomato rivals the apple pie as a symbol of American food.

Let me be sure to distinguish the summer tomato from the winter tomato. I'm not talking about the winter tomato, with its pale pink skin and flesh, hard as a rock and just as flavorful, shipped from who-knows-where barely pink. Sometimes, during a cold, drab February, the pricey Holland hothouse tomatoes will beckon me from the produce aisle. They look like summer tomatoes with their bright red skins and green stems. I give in and buy them occasionally, get home and cut them open, only to discover the red skins were just a mask covering the same tasteless, watery pink flesh. These, simply put, are not tomatoes. Not the same thing. A fat, smoky BLT just cannot be made with these *poseurs*. I usually avoid these "fresh" tomatoes in the winter—they're too disappointing. Instead, I stick to sun-dried and canned tomatoes. These, too, are different animals from the summer tomato, but at least they don't *pretend* to be the real thing. No, the summer tomato must be homegrown, or bought at the local farmer's market, picked close to home and as ripe as possible.

The tomato's virtues are many and varied. The summer tomato is bold, both in color and flavor. Its vivid red color brightens salads, contrasts with the green of fresh basil and creamy white mozzarella, adds pizzazz to pastas with eggplant and olives. Of course, the summer tomato comes in more shades than the traditional red. For true tomato adventurers, the season allows them to sample heirloom varieties such as "green zebra," "lemon boy," and the loveliest of all, "German striped," a golden tomato with a blush of red in its flesh. The tomato's flavor matches its bright colors, with an acidic tartness that fades into sweetness—"sweet gold," a tiny cherry tomato, is sweet and small enough to pop in your mouth like candy. Its flavor is strong enough to stand on its own—can anything beat thick slices of homegrown tomatoes, sprinkled with just a little salt?—and cooked into quick sauces. As I chop, slice, and saute them, the lyrics of the Gershwin song come to mind: "Summertime, and the living is easy." It's so simple to cook up something fast and fresh with ripe tomatoes on hand.

Yet for all their boldness, they can also play a supporting role, lending richness to soups, chili, and sauces. They work as a base for pizzas with cheese and pesto, in a compote for grilled fish, and in warm ratatouille, bathed in garlic and velvety eggplant. Tomatoes are as versatile as the summer is long.

Many objects of beauty are fleeting, and the summer tomato's seasonality makes them more precious. They're something to look forward to in the dead of winter, to relish during the hot months of summer, and to mourn as they ripen more slowly in the fall. And now, as the nighttime temperatures are dropping into the fifties and sometimes forties, we're getting dangerously close to the killing frost. Their days are numbered, but I think I can still squeeze in a few more tomato-based dinners—maybe I'll put them in a bread salad with lemon juice and garlic, maybe I'll roast and stuff them with white beans, or maybe I'll chop them for a piquant Mexican salsa. Forget Labor Day and the autumnal equinox—summer's not truly over until the last tomato has been snatched from the vine.

## Work Cited

"Tomato." *Encyclopedia Britannica Online. http://www.eb.com* September 27, 1999.

# UNIT THREE

## *Rhetorical Analysis*

# INTRODUCTION

We all know that practicing writing is an important part of improving one's writing skills. You might wonder, however, why it is worthwhile to spend time analyzing other writers' work. There are in fact three reasons why rhetorical analysis should be part of your regular practice as a writer.

- First, by studying good examples—by looking at how other writers, especially skilled ones, construct arguments for specific audiences and how they solve problems of presentation or audience adjustment—you can learn techniques that may be useful in your own work.

- Second, by developing a good critical eye for someone else's work, you will also be learning how to critique your own, and thus how to improve it. ("Critical" in this context does not mean "able to find errors" but rather "discerning," that is, able to determine how something is constructed and whether or not it works well.)

- Finally, by learning to analyze the rhetorical elements of a piece of writing, you will become a more effective and insightful reader, better able to dissect other writers' arguments, to identify how they are "spinning" the information they provide, and to ask the crucial questions that will help you better understand the issues that concern you.

This section contains a number of different kinds of arguments for rhetorical analysis. Some stand alone, while some are grouped by theme so you can compare different rhetorical approaches to the same issue.

As you examine these articles, pay close attention to the rhetorical tools selected by each author. Which of the three Rhetorical Appeals does each author rely on most? How is each Appeal presented within the text? How does each author deploy the Common Topics? What organizational devices do you see in each article, and how do these devices contribute to the persuasive force of the text? Pay very close attention, as well, to the way each author adjusts to his or her own audience. Consider the special knowledge and expectations of these audiences and notice the ways in which writers address readers' concerns.

By learning to identify the nuances of skilled writers' rhetorical practices, you will not only hone your own writing skills, but you will develop your abilities as a careful and critical reader and thinker.

**Linda Coleman**

# I

## Single Selections for Rhetorical Analysis

### THE DECLARATION OF INDEPENDENCE

A Transcription

*We are so accustomed to seeing our founding documents as fixed and immutable that we can easily forget that they were written by someone trying to accomplish something very specific at a particular time. They are, in other words, examples of the use of rhetoric. The Declaration of Independence reflects not only the beliefs of the time but Jefferson's understanding of the beliefs of his audience. Notice that the opening treats the separation from Great Britain as something that has been forced on the colonies, not something they are taking action to achieve. Indeed, this unique act of separation has been recast in the very first sentence as the sort of thing that happens "in the course of human events," not a break with the normal workings of things. On the other hand, George III is the subject of a series of active verbs, emphasizing his manipulation of events and his dissociation from the normal course of events. The colonists ("we") only become the subjects of active verbs at the very end of the document when, having been driven to separation by events and by the king's action, they declare their independence.*

*For further discussion of the rhetorical features of the Declaration of Independence, see* Declaring Independence *by Jay Fliegelman. Also, as you read this document, bear in mind that the conventions for spelling, punctuation, and capitalization were different in Jefferson's time.*

**IN CONGRESS, July 4, 1776.**

**The unanimous Declaration of the thirteen United States of America,** When in the Course of human events, it becomes necessary for one people to dissolve the political bands which have connected them with another, and to assume among the powers of the earth, the separate and equal station to which the Laws of Nature and of Nature's God entitle them, a decent respect to the opinions of mankind requires that they should declare the causes which impel them to the separation.

We hold these truths to be self-evident, that all men are created equal, that they are endowed by their Creator with certain unalienable Rights, that among these are Life, Liberty and the pursuit of Happiness.—That to secure these rights, Governments are instituted among Men, deriving their just powers from the consent of the governed,—That whenever any Form of Government becomes destructive of these ends, it is the Right of the People to alter or to abolish it, and to institute new Government, laying its foundation on such principles and organizing its powers in such form, as to them shall seem most likely to effect their Safety and Happiness. Prudence, indeed, will dictate that Governments long established should not be changed for light and transient causes; and accordingly all experience hath shewn, that mankind are more disposed to suffer, while evils are sufferable, than to right themselves by abolishing the forms to which they are accustomed. But when a long train of abuses and usurpations, pursuing invariably the same Object evinces a design to reduce them under absolute Despotism, it is their right, it is their duty, to throw off such Government, and to provide new Guards for their future security.—Such has been the patient sufferance of these Colonies; and such is now the necessity which constrains them to alter their former Systems of Government. The history of the present King of Great Britain is a history of repeated injuries and usurpations, all having in direct object the establishment of an absolute Tyranny over these States. To prove this, let Facts be submitted to a candid world.

He has refused his Assent to Laws, the most wholesome and necessary for the public good.

He has forbidden his Governors to pass Laws of immediate and pressing importance, unless suspended in their operation till his Assent should be obtained; and when so suspended, he has utterly neglected to attend to them.

He has refused to pass other Laws for the accommodation of large districts of people, unless those people would relinquish the right of Representation in the Legislature, a right inestimable to them and formidable to tyrants only.

He has called together legislative bodies at places unusual, uncomfortable, and distant from the depository of their public Records, for the sole purpose of fatiguing them into compliance with his measures.

He has dissolved Representative Houses repeatedly, for opposing with manly firmness his invasions on the rights of the people.

He has refused for a long time, after such dissolutions, to cause others to be elected; whereby the Legislative powers, incapable of Annihilation, have returned to the People at large for their exercise; the State remaining in the mean time exposed to all the dangers of invasion from without, and convulsions within.

He has endeavoured to prevent the population of these States; for that purpose obstructing the Laws for Naturalization of Foreigners; refusing to pass others to encourage their migrations hither, and raising the conditions of new Appropriations of Lands.

He has obstructed the Administration of Justice, by refusing his Assent to Laws for establishing Judiciary powers.

He has made Judges dependent on his Will alone, for the tenure of their offices, and the amount and payment of their salaries.

He has erected a multitude of New Offices, and sent hither swarms of Officers to harrass our people, and eat out their substance.

He has kept among us, in times of peace, Standing Armies without the Consent of our legislatures.

He has affected to render the Military independent of and superior to the Civil power.

He has combined with others to subject us to a jurisdiction foreign to our constitution, and unacknowledged by our laws; giving his Assent to their Acts of pretended Legislation:

For Quartering large bodies of armed troops among us:

For protecting them, by a mock Trial, from punishment for any Murders which they should commit on the Inhabitants of these States:

For cutting off our Trade with all parts of the world:

For imposing Taxes on us without our Consent:

For depriving us in many cases, of the benefits of Trial by Jury:

For transporting us beyond Seas to be tried for pretended offences:

For abolishing the free System of English Laws in a neighbouring Province, establishing therein an Arbitrary government, and enlarging its Boundaries so as to render it at once an example and fit instrument for introducing the same absolute rule into these Colonies:

For taking away our Charters, abolishing our most valuable Laws, and altering fundamentally the Forms of our Governments:

For suspending our own Legislatures, and declaring themselves invested with power to legislate for us in all cases whatsoever.

He has abdicated Government here, by declaring us out of his Protection and waging War against us.

He has plundered our seas, ravaged our Coasts, burnt our towns, and destroyed the lives of our people.

He is at this time transporting large Armies of foreign Mercenaries to compleat the works of death, desolation and tyranny, already begun with circumstances of Cruelty & perfidy scarcely paralleled in the most barbarous ages, and totally unworthy the Head of a civilized nation.

He has constrained our fellow Citizens taken Captive on the high Seas to bear Arms against their Country, to become the executioners of their friends and Brethren, or to fall themselves by their Hands.

He has excited domestic insurrections amongst us, and has endeavoured to bring on the inhabitants of our frontiers, the merciless Indian Savages, whose known rule of warfare, is an undistinguished destruction of all ages, sexes and conditions.

In every stage of these Oppressions We have Petitioned for Redress in the most humble terms: Our repeated Petitions have been answered only by repeated injury. A Prince whose character is thus marked by every act which may define a Tyrant, is unfit to be the ruler of a free people.

Nor have We been wanting in attentions to our Brittish [*sic*] brethren. We have warned them from time to time of attempts by their legislature to extend an unwarrantable jurisdiction over us. We have reminded them of the circumstances of our emigration and settlement here. We have appealed to their native justice and magnanimity, and we have conjured them by the ties of our common kindred to disavow these usurpations, which, would inevitably interrupt our connections and correspondence. They too have been deaf to the voice of justice and consanguinity. We must, therefore, acquiesce in the necessity, which denounces our Separation, and hold them, as we hold the rest of mankind, Enemies in War, in Peace Friends.

We, therefore, the Representatives of the United States of America, in General Congress, Assembled, appealing to the Supreme Judge of the world for the rectitude of our intentions, do, in the Name, and by Authority of the good People of these Colonies, solemnly publish and declare, That these United Colonies are, and of Right ought to be Free and Independent States; that they are Absolved from all Allegiance to the British Crown, and that all political connection between them and the State of Great Britain, is and ought to be totally dissolved; and that as Free and Independent States, they have full Power to levy War, conclude Peace, contract Alliances, establish Commerce, and to do all other Acts and Things which Independent States may of right do. And for the support of this Declaration, with a firm reliance on the protection of divine Providence, we mutually pledge to each other our Lives, our Fortunes and our sacred Honor.

# LETTER FROM BIRMINGHAM JAIL

Martin Luther King, Jr.

> *Martin Luther King, Jr. was an ordained minister who led a boycott of the Montgomery bus system in 1955, resulting in the Supreme Court's ruling that Alabama's bus segregation laws were unconstitutional. Until his assassination in April, 1969, King was one of the most prominent and charismatic leaders in the struggle for African-Americans civil rights, receiving the Nobel Peace Prize in 1964. This famous letter was written from a jail cell in 1963 after King had been arrested at a sit-in demonstration in a segregated diner in Birmingham, Alabama. Although the letter is directly addressed to King's fellow clergy who were critical of his activism, consider that King may also have had an alternative, more friendly audience in mind. As you read, pay attention to the various strategies King uses to construct his argument and to appeal to his audience(s).*

*My Dear Fellow Clergymen:*[1]

While confined here in the Birmingham city jail, I came across your recent statement calling my present activities "unwise and untimely." Seldom do I pause to answer criticism of my work and ideas. If I sought to answer all the criticisms that cross my desk, my secretaries would have little time for anything other than such correspondence in the course of the day, and I would have no time for constructive work. But since I feel that you are men of genuine good will and that your criticisms are sincerely set forth, I want to try to answer your statements in what I hope will be patient and reasonable terms.

I think I should indicate why I am here in Birmingham, since you have been influenced by the view which argues against "outsiders coming in." I have the honor of serving as president of the Southern Christian Leadership Conference, an organization operating in every southern state, with headquarters in Atlanta, Georgia. We have some eighty-five affiliated organizations across the South, and one of them is the Alabama Christian Movement for Human Rights. Frequently we share staff, educational, and financial resources with our affiliates. Several months ago the affiliate here in Birmingham asked us to be on call to engage in a nonviolent direct-action program if such were deemed necessary. We readily consented, and when the hour came we lived up to our promise. So I, along with several members of my staff, am here because I was invited here. I am here because I have organizational ties here.

But more basically, I am in Birmingham because injustice is here. Just as the prophets of the eighth century B.C. left their villages and carried their "thus saith the Lord" far beyond the boundaries of their home towns, and just as the Apostle Paul left his village of Tarsus and carried the gospel of Jesus Christ to the far corners of the Greco-Roman world, so am I compelled to carry the gospel of freedom beyond my own home town. Like Paul, I must constantly respond to the Macedonian call for aid. Moreover, I am cognizant of the interrelatedness of all communities and states. I cannot sit idly by in Atlanta and not be concerned about what happens in Birmingham. Injustice anywhere is a threat to justice everywhere. We are caught in an inescapable network of mutuality, tied in a single garment of destiny. Whatever affects one directly, affects all indirectly. Never again can we afford to live with the narrow, provincial "outside agitator" idea. Anyone who lives inside the United States can never be considered an outsider anywhere within its bounds.

You deplore the demonstrations taking place in Birmingham. But your statement, I am sorry to say, fails to express a similar concern for the conditions that brought about the demonstrations. I am sure that none of you would want to rest content with the superficial kind of social analysis that deals merely with effects and does not grapple with underlying causes. It is unfortunate that demonstrations are taking place in Birmingham, but it is even more unfortunate that the city's white power structure left the Negro community with no alternative.

In any nonviolent campaign there are four basic steps: collection of the facts to determine whether injustices exist; negotiation; self-purification; and direct action. We have gone through all these steps in Birmingham. There can be no gainsaying the fact that racial injustice engulfs this community. Birmingham is probably the most thoroughly segregated city in the United States. Its ugly record of brutality is widely known. Negroes have experienced grossly unjust treatment in the courts. There have been more unsolved bombings of Negro homes and churches in Birmingham than in any other city in the nation. These are the hard, brutal facts of the case. On the basis of these conditions, Negro leaders sought to negotiate with the city fathers. But the latter consistently refused to engage in good-faith negotiation.

Then, last September, came the opportunity to talk with leaders of Birmingham's economic community. In the course of the negotiations, certain promises were made by the merchants—for example, to remove the stores' humiliating racial signs. On the basis of these promises, the Reverend Fred Shuttlesworth and the leaders of the Alabama Christian Movement for Human Rights agreed to a moratorium on all demonstrations. As the weeks and months went by, we realized that we were the victims of a broken promise. A few signs, briefly removed, returned; the others remained.

As in so many past experiences, our hopes had been blasted, and the shadow of deep disappointment settled upon us. We had no alternative except to prepare for direct action, whereby we would present our very bodies as a means of laying our case before the conscience of the local and the national community. Mindful of the difficulties involved, we decided to undertake a process of self-purification. We began a series of workshops on nonviolence, and we repeatedly asked ourselves: "Are you able to accept blows without retaliating?" "Are you able to endure the ordeal of jail?" We decided to schedule our direct-action program for the Easter season, realizing that except for Christmas, this is the main shopping period of the year. Knowing that a strong economic-withdrawal program would be the by-product of direct action, we felt that this would be the best time to bring pressure to bear on the merchants for the needed change.

Then it occurred to us that Birmingham's mayoralty election was coming up in March, and we speedily decided to postpone action until after election day. When we discovered that the Commissioner of Public Safety, Eugene "Bull" Connor, had piled up enough votes to be in the run-off we decided again to postpone action until the day after the run-off so that the demonstrations could not be used to cloud the issues. Like many others, we waited to see Mr. Connor defeated, and to this end we endured postponement after postponement. Having aided in this community need, we felt that our direct-action program could be delayed no longer.

You may well ask: "Why direct action? Why sit-ins, marches, and so forth? Isn't negotiation a better path?" You are quite right in calling for negotiation. Indeed, this is the very purpose of direct action. Nonviolent direct action seeks to create such a crisis and foster such a tension that a community which has constantly refused to negotiate is forced to confront the issue. It seeks to dramatize the issue that it can no longer be ignored. My citing the creation of tension as part of the work of the nonviolent-resister may sound rather shocking. But I must confess that I am not afraid of the word "tension." I have earnestly opposed violent tension, but there is a type of constructive, nonviolent tension which is necessary for growth. Just as Socrates felt that it was necessary to create a tension in the mind so that individuals could rise from the bondage of myths and half-truths to the unfettered realm of creative analysis and objective appraisal, so must we see the need for nonviolent gadflies to create the kind of tension in society that will help men rise from the dark depths of prejudice and racism to the majestic heights of understanding and brotherhood.

The purpose of our direct-action program is to create a situation so crisis-packed that it will inevitably open the door to negotiation. I therefore concur with you in your call for negotiation. Too long has our beloved Southland been bogged down in a tragic effort to live in monologue rather than dialogue.

One of the basic points in your statement is that the action that I and my associates have taken in Birmingham is untimely. Some have asked: "Why didn't you give the new city administration time to act?" The only answer that I can give to this query is that the new Birmingham administration must be prodded about as much as the outgoing one, before it will act. We are sadly mistaken if we feel that the election of Albert Boutwell as mayor will bring the millennium to Birmingham. While Mr. Boutwell is a much more gentle person than Mr. Connor, they are both segregationists, dedicated to maintenance of the status quo. I have hope that Mr. Boutwell will be reasonable enough to see the futility of massive resistance to desegregation. But he will not see this without pressure from devotees of civil rights. My friends, I must say to you that we have not made a single gain in civil rights without determined legal and nonviolent pressure. Lamentably, it is an historical fact that privileged groups seldom give up their privileges voluntarily. Individuals may see the moral light and voluntarily give up their unjust posture; but, as Reinhold Niebuhr has reminded us, groups tend to be more immoral than individuals.

We know through painful experience that freedom is never voluntarily given by the oppressor; it must be demanded by the oppressed. Frankly, I have yet to engage in a direct-action campaign that was "well timed" in the view of those who have not suffered unduly from the disease of segregation. For years now I have heard the word "Wait!" It rings in the ear of every Negro with piercing familiarity. This "Wait" has almost always meant "Never." We must come to see, with one of our distinguished jurists, that "justice too long delayed is justice denied."

We have waited for more than 340 years for our constitutional and God-given rights. The nations of Asia and Africa are moving with jet-like speed toward gaining political independence, but we still creep at horse-and-buggy pace toward gaining a cup of coffee at a lunch counter. Perhaps it is easy for those who have never felt the stinging darts of segregation to say, "Wait." But when you have seen vicious mobs lynch your mothers and fathers at will and drown your sisters and brothers at whim; when you have seen hate-filled policemen curse, kick, and even kill your black brothers and sisters; when you see the vast majority of your twenty million Negro brothers smothering in an airtight cage of poverty in the midst of an affluent society; when you suddenly find your tongue twisted and your speech stammering as you seek to explain to your six-year-old daughter why she can't go to the public amusement park that has just been advertised on television, and see tears welling up in her eyes when she is told that Funtown is closed to colored children, and see ominous clouds of inferiority beginning to form in her little mental sky, and see her beginning to distort her personality by developing an unconscious bitterness toward white people; when you have to concoct an answer for a five-year-old son who is asking: "Daddy, why do white people treat colored people so mean?"; when you take a cross-country drive and find it necessary to sleep night after night in the uncomfortable corners of your automobile because no motel will accept you; when you are humiliated day in and day out by nagging signs reading "white" and "colored"; when your first name becomes "nigger," your middle name becomes "boy" (however old you are) and your last name becomes "John," and your wife and mother are never given the respected title "Mrs."; when you are harried by day and haunted by night by the fact that you are a Negro, living constantly at tiptoe stance, never quite knowing what to expect next, and are plagued with inner fears and outer resentments; when you are forever fighting a degenerating sense of "nobodiness"—then you will understand why we find it difficult to wait. There comes a time when the cup of endurance runs over, and men are no longer willing to be plunged into the abyss of despair. I hope, sirs, you can understand our legitimate and unavoidable impatience.

You express a great deal of anxiety over our willingness to break laws. This is certainly a legitimate concern. Since we so diligently urge people to obey the Supreme Court's decision of 1954 outlawing segregation in the public schools, at first glance it may seem rather paradoxical for us consciously to break laws. One may well ask: "How can you advocate breaking some laws and obeying others?" The answer lies in the fact that there are two types of laws: just and unjust. I would be the first to advocate obeying just laws. One has not only a legal but a moral responsibility to obey just laws. Conversely, one has a moral responsibility to disobey unjust laws. I would agree with St. Augustine that "an unjust law is no law at all."

Now, what is the difference between the two? How does one determine whether a law is just or unjust? A just law is a man-made code that squares with the moral law or the law of God. An unjust law is a code that is out of harmony with the moral law. To put it in the terms of St. Thomas Aquinas: An unjust law is a human law that is not rooted in eternal law and natural law. Any law that uplifts human personality is just. Any law that degrades human personality is unjust. All segregation statutes are unjust because segregation distorts the soul and damages the personality. It gives the segregator a false sense of superiority and the segregated a false sense of inferiority. Segregation, to use the terminology of the Jewish philosopher Martin Buber, substitutes an "I-it" relationship for an "I-thou" relationship and ends up relegating persons to the status of things. Hence segregation is not only politically, economically, and sociologically unsound, it is morally wrong and awful. Paul Tillich said that sin is separation. Is not segregation an existential expression of man's tragic separation, his awful estrangement, his terrible sinfulness? Thus it is that I can urge men to obey the 1954 decision of the Supreme Court, for it is morally right; and I can urge them to disobey segregation ordinances, for they are morally wrong.

Let us consider a more concrete example of just and unjust laws. An unjust law is a code that a numerical or power majority group compels a minority group to obey but does not make binding on itself. This is *difference* made legal. By the same token, a just law is a code that a majority compels a minority to follow and that it is willing to follow itself. This is *sameness* made legal.

Let me give another explanation. A law is unjust if it is inflicted on a minority that, as a result of being denied the right to vote, had no part in enacting or devising the law. Who can say that the legislature of Alabama which set up that state's segregation laws was democratically elected? Throughout Alabama all sorts of devious methods are used to prevent Negroes from becoming registered voters, and there are some counties in which, even though Negroes constitute a majority of the population, not a single Negro is registered. Can any law enacted under such circumstances be considered democratically structured?

Sometimes a law is just on its face and unjust in its application. For instance, I have been arrested on a charge of parading without a permit. Now, there is nothing wrong in having an ordinance which requires a permit for a parade. But such an ordinance becomes unjust when it is used to maintain segregation and to deny citizens the First Amendment privilege of peaceful assembly and protest.

I hope you are able to see the distinction I am trying to point out. In no sense do I advocate evading or defying the law, as would the rabid segregationist. That would lead to anarchy. One who breaks an unjust law must do so openly, lovingly, and with a willingness to accept the penalty. I submit that an individual who breaks a law that conscience tells him is unjust and who willingly accepts the penalty of imprisonment in order to arouse the conscience of the community over its injustice, is in reality expressing the highest respect for law.

Of course, there is nothing new about this kind of civil disobedience. It was evidenced sublimely in the refusal of Shadrach, Meshach, and Abednego to obey the laws of Nebuchadnezzar, on the ground that a higher moral law was at stake. It was practiced superbly by the early Christians, who were willing to face hungry lions and the excruciating pain of chopping blocks rather than submit to certain unjust laws of the Roman Empire. To a degree, academic freedom is a reality today because Socrates practiced civil disobedience. In our own nation, the Boston Tea Party represented a massive act of civil disobedience.

We should never forget that everything Adolf Hitler did in Germany was "legal" and everything the Hungarian freedom fighters did in Hungary was "illegal." It was "illegal" to aid and comfort a Jew in Hitler's Germany. Even so, I am sure that, had I lived in Germany at the time, I would have aided and comforted my Jewish brothers.

If today I lived in a Communist country where certain principles dear to the Christian faith are suppressed, I would openly advocate disobeying that country's antireligious laws.

I must make two honest confessions to you, my Christian and Jewish brothers. First, I must confess that over the past few years I have been gravely disappointed with the white moderate. I have almost reached the regrettable conclusion that the Negro's great stumbling block in his stride toward freedom is not the White Citizen's Counciler or the Ku Klux Klanner, but the white moderate, who is more devoted to "order" than to justice; who prefers a negative peace which is the absence of tension to a positive peace which is the presence of justice; who constantly says: "I agree with you in the goal you seek, but I cannot agree with your methods of direct action"; who paternalistically believes he can set the timetable for another man's freedom; who lives by a mythical concept of time and who constantly advises the Negro to wait for a "more convenient season." Shallow understanding from people of good will is more frustrating than absolute misunderstanding from people of ill will. Lukewarm acceptance is much more bewildering than outright rejection.

I had hoped that the white moderate would understand that law and order exist for the purpose of establishing justice and that when they fail in this purpose they become the dangerously structured dams that block the flow of social progress. I had hoped that the white moderate would understand that the present tension in the South is a necessary phase of the transition from an obnoxious negative peace, in which the Negro passively accepted his unjust plight, to a substantive and positive peace, in which all men will respect the dignity and worth of human personality. Actually, we who engage in nonviolent direct action are not the creators of tension. We merely bring to the surface the hidden tension that is already alive. We bring it out in the open, where it can be seen and dealt with. Like a boil that can never be cured so long as it is covered up but must be opened with all its ugliness to the natural medicines of air and light, injustice must be exposed, with all the tension its exposure creates, to the light of human conscience and the air of national opinion before it can be cured.

In your statement you assert that our actions, even though peaceful, must be condemned because they precipitate violence. But is this a logical assertion? Isn't this like condemning a robbed man because his possession of money precipitated the evil act of robbery? Isn't this like condemning Socrates because his unswerving commitment to truth and his philosophical inquiries precipitated the act by the misguided populace in which they made him drink hemlock? Isn't this like condemning Jesus because his unique God-consciousness and never-ceasing devotion to God's will precipitated the evil act of crucifixion? We must come to see that, as the federal courts have consistently affirmed, it is wrong to urge an individual to cease his efforts to gain his basic constitutional rights because the quest may precipitate violence. Society must protect the robbed and punish the robber.

I had also hoped that the white moderate would reject the myth concerning time in relation to the struggle for freedom. I have just received a letter from a white brother in Texas. He writes: "All Christians know that the colored people will receive equal rights eventually, but it is possible that you are in too great a religious hurry. It has taken Christianity almost two thousand years to accomplish what it has. The teachings of Christ take time to come to earth." Such an attitude stems from a tragic misconception of time, from the strangely rational notion that there is something in the very flow of time that will inevitably cure all ills. Actually, time itself is neutral; it can be used either destructively or constructively. More and more I feel that the people of ill will have used time much more effectively than have the people of good will. We will have to repent in this generation not merely for the hateful words and actions of the bad people but for the appalling silence of the good people. Human progress never rolls in on wheels of inevitability; it comes through the tireless efforts of men willing to be co-workers with God, and without this hard work, time itself becomes an ally of the forces of social stagnation. We must use time creatively, in the knowledge that the time is always ripe to do right. Now is the time to make real the promise of democracy and transform our pending national elegy into a creative psalm of brotherhood. Now is the time to lift our national policy from the quicksand of racial injustice to the solid rock of human dignity.

You speak of our activity in Birmingham as extreme. At first I was rather disappointed that fellow clergymen would see my nonviolent efforts as those of an extremist. I began thinking about the fact that I stand in the middle of two opposing forces in the Negro community. One is a force of complacency, made up in part of Negroes who, as a result of long years of oppression, are so drained of self-respect and a sense of "somebodiness" that they have adjusted to segregation; and in part of a few middle class Negroes who, because of a degree of academic and economic security and because in some ways they profit by segregation, have become insensitive to the problems of the masses. The other force is one of bitterness and hatred, and it comes perilously close to advocating violence. It is expressed in the various black nationalist groups that are springing up across the nation, the largest and best-known being Elijah Muhammad's Muslim movement. Nourished by the Negro's frustration over the continued existence of racial discrimination, this movement is made up of people who have lost faith in America, who have absolutely repudiated Christianity, and who have concluded that the white man is an incorrigible "evil."

I have tried to stand between these two forces, saying that we need emulate neither the "do-nothingism" of the complacent nor the hatred and despair of the black nationalist. For there is the more excellent way of love and nonviolent protest. I am grateful to God that, through the influence of the Negro church, the way of nonviolence became an integral part of our struggle.

If this philosophy had not emerged, by now many streets of the South would, I am convinced, be flowing with blood. And I am further convinced that if our white brothers dismiss as "rabble-rousers" and "outside agitators" those of us who employ nonviolent direct action, and if they refuse to support our nonviolent efforts, millions of Negroes will, out of frustration and despair, seek solace and security in black-nationalist ideologies—a development that would inevitably lead to a frightening racial nightmare.

Oppressed people cannot remain oppressed forever. The yearning for freedom eventually manifests itself, and that is what has happened to the American Negro. Something within has reminded him of his birthright of freedom, and something without has reminded him that it can be gained. Consciously or unconsciously, he has been caught up by the *Zeitgeist*, and with his black brothers of Africa and his brown and yellow brothers of Asia, South America, and the Caribbean, the United States Negro is moving with a sense of great urgency toward the promised land of racial justice. If one recognizes this vital urge that has engulfed the Negro community, one should readily understand why public demonstrations are taking place. The Negro has many pent-up resentments and latent frustrations, and he must release them. So let him march; let him make prayer pilgrimages to the city hall; let him go on freedom rides—and try to understand why he must do so. If his repressed emotions are not released in nonviolent ways, they will seek expression through violence; this is not a threat but a fact of history. So I have not said to my people: "Get rid of your discontent." Rather, I have tried to say that this normal and healthy discontent can be channeled into the creative outlet of nonviolent direct action. And now this approach is being termed extremist.

But though I was initially disappointed at being categorized as an extremist, as I continued to think about the matter I gradually gained a measure of satisfaction from the label. Was not Jesus an extremist for love: "Love your enemies, bless them that curse you, do good to them that hate you, and pray for them which despitefully use you, and persecute you." Was not Amos an extremist for justice: "Let justice roll down like waters and righteousness like an ever-flowing stream." Was not Paul an extremist for the Christian gospel: "I bear in my body the marks of the Lord Jesus." Was not Martin Luther an extremist: "Here I stand; I cannot do otherwise, so help me God." And John Bunyan: "I will stay in jail to the end of my days before I make a butchery of my conscience." And Abraham Lincoln: "This nation cannot survive half slave and half free." And Thomas Jefferson: "We hold these truths to be self-evident, that all men are created equal. . . ." So the question is not whether we will be extremists, but what kind of extremists we will be. Will we be extremists for hate or for love? Will we be extremists for the preservation of injustice or for the extension of justice? In that dramatic scene on Calvary's hill three men were crucified. We must never forget that all three were crucified for the same crime—the crime of extremism. Two were extremists for immorality, and thus fell below their environment. The other, Jesus Christ, was an extremist for love, truth, and goodness, and thereby rose above his environment. Perhaps the South, the nation, and the world are in dire need of creative extremists.

I had hoped that the white moderate would see this need. Perhaps I was too optimistic; perhaps I expected too much. I suppose I should have realized that few members of the oppressor race can understand the deep groans and passionate yearnings of the oppressed race, and still fewer have the vision to see that injustice must be rooted out by strong, persistent, and determined action. I am thankful, however, that some of our white brothers in the South have grasped the meaning of this social revolution and committed themselves to it. They are still too few in quantity, but they are big in quality. Some—such as Ralph McGill, Lillian Smith, Harry Golden, James McBride Dabbs, Ann Braden, and Sarah Patton Boyle—have written about our struggle in eloquent and prophetic terms. Others have marched with us down nameless streets of the South. They have languished in filthy, roach-infested jails, suffering the abuse and brutality of policemen who view them as "dirty nigger lovers." Unlike so many of their moderate brothers and sisters, they have recognized the urgency of the moment and sensed the need for powerful "action" antidotes to combat the disease of segregation.

Let me take note of my other major disappointment. I have been so greatly disappointed with the white church and its leadership. Of course, there are some notable exceptions. I am not unmindful of the fact that each of you has taken some significant stands on this issue. I commend you, Reverend Stallings, for your Christian stand on this past Sunday, in welcoming Negroes to your worship service on a nonsegregated basis. I commend the Catholic leaders of this state for integrating Spring Hill College several years ago.

But despite these notable exceptions, I must honestly reiterate that I have been disappointed with the church. I do not say this as one of those negative critics who can always find something wrong with the church. I say this as a minister of the gospel, who loves the church; who was nurtured in its bosom; who has been sustained by its spiritual blessings and who will remain true to it as long as the cord of life shall lengthen.

When I was suddenly catapulted into the leadership of the bus protest in Montgomery, Alabama, a few years ago, I felt we would be supported by the white church. I felt that the white ministers, priests, and rabbis of the South would be among our strongest allies. Instead, some have been outright opponents, refusing to understand the freedom movement and misrepresenting its leaders; all too many others have been more cautious than courageous and have remained silent behind the anesthetizing security of stained-glass windows.

In spite of my shattered dreams, I came to Birmingham with the hope that the white religious leadership of this community would see the justice of our cause and, with deep moral concern, would serve as the channel through which our just grievances could reach the power structure. I had hoped that each of you would understand. But again I have been disappointed.

I have heard numerous Southern religious leaders admonish their worshipers to comply with a desegregation decision because it is the law, but I have longed to hear white ministers declare: "Follow this decree because integration is morally right and because the Negro is your brother." In the midst of blatant injustices inflicted upon the Negro, I have watched white churchmen stand on the sideline and mouth pious irrelevancies and sanctimonious trivialities. In the midst of a mighty struggle to rid our nation of racial and economic injustice, I have heard many ministers say: "Those are social issues, with which the gospel has no real concern." And I have watched many churches commit themselves to a completely otherworldly religion which makes a strange, and Biblical distinction between body and soul, between the sacred and the secular.

I have traveled the length and breadth of Alabama, Mississippi, and all the other Southern states. On sweltering summer days and crisp autumn mornings I have looked at the South's beautiful churches with their lofty spires pointing heavenward. I have beheld the impressive outlines of her massive religious-education buildings. Over and over I have found myself asking: "What kind of people worship here? Who is their God? Where were their voices when the lips of Governor Barnett dripped with words of interposition and nullification? Where were they when Governor Wallace gave a clarion call for defiance and hatred? Where were their voices of support when bruised and weary Negro men and women decided to rise from the dark dungeons of complacency to the bright hills of creative protest?"

Yes, these questions are still in my mind. In deep disappointment I have wept over the laxity of the church. But be assured that my tears have been tears of love. There can be no deep disappointment where there is not deep love. Yes, I love the church. How could I do otherwise? l am in the rather unique position of being the son, the grandson and the great-grandson of preachers. Yes, I see the church as the body of Christ. But, oh! How we have blemished and scarred that body through social neglect and through fear of being nonconformists.

There was a time when the church was very powerful—in the time when the early Christians rejoiced at being deemed worthy to suffer for what they believed. In those days the church was not merely a thermometer that recorded the ideas and principles of popular opinion; it was a thermostat that transformed the mores of society. Whenever the early Christians entered a town, the people in power became disturbed and immediately sought to convict the Christians for being "disturbers of the peace" and "outside agitators." But the Christians pressed on, in the conviction that they were "a colony of heaven," called to obey God rather than man. Small in number, they were big in commitment. They were too God intoxicated to be "astronomically intimidated." By their effort and example they brought an end to such ancient evils as infanticide and gladiatorial contests.

Things are different now. So often the contemporary church is a weak, ineffectual voice with an uncertain sound. So often it is an arch-defender of the status quo. Far from being disturbed by the presence of the church, the power structure of the average community is consoled by the church's silent and often even vocal sanction of things as they are.

But the judgment of God is upon the church as never before. If today's church does not recapture the sacrificial spirit of the early church, it will lose its authenticity, forfeit the loyalty of millions, and be dismissed as an irrelevant social club with no meaning for the twentieth century. Every day I meet young people whose disappointment with the church has turned into outright disgust.

Perhaps I have once again been too optimistic. Is organized religion too inextricably bound to the status quo to save our nation and the world? Perhaps I must turn my faith to the inner spiritual church, the church within the church, as the true *ekklesia* and the hope of the world. But again I am thankful to God that some noble souls from the ranks of organized religion have broken loose from the paralyzing chains of conformity and joined us as active partners in the struggle for freedom. They have left their secure congregations and walked the streets of Albany, Georgia, with us. They have gone down the highways of the South on torturous rides for freedom. Yes, they have gone to jail with us. Some have been dismissed from their churches, have lost the support of their bishops and fellow ministers. But they have acted in the faith that right defeated is stronger than evil triumphant. Their witness has been the spiritual salt that has preserved the true meaning of the gospel in these troubled times. They have carved a tunnel of hope through the dark mountain of disappointment.

I hope the church as a whole will meet the challenge of this decisive hour. But even if the church does not come to the aid of justice, I have no despair about the future. I have no fear about the outcome of our struggle in Birmingham, even if our motives are at present misunderstood. We will reach the goal of freedom in Birmingham and all over the nation, because the goal of America is freedom. Abused and scorned though we may be, our destiny is tied up with America's destiny. Before the pilgrims landed at Plymouth, we were here. Before the pen of Jefferson etched the majestic words of the Declaration of Independence across the pages of history, we were here. For more than two centuries our forebears labored in this country without wages; they made cotton king; they built the homes of their masters while suffering gross injustice and shameful humiliation—and yet out of a bottomless vitality they continued to thrive and develop. If the inexpressible cruelties of slavery could not stop us, the opposition we now face will surely fail. We will win our freedom because the sacred heritage of our nation and the eternal will of God are embodied in our echoing demands.

Before closing I feel impelled to mention one other point in your statement that has troubled me profoundly. You warmly commended the Birmingham police force for keeping "order" and "preventing violence." I doubt that you would have so warmly commended the police force if you had seen its dogs sinking their teeth into unarmed, nonviolent Negroes. I doubt that you would so quickly commend the policemen if you were to observe their ugly and inhumane treatment of Negroes here in the city jail; if you were to watch them push and curse old Negro women and young Negro girls; if you were to see them slap and kick old Negro men and young boys; if you were to observe them, as they did on two occasions, refuse to give us food because we wanted to sing our grace together. I cannot join you in your praise of the Birmingham police department.

It is true that the police have exercised a degree of discipline in handling the demonstrators. In this sense they have conducted themselves rather "nonviolently" in public. But for what purpose? To preserve the evil system of segregation. Over the past few years I have consistently preached that nonviolence demands that the means we use must be as pure as the ends we seek. I have tried to make clear that it is wrong to use immoral means to attain moral ends. But now I must affirm that it is just as wrong, or perhaps even more so, to use moral means to preserve immoral ends. Perhaps Mr. Connor and his policemen have been rather nonviolent in public, as was Chief Pritchett in Albany, Georgia, but they have used the moral means of nonviolence to maintain the immoral end of racial injustice. As T. S. Eliot has said: "The last temptation is the greatest treason: To do the right deed for the wrong reason."

I wish you had commended the Negro sit-inners and demonstrators of Birmingham for their sublime courage, their willingness to suffer, and their amazing discipline in the midst of great provocation. One day the South will recognize its real heroes. They will be the James Merediths, with the noble sense of purpose that enables them to face jeering and hostile mobs, and with the agonizing loneliness that characterizes the life of the pioneer. They will be old, oppressed, battered Negro women, symbolized in a seventy-two-year-old woman in Montgomery, Alabama, who rose up with a sense of dignity and with her people decided not to ride segregated buses, and who responded with ungrammatical profundity to one who inquired about her weariness: "My feets is tired, but my soul is at rest." They will be the young high school and college students, the young ministers of the gospel and a host of their elders, courageously and nonviolently sitting in at lunch counters and willingly going to jail for conscience' sake. One day the South will know that when these disinherited children of God sat down at lunch counters, they were in reality standing up for what is best in the American dream and for the most sacred values in our Judaeo-Christian heritage, thereby bringing our nation back to those great wells of democracy which were dug deep by the founding fathers in their formulation of the Constitution and the Declaration of Independence.

Never before have I written so long a letter. I'm afraid it is much too long to take your precious time. I can assure you that it would have been much shorter if I had been writing from a comfortable desk, but what else can one do when he is alone in a narrow jail cell, other than write long letters, think long thoughts and pray long prayers?

If I have said anything in this letter that overstates the truth and indicates an unreasonable impatience, I beg you to forgive me. If I have said anything that understates the truth and indicates my having a patience that allows me to settle for anything less than brotherhood, I beg God to forgive me.

I hope this letter finds you strong in the faith. I also hope that circumstances will soon make it possible for me to meet each of you, not as an integrationist or a civil rights leader but as a fellow clergyman and a Christian brother. Let us all hope that the dark clouds of racial prejudice will soon pass away and the deep fog of misunderstanding will be lifted from our fear-drenched communities, and in some not too distant tomorrow the radiant stars of love and brotherhood will shine over our great nation with all their scintillating beauty.

Yours for the cause of Peace and Brotherhood,
Martin Luther King, Jr.

### Note

1. This response to a published statement by eight fellow clergymen from Alabama (Bishop C. C. J. Carpenter, Bishop Joseph A. Durick, Rabbi Hilton L. Grafman, Bishop Paul Hardin, Bishop Holan B. Harmon, the Reverend George M. Murray, the Reverend Edward V. Ramage, and the Reverend Earl Stallings) was composed under somewhat constricting circumstances. Begun on the margins of the newspaper in which the statement appeared while I was in jail, the letter was continued on scraps of writing paper supplied by a friendly Negro trusty, and concluded on a pad my attorneys were eventually permitted to leave me. Although the text remains in substance unaltered, I have indulged in the author's prerogative of polishing it for publication.

# II

## *Thematic Selections for Paired Analysis*

### SCOLDING SCHOLARS: ACADEMIA, HISTORY WRITERS GETTING BLACK EYE

Editorial, *The Columbus Dispatch*

> *In the first weeks of 2002, plagiarism became a national issue after well-known historian Stephen Ambrose was accused of having used passages from other authors' works in his own books without proper acknowledgement of his sources. Soon after, other authors admitted to or were accused of falsifying research and too-close paraphrasing. The editorials that follow consider the ethics and repercussions of plagiarism. While both articles assert strongly that plagiarism is wrong, they predict very different results from these particular cases of plagiarism. While Heather Lee Schroder, writing for the Madison, Wisconsin newspaper* The Capital Times, *laments that the supposedly unintentional plagiarism of some famous historians will damage their reputations, the unsigned editorial from the Columbus, Ohio newspaper* The Columbus Dispatch *argues that the moral failing of historians who plagiarize indicates our culture has little concern for ethics.*

In virtually every culture, the recording and transmission of history is considered a crucial task, and those entrusted with it often enjoy a privileged place in their society.

Whether that history is preserved in oral fashion by tribal storytellers or in written classics such as the history of the ancient world penned by Herodotus, these tales become the repository of a culture's identity and character, not to mention political legitimacy.

Because of this, those who control the recording and transmission of history often wield great power, a fact not lost on monarchs and governments throughout history.

In totalitarian nations, such as the Soviet Union, the rewriting of history became a major industry, needed to make the past conform to the current political line by excising inconvenient facts and people from official memory. This practice was carried to such extremes that daring Soviet citizens were known to joke (very carefully) that "the past is getting harder and harder to predict." But manipulation of history is not limited to totalitarian regimes, as a controversy now rocking academia demonstrates.

This month, Emory University launched a formal investigation into the research methods used by historian Michael Bellesiles in writing *Arming America: The Origins of a National Gun Culture.*

The book set off a nationwide argument when it was published in 2000, because it purports to show that until the Civil War, gun ownership in America was relatively rare. If this were true, it would mean that the United States was not a gun-owning society from the outset and that perhaps the Founding Fathers did not intend the Second Amendment to guarantee an individual right to bear arms.

Naturally, those who regard individual gun ownership to be a freedom as important as any of the others guaranteed in the Bill of Rights were immediately up in arms.

While Bellesiles went on to collect the prestigious Bancroft Prize for the book, other historians were busy double-checking his facts and raising serious questions about his research and objectivity.

For example, Bellesiles claimed that an examination of wills in Vermont showed that only 14 percent of colonial households owned guns. Yet when other scholars checked those same records, they found that 40 percent owned guns.

More disturbing was Bellesiles' assertion that he used San Francisco court records from the 1800s. But when others looked for these same records, they discovered that the records were destroyed nearly a century ago in the 1906 San Francisco earthquake.

Bellesiles then claimed that he found the records at a small historical society in Contra Costa County. But staffers there say they have no such records from San Francisco and no evidence that Bellesiles ever conducted any research at the historical society.

It was this fact that pushed Emory University officials to launch a formal investigation. Bellesiles could lose his tenure as a result.

Meanwhile, the latest edition of *William and Mary Quarterly,* a leading scholarly journal of early American history, contains four essays dealing with Bellesiles' book. Three of these comment directly on his research methods and find them weak or wrong and the book's conclusions heavily biased.

But Bellesiles is not the only high-profile historian whose image has taken a beating. Stephen Ambrose, one of the best-known nonfiction writers in the nation thanks to popular histories such as *Band of Brothers, Citizen Soldiers* and *Undaunted Courage* and his appearances in television productions such as PBS' *Lewis and Clark,* was accused last month of plagiarizing another historian's work.

In his book *The Wild Blue,* about a World War II bombing crew, Ambrose borrowed copiously from *Wings of Morning,* another book about a World War II bomber crew written by Thomas Childers, a history professor at the University of Pennsylvania.

Though Ambrose mentioned Childers in footnotes, readers had no idea that in many cases, Ambrose was copying Childers word for word.

Last week, on his Web site, Ambrose published something approaching an apology for the borrowings and said future editions of the book would attribute the borrowed passages fully.

He may have to do that more than once. Since the allegations about *The Wild Blue*, critics have said that at least half a dozen of Ambrose's books contain passages taken from other authors without proper attribution.

As the Ambrose story was brewing, it was learned that Doris Kearns Goodwin, a bestselling biographer, also borrowed heavily from three other authors when she wrote 1987's *The Fitzgeralds and the Kennedys*. Goodwin lifted passages from three other Kennedy books, including *The Lost Prince: Young Joe, the Forgotten Kennedy*, by Hank Searls, and even from Rose Kennedy's autobiography, *Times to Remember*.

What makes the Goodwin situation particularly appalling is that in 1993, Goodwin very loudly accused author Joe McGinnis of lifting passages without attribution from *The Fitzgeralds and the Kennedys* for his own book, *The Last Brother*. The pot calls the kettle black.

Finally, there is the case of Joseph Ellis, Pulitzer-prize winning author of *Founding Brothers: The Revolutionary Generation*. In a newspaper interview in 2000, Ellis claimed to have served as a paratrooper in Vietnam and as a staffer for Gen. William C. Westmoreland. When these claims were exposed as lies last summer, Ellis was suspended for a year from Mount Holyoke College, where he is a professor of history.

These cases suggest that academia, authors and publishers are overdue for a refresher course in ethics and fundamental standards of research and attribution.

The bad examples they set will have a ripple effect throughout a culture that already appears to be losing its appreciation for such principles.

At the beginning of this month, a school board in Kansas shamelessly abandoned any commitment to standards when it overruled a teacher who had failed 28 biology students who turned in research copied from the Internet. This was exactly the wrong message to send at a time when cheating already appears rampant in the nation's schools. For example, a Rutgers University researcher found that of 4,471 high school students randomly surveyed in the 2000–2001 school year, more than half plagiarized from the Internet and nearly three-quarters had cheated on a test.

It is not comforting to think that from among this generation of students will come the next generation of historians.

## YES, PLAGIARISM IS A SERIOUS BREACH OF TRUST

Heather Lee Schroeder

This week, another noted historian—Doris Kearns Goodwin—has acknowledged that one of her books contains what is known as "unacceptable paraphrasing." The revelation came after and in response to Stephen E. Ambrose's admission that his latest work, *The Wild Blue*, inappropriately used another historian's writing.

Goodwin's 1987 book *The Fitzgeralds and the Kennedys* was the offending work and, in total, five of Ambrose's works have been found to contain passages that are believed to be direct or nearly direct and unattributed quotes from other books. As the year unfolds, other historians may come under fire for their misuse of other scholars' work. I've heard a variety of responses in this university town. Many of them tend toward an "aw, it isn't that bad" point of view. I think all of the controversy begs the question: Is it really plagiarism? And does it matter?

First, I'll point out that we can be pretty sure that both Ambrose and Goodwin didn't knowingly or maliciously steal someone else's work. Rather, it was the result of Goodwin's shoddy note taking and Ambrose's rapid-fire writing of books.

That said, what they did is still plagiarism. Essentially, if you use another person's idea, theory or exact words, you've committed plagiarism—unless it is common knowledge or a direct quote or an attributed paraphrase.

So, why does that matter? The Indiana University Web site has a great segment on "How to Recognize Unacceptable and Acceptable Paraphrases." It says that what often happens in an unacceptable paraphrase is that the writer doesn't cite a source for the ideas or facts, and they often accidentally change the general sense of the meaning of a plagiarized passage.

And these things do matter. If you still aren't convinced, here are a few points to think about:

> *Honesty:* Do you like being lied to? That's what authors are doing when they pass off someone else's work as their own. Now that might not seem important, but consider my next point:

> *Verification:* How can a careful reader verify what the writer has written? How can you weigh the value of the work if you don't know from where or from whom it originated? You can't. And that's a problem. Think about it this way: Imagine reading a news story about the Enron debacle when it first broke that used only unidentified sources. You'd probably dismiss it as smear campaign fodder. Still not convinced? Think about this:

> *Cheating:* You've worked on a project for weeks and weeks—putting in overtime. On the day it's unveiled, one of your co-workers who always rolls out of the office at 4:55 p.m. takes credit for your hard work. Do you like that? That's essentially what an author does in plagiarizing. It devalues the hard work someone else has done.

The sad truth is that Ambrose—and Goodwin to a lesser degree—will always be remembered as "those historians who stole someone else's work." Since they're both gifted theorists and writers and since they both didn't mean to do it, it's a shame that their stars will dim.

# PRIVATIZE SOCIAL SECURITY? HA!

Marianne Means

> *This group of articles was published in response to proposals by Presi-*
> *dent George W. Bush and some members of Congress to "privatize" a*
> *percentage of Social Security funds by giving individuals the ability to*
> *invest this money in the stock market. Since all of these arguments were*
> *constructed in the months following the collapse of large energy corpo-*
> *ration Enron—a bankruptcy that wiped out the retirement savings of*
> *many of that company's employees while damaging the financial port-*
> *folios of many investors—it is not surprising that all of the authors must*
> *consider whether it is too risky to allow private investment of Social*
> *Security funds. Andrea Georgsson favors privatization in her article,*
> *which originally appeared in* The Houston Chronicle, *while Bob Ray*
> *Sanders's piece from* The Fort-Worth Star-Telegram *and Marianne*
> *Means's editorial from* The Milwaukee Journal Sentinel *argue that the*
> *Enron scandal proves privatization is a dangerous idea.*

After the Enron scandal, you'd have to be pretty dense to fall for the Bush administration's dream of transforming the Social Security system from a government-
guaranteed program into a plan under which workers could use some of their
retirement savings to play the stock market.

The warning signals are right up there in neon lights: Even the biggest companies
can't be trusted to tell the truth about the value of their stocks; insiders hold all the
cards; and the laws don't protect investors against fraud.

Yet President Bush's economic adviser, Lawrence Lindsey, vowed on television the
other day that privatizing the retirement safety net remains a high priority with his boss.

Even before Enron collapsed, the recession had seriously undercut the president's
argument that to keep the program financially stable, it would be necessary to put
workers at the mercy of Wall Street financiers. When stocks were booming, there was
a certain political appeal in dangling potential profits in front of ordinary people. But
the realization that stocks that go up can also go down definitely had a chilling effect.
Yet the idea stuck, especially with conservative ideologues, who see the marketplace
as the perfect economic engine and government regulation as an abomination.
Columnist George Will was still promoting the privatization of Social Security after
Enron imploded. He called it "the most direct path to participation in the economy's
wealth creation."

It also can be the most direct path to the loss of retirement benefits and starvation in old age. What the recession began, Enron has finished. The false promise of
unconditional stock market riches has been exposed.

Top Enron executives sold stock for millions of dollars while the company was
riding high and gave themselves big bonuses as bankruptcy neared. Meanwhile, they
lied to employees and stockholders about the company's finances and ultimately forbade workers to bail out of 401(k) retirement plans that held Enron stock. Thousands
of people lost not only their jobs, but also their savings.

The cruelty of greedy Enron executives may not be typical of other companies, but the public is likely to suspect such practices are more common than previously believed. The opportunity for corruption certainly seems to be widespread.

Regulatory oversight is pitiful. Disclosure requirements are easily manipulated. Insiders possess vast power to hoodwink uninformed investors. Accountants often have a vested interest in toadying up to officials for whom they are supposed to produce independent audits.

In theory, executives of publicly traded companies have legal and moral responsibilities to produce honest books. But Enron executives got rich by deceiving the world with secret deals not recorded on their balance sheets. By the time those deals were exposed, it was too late.

Enron's collapse, the largest corporate bankruptcy in American history, doesn't seem to bother Treasury Secretary Paul O'Neill. An early supporter of privatizing Social Security, O'Neill dismisses stock market losses as just a normal part of doing business. "Companies come and go. It's part of the genius of capitalism—people get to make good decisions or bad decisions, and they get to pay the consequence or enjoy the fruits of their decisions," he said.

That's OK if the stocks are meant to supplement your living expenses rather than provide the essentials for survival. But it's callous if you are talking about a government policy that would encourage ordinary people to take risks with their pension and retirement benefits.

The administration's hand-picked commission on Social Security reform recently issued a report warning of future financial shortfalls unless the system is radically overhauled by creating private investment accounts. Individuals would handle their own investments instead of relying solely on benefits that are now automatically calculated by the government.

This assumes financial acumen most working Americans do not possess. And it is such drastic medicine that the commission couldn't agree on the details of a new plan.

The real winners in the privatization proposal would be the mutual fund companies, insurers, banks and stock brokerage firms that would pick up business from the government. Lusting after the fat fees that would be involved, the financial community has contributed millions to the political campaigns of privatization supporters.

The well-being of the organized financial community, however, is not necessarily synonymous with the fiscal security that workers and their families need upon retirement and death. Today, Social Security supports more than 38 million retirees and their surviving spouses and children, plus nearly 7 million disabled workers and their families.

Enron has done great damage to its own employees and stockholders, but the collapse of the company could help future retirees. Social Security as we have always known it may now be safe.

# PRIVATIZE SOCIAL SECURITY OR STRIKE OIL

Andrea Georgsson

Oseola McCarty worked most of her life doing other people's washing and ironing. At her death at age 91 in 1999, she had amassed a small fortune—enough to leave money to a few relatives and her church, as well as $150,000 for scholarships to the University of Southern Mississippi, a school she never attended.

McCarty lived frugally, to say the least, and faithfully made contributions to a bank savings account, eventually dipping into the not-so-high finance world of certificates of deposit and mutual funds.

Florence M. Dailey worked as a bank secretary in Rochester, N.Y., in the early 1900s. She took her boss' advice to buy stock in a company called Eastman Kodak. When she died in 1966, the few thousand dollars she'd invested had appreciated and multiplied to shares worth $20 million. Dailey left the money to Notre Dame and Georgetown universities, schools she never attended.

The stories demonstrate the considerable power of time and compound interest, in McCarty's case, and the jet propulsion force of time and stock market investing, in Dailey's case. Neither woman became wealthy because she depended on a windfall from Social Security.

Women today ought to follow their examples. They do not have to live like paupers. They only have to save and invest for the future, and not count on Social Security to provide a comfortable retirement.

This is where I generally part with the conventional feminist thinking. According to various women's organizations, women should be leery of any attempt by Congress to privatize Social Security, as a presidential commission on the system's reform recommended earlier this month.

As I see it, women not currently close to retirement should count on Social Security being either defunct or unable to meet their financial needs in retirement because the system, for all intents and purposes, is short trillions of dollars for future retirees. By 2016 Social Security likely will be paying out more in benefits than it takes in from payroll taxes—a recipe for collapse.

Furthermore, though women may be highly dependent on Social Security, those benefits have not prevented them from tending to be poorer than men in retirement. This should motivate women to demand reforms that offer them more security. And low-income women, who typically have only Social Security benefits to sustain them in old age, should be doubly interested in a change in the system.

Bills now being considered by Congress to privatize Social Security include plans to let younger workers voluntarily put a portion of their payroll taxes into personal investment accounts that can be used to fund savings or investment accounts.

As owner of her own retirement account, even the poorest working woman could build wealth that she could bequeath to her children. That's better than working for the day that she can collect benefits that end the day she dies, regardless of how much she might have paid into the system and for how long.

The implosion of Enron and the bath its employees took when their company-stock-laden 401(k) accounts tanked has been exploited by those who apparently have no faith in the intelligence of American workers to direct their own financial futures.

The integrity of a government retirement plan that gives workers a choice between a few appropriate stock and bond funds and savings account options will not be subject to wipeout that a fund that is, foolishly, packed with just one company's stock or overloaded in one sector.

Workers would give up some level of traditional Social Security benefits in a privatized plan, but people who invest in the stock market generally do better financially over the long run than people who do not. (And women investors generally do better than men.) No one gets rich off Social Security, but plenty of people have done well by buying and holding shares in a wide variety of sound companies.

Another popular and insulting argument against adding a personal account component to Social Security is that most people, especially the poor, are too unsophisticated to understand investing. Even functionally illiterate women manage to figure out how to secure food stamps and housing vouchers for their families in a system that is notoriously byzantine.

The first time a woman receives a quarterly statement showing the value of her own retirement account, she'll get it. There is nothing overly complicated about realizing that the money being deducted from one's check is growing tax-deferred in an account of one's own. Meanwhile, Einstein's relativity theory is easier to grasp than how payroll taxes—a huge chunk of anyone's paycheck—translate into a Social Security benefit.

A woman can invest her money, or she can take John Paul Getty's advice: "Rise early, work hard, strike oil."

## ENRON'S LESSON FOR SOCIAL SECURITY

Bob Ray Sanders

For anyone who thinks it is a good idea partly to privatize Social Security, I have just one word: "Enron."

Enron is the Houston-based energy company that collapsed this year, sending shock waves through the financial and political communities.

The company, which has filed the largest bankruptcy case in U.S. history, saw its stock fall from a high of $90 a share to just pennies per share. On Thursday, the stock closed at 42 cents on the New York Stock Exchange. Falling with that stock are the hopes and dreams of thousands of employees who lost their jobs and retirees who lost their life savings while many company executives still made off like bandits.

What does all this have to do with Social Security?

A lot.

You will recall that President Bush's campaign platform included a promise that he would find a way to let you keep more of your money rather than sending it all to Washington.

Part of that plan included allowing the taxpayer to keep a percentage (at least one-third) of the money paid to Social Security to invest in private accounts.

The president appointed a commission and charged it ostensibly to find ways to shore up the Social Security system. The commission understood, however, that its role was also to present a plan that would address the president's campaign promise.

Since the Sept. 11 terrorist attacks, there hasn't been much discussion about the commission's work, but a plan is moving forward.

If you were not convinced before that this was a bad idea—reducing the amount of dollars going into the Social Security Trust Fund while gambling on the risky stock market—just think Enron.

The scene in a Senate hearing room this month should have served notice to the members of Congress and the administration that precious retirement funds should not be used for gambling.

Tearful retirees told members of the Senate Commerce subcommittee how they had watched their nest eggs disappear.

A 61-year-old Florida woman said her Enron stock holdings shrank from $700,000 to $20,418.

"It may be too late for you to help me," she told the panel. "It is not too late for you to take some action to make sure this does not happen to anyone else."

While employees remained loyal to their company by holding on to declining stock, some company officials were not remaining loyal to them.

When it was apparent that the Enron stock was definitely headed for the bottom, investors in the company's 401(k) plan were not allowed to sell their stock, but it appears company officials did an "end run" and dumped about $1 billion of their own stock holdings.

In the past year alone, we've seen how fickle the stock market can be, and how it can be manipulated by bad news (and some of it false), economic indicators and a sneeze from the chairman of the Federal Reserve Board.

The market's roller-coaster performance in the past few months is enough to make your head swim.

Think of those who lost their life savings on one company's failure, and imagine what it would be like if millions of people in this country retired and realized that one-third, or half or any portion of their retirement money had disappeared.

That's the fear some people have if we move forward with privatizing any portion of Social Security.

That's my fear.

So, when the subject comes up again, just remember: "Enron."

# THE CASE FOR PROFILING

Charles Krauthammer

> *Following the terrorist attacks of September 11, U.S. airports have implemented new security procedures including random searches of individuals attempting to board planes. In his* Newsweek *article, Charles Krauthammer argues that such searches are ineffective because they focus scrutiny on the people least likely to participate in terrorist attacks. Rather than randomly searching all passengers, he proposes airport security should consider people's identifying characteristics (including race, gender, age, and nationality) and then search only those who fit the profile of a suicide bomber. In contrast, Wendy Kaminer insists in her essay for* The American Prospect *that restricting individual rights through racial profiling, government surveillance, and deportation of non-citizens does not prevent terrorist attacks. As you read both articles, compare how the authors construct their arguments, paying special attention to how each asks readers to remember events that have actually occurred and to "imagine" scenarios contrary to fact. How does each author use commands and other statements directed at the audience to appeal to pathos?*

The latest airport-security scandal is the groping of female flight attendants and passengers during patdowns. Not to worry. The Transportation Security Administration chief is right on it. "We're going to fix that right away," he said recently, announcing the appointment of an ombudsman.

A nice bureaucratic Band-Aid. No one, however, asks the obvious question: Why are we patting down flight attendants in the first place? Why, for that matter, are we conducting body searches of any female passengers?

Random passenger checks at airports are completely useless. We've all been there in the waiting lounge, rolling our eyes in disbelief as the 80-year-old Irish nun, the Hispanic mother of two, the Japanese-American businessman, the House committee chairman with the titanium hip are randomly chosen and subjected to head-to-toe searching for . . . what?

Not for security—these people are hardly candidates for suicide terrorism—but for political correctness. We are engaged in a daily and ostentatious rehearsal of the officially sanctioned proposition that suicide terrorists come from anywhere, without regard to gender, ethnicity, age or religious affiliation.

That is not true, and we know it. Random searches are a ridiculous charade, a charade that not only gives a false sense of security but, in fact, diminishes security because it wastes so much time and effort on people who are obviously no threat.

Everyone now has his nail-clipper, tweezers or X-rayed-shoe story. Can-you-top-this tales of luggage and body searches have become a staple of cocktail chatter. Yet citizens would willingly subject themselves to delay, inconvenience and even indignity if they felt what they were undergoing was actually improving airport security. Since Sept. 11, subjecting oneself to security indignities has been a civic duty. But this has become a parody of civic duty. Random searches are being done purely to defend against the charge of racial profiling.

Imagine that Timothy McVeigh and Terry Nichols had not been acting alone but had instead been part of a vast right-wing, antigovernment, terrorist militia with an ideology, a network and a commitment to carrying out attacks throughout America. Would there have been any objection to singling out young white men for special scrutiny at airports and other public places? Of course not. And if instead, in response to the threat posed by the McVeigh Underground, airport security began pulling young black men or elderly Asian women out of airport lines for full-body searches, would we not all loudly say that this is an outrage and an absurdity?

As it happens, the suicide bombers who attacked us on Sept. 11 were not McVeigh Underground. They were al-Qaeda: young, Islamic, Arab and male. That is not a stereotype. That is a fact. And there is no hiding from it, as there is no hiding from the next al-Qaeda suicide bomber. He has to be found and stopped. And you don't find him by strip searching female flight attendants or 80-year-old Irish nuns.

This is not to say your plane could not be brought down by a suicide bomber of another sort. It could. It could also be brought down by a meteorite. Or by a Stinger missile fired by Vermont dairymen in armed rebellion. These are all possible. But because they are rather improbable, we do not alter our daily lives to defend against the possibility.

True, shoe bomber Richard Reid, while young and Islamic and male, was not Arab. No system will catch everyone. But our current system is designed to catch no one because we are spending 90% of our time scrutinizing people everyone knows are no threat. Jesse Jackson once famously lamented how he felt when he would "walk down the street and hear footsteps and start thinking about robbery—then look around and see somebody white and feel relieved." Jackson is no racist. He was not passing judgment on his own ethnicity. He was simply reacting to probabilities. He would rather not. We all would rather not make any calculations based on ethnicity, religion, gender or physical characteristics—except that on airplanes our lives are at stake.

The pool of suicide bombers is not large. To pretend that it is universal is absurd. Airport security is not permitted to "racially" profile, but every passenger—white or black, male or female, Muslim or Christian—does. We scan the waiting room, scrutinizing other passengers not just for nervousness and shiftiness but also for the demographic characteristics of al-Qaeda. We do it privately. We do it quietly. But we do it. Airport officials, however, may not. This is crazy. So crazy that it is only a matter of time before the public finally demands that our first priority be real security, not political appearances—and puts an end to this charade."

# SAFETY AND FREEDOM

## Wendy Kaminer

Of all the lame excuses offered for the failures of U.S. intelligence and security that facilitated the attacks on the World Trade Center and the Pentagon, the most disingenuous was the repeated claim that antiterrorism efforts have been restrained by respect for America's freedoms. Tell that to the victims of harsh counter-terrorism and immigration laws passed in the aftermath of the Oklahoma City bombing: the Arab Americans who were wrongfully imprisoned for several years on the basis of secret evidence; the asylum seekers who have been turned away from our borders by low-level bureaucrats without ever receiving a hearing; the thousands of lawful immigrants imprisoned and threatened with deportation for minor offenses committed years ago. Tell it to the victims of racial profiling on our highways and in our airports. I don't doubt that some federal law-enforcement agents are honorable and respectful of individual freedom. But in general, the law-enforcement bureaucracy respects our freedoms grudgingly, only when it must, under court order or the pressure of bad publicity. Congress is often just as bad. While both the House and the Senate include some staunch civil libertarians, they haven't had nearly enough influence to stop the antilibertarian and highly ineffective counterterrorism and crime-control laws that recent Democratic and Republican administrations have embraced. Often, law-enforcement agents violate our rights because they've been authorized to do so by law. [See "Taking Liberties," *TAP*, January–February 1999, and "Games Prosecutors Play," September–October 1999, both by Wendy Kaminer.]

Lawmakers have, in turn, been authorized by voters to sacrifice our personal liberties for the empty promise of public safety. Sixty-five percent of people surveyed in 1995, after Oklahoma City, favored giving the FBI power to infiltrate and spy on suspected terrorist groups without evidence of a crime. Fifty-eight percent wanted to give the government power to deport any non-citizen suspected of planning terrorism. Fifty-four percent agreed that in the fight against terrorism, the government should not be hampered by concern for individual rights. I suspect that many more Americans support restrictions on civil liberties today.

It's likely that when people agree to cede liberty for the sake of order, they imagine ceding other people's liberties, not their own: If African Americans were an active political majority in this country, they would probably not be the victims of racial profiling. But many Americans have been willing to tolerate minor bureaucratic intrusions for the sake of feeling safer, even when the feeling is illusory.

Consider our submissive behavior in airports. I understand why we line up at security gates and run bags through an X ray; it's a minor inconvenience that seems to have a rational relationship to safety. But why do we docilely hand over our government-issued picture IDs? The ID requirement doesn't deter terrorists; instead it discourages people from transferring their discount tickets. It probably increases revenue for the airlines more than it enhances security for passengers. After all, terrorists who have access to explosives and other weapons have access to fake IDs. And they probably lie when asked if their bags have been constantly in their possession or if they've received any items from strangers.

It's a small point, but the now passé notion that a picture-ID requirement coupled with a stupid question routine was a meaningful security measure epitomized our sloppy, thoughtless approach to airline safety. Security lapses had nothing to do with the preservation of freedom, as recent reports on inadequate security at Boston's Logan Airport have shown. As *The Boston Globe* reported the day after the terrorist attacks in New York and Washington, D.C., low wages, poor benefits, high turnover, and inadequate background checks by the private companies that were hired to handle airport security contributed to the unsafe conditions at Logan—which had not gone unnoticed. According to *The Wall Street Journal,* in 1998 the Federal Aviation Administration investigated a private cleaning service employed by the Massachusetts Port Authority (which runs Logan). It fined Massport and major airlines $178,000 after a teenager successfully stowed away on a plane in 1999. The airlines themselves have resisted stronger federal oversight of security and mandates that would have affected their bottom lines. What hampered the fight against terrorism are the usual suspects, incompetence and venality—not respect for liberty.

Imagine if federal law enforcers spent all the time, money, and attention that they now devote to an ineffective, repressive war on drugs on understanding and deterring terrorism. Consider the corrosive effect the drug war has had on Fourth Amendment freedoms and on foreign policy: Last spring the Bush administration announced a $40-million gift to Afghanistan's Taliban government in consideration of its promise to ban opium production. If the administration wants to prosecute people who aid and abet terrorists, it should turn itself in immediately. There are evils to blame for the Trade Center attack, as the president observed, but many of them are domestic.

# MAGNET THERAPY: THE PAIN CURE ALTERNATIVE

Ron Lawrence, M.D., Ph.D and Paul J. Rosch, M.D., F.A.C.P.

*Magnet therapy is the practice of placing small magnets on or close to the body in order to cure painful conditions and diseases. Some companies sell magnet therapy "kits" that include magnets said to be especially beneficial, devices for attaching magnets to the body, and books instructing readers how to use magnets effectively. While those who offer or feel they have benefited from these kits claim that magnet therapy has real benefits, most doctors and scientists dismiss the use of magnets as ineffective or condemn those who sell magnet therapy kits as con artists. In the texts that follow, you will encounter authors giving different evaluations of magnet therapy by presenting different types of evidence in arguments aimed at different audiences. By presenting quotes from a number of individuals, the website "Magnet therapy—The pain cure alternative!" demonstrates that the book it is selling offers readers a method for using magnets "that really works!" As you read, notice how this website relies on the ethos of certain types of people in order to make its argument. Robert L. Park, a professor of physics at the University of Maryland, presents the opposite argument in his essay "Magnetic Attraction," offering a history of magnet therapy, a case study, and a brief experiment to convince readers magnets are a "medical scam." Park's essay was electronically published on the site PhysLink.com, which identifies itself as a source for "physics & astronomy online education and reference." Finally, David W. Ramey, a doctor of veterinary medicine, argues in his commentary for* The Scientific Review of Alternative Medicine *that magnet therapy has no scientific basis, and that studies that seem to demonstrate effectiveness of magnet therapy are flawed. By referencing studies from peer-reviewed scientific and medical journals, Ramey presents his argument in a way that will appeal to academic readers. As you read, notice how these articles resemble different types of rhetoric you regularly encounter (such as television advertisements, newspaper editorials, and textbook chapters), and think about the types of arguments and appeals best suited to each rhetorical situation.*

## A Scientifically Proven Method That Really Works!

Did you know that millions of people around the world are using magnets for pain caused by joint problems, repetitive stress, injuries, muscle soreness, and more? In this groundbreaking book you will learn why. Now, two of the most renowned experts on magnet therapy share with you their knowledge of the exciting therapeutic benefits of magnets. You'll discover how magnet therapy:

**Reduces chronic pain caused by joint discomfort**
**Relieves wrist pain**
**Promotes rapid healing**
**Provides restful sleep, lifts fatigue, and much more!**

Here is what some people are saying about magnet therapy.

"I couldn't play golf without wearing magnets. I guarantee you!"

—**Jim Colbert, Professional Golfer, Senior PGA Tour**

"This book is a valuable resource for consumers who are confused about claims for magnets . . . it separates fact from fancy."

—**Martin Blank, Ph.D., Dept. of Physiology and Cellular Biophysics, Columbia University**

"I've had arthritis since it first came out. I tried every pill, nostrum, and treatment; and then at Dr. Lawrence's suggestion, I tried magnets. I now wear them in my shoes and on my lumbar spine. I believe they've kept me functioning in relative comfort."

—**Dick Van Dyke**

"Our players have used magnets for over two years and they have proven to be an effective aid in the recovery of professional football's aches, pains, and injuries."

—**Ryan Vermillion, Director of Rehabilitation for the Miami Dolphins**

"A spectacular, state-of-the-art explanation of how magnetic therapy can relieve pain and promote healing."

—**Professor Alan Bennett, Kings College Medical School, London**

"Finally, a book about the future of drugless medicine—magnets and electromagnetic therapy. Thank you, Dr. Lawrence!"

—**James Coburn, Oscar Award Winning Actor**

"Dr. Lawrence brought magnet therapy to my attention for which I thank him."

—**Andy Griffith**

"Our research has confirmed that magnetic fields can have important effects on nerve growth and regeneration, and may provide other rewards, as clearly outlined in this useful book."

—**Betty Sisken, Ph.D., professor at the Center of Biomedical Engineering, University of Kentucky; president-elect, The Bioelectromagnetics Society**

"Dr. Rosch is probably the world's leading authority on stress."

         **—Konstantin Sudakov, M.D., president, The Russian Academy of Sciences**

"I am well acquainted with Drs. Rosch and Lawrence and can think of few individuals more qualified to provide this valuable resource."

        **—C. Norman Shealy, M.D., Ph.D., president of the Shealy Institute**

"Permanent magnets and electromagnetic therapies offer extraordinary potential for pain relief, promoting healing and other benefits, as this book clearly and authoritatively demonstrates."

       **—Saul Liss, Ph.D., president, MediConsultants, Inc.; chief consultant,**
                 **Bioelectric Technologies, Inc.**

"Wearing magnets helped me feel well and play well."

          **—Donna Andrews, professional golfer, LPGA Tour**

"Dr. Ron Lawrence is a pioneer in pain management."

      **—Anders Sola, M.D., clinical assistant professor, University of Washington**
                  **School of Medicine**

"You have nothing to lose and everything to gain by trying magnetic bracelets."

         **—Bob Murphy, professional golfer, Senior PGA Tour**

"Knowledge of how our bodies operate has been teased slowly from nature—by tribal shamans and medicine men, and in modern times by physical, medical, and psychological scientists. The ancients knew more about the interconnectedness of things and methods of herbal and ritual healing that are only now being confirmed in principle by frontier physical and medical scientists. The problem has been that for over a century Western scientific thought has focused upon a chemical model of how the molecules, tissues, and organs of our bodies are organized and function. However, this biochemical model must be expanded to deeper levels in order to include the electromagnetic and quantum processes that play a major role in how nature (our bodies are an evolutionary product of nature) has organized itself.

Science makes progress by creating models (hypotheses) of nature, then testing our human experiences against these models. Only when an overwhelming preponderance of evidence suggests that certain experiences cannot be explained by the existing model do we reluctantly (often angrily and self-righteously) abandon our cherished hypotheses. Most often it requires an overarching or meta-model that includes the previous model in some form. That is to say that nature consists of processes within processes within processes and our understanding of these processes must be consistent and complete at all levels and scales if our overall understanding is to be complete. And so it is with physical, chemical, biochemical, and electromagnetic, and quantum theories. Each is more perplexing than the previous, but none by itself tells the whole story, as our bodies function on all these levels simultaneously.

Medical scientists have been investigating electrical, magnetic, and now electro-magnetic and quantum influences on bodily functioning for several decades, but without widespread acceptance of their findings. The preponderance of evidence that magnetic fields can relieve pain in the body is sufficiently overwhelming that a major effort is now being mounted to discover how and why this is so. In order to understand all the subtle therapies that are now used in classical and contemporary medicine, we must first understand the electromagnetic properties, and then, the quantum properties of our bodies. This book tells us about some of that effort."

—Edgar Mitchell, Sc.D., astronaut, *Apollo 14*

# MAGNETIC ATTRACTION

Robert L. Park

Paul doesn't let anything get in the way of golf. At 79, he plays almost every day, and he doesn't hold back a thing on his swing. So when Paul got a pain in his shoulder he took the advice of other golfers and bought a magnet therapy kit for $49.95. The cur-rent popularity of magnet therapy, like copper bracelets 20 years ago, seems to have started on the golf course. At first, golf pro shops were about the only place you could buy them. Now you can find therapy magnets in department stores, pharmacies and even my local Safeway.

Paul's handicap dropped from 20 to 17, and the pain in his shoulder went away. He's sure the magnets had something to do with it. His wife thinks so too. Since she began putting magnets in her shoes, she says she doesn't get as tired. Paul says he would recommend magnets for anyone.

But Paul admits he hasn't always followed his own advice. When he got a sore knee he didn't try magnets, he went straight to his doctor. A lot of friends his age have been diagnosed with osteoarthritis. That's really serious; not only will it mess up your golf game, it's not reversible. Fortunately, x-rays showed no sign of osteoarthritis and the pain seemed to go away without any treatment.

Paul's knee got better by itself—and I'd bet his sore shoulder would have too. Most of the things that afflict us get better by themselves. Our bodies have a very sophisticated repair kit for dealing with injury or disease: bones knit, blood clots, antibodies seek out infectious organisms, etc. That can make it pretty hard to tell whether the remedies we take actually help. Whatever we happen to be taking when we get better usually gets the credit.

Paul asked his doctor about magnets, but the doctor advised him that magnet therapy is not scientifically proven. "That didn't surprise me," Paul snorted, "doctors always want to give you a pill. They think everything is internal. I don't know how magnets work, but they were using them in China thousands of years ago." That's true, but the Chinese were also using powdered rhinoceros horn to restore virility.

Unfortunately, they still do, with the result that the world is running out of rhinos. Rhinoceros horn and magnets are traditional treatments.

By contrast, the great medical advances today emerge from a detailed scientific understanding of how the body works. One new wonder drug, Viagra, may yet save the rhino from extinction. The road to modern medicine is littered with the bones of traditional treatments that millions of people once swore by—and are now known to be worthless or even harmful. Treatments such as purges and leeches were finally abandoned only when they were objectively compared to simply allowing the illness to take its course. Magnet therapy, it seems, has been abandoned several times over the centuries—only to be revived.

## Animal Magnetism

In the early 16th century, the power of lodestone (magnetite) to attract iron filings without touching them suggested great power. Paracelsus, the famous Swiss alchemist and physician began using powdered lodestone in salves to promote healing. William Gilbert, however, physician to Queen Elizabeth I, and father of the scientific study of magnetism, pointed out that the process of grinding the lodestone into powder destroyed the magnetism. Nevertheless, a century later, magnetic cures were introduced into England by Robert Fludd as a remedy for all disease. The patient was placed in the "boreal position" with the head north and the feet south during the treatment.

By far the most famous of the magnetizers was Franz Mesmer (1734–1815), who carried the technique from Vienna to Paris in 1778 and soon became the rage of Parisian society. Dressed in colorful robes, he would seat patients in a circle around a vat of "magnetized water." While Mesmer waved magnetic wands over them, the patients held iron rods protruding from the vat. He would later discover that the cure was just as effective if he left the magnets out and merely waved his hand. He called this "animal magnetism."

Benjamin Franklin, in Paris on a diplomatic assignment, suspected that Mesmer's patients did indeed benefit from the strange ritual because it kept them away from the bloodletting and purges of other Paris physicians. Those physicians bitterly resented Mesmer, an outsider who was attracting their most affluent patients. At the urging of the medical establishment, King Louis XVI appointed a royal commission to investigate his claims. This remarkable group included Franklin, then the world's greatest authority on electricity; Antoine Lavoisier, the founder of modern chemistry; and Joseph Guillotine, the physician whose famous invention would one day be used to sever the head of his friend Lavoisier.

The commissioners designed a series of ingenious tests in which some subjects were deceived into thinking they were receiving Mesmer's treatment when they were not, and others received the treatment but were led to believe they had not. The results established beyond any doubt that the effects were due solely to the power of suggestion. Their report, never surpassed for clarity or reason, destroyed Mesmer's reputation in France, and he returned to Vienna.

Nevertheless, magnetic therapy eventually crossed the Atlantic. Its most famous practitioner in the United States was Daniel Palmer, who in 1890 opened Palmer's

School of Magnetic Cure in Davenport, Iowa. Like Mesmer, Palmer soon discovered that his patients recovered just as quickly if he omitted the magnets and merely "laid on hands." Thus was founded "chiropractic therapy," and the school became Palmer's College of Chiropractic.

## New Age Magnetizers

In recent years, an enormous amount of research has been done on the effect of magnetic fields on the human body, driven not by magnetic therapy, but by safety considerations associated with the phenomenal growth in the use of magnetic resonance imaging (MRI) for medical diagnoses and research. MRI subjects the whole body to a magnetic field about a hundred times stronger than the localized field of even the most powerful therapy magnet. Happily, no ill-effects have been found from exposure to MRI fields. Indeed, there are almost no effects at all—just a few reports of faint sensory responses, such as a slight metallic taste and visual sensations of flashing lights if patients move their eyes too rapidly. The fact is that the stuff we're made of just isn't very magnetic.

That's why scientists were surprised two years ago when Dr. Carlos Vallbona at the Baylor College of Medicine in Houston reported results of a double-blind trial of magnets in the treatment of 50 patients suffering post-polio pain. Some of the patients were treated with commercial therapy magnets, others were treated with sham magnets. Seventy-six percent of those treated with real magnets reported a decrease in pain, while only 19 percent receiving the placebo felt an improvement.

But there have been no confirming studies by other researchers, and Leonard Finegold, a biophysicist at Drexel University, found problems in the protocol used in the Baylor trial. Physicists might be more inclined to take the Baylor results seriously if there were some plausible explanation of how the magnets work. The most frequent claim, which Vallbona supports, is that magnets promote the flow of blood to the treated area.

It's easy to check. An excess of blood shows up as a flushing or reddening of the skin. That's why the skin turns red when you apply heat; blood is being diverted to the heated area to serve as a coolant. But you will discover that placing a magnet of any strength against your skin produces no reddening at all. There is no indication that Vallbona tried this.

The argument is that blood, because it contains iron, should be attracted by the magnets. The iron in hemoglobin, however, is not ferromagnetic. The hemoglobin molecule itself is very weakly paramagnetic, but the fluid that carries the red cells, consisting mostly of water, is diamagnetic—it is weakly repelled. Indeed, small animals have even been levitated in powerful magnetic fields.

It has also been suggested that a magnetic field aligns water molecules in the blood, somehow improving circulation. But in fact, no alignment of water molecules is observed even at the field strength of MRI magnets. At the temperature of blood, water molecules are jostling each other so violently that their orientation is randomized. To align them, a magnetic field would have to be strong enough to overcome the thermal energy. Dr. John Schenck, at General Electric's R&D Laboratory, the leading authority on the effect of MRI fields on the body, calculates that fields thousands of times stronger than any that have ever been generated on Earth would be needed to align even one percent of the water molecules.

So how strong are the fields of therapy magnets? In a kit like the one Paul bought, the gold-plated neodymium alloy magnets are rated at 800 gauss, measured at the surface of the magnet. That's not much compared to the 30,000–40,000 gauss electromagnets used in modern MRI, but it's a lot for a small permanent magnet.

The current revival of magnetic therapy is, in fact, due almost entirely to remarkable advances in materials science. New permanent magnet materials based on ferrites and rare-earth alloys are one of the unsung triumphs of modern materials science. These new magnets are essential to high-tech products ranging from miniature walk-man headphones to laptop computers. They can be fabricated into all sorts of shapes, even thin and flexible, allowing them to be inserted into shoes or sewn into mattresses. No one was going to put lodestones in their shoes, or be seen on the golf course wearing old fashioned horseshoe magnets.

The makers of therapy magnets warn against using them "around credit cards or during pregnancy." The instructions with Paul's kit, however, showed a magnet being worn on the wrist. Now your wrist normally passes within an inch or so of your hip pocket when you walk. That's where most men keep their credit cards—and 800 gauss is certainly enough to wipe out the magnetically-coded information on the cards.

Since the people who make these magnets are often paid with credit cards, they presumably have an interest in seeing to it that your cards stay in good working order. Could it be that they make therapy magnets the way refrigerator magnets are made? Since refrigerator magnets are only meant to hold phone messages and Dilbert cartoons, they are designed to have a very short range field. This is done by making them in the form of narrow strips of alternating north and south poles. You can test this. Take two identical refrigerator magnets (the thin flexible kind, not the molded ceramic ones that look like a piece of fruit). Slide one across the other. You can feel them click into place each time the poles line up. Right at its surface, such a magnet may be quite strong, but a very short distance away, depending on the width of the strips, the north and south poles will effectively cancel.

The magnets in Paul's kit were disks about the size of a quarter. They were in little Velcro pouches that can be attached to blue velvet bands that are wrapped around the injured area. They must look dashing in the fitness center. I removed two of the magnets from their pouches and slid one across the other. I could feel them clicking into place—they were just like refrigerator magnets.

To get an idea of how quickly the field falls off, I stuck one of the magnets on a file cabinet. I then held sheets of paper between the magnet and the cabinet until the magnet could no longer support itself. Ten sheets! That's just one millimeter. The field of these magnets would hardly reach through the skin, much less into muscles and joints. Indeed, there was essentially no field extending through the velvet bands. Not only do these magnets have no power to heal, their fields don't even reach the injury. So much for the Baylor study which used commercial alternating-pole magnets. You might characterize them as "homeopathic" magnets.

As medical scams go, magnet therapy may not seem like a big deal. Magnets generally cost less than a visit to the doctor and they certainly do no harm. But magnet therapy can be dangerous if it leads people to forego needed medical treatment.

Worse, it tends to reinforce a sort of upside-down view of how the world works, leaving people vulnerable to predatory quacks if they become seriously ill. It's like trying to find your way around San Francisco with a map of New York. That could be dangerous for someone who is really sick—or really lost.

# MAGNETIC AND ELECTROMAGNETIC THERAPY

David W. Ramey, DVM

One of the more popular therapies for the treatment of a variety of conditions in human and veterinary medicine is the application of a magnetic field. The biological effects of low-level magnetic fields have been studied since the 1500s. The crucial question, however, is whether these effects have any physiological significance. Many claims have been made for the therapeutic effectiveness of magnetic fields, but are there any good reasons for believing them?

## History

The idea that magnetic therapy could be used to treat disease began in the early 16th century with the Swiss physician, philosopher, and alchemist Paracelsus, who used magnets to treat epilepsy, diarrhea, and hemorrhage.[1] Magnetic therapy became more popular in the mid-18th century when Franz Mesmer, an Austrian doctor who also helped begin the fields of hypnotism and psychoanalysis (and from whose name the word "mesmerize" was coined), opened a popular magnetic healing salon in Paris. The purpose of the salon was to treat the untoward effects of the body's innate "animal magnetism." In spite of continued condemnation by the scientific community, magnetic therapy became a popular form of treatment by the lay community.

Over the next few centuries, magnetic therapy developed into a form of quackery. In 1799, Elisha Perkins, a Connecticut physician and sometime mule trader, advocated the use of "metallic tractors" for the treatment of various diseases of humans and horses.[2] The user of the tractors (small metal magnetic wedges) swept the tractors over the injured area for a few minutes to "draw off the noxious electrical fluid that lay at the foot of suffering." Subjects and observers perceived immediate benefits. They reported their testimonials and Perkins became very rich. Magnetic tractors failed to prevent Dr. Perkins' death due to yellow fever in 1799.

In the late 1800s, the Sears catalogue advertised magnetic boot inserts. Magnetic caps and clothing (with over 700 magnets) were available by mail order from Thatcher's Chicago Magnetic Company.[3] Dr. Thatcher asserted that "magnetism properly applied will cure every curable disease no matter what the cause."[4] At the turn of the 20th century, Dr. Albert Abrams, named the "Dean of 20th Century charlatans" by the American Medical Association, postulated that each organ system and patient was "tuned" to a characteristic electromagnetic wavelength. By the time of World War II, physiologic effects of electromagnetic fields no longer received much attention in medical journals.

The history of quackery in the use of magnets has obscured scientific investigations performed on the medical effects of magnetic and electromagnetic fields. From a biophysics standpoint, a distinction is made between the two therapies; magnetic and electromagnetic are not the same.

## Electricity and Magnetism

Electromagnetism was first discovered in the 1800s by the English physicist Michael Faraday, who determined that a magnetic field could be generated by running an electric current through a wire coil. Conversely, a changing magnetic field can generate an electric voltage; the magnetic field must change to have any electrical effect (hence, the term pulsating electromagnetic field therapy, which generates rising and falling levels of a magnetic field.)

The biological effects of pulsating electromagnetic fields are hypothesized to be due to electrical rather than magnetic forces. Magnetism generates a voltage in tissue according to the equation:

$$V = n \times a \times dB/dt$$

V = Voltage
n = number of turns in the electromagnetic coil
a = area of the loop

$dB/dt$ = The rate of change of magnetic field with respect to time, with B representing the strength of the magnetic field (in Teslas). For example, if B goes from zero to 1 Tesla in 1 millisecond, then $dB/dt$ = 1000 Teslas/sec.

Based on this equation, a static magnetic field cannot generate an electrical voltage, as the $dB/dt$ component of the equation, is zero, as is the voltage induced by the field. Thus, any effects of a static magnetic field on tissue cannot be electrical in nature.

## Pulsating Electromagnetic Field Therapy

Extracellular matrix synthesis and repair are subject to regulation both by chemical agents (such as cytokines and growth factors) and physical agents, principally mechanical and electrical stimuli. The precise nature of such electromechanical signals is not known, however. In bone, mechanical and electrical signals may regulate the synthesis of extracellular matrix by stimulating signaling pathways at the cell membrane.[6,7] In soft tissue, alternating current electrical fields induce a redistribution of integral cell membrane proteins which, hypothetically, could initiate signal transduction cascades and cause a reorganization of cytoskeletal structures.[8] However, the hypothesis that electrical signals may be responsible for information transfer in or to cells has neither been proved nor disproved.

There is ample evidence that electrical activity exists in the body at all times. For example, electrical currents can be measured in the beating heart and are also generated in the production of bone. Endogenous electrical current densities produced by mechanical loading of bone under physiologic conditions approximate 1 Hz and 0.1–1.0 microA/cm2.[9] Thus, it is theorized that application of an appropriate electrical current, either directly through wires or indirectly through induction by a magnetic field, may affect tissues in several ways. The word "appropriate" in the preceding sentence is important since cells and tissues respond to a variety of electrical signal configurations in ways that suggest a degree of specificity for both the tissue affected and the signal itself.

The most widely studied application of electromagnetic field therapy in human medicine is in fracture therapy. Although the mechanisms remain undetermined, several studies report that electrical fields generated by pulsating electromagnetic field therapy stimulate biologic processes pertinent to osteogenesis[10,11,12] and bone graft incorporation.[13,14] This form of therapy is approved for the treatment of delayed and non-union fractures in humans in the U.S. by the United States Food and Drug Administration. Effectiveness of the treatment is supported by at least two double-blind studies.[15,16] Pulsating electromagnetic field therapy, however, delays the healing of fresh experimentally induced fractures in rabbits.[17]

Pulsating electromagnetic field therapy has also been evaluated in the treatment of soft tissue injuries, with the results of some studies providing evidence that this form of therapy may be of value in promoting healing of chronic wounds (such as bedsores)[18], in neuronal regeneration,[19,20] and in many other soft tissue injuries.[21,22] Results of a recent study in an experimental Achilles tendinitis model in rats indicated that there was an initial decrease in water content in injured tendons treated with pulsating electromagnetic field therapy but that all treated groups were equal to controls by 14 days.[23] The limited value of this form of therapy in the treatment of tendon injuries may be due in part to the lack of significant electrical activity in tendons, activity that could be altered by a pulsating electromagnetic field.

In contrast, a number of investigators have been unable to show any effect of low-level electromagnetic fields on tissue healing. One study, for example, failed to identify any beneficial effect of applying a magnetic field to a non-healing fracture[24] and concluded that the long periods of immobilization and inactivity required for the application of the magnetic field therapy were just as likely to be responsible for tissue healing.

Criticisms of pulsating electromagnetic field studies include: some of the studies are poorly designed; independent trials have not been conducted to confirm positive results; and the electrical fields induced by the machines are several orders of magnitude lower than are required to alter the naturally occurring electrical fields that exist across biological membranes.[25] Even proponents of the therapy concede that much work needs to be done to optimize such variables as signal configuration and duration of treatment before pulsating electromagnetic field therapy can be generally recommended.[26]

## Static Magnetic Field Therapy

Magnetic devices that radiate an unchanging magnetic field are available in a variety of configurations such as pads, bandages, and even magnetic mattresses. Scientific studies do not support claims of efficacy. Furthermore, a mechanism of action by which such devices might exert these effects remains elusive. Because static magnetic fields do not change, there can be no electrical effect. Hypotheses for an effect of a static field include influencing the electronic spin rate states of chemical reaction intermediates[27,28] and influencing cyclical changes in the physical state(s) of water.[29]

Importantly, neither of these proposed effects has been demonstrated in biological systems under physiological condition.[30]

In spite of a lack of demonstrable mechanism of action, proponents of applying static magnetic field therapy to injured or painful tissues generally attribute their alleged effects to an increase in local blood circulation. Unfortunately, the scientific evidence in supporting this hypothesis is tenuous at best.

Blood, like all tissues, contains electrically charged ions. A physics principle known as Faraday's Law states that a magnetic field will exert a force on a moving ionic current. Furthermore, an extension of Faraday's law called the Hall effect states that when a magnetic field is placed perpendicular to the direction of flow of an electric current, it will tend to deflect and separate the charged ions. While the deflection of ions will be in opposite directions depending on the magnetic pole encountered and the charge of the ion, this force is not based on the attraction or repulsion of like and unlike charges.

The Hall effect implies that when a magnet is placed over flowing blood in which ionic charges (such as Na+ and Cl–) exist, some force will be exerted on the ions. Furthermore, the separation of ionic charges will produce an electromotive force, which is a voltage between points in a circuit. In theory, this produces a very small amount of heat. These physical effects, which do exist, provide the basis for a quasi-scientific theory to account for the purported effects of static magnetic field therapy. For example:

> When a magnetic field with a series of alternating North and South poles is placed over a blood vessel, the influence of the field will cause positive and negative ions (for example, Na+ and Cl–) to bounce back and forth between the sides of the vessel, creating flow currents in the moving blood not unlike those in a river. The combination of the electromotive force, altered ionic pattern, and the currents causes blood vessel dilation with a corresponding increase in blood flow.[31]

The problem with using Faraday's law and the Hall effect to explain the purported effects of static magnetic pads is that the magnitude of that force applied by the field is infinitesimally small. Two facts account for the lack of effect. First, the magnetic field applied to the tissue is extremely weak. Second, the flow of the ionic current (i.e., the blood) is extremely slow, especially when compared to the flow of electric current. However, it is possible to estimate the forces applied to flowing blood by a weak magnetic field as long as the strength of the magnetic field applied, the velocity of the flowing blood, and the number of the ions in the blood are known.

Magnetic field strength is measured in one of two units: 1 Tesla = $10^4$ Gauss. The magnetic field strength of a Norfield's MAGNETIChockwrap™ (for horses) measured at California Institute of Technology had a field strength of 270 Gauss at the level of the pad and 1 Gauss at a distance of 1 cm from the pad. Tissues purportedly affected by the pads lie at least 1 cm away from them; 1 Gauss is approximately the magnetic field strength of the earth.[32] Promotional information for Bioflex pads asserts an "independent laboratory" has measured the field strength of their pads at 350 Gauss and that "optimum" field strength for the purported healing effects is less than 500 Gauss.[33] Regardless, these are very weak magnetic fields.

Considering the applied magnetic field at 250 Gauss (0.025 Tesla) and the velocity of blood flow v as 1 cm/sec (0.01 m/sec), the electric field to which an ion in the blood is exposed can be calculated as:

$$E = v \times B = 2.5 \times 10^{-4} \text{ Volts/meter/sec}$$

Hence, the change in electric potential (a pseudo-Hall effect) across a 1 mm diameter blood vessel can be estimated at a minuscule $2.5 \times 10^{-7}$ Volts.

Ions of opposing charges will move in opposite directions when moving through a static magnetic field. The separation of charges, known as the drift velocity, can also be calculated. In the case of Na+ and Cl– ions in flowing blood under the influence of a 250 Gauss magnetic field, the increased separation of the positive sodium and the negative chloride ions will be about 0.2 Angstroms per second, or about 1/10 the diameter of an atom. This can be compared with the *random* drift distance in one second that results from the thermal agitation imparted by the heat of the horse's body of about 0.25 mm/sec. Stated in another fashion, the ions will travel farther from thermal agitation than from the 250 Gauss magneto-electrical field drift by a factor of about 10 million.[34]

Any magnetic forces generated by a static field affecting fluid movement in blood vessels would have to overcome both the normal, pressure-driven turbulent flow of blood propelled by the heart and the normal thermal-induced Brownian movement of the particles suspended in the blood. Given the strong physical forces that already exist in a blood vessel, any physical forces generated by a static magnetic field on flowing blood, particularly those as weak as those associated with therapeutic magnetic pads, are extremely unlikely to have a biological effect.

## Magnetic Pad Design

At least one manufacturer of magnetic pads (Magnaflex/Bioflex™) asserts that the effect of charge separation can be increased by alternating north and south magnetic poles.

Alternating magnetic poles are most commonly seen in refrigerator magnets. By alternating the magnetic poles, an increased magnetic gradient is created, which increases the ability of the magnets to stick to the refrigerator. Paradoxically, alternating poles decrease the magnetic field strength of the magnet because the fields tend to cancel each other out as they extend from the magnet. Thus, while alternating poles would exert opposite forces on ions flowing through the magnetic field, the decrease in magnetic field strength would lessen any potential influence of the magnetic field on the target ions. Nor does there appear to be any consensus in the industry as to the ideal design for the pads. In fact, a competing manufacturer asserts that, "Leading scientists agree that unipolar magnets are superior to bi-polar,"[35] although neither the scientists nor the supporting research are identified.

Further proprietary design information regarding at least one commercial source of magnetic pads (Bioflex™ pads) would also appear to be irrelevant regarding biologic effects. Promotional information for the pads indicates that the "concentric circle" arrangement of the pads increases the likelihood that the magnetic field would be applied perpendicular to flowing blood, thereby maximizing the Hall effects. In fact, because blood vessels run randomly throughout the three dimensions of any tissue, there can be no "preferred" arrangement of the magnetic field that would favor its perpendicular orientation to the flow of blood.

## Studies on Static Magnetic Fields and Blood Flow

A number of studies have investigated the effects of static magnetic fields on blood flow. Studies commissioned by the makers of one type of magnetic pad showed that exposure of a highly concentrated saline solution in a glass capillary tube increased the flow of the solution. This study has been often cited by manufacturers of static magnetic devices as evidence that magnetic field therapy can potentially affect the circulation of blood. Although the mechanism for the increase in saline flow is not apparent, it certainly could not have been related to any dilatory effect on the walls of the glass capillary tube. The investigator who performed the study concluded that the results of the experiments performed using highly concentrated saline in a glass tube should not be extrapolated to effects that would be expected with flowing blood.[36]

A second study evaluated the effects of the pads in the distal limbs of horses using nuclear scintigraphy, a technique that is useful in identifying areas of blood vessel dilation and inflammation. That study concluded that, "Scintigraphy was performed in the vascular, soft tissue, and bone phase using a cross over trial to demonstrate increased blood flow and metabolic activity as a result of the local application of a permanent magnetic pad on the equine metacarpus. A highly significant increase was evident in the three phases."[37] The results of this study have been used repeatedly to suggest that magnetic pads promote blood circulation to the areas under the pads.

This study, which is apparently the only one to state that a static magnetic field affects blood circulation, is open to criticism. The experimental model, which compared the results of scans on one "treated" limb vs. the non-treated limb is inherently inaccurate, as one forelimb cannot be used as a control for the other in scintigraphic studies (each limb should be used as its own control). Furthermore, the design of the study was flawed, as a bandage and magnetic pad were applied to one limb while a bandage only was applied to the other. A more appropriate control would have been a bandage and a demagnetized pad. The radioisotope chosen for the study was not appropriate to determine blood circulation accurately. Finally, the study measured absolute scintigraphic counts, when the use of relative perfusion ratios would have been more appropriate.[38]

Numerous other studies have failed to show any effect of magnetic fields on blood circulation. For instance, no effect of dental magnets on the circulation of blood in the cheek could be demonstrated.[39] Scintigraphic evaluation of blood flow in mice exposed to two strengths of pulsating electromagnetic field force failed to demonstrate any circulatory effects.[40] A study on the circulatory effects of a magnetic foil was unable to show any effect in the skin of human forearms[41] and application of a magnetic foil to healing wounds in rats showed no significant effects.[42] A study in horses showed that application of a magnetic pad over the tendon region for 24 hours showed no evidence of temperature increase in treated limbs vs. placebo controlled limbs, using thermographic measurements as an indirect assessment of blood circulation to the area.[43]

As a more practical matter, if a magnet caused local increases in circulation, one would expect the area under the magnet to feel warm or become red as a result. Such an effect is not reported when magnets are held in the hand. Furthermore, one would expect any circulatory effects produced by very weak magnetic fields to be magnified in stronger magnetic fields. However, no circulatory effects have ever been reported in magnetic resonance imaging machines, in which the magnetic forces generated are two to four orders of magnitude greater than those produced by therapeutic magnetic pads. In studies of humans exposed to magnetic fields up to 1 Tesla (10,000 Gauss) there was no evidence of alterations in local blood flow at the skin of the thumb or at the forearm.[44] Even a 10 Tesla magnetic field is predicted to change the vascular pressure in a model of human vasculature by less than 0.2%, and experimental results of the effects of strong magnetic fields on concentrated saline solutions are in general agreement with these predictions.[45]

Based on the available scientific data, one must conclude that if there is an effect of static magnetic fields on blood circulation, there is no known biological mechanism by which that effect is generated. One may also postulate that the boots, blankets, and bandages in which the magnets are sewn have some sort of a thermal effect that is independent of the magnetic field (and could be duplicated with any form of bandaging).

## Magnetic Fields and Pain Relief

Both static and pulsating electromagnetic field therapy have also been promoted as being beneficial for the relief of pain. As with other proposed effects, there is no known mechanism of action by which application of a magnetic field produces biological effects. If they are effective in the relief of pain, it is unlikely that the effect is related to a reduction in nerve conductivity; the field required to produce a 10% reduction in nerve conductivity is roughly 24 Tesla.[46]

Studies evaluating the effects of pulsating electromagnetic fields in the relief of pain have shown conflicting results. Pulsating electromagnetic field therapy has reportedly provided pain relief in the treatment of osteoarthritis of the human knee and cervical spine,[47,48] in the treatment of persistent neck pain,[49] and in the treatment of women with chronic refractory pelvic pain.[50] However, electromagnetic therapy showed no benefit in the relief of pain due to shoulder arthritis[51], and a 1994 summary of published trials of non-medicinal and noninvasive therapies for hip and knee osteoarthritis concluded that there were insufficient data available to draw any conclusions on the efficacy of the therapy.[52] Paradoxically, another study in humans showed that magnetic treatment actually induced hyperalgesia in a tooth pain model.[53]

Pads that apply a static magnetic field are also promoted as having pain-relieving effects. Poorly controlled studies from the Japanese literature suggest that static magnetic devices were highly effective in alleviating subjective symptoms such as neck, shoulder, and other muscular pain.[54,55] One controlled, double-blind pilot study suggested that magnetic pads were effective in the relief of myofascial or arthritic-like pain in postpolio syndrome,[56] although every patient in the study, whether being treated with a placebo or a magnet, showed relief from pain. However, other studies have concluded that a magnetic foil offered no advantage over plain insoles in the treatment of pain of the human heel[57] and that a magnetic necklace had no effect on neck and shoulder pain.[58] It has also been suggested that there is a strong placebo effect at work in the perception of pain relief offered by static Magnetic devices.[59]

## Clinical Use of Magnetic Fields in Veterinary Medicine

Magnetic and electromagnetic devices appear not to be used on small animals. However, the devices are widely advertised in magazines targeted at horse owners. Pulsating electromagnetic field therapy is typically applied to horses with boots or blankets. Some of the variables of the magnetic field generated (such as the amplitude and frequency of the signal) can be controlled using this form of magnetic therapy. However, changes in these variables appear to affect different tissues in different ways, and those ways are not well defined, making selection of ideal field strength of the therapy problematic.

The other way to apply a magnetic field to a horse is by attaching a magnetic pad. This form of therapy generates a continuous, static magnetic influence on the targeted tissue; however, the magnetic field cannot be modulated. The principle advantage of this form of magnetic therapy is that it is relatively inexpensive (compared to the cost of the machines) and easy to apply; the disadvantage is that as yet there is no scientific evidence of an effect.

The absence of a plausible scientific theory for a mechanism of action should never override reliable strong clinical evidence of an effect. For example, the mechanism of aspirin was not known for many years, although the drug was clinically effective. However, there appear to be no published scientific studies available that demonstrate that any form of magnetic field therapy is valuable in the treatment of disease conditions of the horse.

Daily electromagnetic therapy did increase the concentration of blood vessels in surgically created defects of equine superficial digital flexor tendon, but the maturation of the repair tissue and the transformation of collagen type (two essential components in the healing process of tendon) actually were delayed by the treatment in tendon samples collected at 8 to 12 weeks after surgery.[60] No benefit could be demonstrated in the healing of freshly created bone injuries treated with pulsating electromagnetic field therapy when compared to untreated control limbs,[61] although another study did suggest an increase in bone activity under pulsating electromagnetic field treatment when holes were drilled in horse cannon bones.[62] Topical treatment with a pulsed electromagnetic field showed little effect on metabolism of normal horse bone in another study.[63] Unfortunately, the principle application of pulsating electromagnetic field therapy in people, for delayed and non-union fractures, is of little apparent use in horses.

## Magnetic Therapy and Pseudoscience

In spite of hundreds of years of investigation, there still appears to be no place for magnetic therapy in scientific medicine. While legitimate investigations are taking place, many aspects of magnetic therapy carry hallmarks of pseudoscience. For example:

- *Vague, unsupported claims of effectiveness.* One device advertises that "leading scientists agree that unipolar magnets are superior to bipolar." The "leading scientists" are not identified. The company also claims to have "tens of thousands of very satisfied users."

- *Misuse of defined scientific terminology.* The discovery of a "unipolar" magnet (see above) or magnetic monopole would lead its discoverer to an almost immediate Nobel prize, as magnetic monopoles have not been shown to exist. One company advertises its "Tectonic" magnets (tectonics is a geologic term referring to the study of the earth's structural features.)

- *Mischaracterization of medicine.* One company warns about the side effects of taking "too many pills" and states that, "Using magnets means you are not putting anything into your stomach that might cause upset or damage." Another company describes their magnets as "natural as nature" and "wholistic" [*sic*]. While magnets may not have any side effects, they may not have any effects, either.

- *Inaccurate claims.* One company states that studies at various universities have "proven" that static magnets increase blood flow. This appears to be contrary to fact.

- *Predicted phenomena remain slippery.* As experimental and theoretical work progresses, more and more sound evidence for the related phenomena should appear.[64] So far, such evidence remains elusive in the field of magnetic therapy.

- *No deepening evidence.* In spite of hundreds of years of experience and investigation, the "state of the art" in magnetic therapy appears to have increased little since the days of Franz Mesmer.

## Summary

Whenever an injury to tissue occurs, the goal of any medical therapy is to help allow healing of that injury so that, to the extent that it can be done, the injured tissue is returned to full normal function as quickly as possible. The quality of tissue repair and the speed with which that repair can be accomplished are the two major variables in the healing of any injury. Any medical therapy that could be demonstrated to affect either variable (or better yet, both of them) would be extremely valuable to the medical field.

However, assessing whether or not a particular medical therapy is effective in those regards is somewhat problematic. The old adage, "Time heals all wounds," is largely true. Many diseases are self-limiting and the body is able to heal itself with no intervention whatsoever. For example, according to one source, approximately 70 per cent of all acute infectious disease conditions of the horse are adequately dealt with by the host's defenses.[65] That suggests that whichever method of treatment is selected, 7 out of 10 times, the problem will get better. If healing occurs while a device touted to promote healing is applied to an injured or infected area, that device often receives the credit.

Explanations that magnetic fields "increase circulation," "reduce inflammation," or "speed recovery from injuries" are simplistic and are not supported by the weight of experimental evidence. The effects of magnetic fields on body tissues are complex and appear to vary from tissue to tissue and from different intensities and duration of the magnetic field applied. The nature of the magnetic devices make them amenable to randomized, controlled, double-blind studies that are, for the most part, lacking. Although the therapies appear to be harmless, that does not also mean that they are useful.

## References

1. Mourino, M. From Thales to Lauterbur, or from the lodestone to MR imaging: magnetism and medicine. *Radiology* 180: 593–612, 1991.

2. Herholdt and Rafn, *Experiments with the Metallic Tractors in Rheumatic and Gouty Affections, Inflammations and Various Tropical Diseases,* Royal Academy of Sciences, Copenhagen, Denmark, 1799.

3. Macklis, R. Magnetic Healing, Quackery and the Debate about the Health Effects of Electromagnetic Fields. *Annals of Medicine* 118(5): 376–383, 1993.

4. Thatcher, C. Plain road to health without the use of medicine. Jameson and Morse, Chicago, IL, 1886.

5. Milstead, K., David, J. and Dobelle, M. Quackery in the medical device field. *Proceedings of the Second National AMA/FDA Congress on Medical Quackery.* Washington, D.C., Oct. 25–26, 1963.

6. Davidovitch, Z., et al. Biochemical mediators of the effects of mechanical forces in electric currents on mineralized tissue. *Calcif Tissue Int* 36: 86–97, 1984.

7. Aaron, R. and Ciombor, D. Acceleration of Experimental Endochondral Ossification by Biophysical Stimulation of the Progenitor Cell Pool. *J Orthop Res* 14(4): 582–89, 1996.

8. Cho, M., et al. Reorganization of microfilament structure induced by ac electric fields. *FASEB J* 10: 1552–1558, 1996.

9. MacGinitie, L.A., Gluzbank, Y.A. and Grodzinski, A.J. Electric Field Stimulation can Increase Protein Synthesis in Articular Cartilage Explants. *J Orthop Res* 12: 151–60, 1994.

10. Shimizu, T., et al. Bone ingrowth into porous calcium phosphate ceramics; influence of pulsating electromagnetic field. *J Orthop Res* 6: 248–258, 1988.

11. Rubin, C., McLeod, K. and Lanyon, L. Prevention of osteoporosis by pulsed electromagnetic fields. *J Bone Joint Surg* [Am] 71: 411–416, 1989.

12. Cruess, R. and Bassett, C.A.L. The effect of pulsing electromagnetic fields on bone metabolism in experimental disuse osteoporosis. *Clin Orthop* 173: 245–250, 1983.

13. Miller, G., et al. Electromagnetic stimulation of canine bone grafts. *J Bone and Joint Surg [Am]* 66: 693–698, 1984.

14. Kold, S. and Hickman, J. Preliminary study of quantitative aspects and the effect of pulsed electromagnetic field treatment on the incorporation of equine cancellous bone grafts. *Eq Vet J* 19(2): 120–124, 1987.

15. Sharrard, W. A double blind trial of pulsed electromagnetic fields for delayed union of tibial fractures. *J Bone and Joint Surg* [Br] 72: 347–355, 1990.

16. Mooney, V. A randomized double blind prospective study of the efficacy of pulsed electromagnetic fields for interbody lumbar fusions. *Spine* 15: 708–712, 1990.

17. De Haas, W.G., Lazarovici, M.A., and Morrison, D.M. The Effect of Low Frequency Magnetic Field on Healing of Osteotomized Rabbit Radius. *Clin Orthop* 145: 245–51, 1979.

18. Ieran, M., et al. Effect of Low Frequency Pulsing Electromagnetic Fields on Skin Ulcers of Venous Origin in Humans: A Double-Blind Study. *J Orthop Res* 8(2): 276–282, 1990.

19. Kort, J., Ito, H. and Basset, C.A.L. Effects of pulsing electromagnetic fields on peripheral nerve regeneration. *J Bone Jt Sug Orthop Trans* 4: 238, 1980.

20. Sisken, B.F., et al. Pulsed electromagnetic fields stimulate nerve regeneration in vitro and in vivo. *Restorative Neurology and Neuroscience* 1: 303–309, 1990b.

21. Polk, C. Electric and Magnetic Fields for Bone and Soft Tissue Repair. In, *Handbook of Biological Effects of Electromagnetic Fields,* 2nd ed. Polk, C. and Postow, E., eds. CRC Press, Boca Raton, FL, 231–246, 1996.

22. Bassett, C.A.L. Beneficial Effects of Electromagnetic Fields. *J of Cell Biochem* 51: 387–393, 1993.

23. Lee, E.W., et al. Pulsed Magnetic and Electromagnetic Fields in Experimental Achilles Tendonitis in the Rat: A Prospective Randomized Study. *Arch Phys Med and Rehab* 78(4): 399–404, 1997.

24. Barker, A.T. Pulsating Electromagnetic Field Therapy for the Treatment of Tibial Non-Union Fractures. *Lancet* 8384 (1): 994–996, 1984.

25. Barker, A.T. Electricity, magnetism and the body: Some Uses and Abuses. *Eng Sci and Edu J,* 249–256, December, 1993.

26. Aaron, R. Department of Orthopedics, Brown University and Orthopedic Research Laboratory, Department of Surgery, Roger Williams Medical Center, Providence, RI. Personal Communication.

27. Schulten, K. Magnetic field effects in chemistry and biology. *Adv. Solid State Phys.* 22: 61, 1982.

28. Steiner, U.E. and Ulrich, T. Magnetic field effects in chemical kinetics and related phenomena. *Chem Rev,* 89: 51, 1989.

29. Beall, P.T., Hazlewood, C.F. and Rao, P.N. Nuclear magnetic resonance patterns of intracellular water as a function of HeLa cell cycle. *Science* 192: 904–907, 1976.

30. Frankel, R.B. and Liburdy, R.P. Biological Effects of Static Magnetic Fields. In, Polk, C. and Postow, E. *Handbook of Biological Effects of Electromagnetic Fields,* 2nd Ed. CRC Press, Boca Raton, FL, 149–183, 1996.

31. Porter, M. *Magnetic Therapy.* Equine Vet Data, 17(7): 371, 1997.

32. Kirschvink, J. Professor of Geobiology, California Institute of Technology, Pasadena, CA. Personal Communication, 1997.

33. Baermann, H. Bioflex, *Flexible Concentric Circle Magnets vs. Elekiban Style Magnets.* www.magnaflex.com

34. Adair, R.K. Sterling Professor Emeritus of Physics, Yale University, New Haven, CT. Personal Communication.

35. Tectonic Magnets, Riviera Beach, FL.

36. Pratt, G. Professor of Electrical Engineering, The Massachusetts Institute of Technology, Cambridge, MA. Personal Communication, 1997.

37. Kobluk, C., Johnston, G. and Lauper, L. A Scintigraphic Investigation of Magnetic Field Therapy on the Equine Third Metacarpus. *Vet and Comp Orthop and Traum* 7(1): 9–13, 1994.

38. Steyn, P. Professor of Radiology, Department of Veterinary Medicine, Colorado State University, Personal Communication, 1997.

39. Saygili, G., et al. Investigation of the Effect of Magnetic Retention Systems Used in Prosthodontics on Buccal Mucosal Blood Flow. *Int J of Prosthodont,* 5(4): 326–332, 1992.

40. Belossi, A., et al. No Effect of a Low-Frequency Pulsed Magnetic Field on the Brain Blood Flow Among Mice. *Panminerva Med,* 35(1): 57–59, 1993.

41. Barker, A. and Cain, M. The claimed vasodilatory effect of a commercial permanent magnet foil; results of a double blind trial. *Clin Phys Physiol Meas* 6(3): 261–263, 1985.

42. Leaper, D.J. Do Magnetic Fields Influence Soft Tissue Wound Healing? *Eq Vet J* 17(3): 178–180, 1985.

43. Turner, T., Wolfsdorf, K. and Jourdenais, J. Effects of Heat, Cold, Biomagnets and Ultrasound on Skin Circulation in the Horse. *Proc 37th AAEP,* 249–257, 1991.

44. Stick, C., et al. Do Strong Magnetic Fields in NMR tomography modify tissue perfusion? *Nuklearmedizin* 154: 326, 1991.

45. Keltner, J., et al. Magnetohydrodynamics of Blood Flow. *Mag Res in Med* 16: 139, 1990.

46. Wikswo, J.P. and Barach, J.P. An estimate of the Steady Magnetic Field Strength required to influence nerve conduction. IEEE *Transactions on Biomedical Engineering* BME-27(12): 722–723, 1980.

47. Trock, D.H., Bollet, A.J. and Markill, R. The effect of pulsed electromagnetic fields in the treatment of osteoarthritis of the knee and cervical spine. Report of randomized, double blind, placebo controlled trials. *J Rheumatol* 21(10): 1903–1911, 1994.

48. Trock, D.H., et al. A double-blind trial of the clinical effects of pulsed electromagnetic fields in osteoarthritis. *J Rheumatol* 20(3): 456–460, 1993.

49. Foley-Nolan, D., et al. Pulsed High Frequency (27MHz) Electromagnetic Therapy for Persistent Neck Pain: A Double Blind, Placebo-Controlled Study of 20 Patients. *Orthopedics* 13(4): 445–451, 1990.

50. Varcaccia-Garofalo, G., et al. Analgesic properties of electromagnetic field therapy in patients with chronic pelvic pain. *Clin Exp Obstet Gynecol* 22(4): 350–354, 1995.

51. Leclaire, R. and Bourgouin, J. Electromagnetic treatment of shoulder periarthritis: a randomized controlled trial of the efficiency and tolerance of magnetotherapy. *Arch Phys Med Rehabil* 72(5): 284–287, 1991.

52. Puett, D.W. and Griffin, M.R. Published trials of nonmedicinal and noninvasive therapies for hip and knee osteoarthritis. *Ann Intern Med* 121(2): 133–140, 1994.

53. Papi, F., et al. Exposure to Oscillating Magnetic Fields Influences Sensitivity to Electrical Stimuli. II. Experiments on Humans. *Bioelectromagnetics* 16: 295–300, 1995.

54. Nakagawa, K. Clinical Application of Magnetic Field. *J Soc Non-trad. Technol.*, 66: 6–17, 1974.

55. Nakagawa, K. Magnetic field-deficient syndrome and magnetic treatment. *Jap Med J* 2745: 24–32, 1976.

56. Vallbonna, C., Hazlewood, C.F. and Jurida, G. Response of Pain to Static Magnetic Fields in Postpolio Patients: A Double-Blind Pilot Study. *Arch Phys Med Rehabil* 78: 1200–1204, 1997.

57. Casselli, M.A., et al. Evaluation of magnetic foil and PPT Insoles in the treatment of heel pain. *J Am Podiatr Med Assoc* 87(1): 11–16, 1997.

58. Hong, C., et al. Magnetic necklace: its therapeutic effectiveness on neck and shoulder pain. *Arch Phys Med Reab.* 63: 464–466, 1982.

59. Lin, J.C., et al. Geophysical Variables and Behavior: XXVII. Magnetic Necklace: Its Therapeutic Effectiveness on Neck and Shoulder Pain: 2. Psychological Assessment. *Psychological Reports* 56: 639–649, 1985.

60. Watkins, J., et al: Healing of surgically created defects in the Equine Superficial Digital Flexor Tendon: Effects of PEMF on collagen-type transformation and tissue morphologic reorganization. *AJVR* 46: 2097–2103, 1985.

61. Bramlage, L., Weisbrode, S. and Spurlock, G. The Effect of a Pulsating Electromagnetic Field on the Acute Healing of Equine Cortical Bone. Proc 30th *AAEP,* 43–48, 1984.

62. Cane, V., Botti, P. and Soana, S. Pulsed Magnetic Fields Improve Osteoblast Activity During the Repair of an Experimental Osseous Defect. *J Ortho Research,* 11(5): 664–670, 1993.

63. Collier, M., et al. Radioisotope uptake in normal equine bone under the influence of a pulsed electromagnetic field. *Mod Vet Prac* 66: 971–974, 1985.

64. Turpin, R. Characterization of Quack Theories. http://www.chewable.com/ hypatian/quack.htm.

65. Walker, R.D. Antimicrobial Chemotherapy. In, *Current Therapy in Equine Medicine, III,* Robinson, N.E., ed. W.B. Saunders Co, Philadelphia, PA, 1992.

# UNIT FOUR

## Mapping the Debate

# INTRODUCTION

By this point in the semester, you have probably realized that many issues do not divide themselves neatly into two positions, "for" and "against." Rather, people take a range of perspectives. One way to get a handle on these perspectives is to write an overview of the debate. Doing this allows you to sort through and identify the different positions people take and reasons why they support their positions. The overview articles that follow do just that. In addition, they provide their readers with background information about the debate, sometimes giving a history of the issue, sometimes giving a set of questions that need to be answered. Although these articles do not purport to be opinion articles, keep in mind that biases are often apparent even in "neutral" writing. Be on the lookout for the writers' biases: consider the placement of the arguments they present—which ones do they begin and end their articles with?—and how much attention they give to each viewpoint.

Section two of this unit is a collection of articles that explore the debate surrounding media violence and its effect on society and particularly on children. The articles provide examples of the multitude of perspectives people can take on a single, complex issue. Although most of the writers here agree that the media has a negative impact on society, not all agree on why we have seen such horrifying violence of late, nor do they agree on what should be done about it.

**Elisa Warford**

# I

## Overview Articles

### GAYS REACT TO ADS THAT CALL THEM SINNERS

Caryle Murphy

> *In this article Caryle Murphy reports on the controversy surrounding a series of newspaper ads that called homosexuality a "sexual sin." Note how she introduces the article before giving background information on the advertisements. It is also significant that, although Murphy quotes many religious leaders, they do not all share the same opinions regarding the ads. This demonstrates that it is perhaps not as easy to generalize about "religious" people as we would like to think. The article was published in July 1998 in* The Washington Post.

Since graduating from the U.S. Merchant Marine Academy three decades ago, Mick Ellis has been an active churchgoer whose religion "has always been Christ-centered." For a time, he served as a Roman Catholic Eucharistic minister, helping distribute Holy Communion at Mass.

As a gay man, said Ellis, now director of student activities at American University, "I just knew in my heart that God accepted me for who I was, that God created me and that God doesn't make mistakes. And I knew that my sexual orientation wasn't a choice."

The relationship between religious life and homosexuality burst into public debate again last week when a coalition of conservative, politically active Christian groups ran several full-page advertisements in national newspapers calling homosexuality a "sexual sin."

Placed by the Christian Coalition, the Family Research Council and 13 other groups, the ads state that homosexuals choose that lifestyle and can change what the

123

groups regard as aberrant behavior through therapy and accepting "the truth of God's healing love." Gay people, the ads strongly imply, are sinful people who do not have a spiritual relationship with God—and need to know "the truth that sets them free."

The ads, which appeared in newspapers over three days, have drawn sharp rebukes from the local gay community and many Washington area church leaders.

"They are basically saying you cannot be gay or lesbian and have a relationship with God," said Cathy Renna, spokeswoman for the Gay and Lesbian Alliance Against Defamation. "I find that particularly offensive. They are denying the spirituality of hundreds of thousands of people across this country."

A great many individual churches around the country have been supportive and accepting of the estimated 1 to 10 percent of the population that is gay. Still, the issue of homosexuality—which has surfaced in disputes over gay clergy members and same-sex unions—has been a divisive one among several denominations, including Catholics, Episcopalians, Presbyterians, United Methodists and Mennonites.

And the ads, according to critics, seem to be both a personal attack on homosexuals—and a political effort to keep the controversy in the public eye.

"They represent a very simplistic arrogance on the part of the religious right," said the Rev. C. Welton Gaddy, executive director of the District-based Interfaith Alliance. "They're assuming their interpretation of the Bible is the only accurate one, their understanding of homosexuality is the only correct one and their statement of faith represents the view of all Christians."

The implication in one of the ads, Gaddy added, "was that unless you experience Christian conversion, you have no place in our society." That message, he said, could also be "directed at Jews, Muslims, Hindus and Catholics."

"You begin to see the potential danger of this kind of narrow theology."

Other local Christian pastors, however, called the ads appropriate and helpful.

"My desire is for homosexuals to see in these ads that Christians genuinely love them and care enough about them to offer a message of forgiveness and power to change, even if it challenges how they think and live," said the Rev. John Loftness, executive pastor of Covenant Life Church in Gaithersburg. He saw the ads as delivering "a message of hope and compassion."

In Springfield, the Rev. Jack Elwood, a pastor at Immanuel Bible Church, said he hoped the ads will "spark a national debate about homosexuality," which he called "one of the crucial issues of our time." Homosexuality, he said, is not only an issue of morality but it is "spilling over into public policy. It's in the court system. It's in the political process. It's one of the things that is reflective of our current culture."

But the Rev. J. Philip Wogaman, pastor of Foundry United Methodist Church in Northwest Washington, said that describing homosexuality as a sin "implies that it's a matter of choice, and it does seem pretty clear that sexual orientation is not a choice, at least with most people."

It also "lays on a homosexual person the burden that their basic identity is disapproved by God," Wogaman added. "And to suggest that they are not really Christians is a terrible thing to say. It's a little like saying that if you had enough faith, you'd be cured of your cancer."

The Rev. Stephen Welch, director of missions for the Mount Vernon Association of Baptist Churches, would not discuss his group's attitude about the ads, saying the issue of homosexuality is not high on its agenda. He would rather, he said, "talk about our work with Habitat for Humanity or the summer camps we sponsor for low-income families or . . . new churches."

Charles L. Cox, executive director of Dignity/USA, which represents Roman Catholic gay, bisexual and transgendered people, said he was struck by the "stark contrast" between the ads and the pastoral letter issued by U.S. Catholic bishops in the fall.

That letter, titled "Always Our Children," stressed that while the church considers homosexual activity sinful, sexual orientation is "a deep-seated dimension of one's personality." Generally, the bishops added, "homosexual orientation is experienced as a given, not as something freely chosen. By itself, therefore, a homosexual orientation cannot be considered sinful for morality presumes the freedom to choose."

Cox said that speaking from personal experience, "I can tell you there are many of us who prayed to God [to] change this orientation. And it didn't happen."

The Rev. Kenneth T. South, executive director of AIDS National Interfaith Network and a United Church of Christ minister who is gay, said he has often wondered why Jesus made so many references to the spiritual perils of being rich but said nothing about homosexuality. "If it was such a horrible concern for Jesus, you would have thought he would have said something about it," South said.

American University's Ellis now attends Metropolitan Community Church in Northwest Washington, which ministers primarily to gay people. He said the ads fly in the face of Christ's famous Bible admonishment to a crowd about to attack an adulterous woman: "Let he who is without sin cast the first stone."

"If Jesus Christ was not in a position to judge," Ellis said, "how does it become religious to place all these judgments on a whole class of people?"

# THE CHANGING FACE OF BILINGUAL EDUCATION

Russell Gersten

*Russell Gersten, who is a professor at the University of Oregon and Senior Researcher at the Eugene Research Institute, gives an overview of the bilingual education debate in this article, which appeared in the scholarly journal* Educational Leadership *in April, 1999. He gives a recent history of bilingual education programs, aside from noting the significant figures in this debate, and he also lists a series of questions that need to be answered by further research. As you read, consider where Gersten's biases lie: what is his position on these issues?*

As bilingual education shifts toward more instruction in English and less in native languages, we need to focus on what research tells us about effective practices.

The past year or so has brought a virtual avalanche of dramatic events in the field of bilingual education, portending a significant shift in how English language learners are taught in the United States. In April 1998, Secretary of Education Richard Riley announced a major shift in policy, calling for a goal of English language proficiency in three years for virtually all English language learners. Riley asserted that "new immigrants have a passion to learn English, and they want the best for their children" (p. 2). A survey of 420 randomly selected members of the Association of Texas Educators (both inside and outside the field of bilingual education) found that the majority agreed with the secretary. They believed that children spend too much time in native language instruction (Tanamachi, 1998). Traub (1999) also argues that Latino students spend far too much time in native language instruction, concluding that, in its current form, "bilingual education seems to be hurting" Latino students the most—"the one group it was initially designed to help" (p. 33).

This view stands in stark contrast to the position of several noted scholars in the field, who feel that English language learners should be taught all academic subjects in their native language for no fewer than five, and preferably seven, years (for example, Cummins, 1994). These scholars believe that extensive academic instruction in the native language is necessary for students to benefit from mainstream classrooms.

Recent events indicate that some large school districts (for example, New York and Denver) and some states (for example, California) are seriously rethinking how they educate English language learners. Invariably, the initiatives call for students to enter English language academic instruction at a much earlier age, and they propose a significant reduction in academic instruction in native languages. An article in the New York Times reports that "in response to years of criticism of the city's bilingual education programs . . . New York City plans to dramatically increase the amount of time devoted to English language development" (Archibold, 1998). The article concludes with a summary of major lawsuits. Lawsuits or threatened litigation in Sacramento, Denver, and Albuquerque convey the emotional tenor of the debate.

Increasingly, parents and teachers (most notably Jaime Escalante and Gloria Tuchman) have begun to question the small amount of time devoted to English language development in many bilingual education programs in the primary grades. Advocacy groups have consistently raised such issues as parental choice in the amount of English language instruction each child receives, how early a child is introduced to substantive English language instruction, and when a child should exit classrooms that use a great deal of native language instruction.

It seems reasonable to expect that after so much attention, controversy, and discussion, research would provide answers to questions such as these:

- At what age is it best to introduce academic instruction in English to young students?
- To what extent—if any—does native language instruction benefit students' cognitive and academic growth?
- Which are the best instructional methods for developing English language proficiency?

Unfortunately, research findings have stubbornly failed to provide answers to the first two questions. Ironically, we have more research-based information on the third—and least emotional—of these guiding research questions.

## Searching for Answers

An unbiased review of research addressing the first question indicates that we do not have adequate information to determine the optimal time for a child to be taught academic content in English (n1). This is not to say that researchers have not passionately debated the issue or that they have not developed and disseminated a vast array of complex theories. This issue has been debated extensively and serves as the basis of some of the aforementioned lawsuits.

The cornerstone of most contemporary models of bilingual education is that content knowledge and skills learned in a student's primary language will transfer to English once the student has experienced between five and seven years of native language instruction. Yet absolutely no empirical research supports this proposition. Methodological problems so severe that the question cannot be adequately answered plague the research on the subject (August & Hakuta, 1997). These problems appear to be most severe in some of the larger studies intended to "answer" major policy questions.

The recent report released by the National Academy of Sciences, "Improving Schooling for Language Minority Children" (August & Hakuta, 1997), offers a laundry list of complaints concerning these studies:

The major national-level program evaluations suffer from design limitations, lack of documentation of study objectives, poorly articulated goals, lack of fit between goals and research designs and excessive use of elaborate statistical designs to overcome shortcomings (p. 138).

In addition, the report concludes that "it is difficult to synthesize the program evaluations of bilingual education because of the extreme politicization of the process" (p. 138). The report makes clear that the prevalence of writings by "advocates who are convinced of the absolute correctness of their positions" (p. 138) presents serious barriers to attempts to improve the quality of instruction for English language learners.

Trying to unravel the issues behind these conflicts and debates can be frustrating. Even the National Academy of Sciences report is of little immediate help. It is as filled with contradictions as most other writing in the field. For example, the authors savagely critique the research on effective schooling and classroom processes, yet report the findings from these seriously flawed studies as if they represented solid facts. Similarly, the authors indicate that there is no empirical support for the effectiveness of native language instruction in the early grades, yet still advocate its use. However, the report also demonstrates an awareness of the contradictory nature of the database by noting:

> It is clear that many children first learn to read in a second language without serious negative consequences. These include children who successfully go through early-immersion, two-way, and English as a second language (ESL)-based programs in North America (p. 23).

Michael Kirst of Stanford University (Schnaiberg, 1998) recently provided some valuable insight into the problems within the bilingual education knowledge base. In discussing California, he noted:

> From its inception . . . in the 1970s, bilingual education has been oriented toward inputs, process and compliance. . . . The assumption was if you have this input, the outputs would take care of themselves. So . . . [we monitor] . . . , whether you mounted the program, and not its results (p. 16).

Although Kirst was discussing California, similar problems have been noted in states such as Texas and Massachusetts. This concern with compliance as opposed to learning outcomes helps explain why the bilingual education knowledge base is so inadequate—which in turn contributes to many of the current problems in the field.

Increasingly, researchers argue that we need to focus on aspects of instruction that lead to improved learning outcomes as opposed to political labels that at best crudely describe complex instructional interventions. Several years ago, my colleagues and I received support from the U.S. Department of Education to begin to articulate these components. Our charge was to synthesize the knowledge base on effective classroom practices that simultaneously promote English language development and academic learning. We intentionally eschewed the ongoing political debates. Our goal was to delineate specific techniques that teachers could use to simultaneously promote learning and English language development.

## English Language Development

Although questions about optimal age remain unanswered, at some point all English language learners begin academic instruction in English. The initial transition is often called "content area ESOL," "structured immersion," or "sheltered content instruction." The common feature is teachers' use of English designed for students who are not proficient in the language. In sheltered instruction, teachers modulate their use of

English so that it is comprehensible to the student and base their degree of support on their knowledge of that student. In some cases, teachers use native language to help a child complete a task, to clarify a point, or to respond to a question.

Almost invariably, sheltered content instruction is coupled with instruction geared toward building the student's knowledge of the English language. In years past, this component has been referred to as ESL or ESOL. Increasingly, educators are using "English language development" (ELD). Historically, teachers focused on the formal structure of language (for example, grammar and mechanics). Critics routinely attacked this approach, however, because it failed to capitalize on the communication function of language, did not generate student interest, and resulted in very limited generalization.

The 1980s brought more "natural" conversational approaches to teaching English. These also attracted criticism, primarily because they did not necessarily help students learn the highly abstract, often decontextualized language of academic discourse. A movement began about 10 years ago to merge English language learning with content acquisition. The rationale is that students can learn English while learning academic content and that this type of learning will build academic language (Cummins, 1994)—that is, the abstract language of scientific, mathematical, or literary discourse. However, too often teachers merely "hope that language occurs [during lessons]. There is a risk during content instruction of neglecting language development" (Gersten & Baker, in press).

The erratic quality of ELD instruction is at the root of the growing dissatisfaction with current practice. Inadequate attention has been devoted to curriculum development, pragmatic teacher training and professional development, and applied research. In a recent professional work group that I conducted in California for the U.S. Department of Education (Gersten & Baker, in press), an educator from the district bilingual education office articulated the problem: "It's important for teachers to be clear about objectives and goals . . . yet an explicit statement of goals does not exist [in district or state curricular materials]."

I would argue, however, that we have made definite progress in understanding what instructional goals are feasible for this group of students and what specific classroom practices are likely to help meet these goals. In our two-year research synthesis project (Gersten & Baker, in press), we concluded that the beginning of an empirical knowledge base on effective instructional practices for English language learners exists. It is important to emphasize, however, that this knowledge base is emerging and should be the topic of controlled, high-quality classroom research.

## References

Archibold, R. C. (1998, June 21). Crew plans an overhaul of bilingual education. *New York Times*, p. 27.

Arreaga-Mayer, C. (1998). Language sensitive peer mediated instruction for culturally and linguistically diverse learners in the intermediate elementary grades. In R. R. Gersten & R. Jimenez (Eds.), *Promoting learning for culturally and linguistically diverse students: Classroom applications from contemporary research* (pp. 73–90). Belmont, CA: Wadsworth.

August, D., & Hakuta, K. (Eds.). (1997). *Improving schooling for language minority children.* Washington, DC: National Academy Press.

Calderon, M., Hertz-Lazarowitz, R., & Slavin, R. (1998). Effects of bilingual cooperative integrated reading and composition on students making the transition from Spanish to English reading. *Elementary School Journal, 99*(2), 153–165.

Chamot, A. U. (1998). Effective instruction for high school English language learners. In R. Gersten & R. Jimenez (Eds.), *Promoting learning for culturally and linguistically diverse students: Classroom applications from contemporary research* (pp. 187–209). Belmont, CA: Wadsworth.

Cummins, J. (1994). Primary language instruction and the education of language minority students. In *Schools and language minority students: A theoretical framework* (2nd ed.). Los Angeles: California State University, National Evaluation, Dissemination and Assessment Center.

Echevarria, J., & Graves, A. (1998). *Sheltered content instruction: Teaching English-language learners with diverse abilities.* Des Moines, IA: Allyn & Bacon.

Fashola, O. S., Drum, P. A., Mayer, R. E., & Kang, S. (1996). A cognitive theory of orthographic transitions: Predictable errors in how Spanish-speaking children spell English words. *American Educational Research Journal, 33*, 825–844.

Gersten, R., & Baker, S. (in press). The professional knowledge base on instructional interventions that support cognitive growth for language minority students. In R. Gersten, E. Schiller, S. Vaughn, & J. Schumm (Eds.), *Research synthesis in special education.* Mahwah, NJ: Erlbaum.

Gersten, R., Baker, S., & Marks, S. U. (1998). *Productive instructional practices for English-language learners: Guiding principles and examples from research-based practice.* Reston, VA: Council for Exceptional Children.

Gersten, R., Baker, S., & Otterstedt, J. (1999). Further analysis of "A meta-analysis of the effectiveness of bilingual education," by J. P. Greene (1989). *Technical Report No. 99–01.* Eugene, OR: Eugene Research Institute.

Gersten, R., & Jimenez, R. (1994). A delicate balance: Enhancing literacy instruction for students of English as a second language. *The Reading Teacher, 47*(6), 438–449.

Greene, J. P. (1998). A meta-analysis of the effectiveness of bilingual education. Unpublished technical report. Austin, TX: University of Texas & the Thomas Rivera Policy Institute.

Klingner, J. K., Vaughn, S., & Schumm, J. S. (1998). Collaborative strategic reading during social studies in heterogeneous fourth-grade classrooms. *Elementary School Journal, 99*(1), 3–22.

Reyes, M. (1992). Challenging venerable assumptions: Literacy instruction for linguistically different students. *Harvard Educational Review, 62*(4), 427–446.

Reyes, E., & Bos, C. (1998). Interactive semantic mapping and charting: Enhancing content area learning for language minority students. In R. Gersten & R. Jimenez (Eds.), *Promoting learning for culturally and linguistically diverse students: Classroom applications from contemporary research* (pp. 133–152). Belmont, CA: Wadsworth.

Riley, R. W. (1998, April 27) Helping all children learn English. Washington, DC: U.S. Department of Education: Office of Public Affairs.

Saunders, W., O'Brien, G., Lennon, D., & McLean, J. (1998). Making the transition to English literacy successful: Effective strategies for studying literature with transition students. In R. Gersten & R. Jimenez (Eds.), *Effective strategies for teaching language minority students: Classroom applications from contemporary research* (pp. 99–132). Belmont, CA: Wadsworth.

Schnaiberg, L. (1998, April 29). What price English? *Education Week*, pp. 1, 16.

Tanamachi, C. (1998, July 18). Educators poll: Set bilingual time limit. *Austin American Statesman*, p. B1.

Traub, J. (1999, January 31). The bilingual barrier. *The New York Times Magazine*, pp. 32–35.

# WHAT CLONES?

Gary Stix

> *Author Gary Stix explains the controversy surrounding decisions by online journal* e-biomed *and print magazine* Scientific American *to publish a claim made by Advanced Cell Technology (ACT) in November 2001 that the company had cloned a human embryo. Since some scientists claim that the group of cells produced by ACT was not actually a clone, or at least not a human clone, there is some question as to whether this company misrepresented its work and whether the two publications were wrong to help spread ACT's allegedly misleading statements. In his article, Stix connects this specific debate to the issue of how to define cloning, therapeutic cloning, reproductive cloning, and human cloning. While Stix attempts to present an objective survey of a number of positions, how does the fact that his article was published in the December 24, 2001 issue of* Scientific American *affect your reading of his work?*

## Were Claims of the First Human Embryo Premature?

On November 25, 2001, a Massachusetts biotechnology company, Advanced Cell Technology (ACT), reported in an online journal—*e-biomed: The Journal of Regenerative Medicine*—that it had cloned the first human embryos. In a concurrent article in the January *Scientific American*, the researchers explained that their results could "represent the dawn of a new age in medicine by demonstrating that the goal of therapeutic cloning is within reach." Therapeutic cloning—in contrast to reproductive cloning, intended to create a baby—would produce the stem cells needed to treat diabetes, paralysis and other currently incurable conditions.

Many leading scientists, however, say the work should never have been published, because the research failed on several accounts to achieve its goals. First, ACT didn't produce any stem cells. But more fundamentally, some investigators questioned the company's basic assertion about having actually cloned a human embryo. In the experiment, the ACT researchers injected cumulus cells into eggs that had their nuclei removed. (Cumulus cells nurture eggs in the ovary.) The investigators hoped that the cumulus cells' DNA would launch the process of early embryonic development that leads to a hollow sphere called a blastocyst, which would contain stem cells. Among the eight eggs injected with cumulus cells, two divided until they became four-cell embryos, and one proceeded until it reached six cells. Eleven other eggs injected with the nucleus of a skin cell failed to develop.

According to some biologists, a cloned embryo would attain its true status as an embryo only when the DNA from the cumulus cell transferred into the egg began transcription (in which its genes begin to issue instructions to make proteins for embryonic development). An egg contains genetic material (RNA) and proteins that were made during the formation of the egg within the ovary and can support development up to the eight-cell stage without any signals from the DNA in the nucleus. Thus, the ACT experiment may have been "running on fumes, purely directed by RNA and supported by proteins that were present in the egg," says John Eppig, a developmental and reproductive biologist at Jackson Laboratory in Bar Harbor, Me. Eppig adds that "there's no published information on a cloned human embryo. Whether someone has done it and not published it, your guess is as good as mine. This [result] is not it." (There was one previous claim of multicell embryo clones, but the findings were not published.)

Eppig is not alone. "They did not present in their paper any evidence that the nuclei that they transferred into the eggs were biologically active," notes Brigid Hogan, a developmental biologist at Vanderbilt University and a member of a National Academy of Sciences panel examining the scientific and medical aspects of human cloning. "So therefore, strictly speaking, they cannot say they generated a cloned embryo." She goes on to say, "If that had been [about anything but] human embryos, it would have never gotten accepted in any journal whatsoever, and I'm not the only one that thinks that. I mean, they should have kept quiet until they got some results that were worth publishing." Rudolf Jaenisch, a cloning expert at the Whitehead Institute for Biomedical Research at the Massachusetts Institute of Technology, concurred: "It's shocking to me that this would be published and that they would have attempted to publish it; it's the total failure of an experiment."

Paul Berg, professor emeritus of biology at Stanford University and a Nobel laureate, also expressed his outrage: "It was anything but a reportable result. I have not heard a single person in this field who hasn't rolled his eyes and been extremely puzzled of what the motive for it was. Anyone who wasn't totally naive would have predicted that this would have raised a firestorm among the people who were trying to prohibit this research." Harry Griffin, assistant director at the Roslin Institute, which cloned Dolly the sheep, also questioned whether the work should have been published. But Griffin asserts that, even if the work eventually proves a success, it would be impractical as a routine technique for cell therapy. "The suggestion that the cloning of an embryo would revolutionize stem cell therapy by providing a route for routine immunocompatible cell transplants is simply naive. Such a treatment might be possible for a small number of patients, but there are five million suffering from Parkinson's disease in the U.S. alone. There is, in our view, no way that individual embryos can be created to provide individual treatment for this number of people—it would be incredibly costly, and there are simply not enough human eggs available."

Not everyone was as harsh, however. Peter Braude, head of the division of women and children's health at Guy's and St. Thomas's School of Medicine in London, says that this paper is the first publication that reports having "put donor nuclei into recipient eggs and demonstrated cleavage. They have yet to demonstrate that they have gene activation of the new nucleus, for which they may be criticized as being premature. But with their having put this up online, it is up to the scientific community to either repeat it or refute it." Braude also said he would have difficulty repeating the experiment from the methodology reported by ACT. But he bridled at the suggestion that ACT should have waited until they could publish on stem cells developed through these methods, given the difficulty that researchers have encountered in obtaining stem cells by any methodology. "If people are saying that they ought to have made stem cells as well, I think they're asking a tall order. It strikes me that they may be the stem cell people who are struggling on those grounds as well. I don't know of anybody who has good-quality stem cell lines that are out in the public domain."

Michael D. West, the president and chief executive of ACT, says that his group has adopted an approach that resembles that of Bob Edwards, the British scientist whose research resulted in 1978 in the first test-tube baby. Edwards published each step of his studies. That, in West's view, helped to foster openness about a controversial procedure. "The reason we decided to publish this was purely because we're promoting the idea of human therapeutic cloning, and we felt it was important to be transparent about where we're at and publish frequently," West says. He explains further that "when we were sure that we had gotten this far and had these results, we felt there was a publishable paper there."

West cites papers in other journals that have detailed findings about other animals at an early stage of embryonic development—in particular, he pointed to a research group led by Don Wolf of the Oregon Regional Primate Research Center, who published a paper last year on parthenogenesis (coaxing an unfertilized egg to become an embryo) and cloning in rhesus monkeys in the *Biology of Reproduction*, a well-established journal. The cloned monkey embryos, West says, died at an earlier stage than did the embryos in the ACT experiment. Wolf, however, disagreed with West's assessment of his work: "I guess I just would ask him whether he would ever consider submitting this [human cloning] manuscript to the *Biology of Reproduction*," Wolf says. "It would have been laughed off the stage. I mean it's so inadequate in

---

- **Speaking Parthenogenetically.** In addition to their claim of human cloning, researchers at ACT got six of 22 human eggs to form into balls of cells called blastocysts through a process known as parthenogenesis—in which unfertilized eggs are chemically tricked into becoming embryos. Although none of the blastocysts contained stem cells, a new study at ACT suggests that producing them is possible in primates. In an upcoming issue of *Science*, ACT is scheduled to report harvesting stem cells from monkey blastocysts and prompting them to turn into cultures of beating-heart cells, gut epithelial tissue, nerve cells that made dopamine, and other cell types.

- **Mired in Ire.** Not everyone at *e-biomed*, the online journal that accepted ACT's cloning paper, was happy with its publication. John Gearhart of Johns Hopkins University, an editorial board member and a pioneer in stem cell research, told the BBC that he was going to resign from the board over the matter. "I feel very embarrassed and very chagrined by this publication," he said in the BBC interview. In December the publisher, Mary Ann Liebert, was planning to meet with Gearhart and said she hoped he would change his mind.

terms of the number of experiments that were conducted and the failure of the experiments that were conducted."

William Haseltine, editor in chief of *e-biomed* and chairman of the biotechnology company Human Genome Sciences, defended the decision to publish. "It was a small but significant first step," he says of the research. The paper, Haseltine describes, went through a standard review process in which "two or more" reviewers, not including him, vetted the paper over the course of about three weeks. He refuses to identify the reviewers, saying only that they did not include editorial board members from ACT.

Haseltine also criticizes scientists for voicing their skepticism in the press, instead of writing letters to the journal or attempting to replicate the results: "It is nonscientific and not acceptable for people to make those comments to the press in the form of sound bites where they can't be judged." He says that scientists may have made such sharp comments partly because of "deep frustration" over the prohibition against any federally funded research that destroys human embryos: "There are those who would express frustration that they think they can do the work better and indeed it is possible they could, but [they] cannot do it." He also blames *Scientific American* and *U.S. News and World Report* which released their articles at the same time as *e-biomed*, for the subsequent frenzy. "Part of the public furor," Haseltine says, "was generated by the weight that the *Scientific American* publication also gave to this story and of course *U.S. News and World Report.*"

*Scientific American* editor in chief John Rennie says that he and staff editors debated whether to publish the article. "I think that we were disappointed that it wasn't a more clear-cut demonstration of an embryo that was further along," Rennie says. The likelihood of intense public interest in the result as the first documented human cloning demonstration justified the decision, he explained. "It was also our intention to continue to follow the story and provide other points of view on this, including dissenting ones," Rennie elaborates.

Haseltine has complained that his journal was not kept informed that *Scientific American* was preparing an article to be released concurrently. But ACT has been in the middle of press spats before. In 1998 it made a claim in the *New York Times* and on a CBS broadcast that it had created an embryo by fusing the nucleus of a human skin cell with a cow egg that had its nucleus removed. West says he just wanted to probe public reaction to the bizarre research. But critics say that the study, which has never been published, was intended to tie into the swell of press attention that attended the publications of research on the first isolation of human embryonic stem cells. At the time, stem cell researcher John Gearhart said ACT's claims reminded him of the spurious findings about cold fusion.

Critics of the ACT paper say that the dispute has not helped the case for therapeutic cloning. "In a controversial area you should have at least one part clean and scrutinized, which is the scientific part, and then you can go to the public and discuss all the other considerations like ethical and moral, ideological and religious," remarks M.I.T.'s Jaenisch. The U.S. House of Representatives has already voted to ban cloning, whether for therapeutic or reproductive purposes. Last December the Senate declined to take up a measure to place a moratorium on the procedure, but the debate will resume in 2002.

"I think the debate was progressing, and it was progressing in a fairly orderly manner; things were moving ahead," says Vanderbilt's Hogan. "People were working behind the scenes to make sure that everyone was aware of the biology. People like me were going around giving talks to Rotary clubs and oncology nurses and students, and then this comes out and everybody panicked."

These results may also mislead the public, says one observer. "When relatively underdeveloped science gets touted, first and foremost, patient hopes get raised," says University of Pennsylvania bioethicist Arthur Caplan. "So a lot of people say, 'Hey, I want this research to proceed because I'm dying and I'm very sick.' But it's cruel to offer something everybody knows is going to take a minimum of 10 years."

For his part, West says that the publication has created a healthy awareness about the cloning debate. "This paper," he says, "has certainly made it clear to the U.S. Congress and the U.S. public in general that there may be therapeutic use for nuclear transfer [cloning] that's entirely distinct from cloning a human being. One does not make a pregnancy."

During a December Senate hearing, West stated that he would be disappointed if ACT couldn't obtain cloned stem cells within six months. In an interview, Jose B. Cibelli, the ACT researcher who performed the cloning procedure, also said, "Give me 200 human eggs, and I'll give you cloned human stem cells." Whether such musings prove to be prescience or braggadocio remains to be seen. But one thing that does seem certain is that, one way or another, ACT will find a way to keep its research endeavors squarely in the public eye.

# SURVEY OF THE ISSUES: FEMINISM IN SURREALISM

Bonnie Crawford

*Bonnie Crawford was a student at the University of Maryland in 1998 when she wrote this paper exploring the issues of the role of women in the artistic movement of surrealism. Note how Crawford introduces the paper by giving background information about surrealism, then moves through the stases of definition and action. She also documents her sources clearly, making it easy for anyone to follow up on what she has written.*

It has been agreed that historically, Surrealism arose as a result of the disillusionment felt throughout post-war Paris and as a reaction against rational thought and the bourgeoisie (Chadwick, *Women* 13). Many members of the Surrealist movement had been involved in Dada, the movement that acted as a precursor to Surrealism, during World War I, including Andre Breton, the poet considered to be the founder of Surrealist ideas (Hubert 1). Breton had been preoccupied with the theories of Sigmund Freud and had even used some of Freud's practices while working with the ill or wounded during WWI. Thus, the ideas claimed by the Surrealists were strongly influenced by those of Freud that explore the subconscious and sexual repression (Breton 58). Breton and a few of his male contemporaries formed an avant-garde group based upon the idea of reaching the subconscious through dreams and recording them (Breton 58).

As to a concrete definition of the term, *Surrealism*, no agreement has been met. Surrealism was defined in the first Surrealist manifesto as "pure psychic automatism" (Breton 59). But, as Marcel Jean, an art historian, acknowledges, *automatism* and *surrealism* are both vague and strangely suggestive "imagewords" that have been used to define each other (Jean 118). In the third issue of *La Revolution Surrealiste*, one of the many Surrealist publications, Pierre Naville, the magazine's editor, wrote, "Everyone knows by now that there is no Surrealist painting"(Jean 121). Naville believed that the nature of Surrealism did not allow a true Surrealist painting to be created, that automatic painting could not be achieved, because Surrealism excluded rational thought while painting required ration.

Perhaps more important than a definition of Surrealism is an evaluation of what the Surrealists were attempting to achieve. According to Breton, the express aim of surrealism was "liberation of the mind" (Breton 48). But, since the early 1980s, with the rewriting of Surrealist history to include women, the question has been exactly whose mind was being liberated. Renee Hubert is among many who acknowledge that "especially in its early stages, surrealism has been labeled a male enterprise" (9), that Surrealism only lent to the liberation of male minds. In the context of modern day feminism, however, Chadwick feels that Surrealism "battled the social institutions— church, state, and family—that regulate the place of women in society" (*Mirrors* 5). Chadwick also argues that it was the first Modernist movement in which women could explore female subjectivity thus liberating women and providing a new means of expression. On the other hand, Norma Broude, another feminist art historian, explains that while Surrealism appeared to advocate social liberation and autonomy of women, the ideas of Surrealism celebrated the inequality between men and women by equating women with nature and intuition and males with culture and rational thought (12).

Once Surrealism has been defined and its motives evaluated, the real issue seems to be whether the women artists associated with the Surrealist movement can be labeled as Surrealists. Since the 1980s, women such as Leonora Carrington, Leonor Fini, Lee Miller, Kay Sage, Frida Kahlo, and Claude Cahun have been either labeled as Surrealists or associated with the Surrealist movement. While Lee Miller explored Surrealism through the medium of photography, she also modeled for other Surrealist photographers such as Edward Steichen and Man Ray (Hubert 199). Her presence in the history of Surrealism prior to the 1980s had been defined as model rather than artist. It has been argued that the nature of Surrealism allows no room for women to be active as artists involved in the movement, that a defining characteristic of Surrealism is that the male Surrealists "project their desires outwards" (Chadwick, *Mirrors* 4). According to Chadwick, male Surrealists created works of art unified by the theme of objectification of woman as muse (*Mirrors* 4). Therefore, woman's role in Surrealism is as muse rather than as artist. The artwork of women Surrealists differs from that of male Surrealists in that the women explored self-images in relation to external and internal realities (Chadwick, *Mirrors* 4).

But are the differences between artworks created by male and female Surrealists a substantial argument against the association of female artists with the Surrealist movement? In his essay, "'Vous pour moi?' Marcel Duchamp and Transgender Coupling," Dickran Tashjian, another scholar in the arts, asserts that:

> The inclination of Breton and others to claim the unconscious as feminine challenged the Surrealist women to defy the ideal woman . . . by portraying themselves as embodied, active subjects living through their mortal existence. (Chadwick, *Mirrors* 39)

In other words, Tashjian explains that the Surrealist women created artworks that differed in subject matter from the works of Surrealist men in a reaction against the subject matter of the male Surrealists and that it is important to acknowledge how the art of each gender affected the other.

Whether the female artists associated with the Surrealist movement *can* be considered Surrealists or not, *should* they be included in the history of Surrealism? Whitney Chadwick feels it necessary to include women in the history of Surrealism because "no other movement has had such a large number of active women participants" (*Women* 7). Hubert agrees by saying that Surrealism may have "provided a watershed in women's liberation by encouraging several independent women . . . to become prominent artists" (2). Chadwick also argues that woman's role in Surrealism is significant because it "established new parameters within which women artists might begin to explore the complex and ambiguous relationship between the female body and female identity" (*Mirrors* 4). The "relationship" that Chadwick refers to is a unifying theme among the artwork created by female artists in the Feminists art movement in the 1970s with "Cunt Art." The Guerrilla Girls, a group of anonymous artists began in 1989 to push for equal representation of women in art museums and galleries with the reasoning that discrimination against minority groups in the art industry should be regulated like many of the other industries in America with Equal Opportunity laws. If women are not included in the history of Surrealism, what does that imply for the significance of women artists at any given time in history? Conversely, many of the art critics opposing the protests of the Guerrilla Girls argue that the exclusion of women from the history of Surrealism is "an issue of quality, not prejudice" (Guerrilla Girls 14). Apparently, these critics believe that art done by women in the Surrealist movement is of lesser quality than that created by males. Other critics agree that discrimination against women exists, but "consider the situation hopeless" (Guerrilla Girls 14).

The problem with surveying the issues surrounding female Surrealists is that texts written by individuals who do not feel it necessary to include women in the history of Surrealism were written prior to the 1980s and prior to the arising of issues such as political correctness. Such texts simply do not address the issue of females in Surrealism and the lack of information about women artists in primary texts on Surrealism, because at the time that such books were published, the issues did not exist. John Berger, the author of *Ways of Seeing*, explains this problem. "The past is never waiting to be discovered," explains Berger, "History always constitutes the relation between a present and its past" (11). The same observation was made by Marcel Duchamp, the Surrealist painter when he remarked, "It is curious to note to what an extent memory is unfaithful . . . It is that, indeed, that explains the delightful fantasy of history" (Jean 124). Even Chadwick agrees that rereading Surrealism in its historical context after living in contemporary culture alters the cultural significance of the movement (*Mirrors* 7).

Once Surrealism has been defined and its aims and beliefs determined, perhaps the significance of the role women played in the Surrealist movement can be determined. But, Whitney Chadwick warns that, "The independence of these women serves as a constant warning to the art historian whose language is more often the generalized language of movements and groups than that of individuals" (*Women* 9).

## Works Cited

Berger, John. *Ways of Seeing*. London: Penguin Books, 1972.

Breton, Andre. *What is Surrealism?* New York: Haskell House Publishers Ltd, 1974.

Broude, Norma and Mary D. Garrard. *The Power of Feminist Art*. New York: Harry N. Abrams, Inc, 1994.

Chadwick, Whitney. *Mirrors Images, Women, Surrealism, and Self Representation*. Cambridge: The MIT Press, 1998.

Chadwick, Whitney. *Women Artists and the Surrealist Movement*. Boston: Little Brown and Company, 1985.

Guerrilla Girls. *Confessions of the Guerrilla Girls*. New York: Harper Perennial, 1995.

Hubert, Renee Riese. *Magnifying Mirrors, Women, Surrealism, and Partnership*. Lincoln: University of Nebraska Press, 1994.

Jean, Marcel. *The History of Surrealist Painting*. New York: Grove Press, Inc, 1959.

Melly, George. *Paris and the Surrealists*. New York: Thames and Hudson Inc, 1991.

Nochlin, Linda. "Why Have There Been No Great Women Artists?" *Women, Art, and Power*. 1971.

Parker, Rosita and Griselda Pollock. "Critical Stereotypes: the 'essential feminine' or how essential is femininity?" *Old Mistresses: Women, Art, Ideology*. 1981.

Pauly, Rebecca. "A Revolution is Not a Dinner Party." *Literature Film Quarterly*, Vol 22, Issue 4, 1994, p 232–238.

Spector, Jack J. "Surrealism Redefined". *Art Journal*, Fall 1994, Vol 53, Issue 3, p. 108–111.

Strickland, Carol and John Boswell. *The Annotated Mona Lisa*. Kansas City: Andrews and McMeel, 1992.

Wilkerson, Margaret. *Personal Interview*. 6 November 1998.

# II

# *Exploring a Debate*

## ☆ TELEVISION AND VIOLENT CRIME

Brandon S. Centerwall

> *In this important study on television violence, Brandon Centerwall, who holds a master's degree in public health and a medical degree, reports on several findings he has made on the link between media violence and aggression in children. The article first appeared in the Spring 1993 issue of* Public Interest. *In another essay in this book, Ted Riecken claims that "[s]ocial scientists cannot ... provide predictive statements about causation." As you read, evaluate the data Centerwall presents: does he convincingly show a causal link between television and real violence? Consider also Centerwall's rhetorical strategies of anticipating his opposition and discrediting it.*

Children are born ready to imitate adult behavior. That they can, and do, imitate an array of adult facial expressions has been demonstrated in newborns as young as a few hours old, before they are even old enough to know that they have facial features. It is a most useful instinct, for the developing child must learn and master a vast repertoire of behavior in short order.

But while children have an instinctive desire to imitate, they do not possess an instinct for determining whether a behavior ought to be imitated. They will imitate anything, including behavior that most adults regard as destructive and antisocial. It may give pause for thought, then, to learn that infants as young as fourteen months demonstrably observe and incorporate behavior seen on television.

The average American preschooler watches more than twenty-seven hours of television per week. This might not be bad if these young children understood what they were watching. But they don't. Up through ages three and four, most children are unable to distinguish fact from fantasy on TV, and remain unable to do so despite adult coaching. In the minds of young children, television is a source of entirely factual information regarding how the world works. There are no limits to their credulity. To cite one example, an Indiana school board had to issue an advisory to young children that, no, there is no such thing as Teenage Mutant Ninja Turtles. Children had been crawling down storm drains looking for them.

Naturally, as children get older, they come to know better, but their earliest and deepest impressions are laid down at an age when they still see television as a factual source of information about the outside world. In that world, it seems, violence is common and the commission of violence is generally powerful, exciting, charismatic, and effective. In later life, serious violence is most likely to erupt at moments of severe stress—and it is precisely at such moments that adolescents and adults are most likely to revert to their earliest, most visceral sense of the role of violence in society and in personal behavior. Much of this sense will have come from television.

## The Seeds of Aggression

In 1973, a remote rural community in Canada acquired television for the first time. The acquisition of television at such a late date was due to problems with signal reception rather than any hostility toward TV. As reported in *The Impact of Television* (1986), Tannis Williams and her associates at the University of British Columbia investigated the effect of television on the children of this community (which they called "Notel"), taking for comparison two similar towns that already had television.

The researchers observed forty-five first- and second-graders in the three towns for rates of inappropriate physical aggression before television was introduced into Notel. Two years later, the same forty-five children were observed again. To prevent bias in the data, the research assistants who collected the data were kept uninformed as to why the children's rates of aggression were of interest. Furthermore, a new group of research assistants was employed the second time around, so that the data gatherers would not be biased by recollections of the children's behavior two years earlier.

Rates of aggression did not change in the two control communities. By contrast, the rate of aggression among Notel children increased 160 percent. The increase was observed in both boys and girls, in those who were aggressive to begin with and in those who were not. Television's enhancement of noxious aggression was entirely general and not limited to a few "bad apples."

In another Canadian study, Gary Granzberg and his associates at the University of Winnipeg investigated the impact of television upon Indian communities in northern Manitoba. As described in *Television and the Canadian Indian* (1980), forty-nine third-, fourth-, and fifth-grade boys living in two communities were observed from 1973, when one town acquired television, until 1977, when the second town did as well. The aggressiveness of boys in the first community increased after the introduction of television. The aggressiveness of boys in the second community, which did not receive television then, remained the same. When television was later introduced in the second community, observed levels of aggressiveness increased there as well.

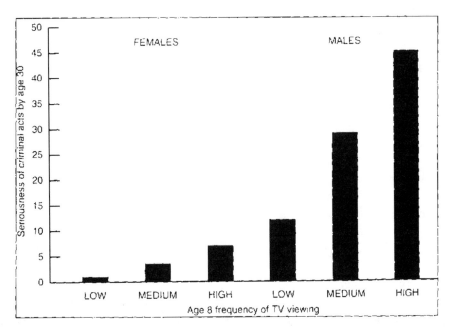

**FIGURE 1.** Relationship of television viewing frequency at age eight to seriousness of crimes committed by age thirty. Columbia County Cohort Study, 1960–1981. (Reprinted by permission from Leonard D. Eron and L. Rowell Huesmann, "The control of aggressive behavior by changes in attitudes, values, and the conditions of learning," *Advances in the Study of Aggression.* Orlando, Florida: Academic Press, 1984.)

In another study conducted from 1960 to 1981, Leonard Eron and L. Rowell Huesmann (then of the University of Illinois at Chicago) followed 875 children living in a semi-rural U.S. county. Eron and Huesmann found that for both boys and girls, the amount of television watched at age eight predicted the seriousness of criminal acts for which they were convicted by age thirty (Figure 1). This remained true even after controlling for the children's baseline aggressiveness, intelligence, and socioeconomic status. Eron and Huesmann also observed second-generation effects. Children who watched much television at age eight later, as parents, punished their own children more severely than did parents who had watched less television as children. Second- and now third-generation effects are accumulating at a time of unprecedented youth violence.

All seven of the U.S. and Canadian studies of prolonged childhood exposure to television demonstrate a positive relationship between exposure and physical aggression. The critical period is preadolescent childhood. Later exposure does not appear to produce any additional effect. However, the aggression-enhancing effect of exposure in preadolescence extends into adolescence and adulthood. This suggests that any interventions should be designed for children and their caregivers rather than for the general adult population.

These studies confirmed the beliefs of most Americans. According to a Harris poll at the time of the studies, 43 percent of American adults believe that television violence "plays a part in making America a violent society." An additional 37 percent think it might. But how important is television violence? What is the effect of exposure upon entire populations? To address this question, I took advantage of an historical accident—the absence of television in South Africa prior to 1975.

## The South African Experience

White South Africans have lived in a prosperous, industrialized society for decades, but they did not get television until 1975 because of tension between the Afrikaner- and English-speaking communities. The country's Afrikaner leaders know that a South African television industry would have to rely on British and American shows to fill out its programming schedule, and they felt that this would provide an unacceptable cultural advantage to English-speaking South Africans. So, rather than negotiate a complicated compromise, the government simply forbade television broadcasting. The entire population of two million whites—rich and poor, urban and rural, educated and uneducated—was thus excluded from exposure to television for a quarter century after the medium was introduced in the United States.

In order to determine whether exposure to television is a cause of violence, I compared homicide rates in South Africa, Canada, and the United States. Since blacks in South Africa live under quite different conditions than blacks in the United States, I limited the comparison to white homicide rates in South Africa and the United States, and the total homicide rate in Canada (which was 97 percent white in 1951).[1] I chose the homicide rate as a measure of violence because homicide statistics are exceptionally accurate.

From 1945 to 1974, the white homicide rate in the United States increased 93 percent. In Canada, the homicide rate increased 92 percent. In South Africa, where television was banned, the white homicide rate declined by 7 percent (Figure 2).

## Controlling for Other Factors

Could there be some explanation other than television for the fact that violence increased dramatically in the U.S. and Canada while dropping in South Africa? I examined an array of alternative explanations. None is satisfactory:

- *Economic growth*. Between 1946 and 1974, all three countries experienced substantial economic growth. Per capita income increased by 75 percent in the United States, 124 percent in Canada, and 86 percent in South Africa. Thus differences in economic growth cannot account for the different homicide trends in the three countries.

- *Civil unrest*. One might suspect that anti-war or civil-rights activity was responsible for the doubling of the homicide rate in the United States during this period. But the experience of Canada shows that this was not the case, since Canadians suffered a doubling of the homicide rate without similar civil unrest.

Other possible explanations include changes in age distribution, urbanization, alcohol consumption, capital punishment, and the availability of firearms. As

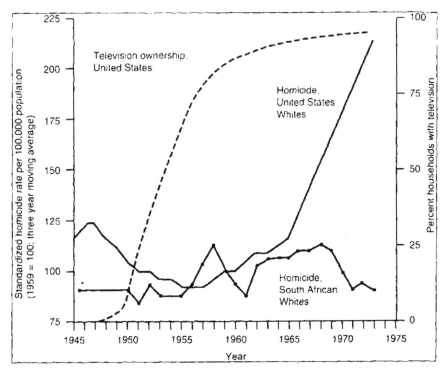

**FIGURE 2.** Television ownership and white homicide rates, United States and South Africa, 1945 through 1973. Asterisk denotes 6-year average. Note that television broadcasting was not permitted in South Africa prior to 1975. (Reprinted by permission from Brandon S. Centerwall, "Exposure to television as a cause of violence," *Public Communication and Behavior*, Vol. 2, Orlando, Florida: Academic Press, 1989.)

discussed in *Public Communication and Behavior* (1989), none provides a viable explanation for the observed homicide trends.

In the United States and Canada, there was a lag of ten to fifteen years between the introduction of television and a doubling of the homicide rate. In South Africa, there was a similar lag. Since television exerts its behavior-modifying effects primarily on children, while homicide is primarily an adult activity, this lag represents the time needed for the "television generation" to come of age.

The relationship between television and the homicide rate holds *within* the United States as well. Different regions of the U.S., for example, acquired television at different times. As we would expect, while all regions saw increases in their homicide rates, the regions that acquired television first were also the first to see higher homicide rates.

Similarly, urban areas acquired television before rural areas. As we would expect, urban areas saw increased homicide rates several years before the occurrence of a parallel increase in rural areas.

The introduction of television also helps explain the different rates of homicide growth for whites and minorities. White households in the U.S. began acquiring television sets in large numbers approximately five years before minority households.

Significantly, the white homicide rate began increasing in 1958, four years before a parallel increase in the minority homicide rate.

Of course, there are many factors other than television that influence the amount of violent crime. Every violent act is the result of a variety of forces coming together—poverty, crime, alcohol and drug abuse, stress—of which childhood TV exposure is just one. Nevertheless, the evidence indicates that if, hypothetically, television technology had never been developed, there would today be 10,000 fewer homicides each year in the United States, 70,000 fewer rapes, and 700,000 fewer injurious assaults. Violent crime would be half what it is.

## The Television Industry Takes a Look

The first congressional hearings on television and violence were held in 1952, when not even a quarter of U.S. households owned television sets. In the years since, there have been scores of research reports on the issue, as well as several major government investigations. The findings of the National Commission on the Causes and Prevention of Violence, published in 1969, were particularly significant. This report established what is now the broad scientific consensus: Exposure to television increases rates of physical aggression.

Television industry executives were genuinely surprised by the National Commission's report. What the industry produced was at times unedifying, but physically harmful? In response, the network executives began research programs that collectively would cost nearly a million dollars.

CBS commissioned William Belson to undertake what would be the largest and most sophisticated study yet, an investigation involving 1,565 teenage boys. In *Television Violence and the Adolescent Boy* (1978), Belson controlled for one hundred variables, and found that teenage boys who had watched above-average quantities of television violence before adolescence were committing acts of serious violence (e.g., assault, rape, major vandalism, and abuse of animals) at a rate 49 percent higher than teenage boys who had watched below-average quantities of television violence. Despite the large sum of money they had invested, CBS executives were notably unenthusiastic about the report.

ABC commissioned Melvin Heller and Samuel Polsky of Temple University to study young male felons imprisoned for violent crimes (e.g., homicide, rape, and assault). In two surveys, 22 and 34 percent of the young felons reported having consciously imitated crime techniques learned from television programs, usually successfully. The more violent of these felons were the most likely to report having learned techniques from television. Overall, the felons reported that as children they had watched an average of six hours of television per day—approximately twice as much as children in the general population at that time.

Unlike CBS, ABC maintained control over publication. The final report, *Studies in Violence and Television* (1976), was published in a private, limited edition that was not released to the general public or the scientific community.

NBC relied on a team of four researchers, three of whom were employees of NBC. Indeed, the principal investigator, J. Ronald Milavsky, was an NBC vice president. The team observed some 2,400 schoolchildren for up to three years to see if watching television violence increased their levels of physical aggressiveness. In *Television and Aggression* (1982), Milavsky and his associates reported that television violence had no effect upon the children's behavior. However, every independent investigator who has examined their data has concluded that, to the contrary, their data show that television violence did cause a modest increase of about 5 percent in average levels of physical aggressiveness. When pressed on the point, Milavsky and his associates conceded that their findings were consistent with the conclusion that television violence increased physical aggressiveness "to a small extent." They did not concede that television violence actually caused an increase, but only that their findings were consistent with such a conclusion.

The NBC study results raise an important objection to my conclusions. While studies have repeatedly demonstrated that childhood exposure to television increases physical aggressiveness, the increase is almost always quite minor. A number of investigators have argued that such a small effect is too weak to account for major increases in rates of violence. These investigators, however, overlook a key factor.

Homicide is an extreme form of aggression—so extreme that only one person in 20,000 committed murder each year in the United States in the mid-1950s. If we were to rank everyone's degree of physical aggressiveness from the least aggressive (Mother Theresa) to the most aggressive (Jack the Ripper), the large majority of us would be somewhere in the middle and murderers would be virtually off the chart (Figure 3). It is an intrinsic property of such "bell curve" distributions that small changes in the average imply major changes at the extremes. Thus, if exposure to television causes 8 percent of the population to shift from below-average aggression to above-average aggression, it follows that the homicide rate will double. The findings of the NBC Study and the doubling of the homicide rate are two sides of the same coin.

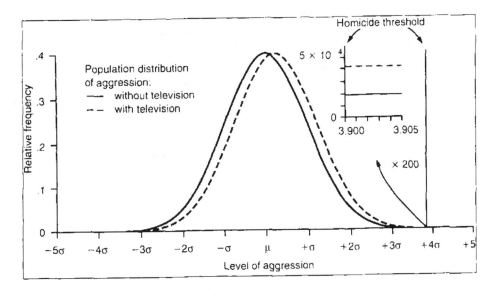

**FIGURE 3.** Relationships between television, aggression, and homicide in the general population: a model. (Reprinted by permission of Academic Press.)

After the results of these studies became clear, television industry executives lost their enthusiasm for scientific research. No further investigations were funded. Instead, the industry turned to political management of the issue.

## The Television Industry and Social Responsibility

The television industry routinely portrays individuals who seek to influence programming as un-American haters of free speech. In a 1991 letter sent to 7,000 executives of consumer product companies and advertising agencies, the president of the Network Television Association explained:

> Freedom of expression is an inalienable right of all Americans vigorously supported by ABC, CBS, and NBC. However, boycotts and so-called advertiser "hit lists" are attempts to manipulate our free society and democratic process.

The letter went on to strongly advise the companies to ignore all efforts by anyone to influence what programs they choose to sponsor. By implication, the networks themselves should ignore all efforts by anyone to influence what programs they choose to produce.

But this is absurd. All forms of public discourse are attempts to "manipulate" our free society and democratic process. What else could they be? Consumer boycotts are no more un-American than are strikes by labor unions. The Network Television Association is attempting to systematically shut down all discourse between viewers and advertisers, and between viewers and the television industry. Wrapping itself in patriotism, the television industry's response to uppity viewers is to put them in their place. If the industry and advertisers were to actually succeed in closing the circle between them, the only course they would leave for concerned viewers would be to seek legislative action.

In the war against tobacco, we do not expect help from the tobacco industry. If someone were to call upon the tobacco industry to cut back production as a matter of social conscience and concern for public health, we would regard that person as simpleminded, if not frankly deranged. Oddly enough, however, people have persistently assumed that the television industry is somehow different—that it is useful to appeal to its social conscience. This was true in 1969 when the National Commission on the Causes and Prevention of Violence published its recommendations for the television industry. It was equally true in 1989 when the U.S. Congress passed an anti-violence bill that granted television industry executives the authority to hold discussions on the issue of television violence without violating antitrust laws. Even before the law was passed, the four networks stated that there would be no substantive changes in their programming. They have been as good as their word.

For the television industry, issues of "quality" and "social responsibility" are peripheral to the issue of maximizing audience size—and there is no formula more tried and true than violence for generating large audiences. To television executives, this is crucial. For if advertising revenue were to decrease by just 1 percent, the television industry would stand to lose $250 million in revenue annually. Thus, changes in audience size that appear trivial to most of us are regarded as catastrophic by the industry. For this reason, industry spokespersons have made innumerable protestations of good intent, but nothing has happened. In the more than twenty years that levels of television violence have been monitored, there has been no downward movement. There are no recommendations to make to the television industry. To make any would not only be futile but could create the false impression that the industry might actually do something constructive.

On December 11, 1992, the networks finally announced a list of voluntary guidelines on television violence. Curiously, reporters were unable to locate any network producers who felt the new guidelines would require changes in their programs. That raises a question: Who is going to bell the cat? Who is going to place his or her career in jeopardy in order to decrease the amount of violence on television? It is hard to say, but it may be revealing that when Senator Paul Simon held the press conference announcing the new inter-network agreement, no industry executives were present to answer questions.

## Meeting the Challenge

Television violence is everybody's problem. You may feel assured that your child will never become violent despite a steady diet of television mayhem, but you cannot be assured that your child won't be murdered or maimed by someone else's child raised on a similar diet.

The American Academy of Pediatrics recommends that parents limit their children's television viewing to one or two hours per day. But why wait for a pediatrician to say it? Limiting children's exposure to television violence should become part of the public health agenda, along with safety seats, bicycle helmets, immunizations, and good nutrition. Part of the public health approach should be to promote child-care alternatives to the electronic baby-sitter, especially among the poor.

Parents should also guide what their children watch and how much. This is an old recommendation that can be given new teeth with the help of modern technology. It is now feasible to fit a television set with an electronic lock that permits parents to pre-set the channels and times for which the set will be available; if a particular program or time of day is locked, the set will not operate then. Time-channel locks are not merely feasible; they have already been designed and are coming off the assembly line.

The model for making them widely available comes from closed-captioning circuitry, which permits deaf and hard-of-hearing persons access to television. Market forces alone would not have made closed-captioned available to more than a fraction of the deaf and hard-of-hearing. To remedy this problem, Congress passed the Television Decoder Circuitry Act in 1990, which requires that virtually all new television sets be manufactured with built-in closed-captioning circuitry. A similar law should require that all new television sets be manufactured with built-in time-channel lock circuitry—and for a similar reason. Market forces alone will not make this technology available to more than a fraction of households with children and will exclude most poor families, the ones who suffer the most from violence. If we can make television technology available to benefit twenty-four million deaf and hard-of-hearing Americans, surely we can do no less for the benefit of fifty million American children.

A final recommendation: Television programs should be accompanied by a violence rating so that parents can judge how violent a program is without having to watch it. Such a rating system should be quantitative, leaving aesthetic and social judgments to the viewers. This approach would enjoy broad popular support. In a *Los*

*Angeles Times* poll, 71 percent of adult Americans favored the establishment of a TV violence rating system. Such a system would not impinge on artistic freedom since producers would remain free to produce programs with high violence ratings. They could even use high violence ratings in the advertisements for their shows.

None of these recommendations would limit freedom of speech. That is as it should be. We do not address the problem of motor vehicle fatalities by calling for a ban on cars. Instead, we emphasize safety seats, good traffic signs, and driver education. Similarly, to address the problem of television-inspired violence, we need to promote time-channel locks, program rating systems, and viewer education about the hazards of violent programming. In this way we can protect our children and our society.

### Note

1. The "white homicide rate" refers to the rate at which whites are the victims of homicide. Since most homicide is intra-racial, this closely parallels the rate at which whites commit homicide.

### References

*Following is a partial list of studies and articles on this topic.*

William A. Belson, *Television Violence and the Adolescent Boy*. Westmead, England: Saxon House (1978).

Brandon S. Centerwall, "Exposure to Television as a Cause of Violence," *Public Communication and Behavior*, Vol. 2. Orlando, Florida: Academic Press (1989), pp. 1–58.

Leonard D. Eron and L. Rowell Huesmann, "The Control of Aggressive Behavior by Changes in Attitudes, Values, and the Conditions of Learning," *Advances in the Study of Aggression*. Orlando, Florida: Academic Press (1984), pp. 139–171.

Gary Granzberg and Jack Steinbring (eds.), *Television and the Canadian Indian*. Winnipeg, Manitoba: University of Winnipeg (1980).

L. Rowell Huesmann and Leonard D. Eron, *Television and the Aggressive Child*. Hillsdale, New Jersey: Lawrence Erlbaum Associates (1986), pp. 45–80.

Candace Kruttschnitt, et al., "Family Violence, Television Viewing Habits, and Other Adolescent Experiences Related to Violent Criminal Behavior," *Criminology*, Vol 24 (1986), pp. 235–267.

Andrew N. Meltzoff, "Memory in Infancy," *Encyclopedia of Learning and Memory*. New York: Macmillan (1992), pp. 271–275. .

J. Ronald Milavsky, et al., *Television and Aggression*. Orlando, Florida: Academic Press (1982).

Jerome L. Singer, et al., "Family Patterns and Television Viewing as Predictors of Children's Beliefs and Aggression," *Journal of Communication*, Vol. 34, No. 2 (1984), pp. 73–89.

Tannis M. Williams (ed.), *The Impact of Television*. Orlando, Florida: Academic Press (1986).

# MORAL INERTIA IN AN ACCELERATED CULTURE

## Ted Riecken

*In this article, Ted Riecken establishes a double ethos: on one hand, he is a father who is concerned about the violent and graphic nature of his children's entertainment; on the other, he is a "teacher and researcher who has explored youth violence and worked with digital technologies for over a decade." He moves between these two personas throughout the essay, backing up his personal experience with research, and vice versa, to convince his audience of teachers and parents that we should ask questions about the media we encounter and encourage our children to do the same. This article was originally published in the* Emergency Librarian *in 1997.*

Thanksgiving Day snapshot: Living traditionally in a digital world. It is 6:00 p.m. on Thanksgiving Day, 1995. My wife and I are shuttling dishes of turkey and stuffing, potatoes and gravy, vegetables and cranberry sauce from the stove to the dining room table. My two kids are relaxing in front of their preferred digital appliances: for six-year-old Tessa it is the TV, and for 14-year-old, Theo, it is a 486 Windows computer.

Tessa calls "Hey Dad! Come here! Look at this!" Walking into the room I find her wide-eyed as she watches footage of a baby being born. The depiction of the birth is explicit. The cameras and microphones capture the entirety of the moment as the baby emerges from the birth canal and enters the world outside the womb. Watching Tessa, I can tell she is deep in thought. After another minute of watching, Tessa, without comment, raises her arm, points the TV's remote at the screen and switches to a six o'clock news report. The TV screen fills with the frightened faces of Muslim prisoners of war held in a Serbian run concentration camp. The camera pans down a line of men who are standing behind barbed wire. The look in their eyes and their skeletal frames are reminiscent of the black and white pictures of the survivors of Auschwitz, Bergen Belsen and Dachau.

Tessa stares in silence for a moment and then again, without comment, raises her arm and clicks her way to another channel. This time she has landed upon the Itchy and Scratchy show. It is a show within a show; it plays as Bart and Lisa Simpson's favorite TV cartoon within the half hour *Simpsons* show. Tessa watches Bart and Lisa watch TV. In the 15 second vignette that follows, Itchy, the rat jams a lit stick of dynamite down the throat of Scratchy, the cat. The dynamite explodes and bits of the cat splatter all over the screen. The show cuts to a scene of Bart and Lisa laughing uproariously. Tessa laughs too. It is now 6:05.

In five minutes Tessa has witnessed a baby's birth, gazed upon one of the horrific outcomes of an ideology called "ethnic cleansing" and has laughed along with the Simpson children as one character blows another to bits. She has consumed all this content in the space of five minutes; the average Canadian child between the ages of two and eleven watches 3.1 hours of television a day.

Moving from the TV room to bedroom, I find Theo playing a computer game called *DOOM*. In this popular shareware game, the player moves through a series of amazingly life-like three dimensional labyrinths, while killing as many alien-like "enemies" as possible. The game is fast, bloody and filled with realistic auditory and visual effects. Theo's weapon of choice for this session is a chainsaw. He tells me that because this is the downloaded Internet version, his arsenal doesn't include the nail gun which is actually a better weapon. He should do okay though, he says, because he has set the game to provide him with an infinite number of lives.

The 1994 version of *DOOM* has since been replaced by a more popular game called *DUKE NUKEM*. The game action is the same as in *DOOM*. However, the enemies are different. They now have more lifelike appearances, having been generated with "rendering" software that imparts shadow and texture to their forms. Their image has also changed. As Duke Nukem, you now kill enemies that have human bodies and the facial features of pigs.

## Reflecting on the Narrative

As a teacher and researcher who has explored youth violence and worked with digital technologies for over a decade, I cannot help but wonder where our continually expanding use of technologies will take us. Statistics from a variety of sources indicate that during the past decade there has been a dramatic rise in the number of violent crimes committed by young people (Frank, 1994; Uniform crime reports, 1996). At the same time, studies of teenagers' values and beliefs (Bibby & Posterski, 1992; Artz & Riecken, 1995) have shown that over the past fifteen years there has been a significant decline in the percentage of young people who are willing to endorse key values such as honesty, politeness, generosity, and concern for others as being very important. One could characterize our current social landscape as one of moral inertia in a time of accelerated technological change.

Is there a link between widespread media violence and the well documented rise in violent behavior among young people? Social scientists who study trends in human social behavior quickly point out that answering such research questions is difficult. The complexities of such research and the qualifications that must accompany studies of human behavior allow researchers to point only to correlation. Social scientists cannot, as the media would have us believe, provide predictive statements about causation. At best, they can suggest theories and tentative explanations about complex social phenomena which are continually changing.

A sociologist whose work has considerable relevance for the age in which we live is the French postmodern theorist, Jean Baudrillard. Baudrillard argued that the culture of affluent societies of the late 20th century is best characterized as consisting of what he calls "ambient consumerism" (Horrocks & Jevtic, 1996). According to Baudrillard, an individual's placement within the social hierarchy of a culture based on ambient consumerism depends upon one's acquisition of particular products which have a "sign" value that convey messages about that individual's status and purchasing power. For example, consider the status-sign-product value of the three letter automobile logos for the BMW and the GEO. Each consists of three letters, and each machine serves the same function (i.e., transportation). However as we all know, the status accorded the owners of these two vehicles is much different. In the same vein, we see children (and their parents) who agonize over their ability or inability to acquire the "right" brand of clothing or running shoes. The agonizing associated with such purchases has little to do with the comfort, durability or any other functional aspect of the clothing. Rather, the agonizing is simply concerned with the status or lack thereof associated with particular products/signs. At a personal level, I witnessed an example of this phenomenon with my young daughter when she would rush to the "Goosebumps" section whenever we would visit our local public library. As a beginning reader, the books were obviously too difficult for her and she never actually read the "Goosebumps" books she signed out. And yet, it was important for her to have association with R. L. Stine's books. For her the books were "cool," and having them was not important for their literary or educational value, but for their status enhancing dimension.

## Whither Tradition?

This kind of ambient consumerism leads to a cultural landscape in which primary sources of meaning stem from the acquisition of signs/products. We are faced, in essence, with a dilution of culture in which tradition plays less of a role in the creation of meaning and the transmission of values, morals and beliefs. What is "good" is often defined by the status enhancing value a product/sign has accorded to it, and the measure of one's success in the status hierarchy is based primarily on one's income and ability to acquire status enhancing signs. Recognition of this kind of social dynamic proclaims itself in bumper stickers such as, "Whoever dies with the most toys wins."

The impact of traditional institutions on the transmission of values and morals is further reduced by combining the dynamics of an ambient consumer culture with the economic restructuring of the family. Add to this, the effects of a revolution in information technologies, and the implications for the maintenance of tradition are profound.

## Information Consumption in An Age of Ambient Consumerism

It is arguable that the same features that characterize ambient consumerism also describe the consumption of information. As we surf the Internet, flip from channel to channel on the television, or blast our way through video games, our engagement with the information encountered along the way usually remains at the surface level. A shallow affiliation with snippets of information obtained through the Internet, television, or video games does little to promote sustained inquiry or deep processing of information. In fact, within the computer gaming industry, the high speed, reflex driven video games popular with so many adolescents today are referred to as "twitch games" because of the response speed required for successful game play.

Ironically, in an information age that has as part of its rhetoric the notions of "getting connected" and becoming part of the "global network", our real life links with tradition and connectedness to home, family, and school appear to be waning. One of the key challenges for parents and educators is nurturing a sense of tradition and connectedness in young people whilst living in an age of learning in which browsing and random clicking can virtually transport one anywhere on the planet. Channel surfing and grazing over a vast array of television content, along with point and click movement through the online word, represent an information medium in which the media itself not only structures, but creates, its own content and the manner in which it is consumed. Marshall McLuhan's adage that the "medium is the message" has never been more true than it is today. As part of the advertising campaign to promote their vision of the Internet world Microsoft Corporation has copyrighted the question, "Where do you want to go today?" Sega Corporation now offers 24 hour a day video game play through many local cable channels and has as its advertising slogan, "No Limits!" A major telephone company has recently named its Internet service division "Ubiquity."

Clearly, as we approach the 21st century, information is seen as a consumable and our access to it is almost ubiquitous. And yet, what is not clear, is whether we as a society are collectively any wiser, or even more important, any more compassionate, caring, or tolerant as a result of our exposure to all the digital information available to us. A number of studies indicate we live in an age of moral inertia, if not outright decline. As I think about where we are headed as a society, the metaphor I keep returning to is that of being collectively lost in a digital labyrinth. Just as in King Minos' labyrinth a minotaur dwelt, so too in the digital labyrinth there dwells a dark element. Anyone who has spent much time surfing the Internet, playing video games, or even watching television does not have to wait long before the baser dimensions of human nature make their presence known. Sex and violence are never far away; in many respects they are in closer reach than they have ever been, only a "click" away.

Where our wanderings within the digital labyrinth will take us no one knows. However, while we wander, we must continue to wonder about the things we encounter. As teachers and parents, we should ask questions about the underlying messages and values embodied in the material we encounter. Are the messages and values congruent with where we have come from and where we think we should be headed? We should also encourage children to question what they encounter. We should help them examine the underlying messages and assumptions embodied within the content of the digital world. Doing so not only helps us maintain a connectedness to where we have come from, but to a larger whole. Remember, in the myth of the labyrinth, it was such a connectedness, in the form of Ariadne's ball of thread along with her caring and compassion, that allowed Theseus to defeat the minotaur, escape from the labyrinth and continue his adventures elsewhere.

## References

Artz, S. & Riecken, T. (1995). A study of violence among adolescent female students in a suburban school district. Stopping the violence: Changing families, changing futures. B.C. Institute on Family Violence, Vancouver, BC.

Bibby, R. & Posterski, D. (1992). Teen trends. Toronto, ON: Stoddart.

Frank, F. (1994). Violent youth crime. In Canadian social trends: A Canadian Studies reader. Vol 2. pp. 373–376, Toronto, ON: Thompson Educational.

Horrocks, C. & Jevtic, Z. (1996). Baudrillard for beginners. Cambridge, England: Icon.

Uniform crime reports. (1996). British Columbia Ministry of the Attorney General, Victoria, BC.

# TAMING THE MEDIA-VIOLENCE HYSTERIA

Morris Freedman

*Published on June 5, 1996 in* Education Week, *Morris Freedman takes issue with Brandon Centerwall's study by arguing that we should not automatically rush to censor disturbing images in the media or literature because "as children and adults, we have always allowed ourselves to get lost in imagined worlds without inevitable catastrophe." He argues that we should prepare our children to respond seriously to complex works rather than to censor them. Freedman is professor Emeritus of English at the University of Maryland.*

We continue living in fear of exposing children to written or depicted violence even though our panic has been largely intuitive rather than the result of study, analysis, and informed discussion. A 1993 report in *The Public Interest*, however, by University of Washington epidemiologist Brandon S. Centerwall, statistically links aggressive behavior specifically to television violence. His article offers many numbers, but it expresses typical feelings: "[By] the age of 18, the average American young person has witnessed 200,000 acts of violence on television, including 40,000 murders. . . . [If], hypothetically, television technology had never been developed, there would be 10,000 fewer homicides each year in the United States, 70,000 fewer rapes, and 700,000 fewer injurious assaults. Violent crime would be half what it is."

Even if the somewhat apocalyptic tone of these summations didn't give us pause, the failure of the cited studies to distinguish between television fact and television fiction should. Official bodies and prestigious persons react almost reflexively, without rumination or a request for hard evidence, to every charge that depictions and reports of violence are intrinsically pernicious. Under pressure from Congress, especially from Sen. Paul Simon, D-Ill., the television networks recently promised, once again, to police themselves. The film industry already has instituted warnings about excessively violent works, although complaints continue to be made about such popular films among the young as *Batman* and *Jurassic Park*.

Four decades ago, horror comics provoked the great national fear. Dr. Frederic Wertham, a psychiatrist and the author of *Seduction of the Innocent*, agitatedly testified before a congressional committee that horror comics incited children to horrible acts, including suicide. At the time, Congress immediately considered legislation but finally did nothing.

How far should we go not to let television, movies, books, comic strips, rap lyrics, classical paintings about the martyrdoms of saints, anything at all, trouble children? The conservative commentator, Phyllis Schlafly has suggested that Greek and Elizabethan tragedy depresses them and should be edited or suppressed. Should we have our elementary and high schools ban *Oedipus Rex* and *Romeo and Juliet*? Do we outlaw Charles Dickens' *A Child's History of England*, a compendium of grisly maimings and tortures? Do we rewrite "Little Red Riding Hood," "Hansel and Gretel," and other such grim tales from the Brothers Grimm, as some school districts already have done?

Do we delete "nasty" words from school dictionaries? Should we white-out parts of the Bible?

Suppose we sanitize, without dispute, every offensive fictional work we identified, would we also censor reports or depictions of starvation in Somalia, genocide in Bosnia, serial rapes, our own Civil War prisons, Jeffrey Dahmer's cannibalism, the O.J. Simpson trial, public executions in China, lynchings, sharks and lions tearing apart their prey, mass deaths of cultists? Most of these have appeared on television news broadcasts, and some, like nature films, on what we commonly regard as educational channels.

The world was outraged when Japanese textbooks rewrote history to expunge reference to Japanese atrocities in World War II. Should we join Japan in acts of censorship?

The depredations of Medea, Lady Macbeth, J. R. Ewing, Bugs Bunny, the characters portrayed by Clint Eastwood, Sylvester Stallone, Susan Lucci, and Arnold Schwarzenegger hardly equal the gamut of evil offered by reality. If mankind had never invented printing or photography, there'd still be horror in the world that children have always been well aware of.

Children are normally more resilient, armored, judicious, even more aesthetically discriminating than we allow ourselves to believe. Rooting lions fascinate them as much as purring kittens. Veteran students of children's psyches, like Drs. Bruno Bettelheim and Robert Coles, have shown how much reality children comfortably absorb and how they defend themselves. Yet we seem reluctant to credit the young with psychological strength or moral instinct.

We learn as adults to accommodate to the most outrageous inevitabilities of life, like earthquakes and epidemics. We do not make hysteria a habitual reaction to realities we may confront for the first time.

Consider some of the messages youthful filmmakers keep sending out. *E.T.* showed children defeating adult authorities who couldn't recognize plain goodness. The *Home Alone* movies depicted the ingenious extremes of self-defense and self-assertion a child can summon against adult thoughtlessness and meanness. The decoded sense is that youth can hold its own when forced to.

So called "children's classics," like *Gulliver's Travels, Robinson Crusoe*, and *Alice's Adventures in Wonderland*, are filled with "disturbing" events. Adult literary classics, like *High Wind in Jamaica* by Robert Hughes and the play *The Children's Hour* by Lillian Hellman, depict the havoc that children can deliberately create, defensively or maliciously, among adults. Children's playtime rhymes linger over details that adults regard as disgusting.

As children and as adults, we have always allowed ourselves to get lost in imagined worlds without inevitable catastrophe. Responding to art seriously does not mean responding to it literally. Although few of us may have tried to fly like Peter Pan when we saw the musical adaptation of James Barrie's classic, we did join in the applause to revive Tinker Bell. Only to the degree that we can be deeply moved can we share in the catharsis of tragedy.

In his *Public Interest* overview of media violence's impact on children, Dr. Centerwall reported that "an Indiana school board had to issue an advisory to young children that . . . there is no such thing as Teenage Mutant Ninja Turtles. Children had been crawling down storm drains looking for them." I find it hard to accept that such "advice" could extinguish a child's fascination with these engaging fauna. Dr. Centerwall did not say whether any child actually came to harm looking for the turtles' habitat.

Nevertheless, it remains the family's and society's responsibility to ensure that the imaginative lives of our young remain wholesomely related to reality, that we all learn, beginning as children, to sort out our responses to art from those to life, and not let ourselves be mindlessly affected by uncivilized behavior and outlandish inventions. Those unfortunately disturbed young persons who cite a created work as the source of their violent acts hardly needed artistic inspiration to lose their balance.

Teachers and parents should properly filter art and history at certain times for certain groups. We must candidly recognize that some words and situations do call for sensitive and wise orientation. Not every fabricated work can claim aesthetic justification: A range of critics have not found Oliver Stone's film exercises in contrived nastiness acceptable on any grounds.

We lose little, and arguably gain a good deal, by preparing students sensibly to approach complex works, to read "The Merchant of Venice," *Huckleberry Finn*, or *The Catcher in the Rye*, or stories about the early days of slavery, gay couples, or the travails of adolescence, or to see disturbing films, like the *The Color Purple* or *Holocaust*. Viewing the gruesome exhibits in the old medical museum of the U.S. Army on the Mall in Washington used to be a favorite pastime of adolescents until the museum was moved. Young persons, like myself, who happened to wander alone through the museum had to deal with their responses privately. By contrast, the newly opened U.S. Holocaust Museum in Washington, not far from the old medical one, erected barriers to prevent children from seeing gruesome documentary films about the concentration camps inadvertently or without the presence of elders.

In the end, what Dr. Centerwall's data may prove is only that, as a society, we have coarsened our adult capacity to differentiate art from actuality. We may be so overcome by the genuine violence television brings us so vividly and so regularly, that we blur, and blend what mankind has imagined with what it has done.

Nor should we fail to acknowledge our own adult reluctance or squeamishness to expose ourselves to works that, however intellectually rationalized, may disturb us too deeply. Although I have twice visited Dachau, I have not seen the television miniseries, now on video, *Holocaust*, nor do I intend to see it. Reviews and articles have persuaded me that while it does not and perhaps could not do justice to the facts, it distorts them in the very act of intensifying them. I do not need the movie to know about the Holocaust. We should scrupulously avoid burdening our children in ways that we cringe to burden ourselves.

We can hardly diminish our guilt, however, about obscuring the existence of evil, or minimize any real effects of violence in fiction or the news, by automatically attacking or canceling out powerful literature and painting, or television, or all of Hollywood, or by mistrusting the normal reactions of our own children.

Recognizing that violence exists and is part of human history and that reports of it in any form can affect us profoundly may not be one of the prettier functions of education but it is as essential to full learning as teaching the nature of beauty, of good, of civilization.

# WE ARE TRAINING OUR KIDS TO KILL

Dave Grossman

> *Dave Grossman describes himself as "an expert in the field of 'killology,'"*
> *having served in the army as an infantry officer and psychologist who*
> *studied how to train people to kill, which he says does not come natural-*
> *ly. In his essay, which appeared in the July/August, 1999, edition of* The
> Saturday Evening Post, *he makes several analogies: between people and*
> *animals, between tobacco and media violence, between AIDS and tele-*
> *vision violence, and between military tactics of desensitization and the*
> *violence children see on television. Note also how Grossman uses the*
> *common topic of testimony and authority to back up his arguments.*

The desensitizing techniques used for training soldiers are being replicated in contemporary mass media—movies, television, and video games, giving rise to the
alarming rate of homicide and violence in our schools and communities.

I am from Jonesboro, Arkansas. I travel the world training medical, law enforcement, and U. S. military personnel about the realities of warfare. I try to make those
who carry deadly force keenly aware of the magnitude of killing. Too many law
enforcement and military personnel act like "cowboys," never stopping to think about
who they are and what they are called to do. I hope I am able to give them a reality
check.

So here I am, a world traveler and an expert in the field of "killology," when the
(then) largest school massacre in American history happens in my hometown of
Jonesboro, Arkansas. That was the March 24, 1998, schoolyard shooting deaths of
four girls and a teacher. Ten others were injured, and two boys, ages 11 and 13, were
jailed, charged with murder.

## Virus of Violence

To understand the why behind Littleton, Jonesboro, Springfield, Pearl, and Paducah,
and all the other outbreaks of this "virus of violence," we need to first understand
the magnitude of the problem. The per capita murder rate doubled in this country
between 1957—when the FBI started keeping track of the data—and 1992. A fuller
picture of the problem, however, is indicated by the rate at which people are
attempting to kill one another—the aggravated assault rate. That rate in America
has gone from around 60 per 100,000 in 1957 to over 440 per 100,000 in the middle of this decade. As bad as this is, it would be much worse were it not for two
major factors.

The first is the increased imprisonment of violent offenders. The prison population in America nearly quadrupled between 1975 and 1992. According to criminolo-
gist John A. Dilulio, "dozens of credible empirical analyses . . . leave no doubt that the
increased use of prisons averted millions of serious crimes." If it were not for our
tremendous imprisonment rate (the highest of any industrialized nation), the aggravated assault rate and the murder rate would undoubtedly be even higher.

The second factor keeping the murder rate from being even worse is medical technology. According to the U.S. Army Medical Service Corps, a wound that would have killed nine out of ten soldiers in World War II, nine out of ten could have survived in Vietnam. Thus, by a very conservative estimate, if we still had a 1940-level medical technology today, our murder rate would be ten times higher than it is. The murder rate has been held down by the development of sophisticated lifesaving skills and techniques, such as helicopter medevacs, 911 operators, paramedics, CPR, trauma centers, and medicines.

Today, both our assault rate and murder rate are at phenomenally high levels. Both are increasing worldwide. In Canada, according to their Center for Justice, per capita assaults increased almost five-fold between 1964 and 1993, attempted murder increased nearly sevenfold, and murders doubled. Similar trends can be seen in other countries in the per capita violent crime rates reported to Interpol between 1977 and 1993. In Australia and New Zealand, the assault rate increased approximately four-fold, and the murder rate nearly doubled in both nations. The assault rate tripled in Sweden and approximately doubled in Belgium, Denmark, England and Wales, France, Hungary, the Netherlands, and Scotland. Meanwhile, all these nations had an associated (but smaller) increase in murder.

This virus of violence is occurring worldwide. The explanation for it has to be some new factor that is occurring in all of these countries. There are many factors involved, and none should be discounted: for example, the prevalence of guns in our society. But violence is rising in many nations with Draconian gun laws. And though we should never downplay child abuse, poverty, or racism, there is only one new variable present in each of these countries that bears the exact same fruit: media violence presented as entertainment for children.

## Killing Is Unnatural

Before retiring from the military, I spent almost a quarter of a century as an army infantry officer and a psychologist, learning and studying how to enable people to kill. Believe me, we are very good at it. But it does not come naturally; you have to be taught to kill. And just as the army is conditioning people to kill, we are indiscriminately doing the same thing to our children, but without the safeguards.

After the Jonesboro killings, the head of the American Academy of Pediatrics Task Force on Juvenile Violence came to town and said that children don't naturally kill. It is a learned skill. And they learn it from abuse and violence in the home and, most pervasively, from violence as entertainment in television, the movies, and interactive video games.

Killing requires training because there is a built-in aversion to killing one's own kind. I can best illustrate this fact by drawing on my own military research into the act of killing.

We all know how hard it is to have a discussion with a frightened or angry human being. Vasoconstriction, the narrowing of the blood vessels, has literally closed down the forebrain—that great gob of gray matter that makes one a human being and distinguishes one from a dog. When those neurons close down, the midbrain takes over and your thought processes and reflexes are indistinguishable from your dog's. If you've worked with animals, you have some understanding of what happens to frightened human beings on the battlefield. The battlefield and violent crime are in the realm of midbrain responses.

Within the midbrain there is a powerful, God-given resistance to killing your own kind. Every species, with a few exceptions, has a hardwired resistance to killing its own kind in territorial and mating battles. When animals with antlers and horns fight one another, they head-butt in a nonfatal fashion. But when they fight any other species, they go to the side to gut and gore. Piranhas will turn their fangs on anything, but they fight one another with flicks of the tail. Rattlesnakes will bite anything, but they wrestle one another. Almost every species has this hard-wired resistance to killing its own kind.

When we human beings are overwhelmed with anger and fear, we slam head-on into that midbrain resistance that generally prevents us from killing. Only sociopaths—who by definition don't have that resistance—lack this innate violence immune system.

Throughout all human history, when humans have fought each other, there has been a lot of posturing. Adversaries make loud noises and puff themselves up, trying to daunt the enemy. There is a lot of fleeing and submission. Ancient battles were nothing more than great shoving matches. It was not until one side turned and ran that most of the killing happened, and most of that was stabbing people in the back. All of the ancient military historians report that the vast majority of killing happened in pursuit when one side was fleeing.

In more modern times, the average firing rate was incredibly low in Civil War battles. British author Paddy Griffith demonstrates in his book *The Battle Tactics of the Civil War* that the killing potential of the average Civil War regiment was anywhere from five hundred to a thousand men per minute. The actual killing rate was only one or two men per minute per regiment. At the Battle of Gettysburg, of the 27,000 muskets picked up from the dead and dying after the battle, 90 percent were loaded. This is an anomaly, because it took 90 percent of their time to load muskets and only 5 percent to fire. But even more amazing, of the thousands of loaded muskets, only half had multiple loads in the barrel—one had 23 loads in the barrel.

In reality, the average man would load his musket and bring it to his shoulder, but he could not bring himself to kill. He would be brave, he would stand shoulder to shoulder, he would do what he was trained to do; but at the moment of truth, he could not bring himself to pull the trigger. And so he lowered the weapon and loaded it again. Of those who did fire, only a tiny percentage fired to hit. The vast majority fired over the enemy's head.

During World War II, U.S. Army Brig. Gen. S. L. A. Marshall had a team of researchers study what soldiers did in battle. For the first time in history, they asked individual soldiers what they did in battle. They discovered that only 15 to 20 percent of the individual riflemen could bring themselves to fire at an exposed enemy soldier.

That is the reality of the battlefield. Only a small percentage of soldiers are able and willing to participate. Men are willing to die. They are willing to sacrifice themselves for their nation; but they are not willing to kill. It is a phenomenal insight into human nature; but when the military became aware of that, they systematically went about the process of trying to fix this "problem." From the military perspective, a 15 percent firing rate among riflemen is like a 15 percent literacy rate among librarians. And fix it the military did. By the Korean War, around 55 percent of the soldiers were willing to fire to kill. And by Vietnam, the rate rose to over 90 percent.

The method in this madness: desensitization.

How the military increases the killing rate of soldiers in combat is instructive because our culture today is doing the same thing to our children. The training methods militaries use are brutalization, classical conditioning, operant conditioning, and role modeling. I will explain each of these in the military context and show how these same factors are contributing to the phenomenal increase of violence in our culture.

Brutalization and desensitization are what happens at boot camp. From the moment you step off the bus, you are physically and verbally abused: countless push-ups, endless hours at attention or running with heavy loads, while carefully trained professionals take turns screaming at you. Your head is shaved; you are herded together naked and dressed alike, losing all individuality. This brutalization is designed to break down your existing mores and norms, and force you to accept a new set of values that embraces destruction, violence, and death as a way of life. In the end, you are desensitized to violence and accept it as a normal and essential survival skill in your brutal new world.

Something very similar to this desensitization toward violence is happening to our children through violence in the media—but instead of 18-year-olds, it begins at the age of 18 months when a child is first able to discern what is happening on television. At that age, a child can watch something happening on television and mimic that action. But it isn't until children are six or seven years old that the part of the brain kicks in that lets them understand where information comes from. Even though young children have some understanding of what it means to pretend, they are developmentally unable to distinguish clearly between fantasy and reality.

When young children see somebody shot, stabbed, raped, brutalized, degraded, or murdered on TV, to them it is as though it were actually happening. To have a child of three, four, or five watch a "splatter" movie, learning to relate to a character for the first 90 minutes and then in the last 30 minutes watch helplessly as that new friend is hunted and brutally murdered, is the moral and psychological equivalent of introducing your child to a friend, letting her play with that friend, and then butchering that friend in front of your child's eyes. And this happens to our children hundreds upon hundreds of times.

Sure, they are told: "Hey, it's all for fun. Look, this isn't real; it's just TV." And they nod their little heads and say OK. But they can't tell the difference. Can you remember a point in your life or in your children's lives when dreams, reality, and television were all jumbled together? That's what it is like to be at that level of psychological development. That's what the media are doing to them.

The Journal of the American Medical Association published the definitive epidemiological study on the impact of TV violence. The research demonstrated what happened in numerous nations after television made its appearance as compared to nations and regions without TV. The two nations or regions being compared are demographically and ethnically identical; only one variable is different: the presence of television. In every nation, region, or city with television, there is an immediate explosion of violence on the playground, and within 15 years there is a doubling of the murder rate. Why 15 years? That is how long it takes for the brutalization of a three- to five-year-old to reach the "prime crime age." That is how long it takes for you to reap what you have sown when you brutalize and desensitize a three-year-old.

Today the data linking violence in the media to violence in society are superior to those linking cancer and tobacco. Hundreds of sound scientific studies demonstrate the social impact of brutalization by the media. The *Journal of the American Medical Association* concluded that "the introduction of television in the 1950s caused a subsequent doubling of the homicide rate, i.e., long-term childhood exposure to television is a causal factor behind approximately one half of the homicides committed in the United States, or approximately 10,000 homicides annually." The article went on to say that ". . . if, hypothetically, television technology had never been developed, there would today be 10,000 fewer homicides each year in the United States, 70,000 fewer rapes, and 700,000 fewer injurious assaults" (June 10, 1992).

## Classical Conditioning

Classical conditioning is like the famous case of Pavlov's dogs they teach in Psychology 101. The dogs learned to associate the ringing of the bell with food, and once conditioned, the dogs could not hear the bell without salivating.

The Japanese were masters at using classical conditioning with their soldiers. Early in World War II, Chinese prisoners were placed in a ditch on their knees with their hands bound behind them. And one by one, a select few Japanese soldiers would go into the ditch and bayonet "their" prisoner to death. This is a horrific way to kill another human being. Up on the bank, countless other young soldiers would cheer them on in their violence. Comparatively few soldiers actually killed in these situations, but by making the others watch and cheer, the Japanese were able to use these kinds of atrocities to classically condition a very large audience to associate pleasure with human death and suffering. Immediately afterwards, the soldiers who had been spectators were treated to sake, the best meal they had in months, and to so-called comfort girls. The result? They learned to associate committing violent acts with pleasure.

The Japanese found these kinds of techniques to be extraordinarily effective at quickly enabling very large numbers of soldiers to commit atrocities in the years to come. Operant conditioning (which we will look at shortly) teaches you to kill, but classical conditioning is a subtle but powerful mechanism that teaches you to like it.

This technique is so morally reprehensible that there are very few examples of it in modern U.S. military training, but there are some clear-cut examples of it being done by the media to our children. What is happening to our children is the reverse of the aversion therapy portrayed in the movie *A Clockwork Orange*. In *A Clockwork Orange*, a brutal sociopath, a mass murderer, is strapped to a chair and forced to watch violent movies while he is injected with a drug that nauseates him. So he sits and gags and retches as he watches the movies. After hundreds of repetitions of this, he associates violence with nausea. And it limits his ability to be violent.

We are doing the exact opposite: Our children watch vivid pictures of human suffering and death, and they learn to associate it with their favorite soft drink and candy bar, or their girlfriend's perfume.

After the Jonesboro shootings, one of the high-school teachers told me how her students reacted when she told them about the shootings at the middle school. "They laughed," she told me with dismay. A similar reaction happens all the time in movie theaters when there is bloody violence. The young people laugh and cheer and keep right on eating popcorn and drinking pop. We have raised a generation of barbarians who have learned to associate violence with pleasure, like the Romans cheering and snacking as the Christians were slaughtered in the Coliseum.

The result is a phenomenon that functions much like AIDS, a phenomenon I call AVIDS—Acquired Violence Immune Deficiency Syndrome. AIDS has never killed anybody. It destroys your immune system, and then other diseases that shouldn't kill you become fatal. Television violence by itself does not kill you. It destroys your violence immune system and conditions you to derive pleasure from violence. And once you are at close range with another human being, and it's time for you to pull that trigger, Acquired Violence Immune Deficiency Syndrome can destroy your midbrain resistance.

## Operant Conditioning

The third method the military uses is operant conditioning, a very powerful repetitive procedure of stimulus-response, stimulus-response. A benign example is the use of flight simulators to train pilots. An airline pilot in training sits in front of a flight simulator for endless hours; when a particular warning light goes on, he is taught to react in a certain way. When another warning light goes on, a different reaction is required. Stimulus-response, stimulus-response, stimulus-response. One day the pilot is actually flying a jumbo jet; the plane is going down, and 300 people are screaming behind him. He is wetting his seat cushion, and he is scared out of his wits; but he does the right thing. Why? Because he has been conditioned to respond reflexively to this particular crisis.

When people are frightened or angry, they will do what they have been conditioned to do. In fire drills, children learn to file out of the school in orderly fashion. One day there is a real fire, and they are frightened out of their wits; but they do exactly what they have been conditioned to do, and it saves their lives.

The military and law enforcement community have made killing a conditioned response. This has substantially raised the firing rate on the modern battlefield. Whereas infantry training in World War II used bull's-eye targets, now soldiers learn to fire at realistic, man-shaped silhouettes that pop into their field of view. That is the stimulus. The trainees have only a split second to engage the target. The conditioned response is to shoot the target, and then it drops. Stimulus-response, stimulus-response, stimulus-response—soldiers or police officers experience hundreds of repetitions. Later, when soldiers are on the battlefield or a police officer is walking a beat and somebody pops up with a gun, they will shoot reflexively and shoot to kill. We know that 75 to 80 percent of the shooting on the modern battlefield is the result of this kind of stimulus-response training.

Now, if you're a little troubled by that, how much more should we be troubled by the fact that every time a child plays an interactive point-and-shoot video game, he is learning the exact same conditioned reflex and motor skills?

I was an expert witness in a murder case in South Carolina offering mitigation for a kid who was facing the death penalty. I tried to explain to the jury that interactive video games had conditioned him to shoot a gun to kill. He had spent hundreds of dollars on video games learning to point and shoot, point and shoot. One day he and his buddy decided it would be fun to rob the local convenience store. They walked in, and he pointed a snub-nosed .38 pistol at the clerk's head. The clerk turned to look at him, and the defendant shot reflexively from about six feet. The bullet hit the clerk right between the eyes—which is a pretty remarkable shot with that weapon at that range—and killed this father of two. Afterward, we asked the boy what happened and why he did it. It clearly was not part of the plan to kill the guy—it was being video-taped from six different directions. He said, "I don't know. It was a mistake. It wasn't supposed to happen."

In the military and law-enforcement worlds, the right option is often not to shoot. But you never, ever put your money in that video machine with the intention of not shooting. There is always some stimulus that sets you off. And when he was excited, and his heart rate went up, and vasoconstriction closed his forebrain down, this young man did exactly what he was conditioned to do: he reflexively pulled the trigger, shooting accurately just like all those times he played video games.

This process is extraordinarily powerful and frightening. The result is ever more "homemade" sociopaths who kill reflexively. Our children are learning how to kill and learning to like it the idea killing [sic]; and then we have the audacity to say, "Oh my goodness, what's wrong?"

One of the boys involved in the Jonesboro shootings (and they are just boys) had a fair amount of experience shooting real guns. The other one, to the best of our knowledge, had almost no experience shooting. Between them, those two boys fired 27 shots from a range of over 100 yards, and they hit 15 people. That's pretty remark-able shooting. We run into these situations often—kids who have never picked up a gun in their lives pick up a real gun and are incredibly accurate. Why? Video games.

# UNIT FIVE

## Definition

# INTRODUCTION

To define is to explain what a term means, but the process of definition defies the simplicity implied by that statement. Everyone has an individual sense of the meaning of many terms, a meaning in part determined by the social groups to which they belong. When you consider this variation in meaning, it becomes clear that the way people think about terms determines, to a large degree, how they react during debates over the way those terms should be applied. Writers will often develop a coherent and persuasive definition of important terms precisely for this reason.

Disagreements over the definition of important terms are often a reason that the debates progress with such difficulty. In essence, the debaters are arguing over different things. Clarifying and attempting to arrive at mutual definitions of terms is a first step. For example, you have to know what you mean by equality before you can begin to assess what, if anything, causes inequality in our society, and what action to take to correct it.

Abstract terms like *equality*, and another American ideal, *democracy*, are often contested. Controversies sometimes circle around the best way to run a democracy. If different groups have different ideas about what a democracy is, then there is little chance they will agree over how a democracy can best be run.

Even terms that seem on the surface to be concrete may need explaining. For example, most people in America today have heard the term *recycling*, but what exactly is the process involved? Once the tin cans, old newspapers, and plastic bottles have been taken from your curb, what machinery and what chemicals, at what cost, are involved in getting new containers and paper made? Understanding how recycling is accomplished would be essential to making decisions about how to organize recycling efforts more effectively. If recycling, which is supposed to help us not pollute our environment, actually resulted in waste and pollution, we might have to reevaluate our implementation of it. A large quantity of writing in the sciences and social sciences involves explaining new concepts and techniques; depending on the audience, defining terms like schizophrenia and greenhouse effect can require great rhetorical skill.

Identifying shades of difference, the meanings instead of the meaning, is another form of argument in the definition stasis. Consider the term *lying*. Most people would agree that lying is deliberately telling an untruth to mislead someone, and that lying in general is immoral behavior. Yet most people tell little white lies on a regular basis to get through social situations graciously. What, then, is the essential difference between lying in general and little white lies? If someone could persuade you that the little white lies you find so innocuous now are no different from the lying you find offensive, they might change the way you evaluate your own and other people's actions. They might even change your future behavior.

Even when you believe your audience already agrees with your definition, it is often useful to provide an argument to remind them of the importance of thinking about the term the way they do, because rhetoric that reinforces a cohesive set of values makes motivation to action more likely. When you feel that your audience has a different or imprecise sense of the meaning of a term important to your argument, you should provide them with compelling reasons to think about the term in new ways. Because defining or redefining terms offers the possibility of changing people's values and behavior, definition is a crucial skill for a rhetor to develop.

**Sonya Brown**

# I

## Cartoons as Definitions

*Like most types of rhetorical moves, definitions can be found in many different forms. Here we have presented two cartoons, each illustrating different tactics of definition. While definition occupies a stasis in itself, and so can be the point of an argument, definition is also a common topic, so that a definition, once established, can be used to support another argument. You might, accordingly, consider what kinds of arguments might be supported by the definitions in each of these cartoons.*

A30 THURSDAY, MARCH 11, 1999    THE WASHINGTON POST

**CATHY** CATHY GUISEWITE

# II

## Single Definitions

### THE BILL OF RIGHTS: THE FIRST 10 AMENDMENTS TO THE CONSTITUTION

*Issues of definition often have real-world consequences, as we can see by looking at the Bill of Rights, a piece of text which is (or ought to be) familiar to all of us. As you read over this document, you might notice that the Bill of Rights is itself a definition: it lists the rights guaranteed, after the Amendments were ratified, by the Constitution of the United States. You should also notice that definitional issues are raised both explicitly and implicitly by the Bill of Rights. Explicitly, the document cannot be implemented unless there are accepted or mandated definitions of some of the terms it uses: what is a* well-regulated militia, *for example,* unreasonable search and seizure, *an* impartial jury? *Legal contests have been waged over what constitutes a* speedy trial *and what kinds of punishments are* cruel *and* unusual. *Notice that there are also implicit definitional issues: what exactly is a* right, *and what particular group of people is entitled to these specific rights? Note as well that some of these definitions have changed markedly since the Bill of Rights was originally written.*

**Note:** The following text is a transcription of the first 10 amendments to the Constitution in their original form. These amendments were ratified December 15, 1791, and form what is known as the "Bill of Rights."

### Amendment I

Congress shall make no law respecting an establishment of religion, or prohibiting the free exercise thereof; or abridging the freedom of speech, or of the press; or the right of the people peaceably to assemble, and to petition the Government for a redress of grievances.

## Amendment II

A well regulated Militia, being necessary to the security of a free State, the right of the people to keep and bear Arms, shall not be infringed.

## Amendment III

No Soldier shall, in time of peace be quartered in any house, without the consent of the Owner, nor in time of war, but in a manner to be prescribed by law.

## Amendment IV

The right of the people to be secure in their persons, houses, papers, and effects, against unreasonable searches and seizures, shall not be violated, and no Warrants shall issue, but upon probable cause, supported by Oath or affirmation, and particularly describing the place to be searched, and the persons or things to be seized.

## Amendment V

No person shall be held to answer for a capital, or otherwise infamous crime, unless on a presentment or indictment of a Grand Jury, except in cases arising in the land or naval forces, or in the Militia, when in actual service in time of War or public danger; nor shall any person be subject for the same offence to be twice put in jeopardy of life or limb; nor shall be compelled in any criminal case to be a witness against himself, nor be deprived of life, liberty, or property, without due process of law; nor shall private property be taken for public use, without just compensation.

## Amendment VI

In all criminal prosecutions, the accused shall enjoy the right to a speedy and public trial, by an impartial jury of the State and district wherein the crime shall have been committed, which district shall have been previously ascertained by law, and to be informed of the nature and cause of the accusation; to be confronted with the witnesses against him; to have compulsory process for obtaining witnesses in his favor, and to have the Assistance of Counsel for his defence.

## Amendment VII

In suits at common law, where the value in controversy shall exceed twenty dollars, the right of trial by jury shall be preserved, and no fact tried by a jury, shall be otherwise reexamined in any Court of the United States, than according to the rules of the common law.

## Amendment VIII

Excessive bail shall not be required, nor excessive fines imposed, nor cruel and unusual punishments inflicted.

## Amendment IX

The enumeration in the Constitution, of certain rights, shall not be construed to deny or disparage others retained by the people.

## Amendment X

The powers not delegated to the United States by the Constitution, nor prohibited by it to the States, are reserved to the States respectively, or to the people.

# WHAT IS A PRION?

Anders Hedberg

> *In the February 21, 2002 issue of* Scientific American, *the magazine's "Ask the Experts" column addresses the question "What is a prion?" Notice how each expert implies an exigence for defining the term from the perspective of his or her own scientific specialty. Also, consider the different tactics of definition used by each expert; why might the cell biology researcher choose to give an etymology of the word while the professor of microbiology and immunology describes the process by which prions cause disease?*

Specifically, what is known about the molecular structure of prions and how they cause infections such as Creutzfeldt-Jakob disease?

Susan Lindquist is a researcher at the Howard Hughes Medical Institute, located in the department of molecular genetics and cell biology at the University of Chicago. She responds:

"'Prion' is a term first used to describe the mysterious infectious agent responsible for several neurodegenerative diseases found in mammals, including Creutzfeldt-Jakob disease (CJD) in humans. The word itself derives from 'proteinaceous infectious particle'; it refers to the initially heretical hypothesis that the infectious agent causing those diseases consists only of protein, with no nucleic acid genome. (All previously known pathogens, such as bacteria and viruses, contain nucleic acids, which enable them to reproduce.) The prion hypothesis explained why the mysterious infectious agent is resistant to ultraviolet radiation, which breaks down nucleic acids, but is susceptible to substances that disrupt proteins.

"A major breakthrough occurred when researchers discovered that the infectious agent consists primarily of a protein found in the membranes of normal cells, but in this case the protein has an altered shape, or conformation. Some scientists hypothesized that the distorted protein could bind to other proteins of the same type and induce them to change their conformation as well, producing a chain reaction that propagates the disease and generates new infectious material. Since then, the gene for this protein has been successfully cloned, and studies using transgenic mice have bolstered the prion hypothesis. The evidence in support of the hypothesis is now very strong, though not incontrovertible.

"Research on prion diseases has recently accelerated for several reasons. First, the mounting experimental evidence has generated great interest in what appears to be a totally new kind of mechanism of disease. Second, the demonstration that prions are responsible for 'mad cow' disease (bovine spongiform encephalopathy), which has infected large numbers of cattle in Great Britain and panicked the public, has lent new urgency to the quest for a cure—especially since the discovery that infected cows might be responsible for several new cases of CJD in humans. Finally, I and my colleagues have recently determined that a phenomenon much like prion infection exists in yeast.

"In the case of yeast, the phenomenon involves the passing of a particular genetic trait from mother cells to daughter cells, rather than the transmission of an infectious agent from one individual to another. These genetic traits had been known for many years, but their baffling patterns of inheritance (for example, they can be passed along through a cell's cytoplasm, rather than the nucleus where the DNA resides) had eluded explanation. We now know that the genetic trait is transmitted by proteins that are encoded in the nucleus but that can change their conformation in the cytoplasm. Once this change has occurred, the reconfigured proteins induce other newly made proteins of the same type to change their conformation, too. Molecular genetic research on yeast should speed up the resolution of fundamental questions about the workings of protein-folding chain reactions. And more important, it suggests that the prion mechanism is ubiquitous among living things and may be responsible for many phenomena other than neurodegenerative diseases like CJD."

Mark Rogers in the department of zoology and the Biotechnology Centre at University College, Dublin, adds some further information:
"The term 'prion' was coined by Stanley B. Prusiner of the University of California School of Medicine at San Francisco in 1982 to distinguish the infectious agent that causes scrapie in sheep, Creutzfeldt-Jakob disease (CJD) in humans and bovine spongiform encephalopathy (BSE) in cattle from other, more typical infectious agents. The prion hypothesis postulates that these diseases are caused not by a conventional virus or bacterium but by a protein that has adopted an abnormal form.
"The process by which this change occurs is not clear and there is a great deal of work under way to establish the structure of the prion protein in both its normal and aberrant forms. Recently scientists have developed a molecular model of both variants and have published papers describing the structure of prion proteins (as manufactured by *E. coli* bacteria that were altered through recombinant DNA techniques). Further work using magnetic resonance imaging and x-ray crystallography should help us understand the key structural elements that allow the prion to co-opt the normal cellular form into the disease-producing variant. It is likely that other cellular components assist in this process, so work on understanding the cell biology of both forms of the protein is also vital."

Shaun Heaphy in the department of microbiology and immunology at Leicester University provides this overview:
"A number of fatal neurodegenerative diseases in humans—such as Creutzfeldt-Jakob disease (CJD), kuru and Gerstmann-Sträussler-Scheinker (GSS) disease—are thought to be caused by an infectious agent known as a prion. Prions also cause disease in a wide variety of other animals, including scrapie in sheep and bovine spongiform encephalopathy (BSE) in cows. Collectively these diseases are known as transmissible spongiform encephalopathies.
"The cause of CJD was unknown for many years; it occurred seemingly randomly, at a very low incidence. In the 1950s an epidemic transmissible disease called kuru, similar to CJD, was identified in the Fore tribe of Papua New Guinea. Transmission of the disease occurred during a ritual funeral process in which the brain of a dead tribe member was removed from the skull, cooked and eaten. Scientific analysis of the

brains of people who had died from CJD or kuru showed that their brain tissue had a spongiform appearance, that is, there were holes where cells ought to be, indicating an encephalopathy, or reduction in the number of brain cells.

"D. Carleton Gajdusek, working at the U.S. National Institutes of Health, demonstrated that extracts of brain prepared from people who had died of CJD or kuru could cause a similar disease when inoculated into the brain of chimpanzees. These experiments obviously suggested the presence of an infectious agent. That inference has been confirmed by the inadvertent transmission of CJD to patients undergoing various medical treatments, such as corneal transplants and human growth hormone therapy.

"Confusingly, researchers also recognized that some prion diseases, such as GSS, were inherited. The pattern of inheritance was recognized as being autosomal and dominant, meaning that if a parent developed GSS, there was a 50 percent chance that a child of either sex would also develop the disease. Any explanation for the cause of a prion disease therefore has to account for random, inherited and transmitted variants of the disease.

"Although there is not yet a universally accepted explanation of this puzzle, progress is being made. We now know that a normal cellular protein, called PrP (for proteinaceous infectious particle) and which is found in all of us, is centrally involved in the spread of prion diseases. This protein consists of about 250 amino acids.

"Some researchers believe that the prions are formed when PrP associates with a foreign pathogenic nucleic acid. This is called the virino hypothesis. (Viruses consist of proteins and nucleic acids that are specified by the virus genome. A virino would also consist of proteins and nucleic acids, but the protein component is specified by the host genome, not the pathogen genome). In support of the virino hypothesis is the existence of different strains of prions that cause differing patterns of disease and breed true; the existence of strains in pathogens is usually the result of changes in the nucleic acid sequence of the infectious agent. Scientists have not found any nucleic acid associated with a prion, however, despite intensive efforts in many laboratories. Furthermore, prions appear to remain infectious even after being exposed to treatments that destroy nucleic acids.

"This evidence has led to the now widely accepted prion theory, which states that the cellular protein PrP is the sole causative agent of prion diseases; there is no nucleic acid involved. The theory holds that PrP is normally in a stable shape (pN) that does not cause disease. The protein can be flipped, however, into an abnormal shape (pD) that does cause disease. pD is infectious because it can associate with pN and convert it to pD, in an exponential process—each pD can convert more pN to pD.

"Prions can be transmitted, possibly by eating and certainly by inoculation either directly into the brain or into skin and muscle tissue. Exponential amplification of the prion (converting pN into pD in the body) would then result in disease. Occasional, sporadic cases of prion diseases arise in middle or old age, presumably because there is a very small but real chance that pN can spontaneously flip to pD; the cumulative likelihood of such a flip grows over the years. Inherited cases of CJD and GSS may result from mutations in the PrP gene, which gives rise to changes in the amino acid sequence of the PrP protein. This change would increase the probability of pN transforming into pD, so that the disease would almost certainly occur.

"Physical analysis of the structure of PrP provides some direct evidence for the existence of two different (normal and aberrant) shapes. Recently the structure of the core part of the PrP protein was determined by magnetic resonance image analysis. Mutations that cause prion disease are clustered within or adjacent to key structural elements in the protein, so it is easy to imagine that mutations destabilize the structure of pN and cause it to reconfigure into pD.

"The prion theory has not been proved correct, but much evidence now supports it. We do not yet know why the pD structure of a prion would result in neurodegeneration, but we do know that prion protein accumulates in brain tissue. One part of the prion protein can cause apoptosis, or programmed cell death; perhaps this mechanism explains the pattern of the disease.

"Prions have long intrigued scientists because of their unusual properties. Recently the general public has become interested in them as well because of the epidemic of BSE, more dramatically known as mad cow disease. Hundreds of thousands of infected animals have been eaten by Europeans and particularly the British over the past 10 years. The latest research suggests that the infected meat may pose a threat to human health, but the significance of that threat may not become apparent for years. Although it is generally considered a British problem, BSE is almost certainly a natural disease of cattle, so it is undoubtedly found in other countries as well. The normal incidence of BSE is vanishingly small, however. The U.S. Department of Agriculture claims that BSE has not been identified in any U.S. cattle."

# THE RETURN TO THE MELTING POT

Arthur Schlesinger, Jr.

> *Arthur Schlesinger, Jr., is a two-time Pulitzer Prize winner for history. In this article, which appeared in the Wall Street Journal in 1990, Schlesinger draws on his knowledge of American history to show the evolution of the idea of "the melting pot." The title of Schlesinger's 1992 book,* The Disuniting of America: Reflections on a Multicultural Society, *reflects, to some degree, the political outlook represented here. As you read, consider why Schlesinger argues that it is necessary to reexamine our contemporary definition of the melting pot, and how a change in our sense of what the term means might impact the things we value and teach.*

"What then is the American, this new man?" a French immigrant asked two centuries ago. Hector St. John de Crevecoeur gave the classic answer to his own question. "He is an American, who, leaving behind him all his ancient prejudices and manners, receives new ones from the new mode of life he has embraced, the new government he obeys, and the new rank he holds. . . . Here individuals of all nations are melted into a new race of man."

The conception of America as a transforming nation, banishing old identities and creating a new one, prevailed through most of American history. It was famously reformulated by Israel Zangwill, an English writer of Russian Jewish origin, when he called America "God's crucible, the great melting pot where all the faces of Europe are melting and re-forming." Most people who came to America expected to become Americans. They wanted to escape a horrid past and to embrace a hopeful future. Their goals were deliverance and assimilation.

Thus Crevecoeur wrote his "Letters from an American Farmer" in his acquired English, not in his native French. Thus immigrants reared in other tongues urged their children to learn English as speedily as possible. German immigrants tried for a moment to gain status for their language, but the effort got nowhere. The dominant culture was Anglo-Saxon and, with modification and enrichment, remained Anglo-Saxon.

## Repudiation of the Melting Pot

The melting pot was one of those metaphors that turned out only to be partly true, and recent years have seen an astonishing repudiation of the whole conception. Many Americans today righteously reject the historic goal of "a new race of man." The contemporary ideal is not assimilation but ethnicity. The escape from origins has given way to the search for "roots." "Ancient prejudice and manners"—the old-time religion, the old-time diet—have made a surprising comeback.

These developments portend a new turn in American life. Instead of a transformative nation with a new and distinctive identity, America increasingly sees itself as preservative of old identities. We used to say *e pluribus unum*. Now we glorify *pluribus* and belittle *unum*. The melting pot yields to the Tower of Babel.

The new turn has had marked impact on the universities. Very little agitates academia more these days than the demands of passionate minorities for revision of the curriculum: in history, the denunciation of Western civilization courses as cultural imperialism; in literature, the denunciation of the "canon," the list of essential books, as an instrumentality of the existing power structure.

A recent report by the New York State Commissioner of Education's task force on "Minorities: Equity and Excellence" luridly describes "African Americans, Asian Americans, Puerto Ricans/Latinos and Native Americans" as "victims of an intellectual and educational oppression." The "systematic bias toward European culture and its derivatives," the report claims, has "a terribly damaging effect on the psyche of young people of African, Asian, Latino and Native American descent"—a doubtful assertion for which no proof is vouchsafed.

Of course teachers of history and literature should give due recognition to women, black Americans, Indians, Hispanics and other groups who were subordinated and ignored in the high noon of male Anglo-Saxon dominance. In recent years they have begun belatedly to do so. But the *cult of ethnicity*, pressed too far, exacts costs—as, for example, the current pressure to teach history and literature not as intellectual challenges but as psychological therapy.

There is nothing new, of course, about the yearnings of excluded groups for affirmations of their own historical and cultural dignity. When Irish-Americans were thought beyond the pale, their spokesmen responded much as spokesmen for blacks, Hispanics and others respond today. Professor John V. Kelleher, for many years Harvard's distinguished Irish scholar, once recalled his first exposure to Irish-American history—"turgid little essays on the fact that the Continental Army was 76 percent Irish, or that many of George Washington's closest friends were nuns and priests, or that Lincoln got the major ideas for the Second Inaugural Address from the Hon. Francis P. Mageghegan of Alpaca, New York, a pioneer manufacturer of cast-iron rosary beads." John Kelleher called this "the there's-always-an-Irishman-at-the-bottom-of-it-doing-the-real-work approach to American history."

Fortunately most Irish-Americans disregarded their spokesmen and absorbed the American tradition. About 1930, Kelleher said, those "turgid little essays began to vanish from Irish-American papers." He added, "I wonder whose is the major component in the Continental Army these days?" The answer, one fears, is getting to be blacks, Jews and Hispanics.

There is often artificiality about the attempts to use history to minister to psychological needs. When I encounter black insistence on inserting Africa into mainstream curricula, I recall the 1956 presidential campaign. Adlai Stevenson, for whom I was working, had a weak record on civil rights in America but was a champion of African nationalism. I suggested to a group of sympathetic black leaders that maybe if Stevenson talked to black audiences about Africa, he could make up for his deficiencies on civil rights. My friends laughed and said that American blacks couldn't care less about Africa. That is no longer the case; but one can't escape the feeling that present emotions are more manufactured than organic.

Let us by all means teach women's history, black history, Hispanic history. But let us teach them as *history*, not as a means of *promoting group self-esteem*. I don't often agree with Gore Vidal, but I liked his remark the other day: "What I hate is good citizenship history. That has wrecked every history book. Now we're getting 'The Hispanics are warm and joyous and have brought such wonder into our lives,' you know, and before them the Jews, and before them the blacks. And the women. I mean, cut it out!"

Novelists, moralists, politicians, fabulators can go beyond the historical evidence to tell inspiring stories. But historians are custodians of professional standards. Their objective is critical analysis, accuracy and objectivity, not making people feel better about themselves.

Heaven knows how dismally historians fall short of their ideals; how sadly our interpretations are dominated and distorted by unconscious preconceptions; how obsessions of race and nation blind us to our own bias. All historians may in one way or another mythologize history. But the answer to bad history is not "good citizenship history"—more bad history written from a different view point. The answer to bad history is better history.

The ideological assault in English departments on the "canon" as an instrument of political oppression implies the existence of a monolithic body of work designed to enforce the "hegemony" of a class or race or sex. In fact, most great literature and much good history are deeply subversive in their impact on orthodoxies. Consider the American canon: Emerson, Whitman, Melville, Hawthorne, Thoreau, Mark Twain, Henry Adams, William and Henry James, Holmes, Dreiser, Faulkner. Lackeys of the ruling class? Agents of American imperialism?

Let us by all means learn about other continents—and other cultures. But, lamentable as some may think it, we inherit an American experience, as America inherits a European experience. To deny the essentially European origins of American culture is to falsify history.

We should take pride in our distinctive inheritance as other nations take pride in their distinctive inheritances. Certainly there is no need for Western civilization, the source of the ideas of individual freedom and political democracy to which most of the world now aspires, to apologize to cultures based on despotism, superstition, tribalism, and fanaticism. Let us abjure what Bertrand Russell called the fallacy of "the superior virtue of the oppressed."

Of course we must teach the Western democratic tradition in its true proportions—not as a fixed, final and complacent orthodoxy, intolerant of deviation and dissent, but as an ever-evolving creed fulfilling its ideals through debate, self-criticism, protest, disrespect and irreverence, a tradition in which all groups have rights of heterodoxy and opportunities for self-assertion. It is a tradition that has empowered people of all nations and races. Little can have a more "terribly damaging effect on the psyche" than for educators to tell young blacks and Hispanics and Asians that it is not for them.

## One Step at a Time

Belief in one's own culture does not mean disdain for other cultures. But one step at a time: No culture can hope to ingest other cultures all at once, certainly not before it ingests its own. After we have mastered our own culture, we can explore the world.

If we repudiate the quite marvelous inheritance that history has bestowed on us, we invite the fragmentation of our own culture into a quarrelsome spatter of enclaves, ghettos and tribes. The bonds of cohesion in our society are sufficiently fragile, or so it seems to me, that it makes no sense to strain them by encouraging and exalting cultural and linguistic apartheid. The rejection of the melting pot points the republic in the direction of incoherence and chaos.

In the 21st century, if present trends hold, non-whites in the U.S. will begin to outnumber whites. This will bring inevitable changes in the national ethos but not, one must hope, at the expense of national cohesion. Let the new Americans foreswear the cult of ghettoization and agree with Crevecoeur, as with most immigrants in the two centuries since, that in America "individuals of all nations are melted into a new race of man."

# THE TERRORISTS HERE AT HOME

Anna Quindlen

> *Almost as soon as President Bush announced that America was at war on terrorism, people began thinking seriously about the definitions of terrorism and terrorist. In this article, essayist Anna Quindlen uses standard and accepted definitions of both terms to make her point. As you read the essay, notice the tactics of definition she employs and how she adjusts her argument to the audience of a major news magazine.*

Letters filled with white powder and anthrax warnings in insistent capitals. Constant bomb scares and the ever-present sensation of something worse to come. And a single-minded cadre of men who believe that their religious convictions justify violence, destruction and the murder of those whose choices they abhor.

That's what the people who work in family-planning clinics have been living with for years and years.

What most citizens of this country felt this fall is what those who are involved in reproductive services, some of them at facilities that have never performed a single abortion, have lived with a long time. Last week the immediate enemy was a wacko named Clayton Lee Waagner, who was busted at a Kinko's in Ohio after doing time on the FBI's Most Wanted list for sending faux anthrax to hundreds of clinics. Waagner had allegedly told Neal Horsley, who runs an anti-abortion Web site, that he also had plans to kill 42 clinic workers. Horsley quotes him as saying, "If I kill 42 people, by golly I'm going to get some attention!"

But Americans haven't really paid much attention to the campaign of systematic destruction being waged by this group of domestic terrorists over the past quarter century. There's that vague feeling that anti-abortion fervor is largely the purview of principled human beings, women with rosaries and strollers who pray on the sidewalks across from clinics.

Here are some of the principles involved: Arson. Assault. Molotov cocktails. Nail bombs. Glued locks. Blocked sewers. Coming in to work every day wondering if holes have been punched in the roof, the phone lines cut or the files vandalized. If you think a doctor has the right to decide whether to perform abortions, wait until you see the pickets on her lawn or hear strangers yelling at her children as they leave for school. Reading over even thumbnail sketches of what has happened to clinics and clinic owners since abortion became legal makes any sane person wonder how dedicated or stubborn an individual would have to be to continue.

No matter what you believe about abortion, a procedure that more than a million women choose in this country every year, those who believe in human rights have to be repelled by the notion of religious fanatics who believe they can harass, injure or murder people on the say-so of a direct pipeline to God, or Allah. Horsley, who delivered Waagner's threats to the world online, has been in the news before because he is responsible for the site called the Nuremberg List, which provided the names and addresses of clinic workers as well as "miscellaneous spouses and other blood flunkies." If Horsley had a swarthy complexion or the word "al" anywhere in his name and had posted such a list of intelligence officials, he would be in jail now.

There's no real ideological difference between these people and the people who flew planes into the World Trade Center. (One of the leaders of Operation Rescue once sent his followers a letter that concluded, "Return to the training so that God may use you." Sound familiar?) Even law enforcement now refers to them as terrorists. That wasn't always true. Many clinics have stories of local police who responded reluctantly to their calls, and even a few demonstrators who were police officers themselves. In recent years, however, local authorities have gotten sick and tired of the constant drain on their manpower, and the federal authorities have begun to take the threats more seriously. Some of what they've learned about handling letters containing anthrax they learned at clinics, where the staff figured out a long time ago how to open potentially hazardous letters. So far none has contained the real thing. "But you can bet if they could get their hands on real anthrax, it would be real anthrax," says Gloria Feldt, who runs Planned Parenthood.

No matter what you think of abortion, you have to conclude that all this is a waste of scarce resources. If clinics did not need to spend so much for security and insurance, they could be providing more education programs, family-planning services and prenatal care. Instead they are forced to deal with the crazed misogyny of people like members of the so-called Army of God, whose manual offers recipes for plastic explosives and the kinds of bombs used in Oklahoma City.

When will Americans support the clinics in their towns, not because they support abortion but because they support the rule of law? When a wife is followed home from a clinic where she had a Pap test and then harangued on the phone by a zealot who copied down her license-plate number and has a mole in the motor-vehicles office? When a daughter is forced to stand on the cold side-walk in a hospital gown, midprocedure, because of a bomb scare? Patricia Baird-Windle, who ran a clinic in Florida, writes in her book "Targets of Hatred" that the most difficult part of the ordeal was the ignorance of ordinary citizens, "the disbelief of people, the looks that tell me that what I am describing cannot possibly be real."

It is real: the attacks, the destruction, the escalation. In 1989 James Kopp was chaining himself to a car blocking a clinic entrance in Pittsburgh; less than 10 years later he was allegedly training a gun on the silhouette of a doctor seen through the window of a house in Buffalo, N.Y. That doctor, Barnett Slepian, wrote in a 1994 letter to the local paper: "Please don't feign surprise, dismay, or certainly not innocence when a more volatile and less restrained member of the group decides to react to their inflammatory rhetoric by shooting an abortion provider." Four years later he was dead on his own kitchen floor. People like Waagner and Horsley will argue he brought it on himself by unconscionable action. That's precisely what the men who hit the Trade Center and the Pentagon thought about the soldiers, bankers, lawyers and assorted infidels they believed they had a holy right to murder. Dr. Slepian's wife and children are as much victims of terrorism as anyone who lost a loved one on September 11, and the zealots who abetted and applauded his murder just as un-American.

# LOVE: THE RIGHT CHEMISTRY

Anastasia Toufexis

> *Anastasia Toufexis has published a number of articles in* Time, *including this one from February of 1993. Toufexis often examines contemporary issues that demand expert scientific or medical research as evidence, such as euthanasia and the recent debates over tobacco. This article is a comparatively light-hearted example of the way scientific discoveries can impact the way people think about common but confusing human behavior, like falling in love. As you read, consider what sort of demands the science in the article puts on the author as she relates to her audience, and consider the tactics Toufexis uses to handle those demands. You might start by considering the punning title.*

Love is a romantic designation for a most ordinary biological—or, shall we say, chemical?—process. A lot of nonsense is talked and written about it.
    —Greta Garbo to Melvyn Douglas in *Ninotchka*

O.K., let's cut out all this nonsense about romantic love. Let's bring some scientific precision to the party. Let's put love under a microscope.

When rigorous people with Ph.D.s after their names do that, what they see is not some silly, senseless thing. No, their probe reveals that love rests firmly on the foundations of evolution, biology and chemistry. What seems on the surface to be irrational, intoxicated behavior is in fact part of nature's master strategy—a vital force that has helped humans survive, thrive and multiply through thousands of years. Says Michael Mills, a psychology professor at Loyola Marymount University in Los Angeles: "Love is our ancestors whispering in our ears."

It was on the plains of Africa about 4 million years ago, in the early days of the human species, that the notion of romantic love probably first began to blossom—or at least that the first cascades of neurochemicals began flowing from the brain to the bloodstream to produce goofy grins and sweaty palms as men and women gazed deeply into each other's eyes. When mankind graduated from scuttling around on all fours to walking on two legs, this change made the whole person visible to fellow human beings for the first time. Sexual organs were in full display, as were other characteristics, from the color of eyes to the span of shoulders. As never before, each individual had a unique allure.

When the sparks flew, new ways of making love enabled sex to become a romantic encounter, not just a reproductive act. Although mounting mates from the rear was, and still is, the method favored among most animals, humans began to enjoy face-to-face couplings; both looks and personal attraction became a much greater part of the equation.

Romance served the evolutionary purpose of pulling males and females into long-term partnership, which was essential to child rearing. On open grasslands, one parent would have a hard—and dangerous—time handling a child while foraging for food. "If, a woman was carrying the equivalent of a 20-lb. bowling ball in one arm and a pile of sticks in the other, it was ecologically critical to pair up with a mate to rear the young," explains anthropologist Helen Fisher, author of *Anatomy of Love*.

While Western culture holds fast to the idea that true love flames forever (the movie *Bram Stoker's Dracula* has the Count carrying the torch beyond the grave), nature apparently meant passions to sputter out in something like four years. Primitive pairs stayed together just "long enough to rear one child through infancy," says Fisher. Then each would find a new partner and start all over again.

What Fisher calls the "four-year itch" shows up unmistakably in today's divorce statistics. In most of the 62 cultures she has studied, divorce rates peak around the fourth year of marriage. Additional youngsters help keep pairs together longer. If, say, a couple have another child three years after the first, as often occurs, then their union can be expected to last about four more years. That makes them ripe for the more familiar phenomenon portrayed in the Marilyn Monroe classic *The Seven-Year Itch*.

If, in nature's design, romantic love is not eternal, neither is it exclusive. Less than 5% of mammals form rigorously faithful pairs. From the earliest days, contends Fisher, the human pattern has been "monogamy with clandestine adultery." Occasional flings upped the chances that new combinations of genes would be passed on to the next generation. Men who sought new partners had more children. Contrary to common assumptions, women were just as likely to stray. "As long as prehistoric females were secretive about their extramarital affairs," argues Fisher, "they could garner extra resources, life insurance, better genes and more varied DNA for their biological futures. . . ."

Lovers often claim that they feel as if they are being swept away. They're not mistaken; they are literally flooded by chemicals, research suggests. A meeting of eyes, a touch of hands or a whiff of scent sets off a flood that starts in the brain and races along the nerves and through the blood. The results are familiar: flushed skin, sweaty palms, heavy breathing. If love looks suspiciously like stress, the reason is simple: the chemical pathways are identical.

Above all, there is the sheer euphoria—of falling in love—a not-so-surprising reaction, considering that many of the substances swamping the newly smitten are chemical cousins of amphetamines. They include dopamine, norepinephrine and especially phenylethylamine (PEA). Cole Porter knew what he was talking about when he wrote, "I get a kick out of you." "Love is a natural high," observes Anthony Walsh, author of *The Science of Love: Understanding Love and Its Effects on Mind and Body*. "PEA gives you that silly smile that you flash at strangers. When we meet someone who is attractive to us, the whistle blows at the PEA factory."

But phenylethylamine highs don't last forever, a fact that lends support to arguments that passionate romantic love is short-lived. As with any amphetamine, the body builds up a tolerance to PEA; thus it takes more and more of the substance to produce love's special kick. After two to three years, the body simply can't crank up the needed amount of PEA. And chewing on chocolate doesn't help, despite popular belief. The candy is high in PEA, but it fails to boost the body's supply.

Fizzling chemicals spell the end of delirious passion; for many people that marks the end of the liaison as well. It is particularly true for those whom Dr. Michael Liebowitz of the New York State Psychiatric Institute terms "attraction junkies." They crave the intoxication of falling in love so much that they move frantically from affair to affair just as soon as the first rush of infatuation fades.

Still, many romances clearly endure beyond the first years. What accounts for that? Another set of chemicals, of course. The continued presence of a partner gradually steps up production in the brain of endorphins. Unlike the fizzy amphetamines, these are soothing substances. Natural pain-killers, they give lovers a sense of security, peace, and calm. "That is one reason why it feels so horrible when we're abandoned or a lover dies," notes Fisher. "We don't have our daily hit of narcotics."

Researchers see a contrast between the heated infatuation induced by PEA, along with other amphetamine-like chemicals, and the more intimate attachment fostered and prolonged by endorphins. "Early love is when you love the way the other person makes you feel," explains psychiatrist Mark Goulston of the University of California, Los Angeles. "Mature love is when you love the person as he or she is." It is the difference between passionate and compassionate love, observes Walsh, a psychobiologist at Boise State University in Idaho. "It's Bon Jovi vs. Beethoven."

Oxytocin is another chemical that has recently been implicated in love. Produced by the brain, it sensitizes nerves and stimulates muscle contraction. In women it helps uterine contractions during childbirth as well as production of breast milk, and seems to inspire mothers to nuzzle their infants. Scientists speculate that oxytocin might encourage similar cuddling between adult women and men. The versatile chemical may also enhance orgasms. In one study of men, oxytocin increased to three to five times its normal level during climax, and it may soar even higher in women.

Chemicals may help explain (at least to scientists) the feelings of passion and is compassion, but why do people tend to fall in love with one partner rather than a myriad of others? Once again, it's partly a function of evolution and biology. "Men are looking for maximal fertility in a mate," says Loyola Marymount's Mills. "That is in large part why females in the prime childbearing ages of 17 to 28 are so desirable." Men can size up youth and vitality in a glance, and studies indeed show that men fall in love quite rapidly. Women tumble more slowly, to a large degree because their requirements are more complex; they need more time to check the guy out. "Age is not vital," notes Mills, "but the ability to provide security, father children, share resources and hold a high status in society are all key factors."

Still, that does not explain why the way Mary walks and laughs makes Bill dizzy with desire while Marcia's gait and giggle leave him cold. "Nature has wired us for one special person," suggests Walsh, romantically. He rejects the idea that a woman or a man can be in love with two people at the same time. Each person carries in his or her mind a unique subliminal guide to the ideal partner, a "love map," to borrow a term coined by sexologist John Money of Johns Hopkins University.

Drawn from the people and experiences of childhood, the map is a record of whatever we found enticing and exciting—or disturbing and disgusting. Small feet, curly hair. The way our mothers patted our head or how our fathers told a joke. A fireman's uniform, a doctor's stethoscope. All the information gathered while growing up is imprinted in the brain's circuitry by adolescence. Partners never meet each and every requirement, but a sufficient number of matches can light up the wires and signal, "It's love." Not every partner will be like the last one, since lovers may have different combinations of the characteristics favored by the map.

O.K., that's the scientific point of view. Satisfied? Probably not. To most people—with or without Ph.D.s—love will always be more than the sum of its natural parts. It's a commingling of body and soul, reality and imagination, poetry and phenylethylamine. In our deepest hearts, most of us harbor the hope that love will never fully yield up its secrets, that it will always elude our grasp.

# NOTES OF A NATIVE SPEAKER

Eric Liu

*Originally published as part of the author's book of essays entitled* The Accidental Asian, *this piece makes its points by implicitly or explicity defining a number of terms, most notably* white, Chinese, assimilation, banana, *and* Asian American. *As you read, note how the author incorporates definition into his overall argument that he must be considered, first and foremost, "American."*

*The son of Chinese immigrant parents, Eric Liu is an unrepentant assimilationist. As he details in this essay, he has worked hard to master the codes of the dominant culture. By any measure, he has succeeded, having graduated from an Ivy League university and worked in the U.S. Senate, the State Department, and the White House, where he served as a speech writer for President Clinton. He concedes that he has neglected or lost some measure of Chinese culture along the way, but rejects the idea that this makes him a "traitor" to his heritage. Instead, he suggests that his experience represents a much larger process that is transforming the face of America as a new, multi-ethnic generation comes into its own. "America is white no longer," he concludes, "and it will never be white again." Liu (b. 1968) founded the political journal* The Next Progressive *and has edited an anthology titled* Next: Young American Writers on the New Generation *(1994). Currently he is a fellow at the New American Foundation and writes for MSNBC. This selection is taken from his collection of personal essays,* The Accidental Asian *(1998).*

1

Here are some of the ways you could say I am "white":

I listen to National Public Radio.
I wear khaki Dockers.
I own brown suede bucks.
I eat gourmet greens.
I have few close friends "of color."
I married a white woman.
I am a child of the suburbs.
I furnish my condo à la Crate & Barrel.
I vacation in charming bed-and-breakfasts.
I have never once been the victim of blatant discrimination.
I am a member of several exclusive institutions.
I have been in the inner sanctums of political power.
I have been there as something other than an attendant.

I have the ambition to return.

I am a producer of the culture.

I expect my voice to be heard.

I speak flawless, unaccented English.

I subscribe to *Foreign Affairs.*

I do not mind when editorialists write in the first person plural.

I do not mind how white television casts are.

I am not too ethnic.

I am wary of minority militants.

I consider myself neither in exile nor in opposition.

I am considered "a credit to my race."

I never asked to be white. I am not literally white. That is, I do not have white skin or white ancestors. I have yellow skin and yellow ancestors, hundreds of generations of them. But like so many other Asian Americans of the second generation. I find myself now the bearer of a strange new status: white, by acclamation. Thus it is that I have been described as an "honorary white," by other whites, and as a "banana,"[1] by other Asians. Both the honorific and the epithet take as a given this idea: to the extent that I have moved away from the periphery and toward the center of American life, I have become white inside. *Some are born white, others achieve whiteness, still others have whiteness thrust upon them.* This, supposedly, is what it means to assimilate.

There was a time when assimilation did quite strictly mean whitening. In fact, well into the first half of this century, mimicry of the stylized standards of the WASP[2] gentry was the proper, dominant, perhaps even sole method of ensuring that your origins would not be held against you. You "made it" in society not only by putting on airs of anglitude, but also by assiduously bleaching out the marks of a darker, dirtier past. And this bargain, stifling as it was, was open to European immigrants almost exclusively; to blacks, only on the passing occasion; to Asians, hardly at all.

Times have changed, and I suppose you could call it progress that a Chinaman, too, may now aspire to whiteness. But precisely because the times have changed, that aspiration—and the *imputation* of the aspiration—now seems astonishingly outmoded. The meaning of "American" has undergone a revolution in the twenty-nine years I have been alive, a revolution of color, class, and culture. Yet the vocabulary of "assimilation" has remained fixed all this time: fixed in whiteness, which is still our metonym for power; and fixed in shame, which is what the colored are expected to feel for embracing the power.

I have assimilated. I am of the mainstream. In many ways I fit the psychological profile of the so-called banana: imitative, impressionable, rootless, eager to please. As I will admit in this essay, I have at times gone to great lengths to downplay my difference, the better to penetrate the "establishment" of the moment. Yet I'm not sure that what I did was so cut-and-dried as "becoming white." I plead guilty to the charges above: achieving, learning the ways of the upper middle class, distancing myself from radicals of any hue. But having confessed, I still do not know my crime.

To be an accused banana is to stand at the ill-fated intersection of class and race. And because class is the only thing Americans have more trouble talking about than race, a minority's climb up the social ladder is often willfully misnamed and wrongly portrayed.

There is usually, in the portrayal, a strong whiff of betrayal: the assimilist is a traitor to his kind, to his class, to his own family. He cannot gain the world without losing his soul. To be sure, something *is* lost in any migration, whether from place to place or from class to class. But something is gained as well. And the result is always more complicated than the monochrome language of "whiteness" and "authenticity" would suggest.

My own assimilation began long before I was born. It began with my parents, who came here with an appetite for Western ways already whetted by films and books and music and, in my mother's case, by a father who'd been to the West. My parents, who traded Chinese formality for the more laissez-faire stance of this country. Who made their way by hard work and quiet adaptation. Who fashioned a comfortable life in a quiet development in a second-tier suburb. Who, unlike your "typical" Chinese parents, were not pushy, status-obsessed, rigid, disciplined, or prepared. Who were haphazard about passing down ancestral traditions and "lessons" to their children. Who did pass down, however, the sense that their children were entitled to mix and match, as they saw fit, whatever aspects of whatever cultures they encountered.

I was raised, in short, to assimilate, to claim this place as mine. I don't mean that my parents told me to act like an American. That's partly the point: they didn't tell me to do anything except to be a good boy. They trusted I would find my way, and I did, following their example and navigating by the lights of the culture that encircled me like a dome. As a function of my parents' own half-conscious, half-finished acculturation, I grew up feeling that my life was Book II of an ongoing saga. Or that I was running the second leg of a relay race. *Slap!* I was out of the womb and sprinting, baton in hand. Gradually more sure of my stride, my breathing, the feel of the track beneath me. Eyes forward, never backward.

Today, nearly seven years after my father's death and two years after my marriage into a large white family, it is as if I have come round a bend and realized that I am no longer sure where I am running or why. My sprint slows to a trot. I scan the unfamiliar vista that is opening up. I am somewhere else now, somewhere far from the China that yielded my mother and father; far, as well, from the modest horizons I knew as a boy. I look at my limbs and realize I am no longer that boy; my gait and grasp exceed his by an order of magnitude. Now I want desperately to see my face, to see what time has marked and what it has erased. But I can find no mirror except the people who surround me. And they are mainly pale, powerful.

How did I end up here, standing in what seems the very seat of whiteness, gazing from the promontory of social privilege? How did I cover so much ground so quickly? What was it, in my blind journey, that I felt I should leave behind? And what *did* I leave behind? This, the jettisoning of one mode of life to send another aloft, is not only the immigrant's tale; it is the son's tale, too. By coming to America, my parents made themselves into citizens of a new country. By traveling the trajectory of an assimilist, so did I.

2

As a child, I lived in a state of "amoebic bliss," to borrow the felicitous phrase of the author of *Nisei Daughter*, Monica Sone. The world was a gossamer web of wonder that began with life at home, extended to my friendships, and made the imaginary realm of daydream seem as immediate as the real. If something or someone was in my personal web of meaning, then color or station was irrelevant. I made no distinctions in fourth grade between my best friend, a black boy named Kimathi, and my next-best friend, a white boy named Charlie—other than the fact that one was number one, the other number two. I did not feel, or feel for, a seam that separated the textures of my Chinese life from those of my American life. I was not "bicultural" but omnicultural, and omnivorous, too. To my mind, I differed from others in only two ways that counted: I was a faster runner than most, and a better student. Thus did work blend happily with play, school with home, Western culture with Eastern: it was all the same to a self-confident boy who believed he'd always be at the center of his own universe.

As I approached adolescence, though, things shifted. Suddenly, I could no longer subsume the public world under my private concept of self. Suddenly, the public world was more complicated than just a parade of smiling teachers and a few affirming friends. Now I had to contend with the unstated, inchoate, but inescapable standards of *cool*. The essence of cool was the ability to conform. The essence of conformity was the ability to anticipate what was cool. And I wasn't so good at that. For the first time, I had found something that did not come effortlessly to me. No one had warned me about this transition from happy amoeboid to social animal; no one had prepared me for the great labors of fitting in.

And so in three adjoining arenas—my looks, my loves, my manners—I suffered a bruising adolescent education. I don't mean to overdramatize: there was, in these teenage banalities, usually something humorous and nothing particularly tragic. But in each of these realms, I came to feel I was not normal. And obtusely, I ascribed the difficulties of that age not to my age but to my color. I came to suspect that there was an order to things, an order that I, as someone Chinese, could perceive but not quite crack. I responded not by exploding in rebellion but by dedicating myself, quietly and sometimes angrily, to learning the order as best I could. I was never ashamed of being Chinese; I was, in fact, rather proud to be linked to a great civilization. But I was mad that my difference should matter now. And if it had to matter, I did not want it to defeat me.

Consider, if you will, my hair. For the first eleven years of my life, I sported what was essentially the same hairstyle: a tapered bowl cut, the handiwork of my mother. For those eleven joyful years, this low-maintenance do was entirely satisfactory. But in my twelfth year, as sixth grade got under way, I became aware—gradually at first, then urgently—that bangs were no longer the look for boys. This was the year when certain early bloomers first made the height-weight-physique distribution in our class seem startlingly wide—and when I first realized that I was lingering near the bottom. It was essential that I compensate for my childlike mien by cultivating at least a patina of teenage style.

This is where my hair betrayed me. For some readers the words "Chinese hair" should suffice as explanation. For the rest, particularly those who have spent all your lives with the ability to comb back, style, and part your hair *at will*, what follows should make you count your blessings. As you may recall, 1980 was a vintage year for hair that was parted straight down the middle, then feathered on each side, feathered so immaculately that the ends would meet in the back like the closed wings of angels.

I dreamed of such hair. I imagined tossing my head back casually, to ease into place the one or two strands that had drifted from their positions. I dreamed of wearing the fluffy, tailored locks of the blessed.

Instead, I was cursed. My hair was straight, rigid, and wiry. Not only did it fail to feather back; it would not even bend. Worse still, it grew the wrong way. That is, it all emanated from a single swirl near the rear edge of my scalp. Parting my hair in any direction except back to front, the way certain balding men stage their final retreat, was a physical impossibility. It should go without saying that this was a disaster. For the next three years, I experimented with a variety of hairstyles that ranged from the ridiculous to the sublimely bad. There was the stringy pothead look. The mushroom do. Helmet head. Bangs folded back like curtains. I enlisted a blow-dryer, a Conair set on high heat, to force my hair into stiff postures of submission. The results, though sometimes innovative, fell always far short of cool.

I feigned nonchalance, and no one ever said anything about it. But make no mistake: this was one of the most consuming crises of my inner life as a young teen. Though neither of my parents had ever had such troubles, I blamed this predicament squarely on my Chinese genes. And I could not abide my fate. At a time when homogeneity was the highest virtue, I felt I stood out like a pigtailed Manchu.

My salvation didn't come until the end of junior high, when one of my buddies, in an epiphany as we walked past the Palace of Hair Design, dared me to get my head shaved. Without hesitation, I did it—to the tearful laughter of my friends and, soon afterward, the tearful horror of my mother. Of course, I had moments of doubt the next few days as I rubbed my peach-fuzzed skull. But what I liked was this: I had managed, without losing face, to rid myself of my greatest social burden. What's more, in the eyes of some classmates, I was now a bold (if bald) iconoclast. I've worn a crew cut ever since.

Well-styled hair was only one part of a much larger preoccupation during the ensuing years: wooing girls. In this realm I experienced a most frustrating kind of success. I was the boy that girls always found "sweet" and "funny" and "smart" and "nice." Which, to my highly sensitive ear, sounded like "leprous." Time and again, I would charm a girl into deep friendship. Time and again, as the possibility of romance came within reach, I would smash into what I took to be a glass ceiling.

The girls were white, you see; such were the demographics of my school. I was Chinese. And I was convinced that this was the sole obstacle to my advancement. It made sense, did it not? I was, after all, sweet and funny and smart and nice. Hair notwithstanding, I was not unattractive, at least compared with some of the beasts who had started "going out" with girls. There was simply no other explanation. Yet I could never say this out loud: it would have been the whining of a loser. My response, then, was to secretly scorn the girls I coveted. It was *they* who were subpar, whose small-mindedness and veiled prejudice made them unworthy.

My response, too, was to take refuge in my talents. I made myself into a Renaissance boy, playing in the orchestra but also joining the wrestling team, winning science prizes but also editing the school paper. I thought I was defying the stereotype of the Asian American male as a one-dimensional nerd. But in the eyes of some, I suppose, I was simply another "Asian overachiever."

In hindsight, it's hard to know exactly how great a romantic penalty I paid for being Chinese. There may have been girls who would have had nothing to do with me on account of my race, but I never knew them. There were probably girls who, race aside, simply didn't like me. And then there were girls who liked me well enough but who also shied from the prospect of being part of an interracial couple. With so many boys out there, they probably reasoned, why take the path of greater resistance? Why risk so many status points? Why not be "just friends" with this Chinese boy?

Maybe this stigma was more imagined than real. But being an ABC ("American-born Chinese," as our parents called us) certainly affected me another way. It made me feel like something of a greenhorn, a social immigrant. I wanted so greatly to be liked. And my earnestness, though endearing, was not the sort of demeanor that won girls' hearts. Though I was observant enough to notice how people talked when flirting, astute enough to mimic the forms, I was oblivious to the subterranean levels of courtship, blind to the more subtle rituals of "getting chicks" by spurning them. I held the view that if you were manifestly a good person, eventually someone of the opposite sex would do the rational thing and be smitten with you. I was clueless. Many years would pass before I'd wise up.

It wasn't just dating rituals that befuddled me as a youth. It was ritual of all kinds. Ceremony, protocol, etiquette—all these made me feel like an awkward stranger. Things that came as second nature to many white kids were utterly exotic to me. American-style manners, for instance. Chinese families often have their own elaborate etiquette, but "please" and "may I" weren't the sort of words ever heard around my house. That kind of formality seemed so beside the point. I was never taught by my parents to write thank-you notes. I didn't even have the breeding to *say* "Thank you" after sleeping over at a friend's house. I can recall the awful, sour feeling in my stomach when this friend told me his mother had been offended by my impoliteness. (At that point, I expressed my thanks.)

Eating dinner at the home of a *yangren* could be especially trying. The oaken furniture seemed scaled-up, chairs like thrones. The meal would begin with someone, usually the father, mumbling grace. Furtively, I'd steal a glance at the heads bowed in prayer. What if they asked me to say something? I looked back down and kept my mouth shut. Next was the question of silverware: which pieces to use, in which order, and so forth. I'd realize then that at home I ate by using chopsticks to shove rice and meat straight from bowl to slurping mouth. Then the whole thing about passing platters of food around the table, instead of just reaching over and getting what you wanted. I would hear myself ask, in too-high tones, "Would you please pass the carrots, please?" It was usually at that point that I would notice that my napkin was the only one still folded neatly on the table.

All this, of course, was in the context of being with my friends and having a nice time. But something made me feel vaguely sad while I sat there, swallowing huge servings of gravy-drenched food with this other family. These were the moments when I realized I was becoming something other than my parents. I wanted so badly then just to be home, in my own kitchen, taking in the aroma of stir-fry on the wok and the chattery sounds of Chinglish. And yet, like an amphibian that has just breached the shore, I could not stop inhaling this wondrous new atmosphere. My moist, blinking eyes opened wide, observing and recording the customs and predilections of these "regular" Americans. The more time I spent in their midst, the more I learned to be like them. To make their everyday idioms and idiosyncrasies familiar. To possess them.

This, the mundane, would be the locus of my conversion. It was through the small things that I made myself over. I wish, if only for story-telling purposes, that I could offer a more dramatic tale, a searing incident of racism that sent me into deep, self-abnegating alienation. The truth is, I can't. I was sometimes uncomfortable, but never really alienated. There were one or two occasions in seventh grade when the toughs in the back of the bus taunted me, called me *chink*: shot spitballs at me. I didn't like it. But each time, one of my friends—one of my white friends, in whose house I'd later eat dinner—would stand with me and fire back both spitballs and insults. Our insults were mean, too: scornful references to the trailer parks where these kids lived or the grubby clothes they wore or the crummy jobs their parents had. These skirmishes weren't just about race; they were also about mobility.

The same could be said, ultimately, about my own assimilation. To say simply that I became a banana, that I became white-identified, is somewhat simplistic. As an impressionable teen, I came to identify not with white people in general but with that subset of people, most of them white, who were educated, affluent: *going places*. It was their cues that I picked up, their judgments that I cared about. It was in their presence that old patterns of thought began to fall away like so much scaffolding around my psyche. It was in their presence that I began to imagine myself beyond race.

3

I recently dug up a photograph of myself from freshman year of college that made me smile. I have on the wrong shoes, the wrong socks, the wrong checkered shirt tucked the wrong way into the wrong slacks. I look like what I was: a boy sprung from a middlebrow burg who affected a secondhand preppiness. I look nervous. Compare that image to one from my senior-class dinner: now I am attired in a gray tweed jacket with a green plaid bow tie and a sensible button-down shirt, all purchased at the Yale Co-op. I look confident, and more than a bit contrived.

What happened in between those two photographs is that I experienced, then overcame, what the poet Meena Alexander has called "the shock of arrival." When I was deposited at the wrought-iron gates of my residential college as a freshman, I felt more like an outsider than I'd thought possible. It wasn't just that I was a small Chinese boy standing at a grand WASP temple; nor simply that I was a hayseed neophyte puzzled by the refinements of college style. It was *both:* color and class were all twisted together in a double helix of felt inadequacy.

For a while I coped with the shock by retreating to a group of my own kind—not fellow Asians, but fellow marginal public-school grads who resented the rah-rah Yalies to whom everything came so effortlessly. Aligning myself this way was bearable—I was hiding, but at least I could place myself in a long tradition of underdog exiles at Yale. Aligning myself by race, on the other hand, would have seemed too inhibiting.

I know this doesn't make much sense. I know also that college, in the multicultural era, is supposed to be where the deracinated minority youth discovers the "person of color" inside. To a point, I did. I studied Chinese, took an Asian American history course, a seminar on race politics. But ultimately, college was where the unconscious habits of my adolescent assimilation hardened into self-conscious strategy.

I still remember the moment, in the first week of school, when I came upon a table in Yale Station set up by the Asian American Student Association. The upper-classman staffing the table was pleasant enough. He certainly did not strike me as a fanatic. Yet, for some reason, I flashed immediately to a scene I'd witnessed days earlier, on the corner outside. Several Lubavitcher Jews, dressed in black, their faces bracketed by dangling side curls, were looking for fellow travelers at this busy cross-roads. Their method was crude but memorable. As any vaguely Jewish-looking male walked past, the zealots would quickly approach, extend a pamphlet, and ask, "Excuse me, sir, are you Jewish?" Since most were not, and since those who were weren't about to stop, the result was a frantic, nervous, almost comical buzz all about the corner: Excuse me, are you Jewish? Are you Jewish? Excuse me. Are you Jewish?

I looked now at the clean-cut Korean boy at the AASA table (I think I can distin-guish among Asian ethnicities as readily as those Hasidim thought they could tell Gentile from Jew), and though he had merely offered an introductory hello and was now smiling mutely at me, in the back of my mind I heard only this: *Excuse me, are you Asian? Are you Asian? Excuse me, Are you Asian?* I took one of the flyers on the table, even put my name on a mailing list, so as not to appear impolite. But I had already resolved not to be active in any Asians-only group. I thought then: I would never *choose* to be so pigeonholed.

This allergic sensitivity to "pigeonholing" is one of the unhappy hallmarks of the banana mentality. What does the banana fear? That is, what did *I* fear? The possibil-ity of being mistaken for someone more Chinese. The possibility of being known only, or even primarily, for being Asian. The possibility of being written off by whites as a self-segregating ethnic clumper. These were the threats—unseen and, frankly, unsubstantiated—that I felt I should keep at bay.

I didn't avoid making Asian friends in college or working with Asian classmates; I simply never went out of my way to do so. This distinction seemed important—it marked, to my mind, the difference between self-hate and self-respect. That the two should have been so proximate in the first place never struck me as odd, or telling. Nor did it ever occur to me that the reasons I gave myself for dissociating from Asians as a group—that I didn't want to be part of a clique, that I didn't want to get absorbed and lose my individuality—were the very developments that marked my own assim-ilation. I simply hewed to my ideology of race neutrality and self-reliance. I didn't need that crutch, I told myself nervously, that crutch of racial affinity. What's more, I was vaguely insulted by the presumption that I might.

But again: Who was making the presumption? Who more than I was taking the mere existence of Korean volleyball leagues or Taiwanese social sets or pan-Asian stu-dent clubs to mean that *all* people of Asian descent, myself, included, needed such quasi-kinship groups? And who more than I interpreted this need as infirmity, as a failure to fit in? I resented the faintly sneering way that some whites regarded Asians as an undifferentiated mass. But whose sneer, really, did I resent more than my own?

I was keenly aware of the unflattering mythologies that attach to Asian Ameri-cans: that we are indelibly foreign, exotic, math and science geeks, numbers people rather than people people, followers and not leaders, physically frail but devious and sneaky, unknowable and potentially treacherous. These stereotypes of Asian otherness and inferiority were like immense blocks of ice sitting before me, challenging me to chip away at them. And I did, tirelessly. All the while, though, I was oblivious to rumors of my *own* otherness and inferiority, rumors that rose off those blocks like a fog, wafting into my consciousness and chilling my sense of self.

As I had done in high school, I combated the stereotypes in part by trying to disprove them. If Asians were reputed to be math and science geeks, I would be a student of history and politics. If Asians were supposed to be feeble subalterns, I'd lift weights and go to Marine officer candidate school. If Asians were alien, I'd be ardently patriotic. If Asians were shy and retiring, I'd try to be exuberant and jocular. If they were narrow-minded specialists, I'd be a well-rounded generalist. If they were perpetual outsiders, I'd join every establishment outfit I could and show that I, too, could run with the swift.

I overstate, of course. It wasn't that I chose to do all these things with no other purpose than to cut against a supposed convention. I was neither so Pavlovian nor so calculating that I would simply remake myself into the opposite of what people expected. I actually *liked* history, and wasn't especially good at math. As the grandson of a military officer, I *wanted* to see what officer candidates school would be like, and I enjoyed it, at least once I'd finished. I am *by nature* enthusiastic and allegiant, a joiner, and a bit of a jingo.

At the same time, I was often aware, sometimes even hopeful, that others might think me "exceptional" for my race. I derived satisfaction from being the "atypical" Asian, the only Chinese face at OCS or in this club or that.

The irony is that in working so duteously to defy stereotype, I became a slave to it. For to act self-consciously against Asian "tendencies" is not to break loose from the cage of myth and legend; it is to turn the very key that locks you inside. What spontaneity is there when the value of every act is measured, at least in part, by its power to refute a presumption about why you act? The *typical Asian* I imagined, and the *atypical Asian* I imagined myself to be, were identical in this sense: neither was as much a creature of free will as a human being ought to be.

Let me say it plainly, then: I am not proud to have had this mentality. I believe I have outgrown it. And I expose it now not to justify it but to detoxify it, to prevent its further spread.

Yet it would be misleading, I think, to suggest that my education centered solely on the discomfort caused by race. The fact is, when I first got to college I felt deficient compared with people of *every* color. Part of why I believed it so necessary to achieve was that I lacked the connections, the wealth, the experience, the sophistication that so many of my classmates seemed to have. I didn't get the jokes or the intellectual references. I didn't have the canny attitude. So in addition to all my coursework, I began to puzzle over this, the culture of the influential class.

Over time, I suppose, I learned the culture. My interests and vocabulary became ever more worldly. I made my way onto what Calvin Trillin once described as the "magic escalator" of a Yale education. Extracurriculars opened the door to an alumni internship, which brought me to Capitol Hill, which led to a job and a life in Washington after commencement. Gradually, very gradually, I found that I was not so much of an outsider anymore. I found that by almost any standard, but particularly by the standards of my younger self, I was actually beginning to "make it."

It has taken me until now, however, to appraise the thoughts and acts of that younger self. I can see now that the straitening path I took was not the only or even the best path. For while it may be possible to transcend race, *it is not always necessary to try.* And while racial identity is sometimes a shackle, it is not *only* a shackle. I could have spared myself a great deal of heartache had I understood this earlier, that the choice of race is not simply "embrace or efface."

I wonder sometimes how I would have turned out had I been, from the start, more comfortable in my own skin. What did I miss by distancing myself from race? What friendships did I forgo, what self-knowledge did I defer? Had certain accidents of privilege been accidents of privation or exclusion, I might well have developed a different view of the world. But I do not know just how my view would have differed.

What I know is that through all those years of shadow-dancing with my identity, something happened, something that had only partially to do with color. By the time I left Yale I was no longer the scared boy of that freshman photo. I had become more sure of myself and of my place—sure enough, indeed, to perceive the folly of my fears. And in the years since, I have assumed a sense of expectation, of access and *belonging*, that my younger self could scarcely have imagined. All this happened incrementally. There was no clear tipping point, no obvious moment of mutation. The shock of arrival, it would seem, is simply that I arrived.

## 4

"The world is white no longer, and it will never be white again." So wrote James Baldwin after having lived in a tiny Swiss village where, to his knowledge, no black man had ever set foot. It was there, in the icy heart of whiteness, that the young expatriate began to comprehend the desire of so many of his countrymen to return to some state of nature where only white people existed. It was there too that he recognized just how impossible that was, just how intertwined were the fates and identities of the races in America. "No road whatever will lead Americans back to the simplicity of this European village where white men still have the luxury of looking on me as a stranger," he wrote. "I am not, really, a stranger any longer for any American alive."

That is precisely how I feel when I consider my own journey, my own family's travels. For here I am now, standing in a new country. Not as an expatriate or a resident alien, but as a citizen. And as I survey this realm—this Republic of Privilege—I realize certain things, things that my mother and father might also have realized about *their* new country a generation ago. I realize that my entry has yielded me great opportunities. I realize, as well, that my route of entry has taken a certain toll. I have neglected my ancestral heritage. I have lost something. Yes, I can speak some Mandarin and stir-fry a few easy dishes. I have been to China and know something of its history. Still, I could never claim to be Chinese at the core.

Yet neither would I claim, as if by default, to be merely "white inside." I do not want to be white. I only want to be integrated. When I identify with white people who wield economic and political power, it is not for their whiteness but for their power. When I imagine myself among white people who influence the currents of our culture, it is not for their whiteness but for their influence. When I emulate white people who are at ease with the world, it is not for their whiteness but for their ease. I don't like it that the people I should learn from tend so often to be white, for it says something damning about how opportunity is still distributed. But it helps not at all to call me white for learning from them. It is cruel enough that the least privileged Americans today have colored skin, the most privileged fair. It is crueler still that by our very language we should help convert this fact into rule. The time has come to describe assimilation as something other than the White Way of Being.

The time has also come, I think, to conceive of assimilation as more than a series of losses—and to recognize that what is lost is not necessarily sacred. I have, as I say, allowed my Chinese ethnicity to become diluted. And I often resolve to do more to preserve, to conserve, my inheritance. But have my acts of neglect thus far, my many omissions, been inherently wrong? G. K. Chesterton once wrote that "conservatism is based upon the idea that if you leave things alone, you leave them as they are. But you do not. If you leave a thing alone, you leave it to a torrent of change." I may have been born a Chinese baby, but it would have taken unremitting reinforcement, by my parents and by myself, for me to have remained Chinese. Instead, we left things alone. And a torrent of change washed over me.

This, we must remember, has been an act of creation as much as destruction. Something new is emerging from the torrent, in my case and the many millions like it. Something undeveloped, speaking the unformed tongue of an unformed nation. Something not white, and probably more Chinese than I know. Whatever it is that I am becoming, is it any less authentic for being an amalgam? Is it intrinsically less meaningful than what I might otherwise have been? In every assimilation, there is a mutiny against history—but there is also a destiny, which is to redefine history. What it means to be American—in spirit, in blood—is something far more borrowed and commingled than anything previous generations ever knew. Alongside the pain of migration, then, and the possibility, there is this truth America is white no longer, and it will never be white again.

### Notes

1. *"banana"*: Derogatory term for an assimilated Asian American who is seen as a sellout, "yellow on the outside and white on the inside."
2. *WASP*: Acronym for "White Anglo-Saxon Protestant."

# III

# *Paired Definitions*

*Few words have more controversy surrounding their usage than* nigger. *The next two articles engage in the debate over how the word* nigger *is used, whether it ought to be used at all, and, if so, by whom. You may already be familiar with Gloria Naylor's writing; she is the author of the novel,* The Women of Brewster Place. *In this article, "The Meanings of a Word," Naylor draws on childhood experiences to show how she finally came to understand the troubled history of the term. Leonard Pitts, Jr.'s article, "You Can't Lift Every Voice Until You Change Your Tune," was originally published in the* Washington Post. *In it, Pitts argues that it is impossible for anyone to use the word without summoning the negative associations of its historically racist and demeaning use. As you read, think about the ways each author establishes ethos to engage in this highly charged issue. After reading, consider whether or not Naylor and Pitts ultimately agree on the meanings of the term.*

## THE MEANINGS OF A WORD

Gloria Naylor

Language is the subject. It is the written form with which I've managed to keep the wolf away from the door and, in diaries, to keep my sanity. In spite of this, I consider the written word inferior to the spoken, and much of the frustration experienced by novelists is the awareness that whatever we manage to capture in even the most transcendent passages falls far short of the richness of life. Dialogue achieves its power in the dynamics of a fleeting moment of sight, sound, smell, and touch.

I'm not going to enter the debate here about whether it is language that shapes reality or vice versa. That battle is doomed to be waged whenever we seek intermittent reprieve from the chicken and egg dispute. I will simply take the position that the spoken word, like the written word, amounts to a nonsensical arrangement of sounds or letters without a consensus that assigns "meaning." And building from the meanings of what we hear, we order reality. Words themselves are innocuous; it is the consensus that gives them true power.

\* \* \*

I remember the first time I heard the word *nigger*. In my third-grade class, our math tests were being passed down the rows, and as I handed the papers to a little boy in back of me, I remarked that once again he had received a much lower mark than I did. He snatched his test from me and spit out that word. Had he called me a nymphomaniac or a necrophiliac, I couldn't have been more puzzled. I didn't know what a nigger was, but I knew that whatever it meant, it was something he shouldn't have called me. This was verified when I raised my hand, and in a loud voice repeated what he had said and watched the teacher scold him for using a "bad" word. I was later to go home and ask the inevitable question that every black parent must face— "Mommy, what does *nigger* mean?"

And what exactly did it mean? Thinking back, I realize that this could not have been the first time the word was used in my presence. I was part of a large extended family that had migrated from the rural South after World War II and formed a close-knit network that gravitated around my maternal grandparents. Their ground-floor apartment in one of the buildings they owned in Harlem was a weekend mecca for my immediately family, along with countless aunts, uncles, and cousins who brought assorted friends. It was a bustling and open house with assorted neighbors and tenants popping in and out to exchange bits of gossip, pick up an old quarrel, or referee the ongoing checkers game in which my grandmother cheated shamelessly. They were all there to let down their hair and put up their feet after a week of labor in the factories, laundries, and shipyards of New York.

Amid the clamor, which could reach deafening proportions—two or three conversations going on simultaneously, punctuated by the sound of a baby's crying somewhere in the back rooms or out on the street—there was still a rigid set of rules about what was said and how. Older children were sent out of the living room when it was time to get into the juicy details about "you-know-who" up on the third floor had gone and gotten herself "p-r-e-g-n-a-n-t!" But my parents, knowing that I could spell well beyond my years, always demanded that I follow the others out to play. Beyond sexual misconduct and death, everything else was considered harmless for our young ears. And so among the anecdotes of the triumphs and disappointments in the various workings of their lives, the word *nigger* was used in my presence, but it was set within contexts and inflections that caused it to register in my mind as something else.

In the singular, the word was always applied to a man who had distinguished himself in some situation that brought their approval for his strength, intelligence, or drive:

"Did Johnny *really* do that?"

"I'm telling you, that nigger pulled in $6,000 of overtime last year. Said he got enough for a down payment on a house."

When used with a possessive adjective by a woman—"my nigger"—it became a term of endearment for her husband or boyfriend. But it could be more than just a term applied to a man. In their mouths it became the pure essence of manhood—a disembodied force that channeled their past history of struggle and present survival against the odds into a victorious statement of being: "Yeah, that old foreman found out quick enough—you don't mess with a nigger."

In the plural, it became a description of some group within the community that had overstepped the bounds of decency as my family defined it. Parents who neglected their children, a drunken couple who fought in public, people who simply refused to look for work, those with excessively dirty mouths or unkempt households were all "trifling niggers." This particular circle could forgive hard times, unemployment, the occasional bout of depression—they had gone through all of that themselves—but the unforgivable sin was a lack of self-respect.

A woman could never be a "nigger" in the singular, with its connotation of confirming worth. The noun *girl* was its closest equivalent in that sense, but only when used in direct address and regardless of the gender doing the addressing. *Girl* was a token of respect for a woman. The one-syllable word was drawn out to sound like three in recognition of the extra ounce of wit, nerve, or daring that the woman had shown in the situation under discussion.

"G-i-r-l, stop. You mean you said that to his face?"

But if the word was used in a third-person reference or shortened so that it almost snapped out of the mouth, it always involved some element of communal disapproval. And age became an important factor in these exchanges. It was only between individuals of the same generation, or from any older person to a younger (but never the other way around), that *girl* would be considered a compliment.

\* \* \*

I don't agree with the argument that use of the word *nigger* at this social stratum of the black community was an internalization of racism. The dynamics were the exact opposite: the people in my grandmother's living room took a word that whites used to signify worthlessness or degradation and rendered it impotent. Gathering there together, they transformed *nigger* to signify the varied and complex human beings they knew themselves to be. If the word was to disappear totally from the mouths of even the most liberal of white society, no one in that room was naïve enough to believe it would disappear from white minds. Meeting the word head-on, they proved it had absolutely nothing to do with the way they were determined to live their lives.

So there must have been dozens of times that *nigger* was spoken in front of me before I reached the third grade. But I didn't "hear" it until it was said by a small pair of lips that had already learned it could be a way to humiliate me. That was the word I went home and asked my mother about. And since she knew that I had to grow up in America, she took me in her lap and explained.

# YOU CAN'T LIFT EVERY VOICE UNTIL YOU'VE CHANGED YOUR TUNE

Leonard Pitts, Jr.

As Richard Pryor told it years ago, he was sitting in a hotel lobby on a trip to Africa when he heard a voice within. "What do you see?" it asked. "Look around."

"I looked around and I saw people of all colors and shapes. And the voice said, 'Do you see any niggers?' I said, 'No.' It said, 'Do you know why? There aren't any.'"

Pryor told an audience that he started crying then. The comedian, whose speech had always been peppered with that ugly word, abruptly realized that it had not passed his lips in the three weeks he'd spent among the blacks of Africa. Pryor subsequently renounced the word altogether: The most profane man in America decided that here was a term too profane even for him.

I mention this only because there is, in case you hadn't noticed, a renewed struggle underway over the use and abuse of the N-word. And it's left me a little ticked off at the blatant hypocrisy. Of black people.

I'm sorry, but I just don't get it. Over recent months, black activists have battled the people who put out the Merriam-Webster dictionary, a black educator has challenged Mark Twain's "Huckleberry Finn," and Spike Lee has lambasted Quentin Tarantino, all over the use and abuse of the N-word.

But I haven't seen anybody say a damn thing about black comics who fly it like a dirty flag. Haven't heard a peep about the tiny talents of raunch rap who spill it into the ether like sewage. Haven't heard anyone say the obvious: that if we as African Americans truly abhor this word, then the protest ought to begin on our own doorstep.

Yeah, yeah, I know the rules. It's okay for us to say it, but not for whites. Except that some young blacks say it is okay for whites if those whites are honorary blacks, down with the brothers. Yet if those same whites mistakenly use the word outside their circle of black friends, they're likely to incite a riot.

I know the rules, but the rules are stupid. Contradictory. And confusing. If white people are baffled about what is and isn't allowed, I can't blame them. I blame us.

We've become entirely too casual, too gratuitous, with this instrument of disparagement. These days, one is less likely to hear the word from a white jerk with his bedsheet draped on his head than from a black one with his pants sagging off his butt. I once heard a young black colleague make a point of saying it in front of a white woman, who was properly flummoxed. The colleague explained with blithe self-satisfaction that she enjoyed dropping the word into conversation in order to observe white folks' stunned reaction.

All of which suggests to me that we as black people suffer from historical amnesia. A blindness to the suffering of ancestors. And a stubborn refusal to learn the lesson Pryor did: to grow up and leave this evil thing behind.

So the last word some beaten black man heard before gravity yanked him down and the rope bit into his neck becomes a shock tactic for a callow youth. The word that followed his torn corpse as it was dragged down dusty roads behind the bumper of a car now serves some oafish rapper who can't find anything else to rhyme with trigger.

That's grotesque. It is obscene.

And it renders just slightly hollow all these recent protests of mortal offense.

I'm supposed to be outraged that the word is used—with historical accuracy—in a classic novel that came out 114 years ago? No. Mark Twain doesn't bother me. Snoop Doggy Dogg does. Def comedy does.

Because they suggest to me that behind the facade of arrogant cool, we still hate us.

That self-loathing is slavery's hardiest legacy, Jim Crow's bastard child. And I'm impatient to see it dead. Impatient for a day when we love ourselves enough to be offended by anyone who uses this word. Moreover, love our children enough to stop teaching it to them.

Here's a new and much simpler rule for the use of the N-word:

Don't.

*The following two selections examine the connotations of the word* gay. *The first piece, written by Hanns Ebensten, appeared in his 1997 book,* A Humble Proposal. *Ebensten provides a variety of definitions, drawn from many sources, to demonstrate why he believes the word* gay *is inadequate and even offensive as a label for homosexual men. James Collard, the editor of* Out *magazine, defines what he calls a post-gay sensibility in his article, which was published in* Newsweek *in August of 1998. Both authors argue that the label* gay *can impose a uniformity of character on people who may in fact be quite ideologically diverse. As you read, notice the strategies with which both writers address stereotypes associated with the label* gay. *After reading both pieces, think about whether or not Collard might say Ebensten had a post-gay sensibility.*

## A HUMBLE PROPOSAL

Hanns Ebensten

I am becoming increasingly anti-gay.

I did not understand why this appellation was applied to homosexual men when I first heard it used about fifty years ago, and since then I like it less and less. It is a nauseating word which brings to mind *The Gay Hussar*, one of the most cloying, vapid pieces of music ever composed, and conjures up sickening visions of painfully gay peasants with bells and ribbons around their ankles dancing in the square of some village in Mittel-Europa.[1] I am not gay, I have never been gay in my life, not even at some disastrous New Year's Eve parties in my youth with a mask on my face and dressed as a harlequin or as Nijinsky in *L'Après midi d'un Faune*.[2] To be condemned to go through life being gay seems to me to be a very sad and dismal prospect—how loathsome to be constantly merry, joyous, bright, and lively, happy even at a funeral, blithe in adversity. Does this describe me, or most of us? Are we merely brilliantly flashy, flaunting, gaudy, showy buffoons without a sensible thought in our heads?

No, I am not gay; and I believe that opposition to the concept of accepting homosexuals in the U.S. military is due, to a large extent, to this unfortunate name, which damns us with a total lack of seriousness and purpose.

Who wants a light-hearted, licentiously "gay dog," a hilarious man given only to social life and pleasures, to be beside him in the assault on the enemy beach and in the parachute attack?

No, gay will not do: We must find another and more appealing name for ourselves.

When I was a boy, homosexuality was not a fit subject for discussion. I overheard my parents, their lips primly pursed, acknowledge that Uncle Max was "a confirmed bachelor" and my mother smirked when she confided to the ladies at her coffee parties that her male hairdresser was "quite a lady." It was explained of an unmarried general who was invariably accompanied in public by a handsome young *aide-de-camp* that he "had never met the right woman"; and some actors were rumored to be *so*. Later, at school and in the army, I listened with fascination when the boys talked about weird, mythical creatures of whose existence they had heard but whom none had ever encountered—"queers," men who were "bent," "bum-rushers" and, most distasteful of all, "brown hatters," named thus for the same reason that men who demeaned themselves to their teachers or officers to seek favors were said to have "a brown nose."

Such talk was restricted to all-male environments. When this unpleasant subject was mentioned in mixed company, and in my home, which was seldom, and oblique references had to be made to someone who suffered from this affliction, the wretch was said to be *tapette*, conveniently breaking into French—the word means a chatter-box—as was customary when anything disagreeable was being discussed while servants were in the room.

In Cockney rhyming slang, in England, queer is equated with "ginger beer," so that some people I knew in London would say of an obviously effeminate man that "he's a bit ginger!" Queer was more often, and more aptly, applied to someone who was ill, specifically ill in the head, demented, rather dotty, or irregular in his or her bowel movements. "Mum got taken all queer," they said. Queer, meaning odd, strange, whimsical, suspicious, spurious, cross, crotchety, and erratic, but which is for an inexplicable reason now being used by homosexuals to denigrate themselves, is offensive in any sense of the word. To queer someone's pitch is not doing him a kindness. Bent, meaning crooked, curved, hooked, or deflected in one's purpose, was the favorite term used by "straight" soldiers and sailors who traditionally accommodated any gentleman who paid for their beer and gave them a gratuity for sexual favors—but these men were hardly quite "straight" and their patrons were only occasionally bent with age and knew quite well what they were doing.

When I came to America, I learned that a gay or queer gentleman who had just left the room is called a faggot, which is a bundle of sticks, twigs, or tree branches. In England, where it must not be confused with a "fag," it used to be applied to a shrivelled old woman. A fag, in England's great public (meaning private) schools, is a young boy who has to serve a senior student and is mistreated and abused in order to teach him that life is invariably unfair; but a fag is not necessarily a faggot.

Before we all became very bold and open-minded and outspoken and permissive, if one met a man whom one liked and with whom after several subsequent meetings, such as taking nature hikes or visiting the zoological gardens or the opera, one felt a certain rapport, one then hesitatingly, daringly asked him: "Do you like the color *green*?" or "Are you"—a pregnant pause for effect—"*musical*?" But not everyone who liked the color green was musical, so this circumspect questioning could and not infrequently did lead to embarrassment and confusion. To be "warm" was also occasionally heard, though I never understood why, and Germans still speak, with approbation or derision, according to their sentiments, of a "warmer Bruder," which sounds like something very nice and cozy to have beside one in bed on a cold night.

So there we have our choices: Do we really want to be gay, queer, bent, faggots, brown hatters, or even warm brothers? There are other collective appellations, but we are not all pederasts, catamites, sodomites, perverts, or onanists. The only other name which is neither condescending nor derogatory is long, awkward on the tongue, a dirty ten-letter word which contains those dread letters *s-e-x*, but at least it is correct.

Homosexual women are fortunate. They name themselves and are named after the island of Lesbos in Greece, the birth-place of Sappho, antiquity's greatest lyrical poet who lived there with her female lovers in the 6th Century B.C. It is a sensible and dignified name, devoid of any unpleasant traits and associations.

I suggest that homosexual men also look back to the classical Greek and Roman period for a suitable and honorable name. The ancient Greeks believed (and proved in battles) that troops composed of pairs of lovers were superior in valor to other soldiers. The city states of Sparta and Thebes employed such troops of lovers, and it is tempting for male homosexuals to name themselves Spartans or Thebans; but these names are, on reflection, not suitable—by no means all homosexual men are fighters; few of us today lead what is generally now understood to be a Spartan[3] existence; and the most famous of the ancients' troops of lovers, the Theban Sacred Band which consisted of 150 pairs of lovers, of which Plutarch wrote: "A band that is held together by erotic love is indissoluble and unbreakable," was finally defeated, though by overwhelmingly large numbers of Macedonians.

So, instead of taking our new name from the battlefield, let us consider the most famous, accepted, and documented male homosexual relationship of antiquity, that between the Emperor Hadrian and Antinous, a youth who was born in the Kingdom of Bithynia, in what is now northern Turkey. They met in 124 A.D. and remained inseparable, traveling constantly, until Antinous's death. He was broad-shouldered and exceptionally beautiful, with curly hair, as is attested by more than five hundred statues of him which survive, many of them portraits taken from life, not idealized, three of the finest being in the museums of Delphi, Olympia, and the Vatican. Eighteen centuries after his death, gazing at the statue of Antinous in the British Museum, the Poet Laureate Lord Tennyson exclaimed: "Ah—this is the inscrutable Bithynian. If we knew what he knew, we should understand the ancient world."

Antinous died on October 30, 130 A.D., by drowning in the river Nile. The inquest continues—was it an accident, murder, or suicide? The distraught Emperor founded a city there in memory of his lover and ordered statues to be raised all over the Roman Empire to his "beloved Bithynian" so that he could be worshipped as a god. There is no better, no more romantic, no more uplifting example of a fine love between two men; and I propose that homosexual men everywhere call themselves Bithynians.

It is an unfamiliar word, and few of us have an affinity with a long-forgotten minor Kingdom on the north coast of Turkey; but after a year or more of general, wide-spread use, this name will seem no more strange than does lesbian—and who, after all, apart from lesbians themselves, knows that this is the name for the natives of a Greek island in the Aegean Sea?

Heads of the U.S. Armed Forces, who are averse to having those wanton, frivolous, erratic gays in the military, will, I believe, have fewer reservations about accepting stalwart, courageous, athletic Bithynians.

Shall we start to call ourselves Bithynians?

Who will begin?

### Notes

1. *Mittel-Europa:* Central Europe.

2. *Nijinsky:* Vaslav Nijinsky (1889–1950), the great Russian dancer, choreographed and performed the avant-garde ballet *L'Après midi d'un Faune (The Afternoon of a Faun).*

3. *Spartan:* Characterized by self-discipline or restraint.

# LEAVING THE GAY GHETTO

## James Collard

Six months ago, a dream came true, and I moved from London to New York City to become editor in chief of *OUT*, the magazine for gay men and lesbians. In many ways it's been a soft landing: America is a friendly country, and New Yorkers—despite the pride they take in being feisty—seem gentle in comparison with Londoners. Which made what took place on June 24 such a rude awakening. At a symposium held in the leafy, academic setting of New York's New School, I critiqued the ghettoization of the gay community and the orthodoxy of gay politics, suggesting that self-criticism should no longer be considered treason. I said we should no longer define ourselves solely in terms of our sexuality—even if our opponents do. That gay people were voicing these dissatisfactions, I argued, amounted to a new "post-gay" sensibility. A barrage of hostile questions—a barracking, we Brits would call it—ensued. "Who does this snotty Brit think he is?" "What does he know?" was the general tone. Later the press jumped on, as well, with Duncan Osborne writing in the newspaper *Lesbian & Gay New York* that what I'd said was tantamount to "announcing the death of gay politics." And you, the reader, may be wondering: Why, at a time when gay bashing is a continuing reality—both actual violence and saber-rattling by politicians like Trent Lott—would the editor of *OUT* magazine want to wash the gay community's dirty linen in public? So I'd like to clarify what I meant by post-gay, a term that was coined by the gay British journalist and activist Paul Burston in 1994. It doesn't refer to someone who's simply switched sexuality, like the WIFE, MOTHER, EX-LESBIAN in a recent ad campaign who claims to have filled the God-shaped hole in her life and discovered the joys of heterosexuality. Nor is it anti-gay. Post-gay is simply a critique of gay politics and gay culture—by gay people, for gay people. For me, the post-gay sensibility began when I realized that I preferred the social variety of "mixed" clubs to the more homogenous gay clubs. First for protection and later with understandable pride, gays have come to colonize whole neighborhoods, like West Hollywood in L.A. and Chelsea in New York City. It seems to me that the new Jerusalem gay people have been striving for all these years won't be found in a gay-only ghetto, but in a world where we are free, equal and safe to live our lives.

Another point of disagreement is the obsession many gays have with the male body beautiful. To me, it's overmarketed, commodified and, like the pressure on women to look a certain way, oppressive. At the extremes, it leads to steroid abuse or liposuction. I have as much of a weakness for a broad, manly chest as the next gay guy, but for me the overmuscled Barbie look fails on its own terms, namely esthetic. (It's also very high maintenance, and I for one am more likely to walk on water than achieve it.)

The anger that I provoked with my remarks that night goes back far beyond anything I said. In our community, anger has been a useful muscle, against homophobia and discrimination, and back in that terrible time when gay men were dying of AIDS in droves and governments stood by and did nothing, or next to nothing. At that time anger really was the only legitimate response, other than grief, and anyone who wasn't feeling precisely the same emotion was, in a real sense, the enemy. But anger no longer has the power to unite us. Much has been achieved in the short time since the gay-rights movement leapt out of the closet—and onto the streets—in the Stonewall Riots of 1969. The movement survived the conservative backlash of the '80s, organized itself to fight the AIDS epidemic and won numerous battles for equality and acceptance. In the aftermath many gay people—because of their economic position, where they work or where they live—feel they can live their lives freely and openly. Many others cannot, and there is also a new generation of young gay people emerging who have grown up in a different climate, at a different stage of the health crisis. These disparate groups are unlikely to be united by the orthodox tactics of angry veterans from earlier battles.

Post-gay doesn't mean "The struggle's over, so let's shop!" The struggle isn't over, and neither is the health crisis. But there's a pressure to conform within gay-activist politics, one that ultimately weakens its fighting strength by excluding the many gay people who no longer see their lives solely in terms of struggle.

It is hard to dedicate oneself to a mixed, gay-friendly society while some outside our community still hate us. But if that is our goal, we need to try to keep it alive and not respond with a kind of fundamentalism of our own. And it seems to me that if South Africa's ANC, whose members were being imprisoned exiled, tortured and assassinated, had the heart to debate just what kind of future they were fighting for—including a commitment to gay rights—then gay people here and across the world can do the same.

*The two articles that follow examine self respect. Joan Didion, a highly regarded American journalist, included the essay "On Self-Respect" in her book,* Slouching Towards Bethlehem, *published in 1966. You may want to ask whether Didion's essay is still relevant over thirty years later. While Didion defines self respect by describing the actions of people who she believes have self respect, E. J. Dionne, Jr. takes a very different tack in "Chattering Class: Personal Worth." Dionne's 1998 article appeared in* The Washington Post. *In it, he compares and contrasts the terms* self respect *and* self esteem *to argue that self esteem might not be as worth having as contemporary American culture implies. Think about how the two definitions are similar and dissimilar as you read. What do these different takes on self respect demonstrate about the power of definition to establish and highlight values?*

## ON SELF-RESPECT

Joan Didion

Once, in a dry season, I wrote in large letters across two pages of a notebook that innocence ends when one is stripped of the delusion that one likes oneself. Although now, some years later, I marvel that a mind on the outs with itself should have nonetheless made painstaking record of its every tremor, I recall with embarrassing clarity the flavor of those particular ashes. It was a matter of misplaced self-respect.

I had not been elected to Phi Beta Kappa. This failure could scarcely have been more predictable or less ambiguous (I simply did not have the grades), but I was unnerved by it; I had somehow thought myself a kind of academic Raskolnikov, curiously exempt from the cause-effect relationships which hampered others. Although even the humorless nineteen-year-old that I was must have recognized that the situation lacked real tragic stature, the day that I did not make Phi Beta Kappa, nonetheless marked the end of something, and innocence may well be the word for it. I lost the conviction that lights would always turn green for me, the pleasant certainty that those rather passive virtues which had won me approval as a child automatically guaranteed me not only Phi Beta Kappa keys but happiness, honor, and the love of a good man; lost a certain touching faith in the totem power of good manners, clean hair, and proven competence on the Stanford-Binet scale. To such doubtful amulets had my self-respect been pinned, and I faced myself that day with the nonplused apprehension of someone who has come across a vampire and has no crucifix at hand.

Although to be driven back upon oneself is an uneasy affair at best, rather like trying to cross a border with borrowed credentials, it seems to me now the one condition necessary to the beginnings of real self-respect. Most of our platitudes notwithstanding, self-deception remains the most difficult deception. The tricks that work on others count for nothing in that very well-lit back alley where one keeps assignations with oneself: no winning smiles will do here, no prettily drawn lists of good intentions. One shuffles flashily but in vain through one's marked cards—the kindness done for the wrong reason, the apparent triumph which involved no real effort, the seemingly heroic act into which one had been shamed. The dismal fact is that self-respect has nothing to do with the approval of others—who are, after all, deceived easily enough; has nothing to do with reputation, which, as Rhett Butler told Scarlett O'Hara, is something people with courage can do without.

To do without self-respect, on the other hand, is to be an unwilling audience of one to an interminable documentary that details one's failings, both real and imagined, with fresh footage spliced in for every screening. *There's the glass you broke in anger, there's the hurt on X's face; watch now, this next scene, the night Y came back from Houston, see how you muff this one.* To live without self-respect is to lie awake some night, beyond the reach of warm milk, Phenobarbital, and the sleeping hand on the coverlet, counting up the sins of commission and omission, the trusts betrayed, the promises subtly broken, the gifts irrevocably wasted through sloth or cowardice or carelessness. However long we postpone it, we eventually lie down alone in that notoriously uncomfortable bed, the one we make ourselves. Whether or not we sleep in it depends, of course, on whether or not we respect ourselves.

To protest that some fairly improbable people, some people who *could not possibly respect themselves*, seem to sleep easily enough is to miss the point entirely, as surely as those people miss it who think that self-respect has necessarily to do with not having safety pins in one's underwear. There is a common superstition that "self-respect" is a kind of charm against snakes, something that keeps those who have it locked in some unblighted Eden, out of strange beds, ambivalent conversations, and trouble in general. It does not at all. It has nothing to do with the face of things, but concerns instead a separate peace, a private reconciliation. Although the careless, suicidal Julian English in *Appointment in Samarra* and the careless, incurably dishonest Jordan Baker in *The Great Gatsby* seem equally improbable candidates for self-respect, Jordan Baker had it, Julian English did not. With that genius for accommodation more often seen in women than in men, Jordan took her own measure, made her own peace, avoided threats to that peace: "I hate careless people," she told Nick Carraway. "It takes two to make an accident."

Like Jordan Baker, people with self-respect have the courage of their mistakes. They know the price of things. If they choose to commit adultery, they do not then go running, in an excess of bad conscience, to receive absolution from the wronged parties; nor do they complain unduly of the unfairness, the undeserved embarrassment, of being named co-respondent. In brief, people with self-respect exhibit a certain toughness, a kind of moral nerve; they display what was once called *character*, a quality which, although approved in the abstract, sometimes loses ground to other, more instantly negotiable virtues. The measure of its slipping prestige is that one tends to think of it only in connection with homely children and United States senators who have been defeated, preferably in the primary, for reelection. Nonetheless, character—the willingness to accept responsibility for one's own life—is the source from which self-respect springs.

Self-respect is something that our grandparents, whether or not they had it, knew all about. They had instilled in them, young, a certain discipline, the sense that one lives by doing things one does not particularly want to do, by putting fears and doubts to one side, by weighing immediate comforts against the possibility of larger, even intangible, comforts. It seemed to the nineteenth century admirable, but not remarkable that Chinese Gordon put on a clean white suit and held Khartoum against the Mahdi; it did not seem unjust that the way to free land in California involved death and difficulty and dirt. In a diary kept during the winter of 1846, an emigrating twelve-year-old named Narcissa Cornwall noted coolly: "Father was busy reading and did not notice that the house was being filled with strange Indians until Mother spoke about it." Even lacking any clue as to what Mother said, one can scarcely fail to be impressed by the entire incident: the father reading, the Indians filing in, the mother choosing the words that would not alarm, the child duly recording the event and noting further that those particular Indians were not, "fortunately for us," hostile. Indians were simply part of the *donnée*.

In one guise or another, Indians always are. Again, it is a question of recognizing that anything worth having has its price. People who respect themselves are willing to accept the risk that the Indians will be hostile, that the venture will go bankrupt, that the liaison may not turn out to be one in which *every day is a holiday because you're married to me*. They are willing to invest something of themselves; they may not play at all, but when they do play, they know the odds.

That kind of self-respect is a discipline, a habit of mind that can never be faked but can be developed, trained, coaxed forth. It was once suggested to me that, as an antidote to crying, I put my head in a paper bag. As it happens, there is a sound physiological reason, something to do with oxygen, for doing exactly that, but the psychological effect alone is incalculable: it is difficult in the extreme to continue fancying oneself Cathy in *Wuthering Heights* with one's head in a Food Fair bag. There is a similar case for all the small disciplines, unimportant in themselves; imagine maintaining any kind of swoon, commiserative or carnal, in a cold shower.

But those small disciplines are available only insofar as they represent larger ones. To say that Waterloo was won on the playing fields of Eton is not to say that Napoleon might have been saved by a crash program in cricket; to give formal dinners in the rain forest would be pointless did not the candlelight flickering on the liana call forth deeper, stronger disciplines, values instilled long before. It is a kind of ritual, helping us to remember who and what we are. In order to remember it, one must have known it.

To have that sense of one's intrinsic worth which constitutes self-respect is potentially to have everything; the ability to discriminate, to love and to remain indifferent. To lack it is to be locked within oneself, paradoxically incapable of either love or indifference. If we do not respect ourselves, we are on the one hand forced to despise those who have so few resources as to consort with us, so little perception as to remain blind to our fatal weaknesses. On the other, we are peculiarly in thrall to everyone we see, curiously determined to live out—since our self-image is untenable—their false notions of us. We flatter ourselves by thinking this compulsion to please others an attractive trait: a gift for imaginative empathy, evidence of our willingness to give. Of *course* I will play Francesca to your Paolo, Helen Keller to anyone's Annie Sullivan: no expectation is too misplaced, no role too ludicrous. At the mercy of those we cannot but hold in contempt, we play roles doomed to failure before they are begun, each defeat generating fresh despair at the urgency of divining and meeting the next demand made upon us.

It is the phenomenon sometimes called "alienation from self." In its advanced 12 stages, we no longer answer the telephone, because someone might want something; that we could say *no* without drowning in self-reproach is an idea alien to this game. Every encounter demands too much, tears the nerves, drains the will, and the specter of something as small as an unanswered letter arouses such disproportionate guilt that answering it becomes out of the question. To assign unanswered letters their proper weight, to free us from the expectations of others, to give us back to ourselves—there lies the great, the singular power of self-respect. Without it, one eventually discovers the final turn of the screw: one runs away to find oneself, and finds no one at home.

## PERSONAL WORTH

E.J. Dionne, Jr.

Which would you prefer kids to learn: **self-respect** or **self-esteem?**

I'd make a case that this is not an interesting question only about words but also about philosophy—and perhaps even psychology. The evidence is that self-esteem now far outstrips self-respect in the public discourse—by a huge margin, if my Internet and newspaper searches are any indication. But is self-esteem's apparent victory over self-respect in the conceptual wars a good thing? I'd claim that it's not, though I'd welcome arguments to the contrary.

The word "esteem" does have a noble sound to it, and in the dictionaries, its meaning overlaps with that of the word, "respect." The *New College Edition of the American Heritage Dictionary*, for instance, defines esteem as "to regard as of a high order, think of with respect; prize." Respect, in turn, is defined as "to feel or show esteem for, to honor."

But Ronald Thiemann, dean of Harvard University's Divinity School, notes that the ancient meanings of the two words suggest a difference in emphasis.

In the old "cultures of honor," he said, esteem usually attached to rank. "The king deserved esteem no matter what he did," Dr. Thiemann said. The implication for self-esteem is that "I deserve esteem no matter what I do." Respect, on the other hand, was earned by behaving in a certain way and, he argues, also by accepting limits on one's behavior. Nobody out there needs to be convinced of how big the idea of self-esteem has become. But if you surf the Net, you might be astonished nonetheless at the range of books, activities and organizations that promise to help you raise your self-esteem—or somebody else's.

This being America, there's a National Association for Self-Esteem whose purpose is "to fully integrate self-esteem into the fabric of American society so that every individual, no matter what their age or background, experiences personal worth and happiness." There's the Self-Esteem Shop Online (*www.selfesteemshop.com*), which offers titles such as *Parents as Therapeutic Partners, 101 Ways to Be a Special Mom* and *Cutting Loose: Why Women Who End Their Marriages Do So Well.*

Self-esteem has entered the vocabulary in part as a response by members of groups that have suffered oppression or discrimination to what they see as society's effort to keep them down, and diminish their sense of self-worth. To the extent that the self-esteem movement is about the insistence that all human beings are worthy of respect—from themselves and others—the movement can be seen as a positive force.

My crankiness on the relative merit of self-respect over self-esteem is rooted in something else—the arrogance that can go along with too much self-esteem. As Martha Minow, a Harvard law professor and author of *Not Only for Myself*, explains it, the first definition of esteem "is about ranking, and if you add the 'self' to esteem, it's how you rank yourself." High self-esteem, in other words, can mean ranking yourself above everybody else. That breeds arrogance. Respect, on the other hand, carries a notion of dignity in relationship to others. Can you ever have too much self-respect?

Elisabeth Lasch-Quinn, a historian at Syracuse University, points to another aspect of self-esteem—it reflects the triumph of our therapeutic era.

Therapy is aimed at making people "feel good, feel comfortable." That's why you want self-esteem. "But the drive for self-respect is completely opposite in every way" she says. "It means being uncomfortable because you're in struggle, trying to live up to a standard of excellence or remaining true to your most deeply held moral beliefs."

Following from this, there is a vigorous debate among educators over whether teaching self-esteem helps kids learn by making them believe they can and are personally worthy or whether, on the contrary, the process of learning, performing tasks well and treating others decently must come prior to self-esteem (or, as I'd prefer, self-respect).

Lasch-Quinn suggests that if you want to trace the trajectory of ideas in American education, you could contrast the 19th century's emphasis on "character building" with the late-20th-century focus on self-esteem.

Minow's interest in this subject was inspired by the much-cited thought of the first-century sage Hillel: "If I am not for myself, who will be? If I am only for myself, who am I? If not now, when?" Of course we should have respect and if you must, some esteem for ourselves. But in my gut, I fear that if we spend a few more decades promoting self-esteem, we might convince ourselves to forget that there's anyone of value out there—other than ourselves. "We can't have respect for ourselves if we're only for ourselves," Minow says. "We become egotistical selfish beasts." To feel that way would lower our self-esteem—and our self-respect, too.

# UNIT SIX

## *The Affirmative Argument*

# INTRODUCTION

The argument part of the phrase *affirmative argument* has been defined in earlier chapters and in *IAW*; the affirmative argument is a special type of argument. The word affirmative comes from a French verb that means "to firm up," so an affirmative argument is one designed to intensify or to strengthen a position that your audience has already taken on your issue. The affirmative argument can be more broadly construed as one written to an audience that is not opposed to one's position; that is, written to an audience who agrees with—or at least does not disagree with—your perspectives.

At first glance, writing to an audience who agrees with your position may sound as if it is a waste of time: Why should you bother to argue with people who agree with your position? If you look closely at essays, articles, editorials, or other forms of persuasive argument, however, you will see that many, if not most, of them appear to be written to audiences who agree with the position being presented or are at most mildly at odds with that position. Think back on your own experiences with persuasive argument; you will probably notice that there have been few times where you were able to change someone's perspective on an issue completely. Most effective persuasive arguments begin with an audience that is sympathetic.

So, let's return to the question of why one writes to an audience who supports one's position. The first, and most obvious reason, is to strengthen their belief in a position. Religious leaders, for example, regularly argue in favor of a particular action or behavior to groups who believe as they do. A second reason one might argue to a sympathetic audience would be to modify their perspective on one area of the issue. For example, if you have a group of sociologists who believe that teenagers convicted of crimes should not be sent to prison but to rehabilitation programs, you might argue that teenagers convicted of crimes should be sent to rehabilitation programs rather than jails, *except* for those who commit murder.

In order to strengthen or modify your audience's beliefs, you will need to use the rhetorical tools you have already learned and add some new ones to your kit. The following chapter's articles have been selected to illustrate some of these new skills you will be developing. The first section gives you three individual examples of arguments designed to strengthen or modify their audiences' existing attitudes. The second section offers three pairs of articles—essays which have been written on the same issue, but from different perspectives and for different audiences. These allow you to see some of the ways an argument can be shaped for a particular, sympathetic audience. The third section's selections illustrate some powerful rhetorical tools: figures of speech. Two of the articles in this section are speeches; they were intended to be heard and only secondarily to be read. They show you another approach to thinking about your audience; that is, how will your audience come to your argument—will they hear it? Read it? Will they see your argument in conjunction with an on-going dialog (as is explicitly the case with the first article in this section)? The final section introduces some more light-hearted, but powerful, approaches to persuasion: satire, parody, marked styles, and humor. These pieces vary more in their length, wording, and content than do the other articles of the sections, but each makes a clear argument. The affirmative arguments made here are different in nature from the preceding ones. Instead of extolling the virtues of their own perspectives, the authors show the problems or fallacies with other positions. This approach is affirmative because the authors expect to strengthen their audiences' agreement by showing the pitfalls in the opposition.

**Nancy O. Dickson**

# I

# *Presenting the Affirmative Argument*

The first three articles in this unit offer examples of affirmative arguments addressed to particular audiences.

## WHAT OUR EDUCATION SYSTEM NEEDS IS MORE F'S

Carl Singleton

> *With this essay, Carl Singleton joined an on-going debate being conducted in* The Chronicle of Higher Education, *a journal for postsecondary educators. Here Singleton responds to previously proposed approaches to problems in the American educational system. Although he rejects earlier proposals, he does not see his audience as antagonistic. Rather, by drawing on the common goal of all educators—to provide the best possible education for students—he establishes a bond with his audience.*
>
> *As you read, pay attention to the ways Singleton identifies with his audience. What clues can you find in the article itself that tell you who his audience is? Note your own responses to the essay. What are your reactions? What tells you you are not the intended audience? How would he have to modify his argument for an audience of students? Parents?*

I suggest that instituting merit raises, getting back to basics, marrying the university to industry, and the other recommendations will not achieve measurable success [in restoring quality to American education] until something even more basic is returned to practice. The immediate need for our educational system from prekindergarten through post-Ph.D. is not more money or better teaching but simply a widespread giving of F's.

Before hastily dismissing the idea as banal and simplistic, think for a moment about the implications of a massive dispensing of failing grades. It would dramatically, emphatically, and immediately force into the open every major issue related to the inadequacies of American education.

Let me make it clear that I recommend giving those F's—by the dozens, hundreds, thousands, even millions—only to students who haven't learned the required material. The basic problem of our educational system is the common practice of giving credit where none has been earned, a practice that has resulted in the sundry faults delineated by all the reports and studies over recent years. Illiteracy among high-school graduates is growing because those students have been passed rather than flunked; we have low-quality teaching because of low-quality teachers who never should have been certified in the first place; college students have to take basic reading, writing, and mathematics courses because they never learned those skills in classrooms from which they never should have been granted egress.

School systems have contributed to massive ignorance by issuing unearned passing grades over a period of some 20 years. At first there was tolerance of students who did not fully measure up (giving D's to students who should have received firm F's); then our grading system continued to deteriorate (D's became C's, and B became the average grade); finally we arrived at total accommodation (come to class and get your C's, laugh at my jokes and take home B's).

Higher salaries, more stringent certification procedures, getting back to basics will have little or no effect on the problem of quality education unless and until we insist, as a profession, on giving F's whenever students fail to master the material.

Sending students home with final grades of F would force most parents to deal with the realities of their children's failure while it is happening and when it is yet possible to do something about it (less time on TV, and more time on homework, perhaps?). As long as it is the practice of teachers to pass students who should not be passed, the responsibility will not go home to the parents, where, I hope, it belongs. (I am tempted to make an analogy to then Gov. Lester Maddox's statement some years ago about prison conditions in Georgia—"We'll get a better grade of prisons when we get a better grade of prisoners"—but I shall refrain.)

Giving an F where it is deserved would force concerned parents to get themselves away from the TV set, too, and take an active part in their children's education. I realize, of course, that some parents would not help; some cannot help. However, Johnny does not deserve to pass just because Daddy doesn't care or is ignorant. Johnny should pass only when and if he knows the required material.

Giving an F whenever and wherever it is the only appropriate grade would force principals, school boards, and voters to come to terms with cost as a factor in improving our educational system. As the numbers of students at various levels were increased by those not being passed, more money would have to be spent to accommodate them. We could not be accommodating them in the old sense of passing them on, but by keeping them at one level until they did in time, one way or another, learn the material.

Insisting on respecting the line between passing and failing would also require us to demand as much of ourselves as of our students. As every teacher knows, a failed student can be the product of a failed teacher.

Teaching methods, classroom presentations, and testing procedures would have to be of a very high standard—we could not, after all, conscionably give F's if we have to go home at night thinking it might somehow be our own fault.

The results of giving an F where it is deserved would be immediately evident. There would be no illiterate college graduates next spring—none. The same would be true of high-school graduates, and consequently next year's college freshmen—*all* of them—would be able to read.

I don't claim that giving F's will solve all of the problems, but I do argue that unless and until we start failing those students who should be failed, other suggested solutions will make little progress toward improving education. Students in our schools and colleges should be permitted to pass only after they have fully met established standards; borderline cases should be retained.

The single most important requirement for solving the problems of education in America today is the big fat F, written decisively in red ink millions of times in schools and colleges across the country.

# SINKING FAST: HOW FACTORY TRAWLERS ARE DESTROYING U.S. FISHERIES

Rob King

*This article, taken from the Greenpeace web page, appears to have a dual agenda: first, to strengthen the ideas and attitudes of an audience that already supports Greenpeace's mission; and second to provide information and to persuade an audience that is uncommitted on the issue. What in this excerpt tells you that the article is not written to change the minds of, for example, commercial fishermen?*

*As you read, look at the way the author strengthens his ethos through the use of documentation and citation. Pay attention to the language used—what are the author's assumptions about his audience's education level? Although you have only an excerpt of a longer article, based on what you have read, what do you think the author's solution to this problem might be?*

## THE GLOBAL FISHING CRISIS

### Overfishing and Fisheries Collapse

For the first time in this century, world marine fish catches are declining. The downward trend in marine productivity stands in stark contrast to the remarkable growth in world catches during most of this century—from about 3 million tons in 1900 to a high of 86 million tons in 1989, when harvests peaked. To fisheries experts, recent declines are a warning that current levels of exploitation have exceeded the productive limits of many of the world's marine ecosystems.[1] A 1990 U.N. survey of world fisheries confirmed that view, classifying nearly every commercial species it surveyed as fully exploited, over-exploited, or depleted.

Then, in 1992, the unimaginable happened: after being fished without interruption for almost 500 years, one of the world's most productive fisheries, the Canadian Grand Banks cod fishery of Newfoundland and Labrador, was closed. A resource that once seemed inexhaustible, and whose abundance was legendary, has been fished to the verge of commercial extinction and remains closed today. The immediate impact has thrown 40,000 people out of work in the fishing communities of Canada's maritime provinces, at a cost to the Canadian public of $2 billion in unemployment assistance and retraining programs. The long-term costs of social dislocation, lost biological diversity, and potential ecosystem collapse have yet to be assessed.

The story of the Grand Banks cod fishery is only the most spectacular recent example of a phenomenon seen in other commercial fisheries across the North Atlantic, the North Pacific and Bering Sea, and the west coast of Africa, where four decades of historically unprecedented exploitation have been conducted by the industrial fishing fleets of Europe, the former Soviet Union, and Japan. Today, about 70%

of the world's marine fish stocks are considered heavily exploited, over-exploited, depleted or slowly recovering, and nine of the world's seventeen major fishing grounds are in serious decline. Most are in the developed countries of the Northern Hemisphere, where these fleets have operated the longest.[2]

Fisheries collapse on this scale only becomes intelligible when we understand the extent of industrial fishing operations in recent decades, though other factors contribute to the decline and intensify its effects locally. Complex interactions between global climate and ocean cycles, such as the El Nino, can disrupt marine currents and alter the abundance of microscopic plant and animal life which form the base of the ocean food chain, with profound effects. Destruction of coastal habitat and spawning grounds has cascading effects throughout the marine ecosystem, as do industrial and agricultural pollution. All of these factors are at work today, and they prove particularly lethal in semi-enclosed, low-energy marine environments such as the Baltic Sea and the Black Sea.[3]

Overwhelmingly, however, the global fisheries crisis is a product of industrial overfishing. Modern factory fleets have transformed fishing into a globalized extraction industry dominated by multinational corporations and industrial economies of scale. Their combined fish-catching capacity is such that major fishing nations of the European Union could cut their fishing fleets by 40%, and Norway by 60%, with no reduction in harvests.[4] In the United States, overcapacity is a problem in many major fisheries; in the largest U.S. fishery, the North Pacific pollock fishery off Alaska, the Seattle-based factory trawling fleet has the capacity to harvest two to three times the total allowable catch every year.[5] In every major fishing nation the situation is the same: too many boats and too much fishing pressure on already stressed stocks are accelerating the downward spiral of fisheries production.

## Subsidizing Destructive Fishing

Governments everywhere are responsible for promoting and subsidizing overexpansion of national fishing fleets. The European Union alone increased spending on its commercial fleets from $80 million in 1983 to over half a billion dollars a year in 1990, one-fifth of which went to boat building or refitting.[6] By the early 1990s, Japan had extended an estimated $19 billion worth of credit to its overbuilt commercial fleets.[7] In the United States, $1.6 billion of government and private investment was used to build up the domestic factory trawler fleet to fish in Alaskan waters; now the U.S. government is financing the export of surplus fleet capacity to Russian waters. In some cases, as in Canada and the U.S., fisheries collapse on the Grand Banks and Georges Bank has forced national governments to consider boat buyback programs in order to reduce fishing pressure. Overall, the world fishing fleets receive direct or indirect government support in excess of $50 billion every year.[8]

Over-investment in boats led to a doubling of the world's commercial fishing fleet between 1970-89, when new tonnage was added at an average rate of 4.6% per year. In the same period total marine landings increased from 60 million metric tons to over 86 million metric tons in the peak year of 1989, at an annual rate of only 2.4%.[9] In other words, new fishing capacity was being added at nearly twice the rate of increase in total catches. Today catches are declining, and the reason is a worldwide fleet capacity grossly in excess of what the oceans can sustain.

The most powerful vessels in the world fishing fleet were introduced beginning in the 1950s. Large stern-trawling and processing factory ships, commonly known as "factory trawlers," are the most efficient fish-catching machines in the world. A modern "supertrawler" can catch 400 tons of fish per tow in the largest nets; and process 50–80 tons or more of product per day. Mobility and state-of-the-art electronic gear allow them to track schools of fish and maintain high catch totals even as stocks are declining overall. Mobility also allows them to escape quota restrictions and depleted stocks in one ocean by moving to new fishing grounds in any part of the globe. It is this class of vessel which poses the most serious threat to fisheries around the world today.

## References

1. *Economist*, March 19, 1994: 21.
2. *FAO*, "Review of the State of the World Fishery Resources," 1995.
3. S. M. Garcia and C. Newton, "Current Situation, Trends and Prospects In World Capture Fisheries," *FAO*, June 1994:15–16.
4. *Economist*, March 19, 1994: 21.
5. Greenpeace Inc. (USA), 1996. Extrapolated from calculations of the factory trawler catch and the number of days in the off shore pollock season for 1994.
6. *Economist*, March 19th, 1994: 13.
7. *Economist*, March 19, 1994: 21.
8. Peter Weber, "Worldwatch Paper 120," July 1994: 8.
9. S. M. Garcia and C. Newton, "Current Situation, Trends and Prospects In World Capture Fisheries," *FAO*, June 1994: 18–19.

# MYSTIQUE AND MISTAKES

Abigail Trafford

*Trafford is editor of and regular columnist for the Health Section of The Washington Post. Although it might appear at first that she is writing to persuade motorcyclists to wear helmets, you will see, if you look more closely, that her audience is the "tax-paying public" whom she urges to push for more stringent laws concerning helmets. As you read, notice the ways she tries to make her audience understand the resistance they will face from bikers who reject helmets. Look also at the familiar figures of speech she uses. Who does she exclude from her audience? How does she establish her ethos?*

Evel Knievel and "Easy Rider," the smell of leather and thirst for freedom. Elvis Presley and King Hussein, the suntanned look, the feel of metal. Hell's Angels and James Dean—the biker mystique of noise, youth, sweat and . . .

Brains splattering on the pavement.

For all the rough glamour of riding a motorcycle, suffering a head injury is a major risk if you crash and you're not wearing a helmet. Decades of research have shown that helmets protect riders from serious head injuries.

Yet a number of bikers are enraged that anyone would tell them they have to wear helmets. Their opposition is based not on medical grounds but the principle of individual rights and personal freedom.

House Speaker Newt Gingrich explained it best when, according to news reports, he promised a crowd of 1,500 bandanna-and-leather bikers at the recent Republican Convention that the GOP would oppose laws that require riders to wear helmets. "This party's about freedom. It's about your opportunity to go out and work your heart out and enjoy yourself, lead the kind of life you want," he said.

This captures the essence of the debate on many behavioral health issues, whether it's smoking in office buildings, having unprotected sex, playing Little League baseball or riding a motorcycle without a helmet. In arguments from family rooms to city hall, individual freedom is pitted against intrusive rules. One side argues for the right of the individual to make choices about personal behavior—even foolish ones like smoking or not wearing a helmet. The other side calls for a government or parental role in influencing individual behaviors that present a burden to the society at large.

To emergency room physicians and highway safety experts, the medical case for motorcycle helmet use is overwhelming. To insist on feeling the wind through your hair in the name of individual rights is just "dumb and dumber," says Arthur L. Kellermann, director of the Emory University Center for Injury Control in Atlanta. "It requires a suspension of reality to make this kind of argument."

The reality, he says, is that without strong helmet laws, riders suffer more deaths and serious head injuries. According to estimates by the National Highway Traffic Safety Administration, an unhelmeted rider who has an accident is 40 percent more likely to suffer a fatal head injury and 15 percent more likely to incur nonfatal brain damage. Only about 50 percent of riders wear helmets voluntarily. But in states where a helmet law has been enacted, helmet use approaches 100 percent. As Allan Williams, senior vice president for research at the Insurance Institute for Highway Safety says: "Helmets are very effective. The evidence is very clear. It's common sense."

A study of motorcycle crashes in Nebraska concluded that the reinstitution of the state's helmet law in 1989 had resulted in fewer "fatalities and severe head injuries," according to a report in the Annals of Emergency Medicine. The percentage of serious brain damage among injured riders was "much lower among helmeted motorcyclists (5 percent) than among unhelmeted cyclists (14 percent)," concluded physicians at the University of Nebraska Medical Center.

In California, fatal crashes decreased by more than 35 percent after a 1992 helmet law was enacted, the *Journal of the American Medical Association* reported.

"Our results point uniformly to the effectiveness of unrestricted motorcycle helmet uses laws [with] . . . decreases in motorcycle fatalities . . . head injuries and head injury severity," concluded researchers at the Southern California Injury Prevention Research Center at UCLA.

To be sure, most people who ride motorcycles do not have crashes and motorcycle deaths have been declining since 1980. The 2,135 fatalities reported in 1995 accounted for 5 percent of all motor vehicle deaths.

Still, the Easy Rider life puts you on the edge. It's 20 times riskier to ride on a motorcycle than in a car. Most bikers are young and male. The consequences of a long-term head injury can be devastating.

It gets down to personal choices. Motorcycle mystique has great appeal. My godson started down the Harley culture road by racing dirt bikes in a cornfield in Potomac. But by age 25 he made a pact with a friend to swear off the steel beast. Too many friends in too many accidents, often caused by drivers in cars, he explains. "Sure it's one of the highest highs in the world . . . an adrenaline rush-a-rama. It's tremendous freedom. But anybody's mistake and you're dead."

A significant part of a person's health status is determined by behavior. For those who want to smoke, or drink to excess, or take drugs, or ride a motorcycle without a helmet, it's easy to embrace the principle of individual rights. The question of personal responsibility is more difficult to answer.

In the case of motorcycle injuries, it's usually the tax-paying public that has to pick up the pieces, because many bikers have no private funds to take care of themselves if they are injured. In the Nebraska study, more than 40 percent of injured motorcyclists lacked health insurance or received Medicaid or Medicare. More than 45 percent of motorcyclists treated at Massachusetts General Hospital had no insurance.

That's one reason society has an interest in setting standards for personal behavior. Ultimately society pays the bill. But as every student of human nature knows, when it comes to risky behaviors that make people feel good, it's hard to make people just say no.

# II

## Pairs of Articles

*As you read these two articles, pay attention to the fundamental points of agreement between the two; both authors, for example, agree that we are in the middle of an electronic revolution, a major cultural shift that will have profound effects on all our lives. Look at the language they use (and take the time to look up the words you don't know): what assumptions do both authors make about their audiences' vocabularies? What does this tell you about their intended audience? Both authors use the hive as a metaphor, but they do so with different objectives. Look at the titles. What can you tell about the authors' intended audiences from these titles? Further clues to the authors' assumptions about their audiences can be found in the final paragraphs: Birkerts quotes Stephen Dedalus (a character in James Joyce's* Ulysses*), while Kelly cites George Orwell (as an example of someone who was wrong about computerization). As you read, try to formulate each author's "pro" statement—his thesis or argument.*

## from THE GUTENBERG ELEGIES: THE FATE OF READING IN AN ELECTRONIC AGE

Sven Birkerts

The digital future is upon us. From our President on down, people are smitten, more than they have been with anything in a very long time. I can't open a newspaper without reading another story about the Internet, the information highway. The dollar, not the poet, is the antenna of the race, and right now the dollar is all about mergers and acquisitions: the fierce battles being waged for control of the system that will allow us, soon enough, to cohabit in the all but infinite information space. The dollar is smart. It is betting that the trend will be a juggernaut, unstoppable; that we are collectively ready to round the corner into a new age. We are not about to turn from this millennial remaking of the world; indeed, we are all excited to see just how much power and ingenuity we command. By degrees—it is happening year by year, appliance by appliance—we are wiring ourselves into a gigantic hive.

When we look at the large-scale shift to an electronic culture, looking as if at a time-lapse motion study, we can see not only how our situation has come about but also how it is in our nature that it should have. At every step—this is clear—we trade for ease. And ease is what quickly swallows up the initial strangeness of a new medium or tool. Moreover, each accommodation paves the way for the next. The telegraph must have seemed to its first users a surpassingly strange device, but its newfangledness was overridden by its usefulness. Once we had accepted the idea of mechanical transmission over distances, the path was clear for the telephone. Again, a monumental transformation: Turn select digits on a dial and hear the voice of another human being. And on it goes, the inventions coming gradually, one by one, allowing the society to adapt. We mastered the telephone, the television with its few networks running black-and-white programs. And although no law required citizens to own or use either, these technologies did in a remarkably short time achieve near total saturation.

We are, then, accustomed to the process; we take the step that will enlarge our reach, simplify our communication, and abbreviate our physical involvement in some task or chore. The difference between the epoch of early modernity and the present is—to simplify drastically—that formerly the body had time to accept the graft, the new organ, whereas now we are hurtling forward willy-nilly, assuming that if a technology is connected with communications or information processing it must be good, we must need it. I never cease to be astonished at what a mere two decades have brought us. Consider the evidence. Since the early 1970s we have seen the arrival of— we have accepted, deemed all but indispensable—personal computers, laptops, telephone-answering machines, calling cards, fax machines, cellular phones, VCRs, modems, Nintendo games, E-mail, voice mail, camcorders, and CD players. Very quickly, with almost no pause between increments, these circuit-driven tools and entertainments have moved into our lives, and with a minimum rippling of the waters, really—which, of course, makes them seem natural, even inevitable. Which perhaps they are. Marshall McLuhan called improvements of this sort "extensions of man," and this is their secret. We embrace them because they seem a part of us, an enhancement. They don't seem to challenge our power so much as add to it.

I am startled, though, by how little we are debating the deeper philosophical ramifications. We talk up a storm when it comes to policy issues—who should have jurisdiction, what rates may be charged—and there is great fascination in some quarters with the practical minutiae of functioning, compatibility, and so on. But why do we hear so few people asking whether we might not *ourselves* be changing, and whether the changes are necessarily for the good?

In our technological obsession we may be forgetting that circuited interconnectedness and individualism are, at a primary level, inimical notions, warring terms. Being "on line" and having the subjective experience of depth, of existential coherence, are mutually exclusive situations. Electricity and inwardness are fundamentally discordant. Electricity is, implicitly, of the moment—*now*. Depth, meaning, and the narrative structuring of subjectivity—these are *not* now; they flourish only in that order of time Henri Bergson called "duration." Duration is deep time, time experienced without the awareness of time passing. Until quite recently—I would not want to put a date to it—most people on the planet lived mainly in terms of duration: time not artificially broken, but shaped around natural rhythmic cycles; time bound to the integrated functioning of the senses.

We have destroyed that duration. We have created invisible elsewheres that are as immediate as our actual surroundings. We have fractured the flow of time, layered it into competing simultaneities. We learn to do five things at once or pay the price. Immersed in an environment of invisible signals and operations, we find it as unthinkable to walk five miles to visit a friend as it was once unthinkable to speak across that distance through a wire.

My explanation for our blithe indifference to the inward consequences of our becoming "wired" is simple. I believe that we are—biologically, neuropsychologically—creatures of extraordinary adaptability. We fit ourselves to situations, be they ones of privation or beneficent surplus. And in many respects this is to the good. The species is fit because it knows how to fit.

But there are drawbacks as well. The late Walker Percy made it his work to explore the implications of our constant adaptation. Over and over, in his fiction as well as his speculative essays, he asks the same basic questions. As he writes in the opening of his essay, "The Delta Factor,": "Why does man feel so sad in the twentieth century? Why does man feel so bad in the very age when, more than in any other age, he has succeeded in satisfying his needs and making over the world for his own use?" One of his answers is that the price of adaptation is habit, and that habit—habit of perception as well as behavior—distances the self from the primary things that give meaning and purpose to life. We accept these gifts of technology, these labor-saving devices, these extensions of the senses, by adapting and adapting again. Each improvement provides a new level of abstract to which we accommodate ourselves. Abstraction is, however, a movement away from the natural given—a step away from our fundamental selves rooted for millennia in an awe before the unknown, a fear and trembling in the face of the outer dark. We widen the gulf, and if at some level we fear the widening, we respond by investing more of our faith in the systems we have wrought.

We sacrifice the potential life of the solitary self by enlisting ourselves in the collective. For this is finally even more than the saving of labor—what these systems are all about. They are not only extensions of the sense; they are extensions of the senses that put us in touch with the extended senses of others. The ultimate point of the ever-expanding electronic web is to bridge once and for all the individual solitude that has hitherto always set the terms of existence. Each appliance is a strand, another addition to the virtual place wherein we will all find ourselves together. Telephone, fax, computer networks, E-mail, interactive television—these are the components out of which the hive is being built. The end of it all, the *telos*, is a kind of amniotic environment of impulses, a condition of connectedness. And in time—I don't know how long it will take—it will feel as strange (and exhilarating) for a person to stand momentarily free of it as it feels now for a city dweller to look up at night and see a sky full of stars.

Whether this sounds dire or not depends upon your assumptions about the human condition—assumptions, that is, in the largest sense. For those who ask, with Gauguin, "Who are we? Why are we here? Where are we going?"—and who feel that the answering of those questions is the grand mission of the species—the prospect of a collective life in an electronic hive is bound to seem terrifying. But there are others, maybe even a majority, who have never except fleetingly posed those same questions, who have repressed them so that they might "get on," and who gravitate toward that life because they see it as a way of vanquishing once and for all the anxious gnawings they feel whenever any intimations of depth sneak through the inner barriers.

My core fear is that we are, as a culture, as a species, becoming shallower; that we have turned from depth—from the Judeo-Christian premise of unfathomable mystery—and are adapting ourselves to the ersatz security of a vast lateral connectedness. That we are giving up on wisdom, the struggle for which has for millennia been central to the very idea of culture, and that we are pledging instead to a faith in the web.

There is, finally, a tremendous difference between communication in the instrumental sense and communion in the affective, soul-oriented sense. Somewhere we have gotten hold of the idea that the more all-embracing we can make our communications networks, the closer we will be to that connection that we long for deep down. For change us as they will, our technologies have not yet eradicated that flame of a desire—not merely to be in touch, but to be, at least figuratively, embraced, known and valued not abstractly but in presence. We seem to believe that our instruments can get us there, but they can't. Their great power is all in the service of division and acceleration. They work in—and create—an unreal time that has nothing to do with the deep time in which we thrive: the time of history, tradition, ritual, art, and true communion.

The proselytizers have shown me in their vision, and in my more susceptible moods I have felt myself almost persuaded. I have imagined what it could be like, our toil and misery replaced by a vivid, pleasant dream. Fingers tap keys, oceans of fact and sensation get downloaded, are dissolved through the nervous system. Bottomless wells of data are accessed and manipulated, everything flowing at circuit speed. Gone the rock in the field, the broken hoe, the grueling distances. "History," said Stephen Daedalus, "is a nightmare from which I am trying to awaken." This may be the awakening, but it feels curiously like the fantasies that circulate through our sleep. From deep in the heart I hear the voice that says, "Refuse it."

## from OUT OF CONTROL: THE RISE OF NEO-BIOLOGICAL CIVILIZATION

Kevin Kelly

If twentieth-century science can be said to have a single icon, it is the Atom. As depicted in the popular mind, the symbol of the Atom is stark: a black dot encircled by the hairline orbits of several smaller dots. The Atom whirls alone, the epitome of singleness. It is the metaphor for individuality. At its center is the animus, the It, the life force, holding all to their appropriate whirling station. The Atom stands for power and knowledge and certainty. It conveys the naked power of simplicity.

The iconic reign of the Atom is now passing. The symbol of science for the next century is the dynamic Net. The icon of the Net, in contradistinction to the Atom, has no center. It is a bunch of dots connected to other dots, a cobweb of arrows pouring into one another, squirming together like a nest of snakes, the restless image fading at indeterminate edges. The Net is the archetype displayed to represent all circuits, all intelligence, all interdependence, all things economic and social and ecological, all communications, all democracy, all groups, all large systems. This icon is slippery, ensnaring the unwary in its paradox of no beginning, no end, no center.

The Net conveys the logic of both the computer and nature. In nature, the Net finds form in, for example, the beehive. The hive is irredeemably social, unabashedly of many minds, but it decides as a whole when to swarm and where to move. A hive possesses an intelligence that none of its parts does. A single honeybee brain operates with a memory of six days; the hive as a whole operates with a memory of three months, twice as long as the average bee lives.

Although many philosophers in the past have suspected that one could abstract the laws of life and apply them to machines, it wasn't until computers and human-made systems became as complex as living things—as intricately composed as a beehive—that it was possible to prove this. Just as a beehive functions as if it were a single sentient organism, so does an electronic hive, made up of millions of buzzing, dim-witted personal computers, behave like a single organism. Out of networked parts—whether of insects, neutrons, or chips—come learning, evolution, and life. Out of a planet-wide swarm of silicon calculators comes an emergent self-governing intelligence: the Net.

I live on computer networks. The network of networks—the Net, also known as the Internet—links several million personal computers around the world. No one knows exactly how many millions are connected, or even how many intermediate nodes there are. The Internet Society made an educated guess last year that the Net was made up of 1.7 million host computers and 17 million users. Like the beehive, the Net is controlled by no one: No one is in charge. The Net is, as its users are proud to boast, the largest functioning anarchy in the world. Every day hundreds of millions of messages are passed between its members without the benefit of a central authority.

In addition to a vast flow of individual letters, there exists between its wires that disembodied cyberspace where messages interact, a shared space of written public conversations. Every day authors all over the world add millions of words to an uncountable number of overlapping conversations. They daily build an immense distributed document, one that is under eternal construction, in constant flux, and of fleeting permanence. The users of this media are creating an entirely new writing space, far different from that carved out by a printed book or even a chat around a table. Because of this impermanence, the type of thought encouraged by the Net tends toward the non-dogmatic—the experimental idea, the quip, the global perspective, the interdisciplinary synthesis, and the uninhibited, often emotional, response. Many participants prefer the quality of writing on the Net to book writing because Net writing is of a conversational, peer-to-peer style, frank and communicative, rather than precise and self-consciously literary. Instead of the rigid canonical thinking cultivated by the book, the Net stimulates another way of thinking: telegraphic, modular, nonlinear, malleable, cooperative.

A person on the Internet sees the world in a different light. He or she views the world as decidedly decentralized, every far-flung member a producer as well as a consumer, all parts of it equidistant from all others, no matter how large it gets, and every participant responsible for manufacturing truth out of a noisy cacophony of ideas, opinions, and facts. There is no central meaning, no official canon, no manufactured consent rippling through the wires from which one can borrow a viewpoint. Instead, every idea has a backer, and every backer has an idea, while contradiction, paradox, irony, and multifaceted truth rise up in a flood.

A recurring vision swirls in the shared mind of the Net, a vision that nearly every member glimpses, if only momentarily: of wiring human and artificial minds into one planetary soul. This incipient techno-spiritualism is all the more remarkable because of how unexpected it has been. The Net, after all, is nothing more than a bunch of highly engineered pieces of rock braided together with strands of metal or glass. It is routine technology. Computers, which have been in our lives for twenty years, have made our life faster but not that much different. Nobody expected a new culture, a new thrill, or even a new politics to be born when we married calculating circuits with the ordinary telephone; but that's exactly what happened.

There are other machines, such as the automobile and the air conditioner, that have radically reshaped our lives and the landscape of our civilization. The Net (and its future progeny) is another one of those disrupting machines and may yet surpass the scope of all the others together in altering how we live.

The Net is an organism/machine whose exact size and boundaries are unknown. All we do know is that new portions and new uses are being added to it at such an accelerating rate that it may be more of an explosion than a thing. So vast is this embryonic Net, and so fast is it developing into something else, that no single human can fathom it deeply enough to claim expertise on the whole.

The tiny bees in a hive are more or less unaware of their colony, but their collective hive mind transcends their small bee minds. As we wire ourselves up into a hivish network, many things will emerge that we, as mere neurons in the network, don't expect, don't understand, can't control, or don't even perceive. That's the price for any emergent hive mind.

At the same time the very shape of this network space shapes us. It is no coincidence that the post-modernists arose as the networks formed. In the last half-century a uniform mass market has collapsed into a network of small niches—the result of the information tide. An aggregation of fragments is the only kind of whole we now have. The fragmentation of business markets, of social mores, of spiritual beliefs, of ethnicity, and of truth itself into tinier and tinier shards is the hallmark of this era. Our society is a working pandemonium of fragments—much like the Internet itself.

People in a highly connected yet deeply fragmented society can no longer rely on a central canon for guidance. They are forced into the modern existential blackness of creating their own cultures, beliefs, markets, and identities from a sticky mess of interdependent pieces. The industrial icon of a grand central or a hidden "I am" becomes hollow. Distributed, headless, emergent wholeness becomes the social ideal.

The critics of early computers capitalized on a common fear: that a Big Brother brain would watch over us and control us. What we know now of our own brains is that they too are only networks of mini-minds, a society of dumber minds linked together, and that when we peer into them deeply we find that there is no "I" in charge. Not only does a central-command economy not work: a central-command brain won't either. In its stead, we can make a nation of personal computers, a country of decentralized nodes of governance and thought. Almost every type of large-scale governance we can find, from the body of a giraffe, to the energy regulation in a tidal marsh, to the temperature regulation of a beehive, to the flow of traffic on the Internet, resolves into a swarmy distributed net of autonomous units and heterogeneous parts.

No one has been more wrong about computerization than George Orwell in *1984*. So far, nearly everything about the actual possibility-space that computers have created indicates they are not the beginning of authority but its end. In the process of connecting everything to everything, computers elevate the power of the small player. They make room for the different, and they reward small innovations. Instead of enforcing uniformity, they promote heterogeneity and autonomy. Instead of sucking the soul from human bodies, turning computer users into an army of dull clones, *networked* computers—by reflecting the networked nature of our own brains—encourage the humanism of their users. Because they have taken on the flexibility, adaptability, and self-connecting governance of organic systems, we become more human, not less so, when we use them.

# WOLVES IN YELLOWSTONE

Laura DeLano

> *Laura DeLano, a student at the University of Maryland, has written a pair of essays concerning the fate of the wolves in Yellowstone National Park. The first, written for the Defenders of Wildlife, "The Killing Begins Again?" argues for the continued occupation of the park by the wolves. The second, "Unwanted Guests Are Sent Packing," an article for the* Whipton Daily News, *a newspaper whose audience is predominantly the farmers whose lands abut the park, argues for exterminating the wolves. In both pieces DeLano begins her argument in her titles. Look at the different language selection she uses in the two pieces: "slaughter" in the first piece becomes "removal" in the second.*

## THE KILLING BEGINS AGAIN

### *Audience Analysis*

This piece was written as a special plea to help save the wolves in Yellowstone. It was sent, along with a letter asking for donations, to all those on the Defenders of Wildlife mailing list. In order to be on the mailing list for this publication, one must have already shown support for the causes which they are active in. This means that the people reading are interested in the fate of the environment and the creatures on it.

Do you think that the years of bounty hunters and prize money for endangered wolf pelts are a thing of our past? Well think again. After years of planning and hard work reintroducing gray wolves into Yellowstone, they are now in jeopardy of another mass genocide. On December 12, 1997, Judge Downes ruled that the conservation methods of Bruce Babbitt were illegal and that the reintroduced wolves and their offspring would have to be removed. This would mean either returning the wolves to their homeland in Alberta, Canada, placing them in zoos, or destroying them. The first solution is not possible because the area left behind in Canada when these wolves were moved to the United States has been taken over by other wolf packs. Furthermore, there is no demand for North American gray wolves in zoos. By the process of elimination, slaughter is the only possible option of removal.

Defenders of Wildlife, along with the National Wildlife Federation, filed an appeal on December 30, 1997, which will be tried by Brian O'Neill, the attorney who led the case against the Exxon Corporation following their 1989 Exxon Valdez oil spill ("Defenders Challenge" 1). We are willing to face as many years in court as necessary, taking this matter all the way to the United States Supreme Court if need be. But this will take a great deal of money, which can only come from our faithful supporters.

As Americans, it is our responsibility to set an example for the rest of the world when it comes to saving our endangered species. How can we criticize poachers for killing elephants for their tusks, or South Americans for burning millions of acres of rain forests when we are prepared to slaughter one of our own natural treasures in the interest of profit? Yes, profit. The ranchers' foremost concern when it comes to the wolves in Yellowstone is dollar signs. Rather than take the time and money to develop a way to protect their herds from the natural predators of the land which they have invaded, they would rather place the responsibility on others to remove these animals which are inconveniencing them.

As Mark Van Putten, President of NWF states, "This is a defining issue of right and wrong. . . . It would be morally wrong to exterminate them a second time" (Kluger 3). When the American people were called upon to voice their opinions on the matter of reintroduction, they favored it ("American Say" 1). Well now it is time to back-up your promise made to the wolves.

These magnificent animals were once part of a stable ecosystem in the park before they were subject to the whims of man. First, we nearly slaughtered them out of existence. Then we realized what we were doing was wrong. In effort to compensate for our earlier behavior, we tried to aid the revival of the species by reintroducing them into Yellowstone Park. And now we are expected to begin the cycle all over again with a second wave of killing. Don't you think that it is time we put an end to this vicious cycle?

By supporting the fight to keep the wolves in Yellowstone, you are fighting to conserve one of our greatest natural resources for future generations. Without the graciousness of our supporters, we never would have been able to bring the wolves home in the first place. Please do not abandon this cause at the most critical point, rather continue to show your generosity by continuing to support the efforts of Defenders of Wildlife.

## UNWANTED GUESTS ARE SENT PACKING

### Audience Analysis: *In favor of wolf removal*

> This piece was written to appear on the front page of the *Whipton Daily News*, a local daily newspaper for the small town of Whipton which borders on Yellowstone National Park ground. There are less than 1000 inhabitants of this town and the surrounding areas, of which two-thirds are involved in the cattle industry. Most of them are members of the American Farm Bureau Association, therefore they have anxiously been awaiting a verdict on the trial of the *Farm Bureau Versus Bruce Babbitt*, the man responsible for the wolf reintroduction. In addition, this is the only available news source for these people, so it can be assumed that everyone will not only be reading it, but it will also be the talk of the town.
>
> Note: This paper will be set in the past, as if it is appearing December 13, 1997, the day after the decision was released.

Last night justice was served. After deliberating for nearly three years, on December 12, 1997, Judge Downes ruled in favor of the Farm Bureau in the case, *Farm Bureau v. Babbitt*. For the first time, the haunting cries of the wolves were drowned out by the ecstatic cries of the farmers encompassing Yellowstone National Park.

Whipton's ranchers have been anxiously anticipating this verdict since the Montana, Wyoming, and Idaho Farm Bureau, as well as the American Farm Bureau, filed suit on November 25, 1994, three days after the approval of the plan which would release Canadian gray wolves into Yellowstone National Park ("FB Welcomes" 1). Despite our active pursuit of justice from the onset of this charade, the wolves were released as planned in January 1995.

In a press conference following the verdict, Dean Kleckner, President of The American Farm Bureau Federation, said he was glad that the welfare of the ranchers he represents was finally considered. "This ruling culminates more than three years of litigation on this issue. The ruling vindicates the Farm Bureau's position that the wolf introduction program failed to address the concerns of farmers and ranchers and represented overzealous regulation by the government" ("Wolf Introduction Ruled" 1). According to the decision reached by Judge Downes, and supported by ranchers, all non-native wolves and their offspring will have to be removed from Yellowstone.

The Farm Bureau's case was based upon the Endangered Species Act which states that a species can only be introduced into an area where they no longer exist (Kelly 1). As we can all attest, wolves have always existed in the park. Prior to the release of the Canadian gray wolves, attacks of the livestock by these animals native to the area posed enough of a threat. As Kleckner states, "government workers did not follow the endangered species rule they wrote themselves" ("Wolf Court Case" 1). This victory will hopefully serve as a reminder to the government officials that they too are responsible for following the laws that govern all Americans.

Even though we are one step closer to righting this wrong, most ranchers have already been impacted by the unjust wolf release. In the past three years, over 100 sheep and sixteen cattle have been lost to the insatiable appetite of the wolves ("Wolf Court Case" 1). Even though compensation was granted to these ranchers, this was not a practice that was to continue indefinitely as the wolf population increased. This clearly meant more attacks on livestock with no such reimbursement available in the future if something had not been done to stop the predators.

Yesterday's outcome is evidence that Bruce Babbitt has underestimated the American Farm Bureau. Even though we may be located over a thousand miles from the nation's capital, our voice has definitely been heard loud and clear.

## Bibliography

"Americans Say Wolves Should Stay." National Wildlife Federation 3 Feb. 1998: n. pag. Online. http://www.nwf.org/nrockies/wolves/pollrls.html

Chadwick, Douglas H. "Return of the Gray Wolf." *National Geographic*. vol. 193, no. 5 May 1998: 72–99.

"Defenders Challenge Farm Bureau On Anniversary Of Wolf Reintroduction." Defenders 12 Jan. 1998: n. pag. Online. http://www.defenders.org/pr0ll298.html

"Defenders Will Fight to Save Yellowstone Wolves." *Defenders* vol. 73, no. 1 (1997/1998): 23

"Exxon Valdez Plaintiffs' Attorney Enters Appeal: Conservation Groups Appeal Wolf Extermination Order." *Defenders* 30 Dec. 1997: n. pag. Online. http://www.defenders.org/prl23097.html

"Farmers Relieved by Removal of Gray Wolves." *FARMComm-Farm and Rural News* 5 Jan. 1998: n. pag. Online. http://www.farmcomm.org/98010500.html

"FB Welcomes Judge's Clarification on Wolves." *Farm Bureau News* vol.77, no.4 26 Jan., 1998: n.pag. Online http://www.fb.com/news/f...26/html/fbwelcomes.html

Kelly, David. "Learning to Listen: Illegal government action put gray wolves in danger." *Voice of Agriculture* (1998): n. pag. Online. http://www.fb.com/views/com/listen.html

Kluger, Jeffery. "The Big (Not So Bad) Wolves Of Yellowstone." *Time* 19 Jan. 1998: n. pag. Online. http://www.pathfinder.com/time/maga...0119/nation.the _big_not_so_ba1.html

Maughan, Ralph. "Wolves Released in Idaho." Online. http://www.envirolink.org/arrs/yellowstone2.html

"NWF Howling Mad Over Wolf Removal Order." National Wildlife Federation 13 Dec. 1997: n. pag. Online. http://www.nwf.org/nrockies/wolves/response.html

Putten, Mark Van. "The Wolf Decision—A Blow To Common Sense." National Wildlife Federation (1997) : n. pag. Online. http://www.nwf.org/nrockies/wolves/wolfmvp.html

"Wolf Court Case Big Victory for Farm Bureau." Utah Farm Bureau Federation (1998): n.pag. Online. http://www.fb.com/utfb/lr-wolf.html

"Wolf Introduction Ruled Unlawful." *Farm Bureau News* 22 Dec., 1997: n.pag. Online.

"Wolf Reintroduction in Yellowstone National Park and Central Idaho." National Wildlife Federation (1997): n. pag. Online. http://www.nwf.org/nrockies/wolves/timeline.html

# WOMEN IN COMBAT

Rian Almon

> *Rian Almon, a student at the University of Maryland, has written on the issue of women in combat: one essay, "A Resolution for Women," which supports women's rights to serve in combat, is a speech to be delivered at the national conference of the National Organization for Women; the second, "The Combat 'Privilege,'" is written for* The Stars and Stripes, *a newspaper for service men and women, and opposes women serving in combat.*

## A Resolution for Women

### Persona

For the following article I have assumed the persona of a high-ranking member of the National Organization for Women (NOW). My persona, as a member of NOW, is a devoted feminist who is familiar with many issues relating to women's rights. She is a leader in NOW's campaign for equal rights and opportunities for all women. One particular opportunity she feels women are unfairly denied is the right to serve in combat units in the United States military.

### Audience Analysis

The following speech is written for the audience at the NOW's conference scheduled for December 1999. My audience consists primarily of women in their late twenties and older. These individuals are also members, many of them high ranking, of NOW. The women in the audience are united in the common goal to promote equal opportunities for all women. Many of the members of my audience are familiar with current issues relating to women's rights, and are devoted to combating injustice against women.

Good evening. Tonight I stand before you with mixed emotions. Just three weeks before the New Year I am filled with a sense of accomplishment and a sense of duty. I am proud of this organization and the many advances it fought for and won for women in the past century. We have seen significant growth in areas such as reproductive rights, lesbian rights, and affirmative action. However, this pride is stifled by a heavy burden of responsibility. I assure you that our work at the National Organization for Women is not complete. Women in this country continue to feel the sting of injustice, and the pinch of inequality. Today I'd like to tackle just one of the issues women face in the year 2000. As our New Year's resolution I propose that the United States Government should integrate female soldiers into combat.

The first argument against women in combat that I would like to address is the false notion that women are physically inferior to their male counterparts. Although many men stand by the argument that "bigger is better," I assure you that there is little evidence to support such a theory. The reason being that "with the growing complexity of modern military weapons systems, technical ability and education are becoming far more important than physical strength for determining eligibility or qualifications for many positions" (DeCew 64). I am not suggesting that today's combat is controlled by a "push-button" military, but I do feel that changing technology has shifted some of the emphasis from physical warfare to technological methods (Wilson). Even in cases where direct combat is necessary, physical conditioning is usually an adequate substitute for size. Although it may come as a shock to individuals who throw around the "bigger is better" cliché, history has proven that "size" really "doesn't matter." Take, for instance, the Vietnam War. American troops experienced very little success against the Viet Cong and North Vietnamese, despite the fact that the Americans were usually of much larger stature than their enemies (DeCew 64). Later, in the early 90's, fourteen female Marine officers were presented with Combat Action ribbons for returning fire against Iraqi troops during Operations Desert Storm and Desert Shield. It is through such accomplishments made during the Gulf War that women proved their fitness to serve in combat (Donegan 372).

A second argument aimed at preventing women from gaining combat positions is that women threaten the morale of a traditionally male military. I find this argument to be particularly abhorrent, especially among a society that prides itself on democratic values, because it relies on gender, rather than ability, as the basis for selection. I assure you that "military readiness, especially in emergency situations, is more dependent on leadership, trust, organization for a common goal, the presence of imminent danger, and a willingness to sacrifice, than on any considerations relevant to gender" (DeCew 65). Women should not be excluded from combat based on the unsupported generalization that men work better with men.

A final argument used to prevent women from gaining combat positions is that the inclusion of women in combat will lead to higher rates of sexual misconduct and an increase in discipline problems. Although integrating women into combat may increase instances of love and lust among soldiers, especially on board combat vessels, simple facts of human nature should not be used to ban any individuals from gaining a position they rightly deserve (Eisman). In the past, increased numbers of women have led to an increase in instances of fraternization (Rayner 53). However, "the military's rules concerning sexual behavior are far stricter than those in civilian life" (Noah 40) and if properly enforced, such prohibited behaviors would be lessened. Opponents of women in combat contend that women are also to blame for more serious instances of sexual assault and rape in combat missions. These individuals claim the exclusion of women from combat is actually a preventative measure aimed at protecting women from becoming victims of such crimes. Do not be misled by this argument that incorrectly places the blame on women, rather than their male predators. It is all-male institutions such as the military that are all too often "marred by aggressive behavior that exacerbates tensions" (DeGroot), and women should not be blamed for such attitudes. In addition to such claims, pregnancy is another problem attributed to women. However, if my high-school biology class serves me right, it takes two people—a woman and a MAN—to make a baby. Furthermore, pregnancy leave has little influence on rates of attrition because "women on the average spend a mere one fewer hour per month at work than their male counterparts" (Willens). I suggest that if the military wants to resolve sexual tension, they might want to exclude men and not women.

In conclusion, as members of The National Organization for Women we must work together to ensure women have the same opportunities for advancement as men. Women will never be truly equal if they continue to be excluded from combat. We can't stand by and let this injustice continue. The time for change is NOW!

## THE COMBAT "PRIVILEGE"

### Persona

For the following article I have assumed the persona of a retired Marine Corps Commander. This gentleman was a combat soldier during the Vietnam War, and received the Medal of Honor for his actions in the line of fire. He currently presides on the Marine Corps advisory panel for the Department of Defense. The Commander is adamantly opposed to the integration of women in combat. He knows first hand the responsibilities associated with combat, and does not feel women are capable of completing such tasks. Furthermore, my persona made some of the strongest bonds of his life during Vietnam, and he feels that this would not have occurred in a coed unit.

### Audience Analysis

The following article is written for *The Stars and Stripes*. *The Stars and Stripes* is a reputable veteran's magazine. Although its main audience is veterans, Senators, Congressmen, and other government officials are also primary readers of the periodical. Aside from having served in the Armed Forces, many of these individuals have also participated in combat. These men have a mutual interest in keeping up with issues concerning the military. Furthermore, *The Stars and Stripes* is known for its anti-female sentiment and it is likely that the majority of my reader's share my view that women should be excluded from combat. Despite a largely male audience, there are many women who read *The Stars and Stripes* as overhearers, after it has been "passed along" to them from their husbands or friends.

I am sure many of you, like myself, are familiar with images of war. Even if you have not experienced war first-hand, movies like Steven Spielberg's *Saving Private Ryan* present a relatively accurate portrayal of the horror and brutality of combat. But these pictures are deceiving, in a way, because they are just pictures. They don't tell the whole story. Until you have experienced combat first-hand, as I'm sure many of you have, you can never fully understand what its like to be knee-deep in mud, 20,000 miles from home, dodging bullets coming from "God knows where." I know what it's like because I've been there. It is because of this experience that I left my hometown a cocky kid and came back from Vietnam a man. Today the combat "experience" is at the center of a heated debate. It seems that feminists feel women deserve the "privilege" to serve in combat; that is, if you can call it a privilege. I am writing because I feel otherwise. Women, in my opinion, should be excluded from combat because not only are they physically incapable of completing many of the tasks associated with combat, they also threaten to destroy the cohesive nature of the combat unit.

Before I even attempt to explain the importance of male bonding in combat situations, I would like to point out one undeniable fact: women "simply do not have the physical strength and endurance needed for combat" (Willens). Even feminists cannot deny the fact that obvious physical and biological differences exist between men and women. For instance, the typical female soldier is "on average, about five inches shorter than the male soldier, has half the upper body strength, lower aerobic capacity, and 37% less muscle mass" (Owens). In addition, women also suffer from higher rates of attrition and are four times more likely to ask for leave due to illness (Owens). As a result, female soldiers are held to lower physical standards than male soldiers (United States General Accounting Office). I reject the suggestion that such differences are "minimal" and I assure you that five inches, a lot of upper body strength and 37% muscle mass, do make a difference when carrying a 200 pound wounded soldier a 1/4 mile to safety. I use this example because combat troops, more so than most other divisions of the military, face extreme, often life-threatening circumstances on a regular basis. Male soldiers can never feel fully confident in women's abilities as long as they are held to lesser physical standards (Hackworth). Lowering the standards for combat positions to accommodate women means lowering the standards for the entire military.

My second point is one that is perhaps a bit more difficult to grasp. It is based on the assumption that "a combat unit's very success depends on something that is hard to measure, but too easy to discount: male bonding" (Simons A23). With a United States military that spans fifty states, it is to be expected that most combat units will be composed of individuals from very different social and ethnic backgrounds. The single characteristic that unites these soldiers is the shared experience of being male. A level of comfort develops between men who spend every day together, who eat together, sleep together, fight together and suffer together (Simons A23). I do not doubt that if women were introduced to these combat situations this sense of comfort would be lost due to sexual tension and everyday differences in nature. This opinion is reflected in the statements of Medal of Honor recipients who, when asked what motivated them to overcome great obstacles, most frequently responded "I did it for my buddies," rather than "my country," "my army," or even "my God" (Manzi). I maintain that each of these soldiers, even if they did not know what they were fighting for, knew whom they were fighting for: their fellow soldiers, other men caught in a similar struggle for survival. Although this relationship is difficult to put into words, I assure you that the presence of women in combat will only serve to destroy military morale and decrease military effectiveness.

In conclusion, although my opinion may not be "politically correct" I feel very strongly that women should be excluded from combat. The military is "not designed to be a mirror of society" ("Bush Would Keep Women in Combat"). Military policy should not be decided in the interest of human rights, but rather on the basis of military effectiveness (Mitchell Appendix). When we send our citizens to risk their lives in unfamiliar territories for the sake of our country, we had better be sure we are sending the best.

## Works Cited

"Bush Would Keep Women in Combat." *Human Events* 13 Aug. 1999.

DeCew, Judith Wagner. "The Combat Exclusion and the Role of Women in the Military." *Hypatia* 10.1 (1995) 56–74.

DeGroot, Gerard. "Wanted: More Than a Few Good Women." *The Boston Globe* 5 Sept. 1999.

Donegan, Craig. "New Military Culture." *CQ Researcher* 6.16 (1996) : 361–384.

Eisman, Dale. "Top Admiral Against Women On Subs." *The Virginian-Pilot* 3 Sept. 1999.

Hackworth, John. "Monosex Boot Camp." 20 Oct. 1999 *<http//:www.hackworth.com/index.html>*

Levin, Carl. "Opening Statement of Armed Services Committee Hearing." 29 Sept. 1999. 26 Oct. 1999 *<http://www.senate.gov/levin/floor/092998.htm>*

Luddy, John. "Why the Women-in-Combat Campaign Must Be Resisted." *Human Events* 16 Nov. 1996.

Manzi, Thomas. "Women in Combat: The Opposing View." *The Washington Post* 3 Jan. 1998.

Marks, Alexandra. "US Women in Combat Draw Unfriendly Fire." *Christian Science Monitor.* 18 Apr. 1997.

Mitchell, Brian. *Women in the Military: Flirting with Disaster.* Washington D.C.: Regency Publishing, 1998.

Nantais, Cynthia and Martha Lee. "Women in the U.S. Military: Protectors or Protected?" *Journal of Gender Studies* 8.2 (1999) : 181–192.

Owens, Mackubin T. "Women in Combat." *Human Life Review* Spring 1997.

Noah, Timothy. "Dishonoring the U.S. Uniform." *U.S. News and World Report* 25 Nov. 1996: 41–42.

Priest, Dana. "A Trench Between Women, Jobs." *The Washington Post* 28 Dec. 1997: 1+.

Rayner, Richard. "Women in the Warrior Culture." *The New York Times Magazine* 22 June 1997: 24+.

Simons, Anna. "In War, Let Men be Men." *New York Times* 23 Apr. 1997: A23.

United States. General Accounting Office. *Gender Integration In Basic Training.* Washington: GPO, 1997.

United States. The Navy Public Affairs Library. "Secretary of Defense Aspin Expects to Open New Opportunities for Women with Direct Ground Combat Rule." Washington: GPO, 1994.

Willens, Jake. "Women in the Military." *Intellectual Capital.* 22 Aug. 1997. Center For Defense Information. 20 Oct. 1999.
*<http://www.intellectualcapital.com/isues/issue48/item856.asp>*

Wilson, Barbara A. "Why Not Women in Combat?" 26 Oct. 1999
*<http://www.angelfire.com/ok/4equity?captbarb.html>*

"Women in the Military." 21 July 1999. National Organization for Women. 20 Oct. 1997 *<http://www.now.org/issues/military/policies/wim.html>*

# III

## Figures of Speech

### A GIFT OF OPPRESSION

Leonard Pitts, Jr.

*Pitts is a columnist for the* Chicago Tribune *and the* Detroit Free Press *where this essay first appeared in 1995. How does Pitts create a rapport with his audience? What does he mean by the title? How can "oppression" possibly be a "gift"? Pitts defines himself as intermediary between "young black America" and "people" (those who are not "young black America"). What do the opening paragraphs tell you about his relationships with these two groups?*

This is an open letter to young black America. People are asking me about you again. They're writing and calling, challenging me to explain why you sometimes call each other "nigger," then profess anger and hurt when a white person uses the same word.

They think you're hypocritical. They think you're hypersensitive. They think you should be more like the Italian guy who'll let a friend get away with the word "wop" or the Irish person who, in the spirit of good fun, now and then tolerates being called a "mick."

They think you should emulate those people in other ways, too: Stop whining about the names you are called and the mistreatment you have received. Life here has been no picnic for them, either. They worked, they educated themselves, they moved ahead and assimilated. Why can't you?

But you aren't Irish or Italian, are you? You're African. Skin the color of creamless coffee. Or pecan shell. Or sandy shore. Skin that makes you stand out in a crowd of Europeans like "a fly in the buttermilk," as the old folks used to say.

That's why your forebears and mine were chosen to bear the burden of slavery—the fact that it was beyond their ability to run off and blend in. And there you have the defining difference, the thing that makes our experience unique. With the possible exception of the original tenants of this land, no group of Americans—not Irish, Italian, Chinese, woman nor gay—ever suffered on these shores as we did.

Ten million to 20 million kidnapped from the bosom of home. Half again that many left dead by the horrors of the Middle Passage. Centuries of enslavement, rape, torture, disenfranchisement, theft, poverty, ignorance, murder and hate. And then someone asks in well-meaning innocence why we can't be more like the Irish.

Makes me want to holler.

That's why you call yourself "nigger" sometimes, I know.

Oppression long ago taught us how to build a mansion from a stack of debris, weave a symphony from a moan of pain. Look at the record. Given hog entrails, we made chit'lins. Given agony, we invented the blues. Given the bruising hardness of city streets, we created cool.

And given "nigger," a word white men meant as an emblem of our stupidity, meanness and filth, we made a multipurpose word useful in the expression of everything from anger and humor to sarcasm and fraternity. We made it our word. And the whole weight of history bars white people from using it the way we do—or even understanding it the way we do.

But here's my problem: Unlike chit'lins, unlike cool and unlike the blues, this gift of oppression always took from us more than it gave. Meaning that if there's a certain sense of in-group smugness in greeting your brother as a "nigger," there is also, unspoken between the consonants, an admission that the white man was right when he said we were lower and lesser.

That word is drenched with four centuries of blood and tears. It hates us, even when it issues from our own lips.

And it is time we got beyond self-loathing.

I know what "Action News" says about you. I know how police act like you're a crime waiting to happen. I know the advice the crack man gives, know the terrible things family and friends sometimes say because they don't know better and they don't know you.

Love yourself anyway. Love yourself past the hateful words and the hurtful lies. Love yourself over the empty pockets of poverty and the bare walls of spirit. Love yourself through the narrowness of days and the meanness of nights.

Love yourself with a fierceness and an urgency, and I promise that it will lead you up to this truth: You are the flower of 400 years. You are the dream a slave once had.

And there is no such thing as a nigger.

There never was.

# STATEMENT ON THE ASSASSINATION OF MARTIN LUTHER KING, JR.

Robert F. Kennedy

*Kennedy delivered this speech in Indianapolis, Indiana, on April 4, 1968, following the assassination of civil rights leader Dr. Martin Luther King, Jr. This was a period of great turmoil in this country: the Vietnam War was going badly, and at home anti-war protesters were at their most active. Many people thought that the greatest victories of the Civil Rights movement were behind them, but some, like Kennedy, understood the deep-seated resentment still smoldering from the glacial pace at which change was actually occurring in the lives of African Americans.*

*Kennedy's efforts to avert the riots which followed King's death were unsuccessful and he himself was assassinated shortly after delivering this speech. Either before or after reading this speech you might want to revisit King's "Letter from Birmingham Jail." As you read this address to the nation, pay attention to Kennedy's use of repetition to produce an almost hypnotic rhythm to his prose. What is the effect of this use of language and why do you think he might have chosen it?*

I have bad news for you, for all of our fellow citizens, and people who love peace all over the world, and that is that Martin Luther King was shot and killed tonight.

Martin Luther King dedicated his life to love and to justice for his fellow human beings, and he died because of that effort.

In this difficult day, in this difficult time for the United States, it is perhaps well to ask what kind of a nation we are and what direction we want to move in. For those of you who are black—considering the evidence there evidently is that there were white people who were responsible—you can be filled with bitterness, with hatred, and a desire for revenge. We can move in that direction as a country, in great polarization—black people amongst black, white people amongst white, filled with hatred toward one another.

Or we can make an effort, as Martin Luther King did, to understand and to comprehend, and to replace that violence, that stain of bloodshed that has spread across our land, with an effort to understand with compassion and love.

For those of you who are black and are tempted to be filled with hatred and distrust at the injustice of such an act, against all white people, I can only say that I feel in my own heart the same kind of feeling. I had a member of my family killed, but he was killed by a white man. But we have to make an effort in the United States, we have to make an effort to understand, to go beyond these rather difficult times.

My favorite poet was Aeschylus. He wrote: "In our sleep, pain which cannot forget falls drop by drop upon the heart until, in our own despair, against our will, comes wisdom through the awful grace of God."

What we need in the United States is not division; what we need in the United States is not hatred; what we need in the United States is not violence or lawlessness; but love and wisdom, and compassion toward one another, and a feeling of justice toward those who still suffer within our country, whether they be white or they be black.

So I shall ask you tonight to return home, to say a prayer for the family of Martin Luther King, that's true, but more importantly to say a prayer for our own country, which all of us love—a prayer for understanding and that compassion of which I spoke.

We can do well in this country. We will have difficult times; we've had difficult times in the past; we will have difficult times in the future. It is not the end of violence; it is not the end of lawlessness; it is not the end of disorder.

But the vast majority of white people and the vast majority of black people in this country want to live together, want to improve the quality of our life, and want justice for all human beings who abide in our land.

Let us dedicate ourselves to what the Greeks wrote so many years ago: to tame the savageness of man and make gentle the life of this world.

Let us dedicate ourselves to that, and say a prayer for our country and for our people.

# INAUGURAL ADDRESS

## President John F. Kennedy

*Kennedy delivered this speech on Friday, January 10, 1961 at his inauguration as the thirty-second president of the United States. His election was a real changing of the guard. Eisenhower, an old war hero who had led the Allied forces to victory in Europe, turned over the presidency to a young man (the youngest ever elected to this office) who had been a junior officer in that same war. When Kennedy became president, three major problems faced him. On the international front, the Cold War had begun and the Iron Curtain was firmly in place. At home, our economy, which had remained strong immediately following the war, had started to slip. In addition, several groups, most notably African Americans and the younger generation, were beginning to rebel against the status quo on a number of fronts.*

*As you read this speech, notice the various audiences Kennedy addresses. He uses many figures of speech, some of which will sound familiar to you because they were so effective they have become a part of our political language over the past four decades.*

**[As Actually Delivered]**

Vice President Johnson, Mr. Speaker, Mr. Chief Justice, President Eisenhower, Vice President Nixon, President Truman, Reverend Clergy, Fellow Citizens:

We observe today not a victory of party but a celebration of freedom—symbolizing an end as well as a beginning—signifying renewal as well as change. For I have sworn before you and Almighty God the same solemn oath our forebears prescribed nearly a century and three quarters ago.

The world is very different now. For man holds in his mortal hands the power to abolish all forms of human poverty and all forms of human life. And yet the same revolutionary beliefs for which our forebears fought are still at issue around the globe—the belief that the rights of man come not from the generosity of the state but from the hand of God.

We dare not forget today that we are the heirs of that first revolution. Let the word go forth from this time and place, to friend and foe alike, that the torch has been passed to a new generation of Americans—born in this century, tempered by war, disciplined by a hard and bitter peace, proud of our ancient heritage—and unwilling to witness or permit the slow undoing of those human rights to which this nation has always been committed, and to which we are committed today at home and around the world.

Let every nation know, whether it wishes us well or ill, that we shall pay any price, bear any burden, meet any hardship, support any friend, oppose any foe to assure the survival and the success of liberty.

This much we pledge—and more.

To those old allies whose cultural and spiritual origins we share, we pledge the loyalty of faithful friends. United, there is little we cannot do in a host of cooperative ventures. Divided, there is little we can do—for we dare not meet a powerful challenge at odds and split asunder.

To those new states whom we welcome to the ranks of the free, we pledge our word that one form of colonial control shall not have passed away merely to be replaced by a far more iron tyranny. We shall not always expect to find them supporting our view. But we shall always hope to find them strongly supporting their own freedom—and to remember that, in the past, those who foolishly sought power by riding the back of the tiger ended up inside.

To those peoples in the huts and villages of half the globe struggling to break the bonds of mass misery, we pledge our best efforts to help them help themselves, for whatever period is required—not because the communists may be doing it, not because we seek their votes, but because it is right. If a free society cannot help the many who are poor, it can not save the few who are rich.

To our sister republics south of our border, we offer a special pledge—to convert our good words into good deeds—in a new alliance for progress—to assist free men and free governments in casting off the chains of poverty. But this peaceful revolution of hope cannot become the prey of hostile powers. Let all our neighbors know that we shall join with them to oppose aggression or subversion anywhere in the Americas. And let every other power know that this Hemisphere intends to remain the master of its own house.

To that world assembly of sovereign states, the United Nations, our last best hope in an age where the instruments of war have far outpaced the instruments of peace, we renew our pledge of support—to prevent it from becoming merely a forum for invective—to strengthen its shield of the new and the weak—and to enlarge the area in which its writ may run.

Finally, to those nations who would make themselves our adversary, we offer not a pledge but a request: that both sides begin anew the quest for peace, before the dark powers of destruction unleashed by science engulf all humanity in planned or accidental self-destruction.

We dare not tempt them with weakness. For only when our arms are sufficient beyond doubt can we be certain beyond doubt that they will never be employed.

But neither can two great and powerful groups of nations take comfort from our present course—both sides overburdened by the cost of modern weapons, both rightly alarmed by the steady spread of the deadly atom, yet both racing to alter that uncertain balance of terror that stays the hand of mankind's final war.

So let us begin anew—remembering on both sides that civility is not a sign of weakness, and sincerity is always subject to proof. Let us never negotiate out of fear. But let us never fear to negotiate.

Let both sides explore what problems unite us instead of belaboring those problems which divide us.

Let both sides, for the first time, formulate serious and precise proposals for the inspection and control of arms—and bring the absolute power to destroy other nations under the absolute control of all nations.

Let both sides seek to invoke the wonders of science instead of its terrors. Together let us explore the stars, conquer the deserts, eradicate disease, tap the ocean depths and encourage the arts and commerce.

Let both sides unite to heed in all corners of the earth the command of Isaiah— to "undo the heavy burdens . . . (and) let the oppressed go free."

And if a beach-head of cooperation may push back the jungle of suspicion, let both sides join in creating a new endeavor, not a new balance of power, but a new world of law, where the strong are just and the weak secure and the peace preserved.

All this will not be finished in the first one hundred days. Nor will it be finished in the first one thousand days, nor in the life of this Administration, nor even perhaps in our lifetime on this planet. But let us begin.

In your hands, my fellow citizens, more than mine, will rest the final success or failure of our course. Since this country was founded, each generation of Americans has been summoned to give testimony to its national loyalty. The graves of young Americans who answered the call to service surround the globe.

Now the trumpet summons us again—not as a call to bear arms, though arms we need—not as a call to battle, though embattled we are—but a call to bear the burden of a long twilight struggle, year in and year out, "rejoicing in hope, patient in tribulation"—a struggle against the common enemies of man: tyranny, poverty, disease and war itself.

Can we forge against those enemies a grand and global alliance, North and South, East and West, that can assure a more fruitful life for all mankind? Will you join in that historic effort?

In the long history of the world, only a few generations have been granted the role of defending freedom in its hour of maximum danger. I do not shrink from this responsibility—I welcome it. I do not believe that any of us would exchange places with any other people or any other generation. The energy, the faith, the devotion which we bring to this endeavor will light our country and all who serve it—and the glow from that fire can truly light the world.

And so, my fellow Americans: ask not what your country can do for you—ask what you can do for your country.

My fellow citizens of the world: ask not what America will do for you, but what together we can do for the freedom of man.

Finally, whether you are citizens of America or citizens of the world, ask of us here the same high standards of strength and sacrifice which we ask of you. With a good conscience our only sure reward, with history the final judge of our deeds, let us go forth to lead the land we love, asking His blessing and His help, but knowing that here on earth God's work must truly be our own.

# IV

## Parody, Marked Style, and Humor

*Laughter is an effective tool in the rhetorical arsenal—it is hard to take something seriously once you have laughed at it, and your audience will be more disposed to agree with you if you make them laugh. Laughter, however, can come from a variety of different sources: the ludicrous, the bizarre, the amusing, or the embarrassing all can make us laugh. In the following group of essays, you will see a variety of approaches to making an argument based on coming at the issue from a totally unexpected direction—coming out of left field to deliver a one-two punch (to mix metaphors).*

# BAN THE THINGS. BAN THEM ALL.

Molly Ivins

> *Ivins is a politician and writer from Texas who is known for her blunt, outspoken style. Her first book, for example, was titled* Molly Ivins Can't Say That, Can She? *Gun control is a much debated issue, with nothing much new to say on either side (except for mounting statistics of increasingly youthful killers and victims), but here Ivins shakes up the debate by using satire, ridicule, and figures of speech to make her pro-knife argument.*

Guns. Everywhere guns.

Let me start this discussion by pointing out that I am not anti-gun. I'm pro-knife. Consider the merits of the knife.

In the first place, you have to catch up with someone to stab him. A general substitution of knives for guns would promote physical fitness. We'd turn into a whole nation of great runners. Plus, knives don't ricochet. And people are seldom killed while cleaning their knives.

As a civil libertarian, I of course support the Second Amendment. And I believe it means exactly what it says: "A well-regulated militia being necessary to the security of a free state, the right of the people to keep and bear arms shall not be infringed." Fourteen-year-old boys are not part of a well-regulated militia. Members of wacky religious cults are not part of a well-regulated militia. Permitting unregulated citizens to have guns is destroying the security of this free state.

I am intrigued by the arguments of those who claim to follow the judicial doctrine of original intent. How do they know it was the dearest wish of Thomas Jefferson's heart that teenage drug dealers should cruise the cities of this nation perforating their fellow citizens with assault rifles? Channeling?

There is more hooey spread about the Second Amendment. It says quite clearly that guns are for those who form part of a well-regulated militia, i.e., the armed forces including the National Guard. The reasons for keeping them away from everyone else get clearer by the day.

The comparison most often used is that of the automobile, another lethal object that is regularly used to wreak great carnage. Obviously, this society is full of people who haven't got enough common sense to use an automobile properly. But we haven't outlawed cars yet.

We do, however, license them and their owners, restrict their use to presumably sane and sober adults and keep track of who sells them to whom. At a minimum, we should do the same with guns.

In truth, there is no rational argument for guns in this society. This is no longer a frontier nation in which people hunt their own food. It is a crowded, overwhelmingly urban country in which letting people have access to guns is a continuing disaster. Those who want guns—whether for target shooting, hunting or potting rattlesnakes (get a hoe)—should be subject to the same restrictions placed on gun owners in England—a nation in which liberty has survived nicely without an armed populace.

The argument that "guns don't kill people" is patent nonsense. Anyone who has ever worked in a cop shop knows how many family arguments end in murder because there was a gun in the house. Did the gun kill someone? No. But if there had been no gun, no one would have died. At least not without a good footrace first. Guns do kill. Unlike cars, that is all they do.

Michael Crichton makes an interesting argument about technology in his thriller *Jurassic Park*. He points out that power without discipline is making this society into a wreckage. By the time someone who studies the martial arts becomes a master— literally able to kill with bare hands—that person has also undergone years of training and discipline. But any fool can pick up a gun and kill with it.

"A well-regulated militia" surely implies both long training and long discipline. That is the least, the very least, that should be required of those who are permitted to have guns, because a gun is literally the power to kill. For years, I used to enjoy taunting my gun-nut friends about their psycho-sexual hangups—always in a spirit of good cheer, you understand. But letting the noisy minority in the National Rifle Association force us to allow this carnage to continue is just plain insane.

I do think gun nuts have a power hangup. I don't know what is missing in their psyches that they need to feel they have the power to kill. But no sane society would allow this to continue.

Ban the damn things. Ban them all.

You want protection? Get a dog.

# A MODEST PROPOSAL

Jonathan Swift

> *Swift (1667–1745) was a prolific Irish writer, best known for his scathing political essays. In this article, Swift uses satire to bring attention to the plight of the hordes of starving women and children wandering through Ireland. Instead of caring for the children, Swift argues, they could be harvested and eaten, thus solving the problem of what to do about the children as well as providing delicacies for the tables of the wealthy. Look at Swift's use of detail ("a delicious, nourishing and wholesome food, whether stewed, roasted, baked or boiled") to make his proposal appear more real.*

It is a melancholy object to those who walk through this great town or travel in the country, when they see the streets, the roads, and cabin doors, crowded with beggars of the female sex, followed by three, four, or six children, all in rags and importuning every passenger for an alms. These mothers, instead of being able to work for their honest livelihood, are forced to employ all their time in strolling to beg sustenance for their helpless infants, who, as they grow up, either turn thieves for want of work, or leave their dear native country to fight for the Pretender in Spain, or sell themselves to the Barbados.

I think it is agreed by all parties that this prodigious number of children in the arms, or on the backs, or at the heels of their mothers, and frequently of their fathers, is in the present deplorable state of the kingdom a very great additional grievance; and therefore whoever could find out a fair, cheap, and easy method of making these children sound, useful members of the commonwealth would deserve so well of the public as to have his statue set up for a preserver of the nation.

But my intention is very far from being confined to provide only for the children of professed beggars; it is of a much greater extent, and shall take in the whole number of infants at a certain age who are born of parents in effect as little able to support them as those who demand our charity in the streets.

As to my own part, having turned my thoughts for many years upon this important subject, and maturely weighed the several schemes of other projectors, I have always found them grossly mistaken in their computation. It is true, a child just dropped from its dam may be supported by her milk for a solar year, with little other nourishment; at most not above the value of two shillings, which the mother may certainly get, or the value in scraps, by her lawful occupation of begging; and it is exactly at one year that I propose to provide for them in such a manner as instead of being a charge upon their parents or the parish, or wanting food and raiment for the rest of their lives, they shall on the contrary contribute to the feeding, and partly to the clothing, of many thousands.

There is likewise another great advantage in my scheme, that it will prevent those voluntary abortions, and that horrid practice of women murdering their bastard children, alas, too frequent among us, sacrificing the poor innocent babes, I doubt, more to avoid the expense than the shame, which would move tears and pity in the most savage and inhuman breast.

The number of souls in this kingdom being usually reckoned one million and a half, of these I calculate there may be about two hundred thousand couples whose wives are breeders; from which number I subtract thirty thousand couples who are able to maintain their own children, although I apprehend there cannot be so many under the present distress of the kingdom; but this being granted, there will remain an hundred and seventy thousand breeders. I again subtract fifty thousand for those women who miscarry, or whose children die by accident or disease within the year. There only remain an hundred and twenty thousand children of poor parents annually born. The question therefore is, how this number shall be reared and provided for, which, as I have already said, under the present situation of affairs, is utterly impossible by all the methods hitherto proposed. For we can neither employ them in handicraft or agriculture; we neither build houses (I mean in the country) nor cultivate land. They can very seldom pick up a livelihood by stealing till they arrive at six years old, except where they are of towardly parts; although I confess they learn the rudiments much earlier, during which time they can however be looked upon only as probationers, as I have been informed by a principal gentleman in the county of Cavan, who protested to me that he never knew above one or two instances under the age of six, even in a part of the kingdom so renowned for the quickest proficiency in that art.

I am assured by our merchants that a boy or a girl before twelve years old is no salable commodity; and even when they come to this age they will not yield above three pounds, or three pounds and half a crown at most on the Exchange; which cannot turn to account either to the parents or the kingdom, the charge of nutriment and rags having been at least four times that value.

I shall now therefore humbly propose my own thoughts, which I hope will not be liable to the least objection.

I have been assured by a very knowing American of my acquaintance in London, that a young healthy child well nursed is at a year old a most delicious, nourishing, and wholesome food, whether stewed, roasted, baked, or boiled; and I make no doubt that it will equally serve in a fricassee or a ragout.

I do therefore humbly offer it to public consideration that of the hundred and twenty thousand children, already computed, twenty thousand may be reserved for breed, whereof only one fourth part to be males, which is more than we allow to sheep, black cattle, or swine; and my reason is that these children are seldom the fruits of marriage, a circumstance not much regarded by our savages, therefore one male will be sufficient to serve four females. That the remaining hundred thousand may at a year old be offered in sale to the persons of quality and fortune through the kingdom, always advising the mother to let them suck plentifully in the last month, so as to render them plump and fat for a good table. A child will make two dishes at an entertainment for friends; and when the family dines alone, the fore or hind quarter will make a reasonable dish, and seasoned with a little pepper or salt will be very good boiled on the fourth day, especially in winter.

I have reckoned upon a medium that a child just born will weigh twelve pounds, and in a solar year if tolerably nursed increaseth to twenty-eight pounds.

I grant this food will be somewhat dear, and therefore very proper for landlords, who, as they have already devoured most of the parents, seem to have the best title to the children.

Infant's flesh will be in season throughout the year, but more plentiful in March, and a little before and after. For we are told by a grave author, an eminent French physician, that fish being a prolific diet, there are more children born in Roman Catholic countries about nine months after Lent than at any other season; therefore, reckoning a year after Lent, the markets will be more glutted than usual, because the number of popish infants is at least three to one in this kingdom; and therefore it will have one other collateral advantage, by lessening the number of Papists among us.

I have already computed the charge of nursing a beggar's child (in which list I reckon all cottagers, laborers, and four-fifths of the farmers) to be about two shillings per annum, rags included; and I believe no gentleman would repine to give ten shillings for the carcass of a good fat child, which as I have said, will make four dishes of excellent nutritive meat, when he hath only some particular friend or his own family to dine with him. Thus the squire will learn to be a good landlord, and grow popular among the tenants; the mother will have eight shillings net profit, and be fit for work till she produces another child.

Those who are more thrifty (as I must confess the times require) may flay the carcass; the skin of which artificially dressed will make admirable gloves for ladies, and summer boots for fine gentlemen.

As to our city of Dublin, shambles may be appointed for this purpose in the most convenient parts of it, and butchers we may be assured will not be wanting; although I rather recommend buying the children alive, and dressing them hot from the knife as we do roasting pigs.

A very worthy person, a true lover of his country, and whose virtues highly esteem, was lately pleased in discoursing on this matter to offer a refinement upon my scheme. He said that many gentlemen of his kingdom having of late destroyed their deer, he conceived that the want of venison might be well supplied by the bodies of young lads and maidens, not exceeding fourteen years of age nor under twelve, so great a number of both sexes in every country being now ready to starve for want of work and service; and these to be disposed of by their parents, if alive, or otherwise their nearest relations. But with due deference to so excellent a friend and deserving a patriot, I cannot be altogether in his sentiments; for as to the males, my American acquaintance assured me from frequent experience that their flesh was generally tough and lean, like that of our schoolboys, by continual exercise, and their taste disagreeable; and to fatten them would not answer the charge. Then as to the females, it would, I think with humble submission, be a loss to the public, because they soon would become breeders themselves; and besides, it is not improbable that some scrupulous people might be apt to censure such a practice (although indeed very unjustly) as a little bordering upon cruelty; which, I confess, hath always been with me the strongest objection against any project, how well soever intended.

But in order to justify my friend, he confessed that this expedient was put into his head by the famous Psalmanazar, a native of the island Formosa, who came from thence to London about twenty years ago, and in conversation told my friend that in his country when any young person happened to be put to death, the executioner sold the carcass to persons of quality as a prime dainty; and that in his time the body of a plump girl of fifteen, who was crucified for an attempt to poison the emperor, was sold to his Imperial Majesty's prime minister of state, and other great mandarins of the court, in joints from the gibbet, at four hundred crowns. Neither indeed can I deny that if the same use were made of several plump young girls in this town, who without one single groat to their fortunes cannot stir abroad without a chair, and appear at the playhouse and assemblies in foreign fineries which they never will pay for, the kingdom would not be the worse.

Some persons of a desponding spirit are in great concern about that vast number of poor people who are aged, diseased, or maimed, and I have been desired to employ my thoughts what course may be taken to ease the nation of so grievous an encumbrance. But I am not in the least pain upon that matter, because it is very well known that they are every day dying and rotting by cold and famine, and filth and vermin, as fast as can be reasonably expected. And as to the younger laborers, they are now in almost as hopeful a condition. They cannot get work, and consequently pine away for want of nourishment to a degree that if any time they are accidentally hired to common labor, they have not strength to perform it; and thus the country and themselves are happily delivered from the evils to come.

I have too long digressed, and therefore shall return to my subject. I think the advantages by the proposal which I have made are obvious and many, as well as of the highest importance.

For first, as I have already observed, it would greatly lessen the number of Papists, with whom we are yearly overrun, being the principal breeders of the nation as well as our most dangerous enemies; and who stay at home on purpose to deliver the kingdom to the Pretender, hoping to take their advantage by the absence of so many good Protestants, who have chosen rather to leave their country than to stay at home and pay tithes against their conscience to an Episcopal curate.

Secondly, the poorer tenants will have something valuable of their own, which by law may be made liable to distress, and help to pay their landlord's rent, their corn and cattle being already seized and money a thing unknown.

Thirdly, whereas the maintenance of an hundred thousand children, from two years old and upwards, cannot be computed at less than ten shillings a piece per annum, the nation's stock will be thereby increased fifty thousand pounds per annum, besides the profit of a new dish introduced to the tables of all gentlemen of fortune in the kingdom who have any refinement in taste. And the money will circulate among ourselves, the goods being entirely of our own growth and manufacture.

Fourthly, the constant breeders, besides the gain of eight shillings sterling per annum by the sale of their children, will be rid of the charge of maintaining them after the first year.

Fifthly, this food would likewise bring great custom to taverns, where the vintners will certainly be so prudent as to procure the best receipts for dressing it to perfection, and consequently have their houses frequented by all the fine gentlemen, who justly value themselves upon their knowledge in good eating; and a skillful cook, who understands how to oblige his guests, will contrive to make it as expensive as they please.

Sixthly, this would be a great inducement to marriage, which all wise nations have either encouraged by rewards or enforced by laws and penalties. It would increase the care and tenderness of mothers toward their children, when they were sure of a settlement for life to the poor babes, provided in some sort by the public, to their annual profit instead of expense. We should see an honest emulation among the married women, which of them could bring the fattest child to the market. Men would become as fond of their wives during the time of their pregnancy as they are now of their mares in foal, their cows in calf, or sows when they are ready to farrow; nor offer to beat or kick them (as is too frequent a practice) for fear of a miscarriage.

Many other advantages might be enumerated. For instance, the addition of some thousand carcasses in our exportation of barreled beef, the propagation of swine's flesh, and improvements in the art of making good bacon, so much wanted among us by the great destruction of pigs, too frequent at our tables, which are no way comparable in taste or magnificence to a well-grown, fat, yearling child, which roasted whole will make a considerable figure at a lord mayor's feast or any other public entertainment. But this and many others I omit, being studious of brevity.

Supposing that one thousand families in this city would be constant customers for infants' flesh, besides others who might have it at merry meetings, particularly weddings and christenings, I compute that Dublin would take off annually about twenty thousand carcasses, and the rest of the kingdom (where probably they will be sold somewhat cheaper) the remaining eighty thousand.

I can think of no one objection that will possibly be raised against this proposal, unless it should be urged that the number of people will be thereby much lessened in the kingdom. This I freely own, and it was indeed one principal design in offering it to the world. I desire the reader will observe, that I calculate my remedy for this one individual kingdom of Ireland and for no other that ever was, is, or I think ever can be upon earth. Therefore let no man talk to me of other expedients: of taxing our absentees at five shillings a pound: of using neither clothes nor household furniture except what is of our own growth and manufacture: of utterly rejecting the materials and instruments that promote foreign luxury: of curing the expensiveness of pride, vanity, idleness, and gaming in our women: of introducing a vein of parsimony, prudence, and temperance: of learning to love our country, in the want of which we differ even from Laplanders and the inhabitants of Topinamboo: of quitting our animosities and factions, nor acting any longer like the Jews, who were murdering one another at the very moment their city was taken: of being a little cautious not to sell our country and conscience for nothing: of teaching landlords to have at least one degree of mercy toward their tenants: lastly, of putting a spirit of honesty, industry, and skill into our shopkeepers; who, if a resolution could now be taken to buy only our native goods, would immediately unite to cheat and exact upon us in the price, the measure, and the goodness, nor could ever yet be brought to make one fair proposal of just dealing, though often and earnestly invited to it.

Therefore I repeat, let no man talk to me of these and the like expedients, till he hath at least some glimpse of hope that there will ever be some hearty and sincere attempt to put them in practice.

But as to myself, having been wearied out for many years with offering vain, idle, visionary thoughts, and at length utterly despairing of success, I fortunately fell upon this proposal, which, as it is wholly new, so it hath something solid and real, of no expense and little trouble, full in our own power, and whereby we can incur no danger in disobliging England. For this kind of commodity will not bear exportation, the flesh being of too tender a consistence to admit a long continuance in salt, although perhaps I could name a country which would be glad to eat up our whole nation without it.

After all, I am not so violently bent upon my own opinion as to reject any offer proposed by wise men, which shall be found equally innocent, cheap, easy, and effectual. But before something of that kind shall be advanced in contradiction to my scheme, and offering a better, I desire the author or authors will be pleased maturely to consider two points. First, as things now stand, how they will be able to find food and raiment for an hundred thousand useless mouths and backs. And secondly, there being a round million of creatures in human figure throughout this kingdom, whose sole subsistence put into a common stock would leave them in debt two millions of pounds sterling, adding those who are beggars by profession to the bulk of farmers, cottagers, and laborers, with their wives and children who are beggars in effect; I desire those politicians who dislike my overture, and may perhaps be so bold to attempt an answer, that they will first ask the parents of these mortals whether they would not at this day think it a great happiness to have been sold for food at a year old in this manner I prescribe, and thereby have avoided such a perpetual scene of misfortunes as they have since gone through by the oppression of landlords, the impossibility of paying rent without money or trade, the want of common sustenance, with neither house nor clothes to cover them from the inclemencies of the weather, and the most inevitable prospect of entailing the like or greater miseries upon their breed forever.

I profess, in the sincerity of my heart, that I have not the least personal interest in endeavoring to promote this necessary work, having no other motive than the public good of my country, by advancing our trade, providing for infants, relieving the poor, and giving some pleasure to the rich. I have no children by which I can propose to get a single penny; the youngest being nine years old, and my wife past childbearing.

# A BRIEF REPORT ON CLINICAL ASPECTS OF PROCRASTINATION: BETTER LATE THAN NEVER

Kathy Alberding, M.S.W., David Antonuccio, Ph.D., and
Blake H. Tearnan, Ph.D.

*In this brief but pithy article, the authors manage to lampoon social scientists, scholarly publications, many college students, and stuffed shirts everywhere. It is effective because it mirrors so accurately the form of academic writing. Beyond the humor, however, there is an implicit argument that scholarly writing can mistake the form for the function or take itself too seriously.*

This is a brief report of a full-length article the authors are planning to write on the topic of procrastination as a mature psychological defense. The authors have not, however, had the time to do a thorough literature review, or any, for that matter, but all have experience with the topic and fully intend to do such a review in the near future.

There are several advantages of procrastination, not the least of which is that it allows an individual the opportunity to think a task through (D'Lay, in press). When the authors actually get around to writing the article, they expect to give it the thorough, detailed treatment this topic deserves.

## References

D'Lay, I. (1925). Don't rush into anything. Peoria: Turtle Publications, in press.

Acknowledgments: The authors would like to extend their appreciation to those who expressed interest in contributing to this report but who never found sufficient time to do so: Patricia Chatham, Ph.D., Stephanie Dillon, Ph.D., William Danton, Ph.D., Norman Kerbel, M.A., Kathryn McFadden, M.S., David Hutchison. M.D., Carol Vasso, and Julie Anderson.
(Received: December 3, 1975 Revised: September 12, 1986).

# UNIT SEVEN

## *Putting It All Together*

# INTRODUCTION

As you prepare to write your final position paper, it may be helpful to take stock of what you have learned this semester. By this point in the course, you have quite a large kit of rhetorical tools at your disposal. You have also read many well-constructed essays; in other words, you know what makes a good argument. You have even made a good start on your final position paper: you have explored the issues by doing considerable research, and you have articulated positions on both sides of the debate. Now, you are ready to write.

The essays in this unit are a sampling of successful final position papers written by students at the University of Maryland. As you read these essays, analyze them for the rhetorical strategies they employ. Try to identify in which stases the writers situate their debate and how each essay makes use of the three rhetorical appeals in persuading his or her intended audience. Notice how much background they give, and where they concede and refute opposing positions. See if you can detect any figures of speech in their writing. Finally, notice the clarity of their documentation and how they use their research to strengthen their arguments rather than allowing the research to dominate their personal positions. As you note these writers' rhetorical choices, try to make some conscious decisions about how you want to approach your topic. You should subject your own topic to the same kind of rhetorical analysis you perform on others' writing.

Avoid the temptation to just imitate these papers. Aside from the potential of a serious infraction of academic integrity, what was effective for one writer, message, and audience will probably not be effective for your own message and audience. Besides, the most interesting part of writing is deciding on your own which tactics to use. The possibilities are nearly endless; choose your own perspective.

**Elisa Warford**

# THE QUESTION OF REFORM: ISSUES WITHIN THE UN

Jawad Muaddi

*Written in December of 1999, this essay by Jawad Muaddi explores the
need for reform in the United Nations and suggests three possible solutions. Muaddi presents a very logical argument, one that opposes following tradition merely for tradition's sake. In addition to presenting
his own position in a positive way, he neatly refutes the opposition his
argument might encounter.*

## *Audience Analysis*

The audience members for my paper subscribe to *The Economist*. This group of
informed followers of foreign affairs has read numerous articles about the UN, especially in recent months due to the Kosovo and East Timor crises.

If we are to learn anything from the tragedies of this decade, then our chief concern
as we enter the next millennium must be to secure and ensure human rights. The
recent inhumane acts in Kosovo and East Timor have exposed weaknesses in the
international system, and these problems will continue unless world leaders reform
the UN charter in three ways. First, the charter must allow for intervention by the UN
when deemed necessary by the General Assembly, even if such intervention violates
the sovereignty of other nations. Second, the recent abuse of the veto power belonging to the five permanent members of the Security Council warrants limitations.
Finally, the UN must collect outstanding dues from indebted nations. Many experts
and world leaders, including Kofi Annan, the first UN Secretary General to recognize
these weaknesses, have articulated the need for such reformation and have shocked
traditionalists who vehemently oppose any change to the UN Charter. Indeed, these
recent ideas to reform the UN have met with a powerful tide of resistance; however,
only global support for these reforms will guarantee that productive changes will
result. Although most nations can control and contain hostile activities within their
borders, other nations are simply unable, or unwilling, to maintain order. Thus, for
the sake of the citizens of unstable nations, the international community must
strongly advocate UN reform.

Recent tragedies obviously illustrate the dire need for a change in the UN's
approach to resolving crises. The most glaring example, the well-publicized ethnic
cleansing of the Kosovars by the Serbians, caused a storm of criticism to rain down
on the UN for failing to intervene. Of course, the Security Council members and
world leaders noticed both this horrific atrocity and the UN's inability to handle it.
(Even the America-centric George W. Bush might have read about Serbia's crimes
against its own people). However, the almost helpless UN could not intervene because
the U.N. charter shields sovereign Serbia, a member nation of the General Assembly,
when internal problems occur. In his *Washington Post* editorial, entitled "Murder in
the Name of Sovereignty," Jim Hoagland asserts that Serbia used this shield to "[etch]

in blood its sovereign right to kill as many of its own masses as it sees fit." Although difficult for most people to imagine, this grim reality exists. In the future. the UN must not allow sovereign nations like Serbia to mask atrocities within their borders. In an interview with Hoagland, Annan states one of the best arguments for this necessary change: "Today what is internal doesn't remain internal for very long" (Hoagland A33). By pointing out the differences between present and past conflicts, Annan makes a solid counterargument to traditionalists who subscribe to post-WWII ideology. Indeed, the weak appeal to tradition helps to corroborate Annan's position.

A similar, though less severe, example of the sovereignty issue occurred in East Timor, where the UN needed special permission from Indonesia to intervene. The delay allowed barbaric militias to murder and rape thousands of East Timorese citizens, in addition to annihilating their villages, forcing the few survivors to flee to the mountains. In an article that appeared in *The Christian Science Monitor*, Sander Thoenes (who was killed on September 21 by militiamen) and Minh Vo observed that unarmed police officers who oversaw the elections, "could do little more than watch as militiamen murdered hundreds of East Timorese, including UN staff members" (Thoenes 1). The UN's inability to intervene due to Indonesia's sovereignty left these helpless officers (the only group of trained UN representatives in East Timor during the two-week massacre) in this predicament. Fortunately, these victims have started to return to their homes, or rather the land where their homes once stood. Nevertheless. the victims of this tragedy would have suffered less had the UN acted more expediently.

In the debate over state sovereignty, both traditionalists and reformists agree that the UN charter respects the independence of member nations. Also, both sides agree that the founders of the UN made this rule to end the international conflicts of WWII. For over fifty years, nobody questioned the sovereignty clause. In his address to the UN General Assembly on September 26, Annan opened the door to change when he said aggressive 'intervention to protect citizens from wholesale slaughter is an evolution we should welcome'" (Ford 1). The international community should accept Annan's invitation because the time has come to reconsider this outdated principle. While the problems 55 years ago resulted from conflicts between nations, the problems of our era result from conflicts within nations. Thus, the value of sovereignty as a peacemaking tool has diminished, especially in the past decade.

Critics who fear that reformation will eliminate a great international tool must realize that sovereignty has served its purpose in the last 55 years, but that different times call for a new UN that can keep pace with all the changes in the world. While some traditionalists fear change because of the loss of an existing method, others fear the arrival of aggressive intervention; in fact, they label this new tool as "human rights imperialism." Bernard Kouchner, the UN governor in Kosovo and recipient of the Nobel Peace Prize, strongly refuted such views when he said, "Everywhere, human rights are human rights. Freedom is freedom. Suffering is suffering. Oppression is oppression" (Kouchner 7). Indeed, Kouchner's intentional understatement makes sense in this time of seemingly senseless UN diplomacy.

In addition to intervening at the cost of sovereignty, the UN needs further reform to achieve its goal of ending inhumane atrocities. The five permanent Security Council members, China, England, France. Russia, and the United States, have possessed the right to veto UN diplomacy since the founding of the organization. Once again, times have changed in the last 50 years. The UN will succeed in the future only if these nations agree to allow the consensus of member nations to dictate UN diplomacy. Unfortunately, the national interest of one permanent member often overrides the will of the vast majority of other member nations. The veto essentially makes the UN a democratic dictatorship. The majority vote of the Security Council determines UN diplomacy only if the permanent members unanimously agree. Thus, as a dictator has absolute authority, each superpower has total control of the UN when it exercises its veto right. Because this scenario has recently prevented the UN from carrying out its mission, the irresponsible use of the veto necessitates reform.

As with the concept of state sovereignty, the time has come for the world to reconsider the usefulness of the veto power. After WWII, the five permanent members emerged as the winners and the major powers in the world: Thus, when the UN formed, the organization granted these five nations permanent seats in the Security Council to ensure their loyalty. Perhaps many have forgotten the original intent of the veto when the founders of the UN drew up the charter. Article 24 states that the members of the UN "confer on the Security Council primary responsibility for the maintenance of international peace and security" (5:24:1). Although the charter has no explicit limitations of the veto, the organization expects these nations to use their power responsibly.

Collectively, the vetoes of the five permanent members of the Security Council have recently failed the expectations of the UN. Several experts, including world leaders, believe these nations have used the veto power for the sole purpose of promoting their own national interest. Richard Butler, Diplomat in Residence at the Council on Foreign Relations, criticizes China for its vetoes of minor UN peacekeeping missions, particularly in Macedonia. In an essay that appeared in *Foreign Affairs*, he asserts that China's irresponsible vetoes "abused Security Council procedures." However, China's actions did not surprise Butler, one of the most outspoken critics of the veto power, because Macedonia recognized Taiwan's independence (Butler 9).

The outcries against the veto power range from critics who want to abolish it, such as Butler, to advocates who only want to place minor restrictions, such as Joschka Fischer, the German minister for foreign affairs. Butler believes that China, England, France, and Russia would give up the veto power if the United States only took the initiative (10). Despite Butler's optimism, his solution to the veto problem will likely never happen because the world's premier international superpower, the US, will not give up its veto power in the foreseeable future. However, Fischer's proposed limitations can realistically reform the procedures of the Security Council. In a September address to the UN, he asserts that an "obligation for a state to explain to the General Assembly why it is vetoing a resolution would make it more difficult to do so" (Fischer). If enacted, Fischer's proposal would lead to a more responsible use of the veto because a Security Council member would have to at least give a reasonable and viable explanation for its veto in order to prevent humiliation. Despite their different views on how to reform the Security Council's procedure in relation to the veto, Butler, Fischer, and other critics agree that the veto power has obstructed the UN from achieving its goals.

The lack of funding presents another obstacle on the UN's path to a peaceful world. Because more aggressive intervention will require more finances, world leaders must address this issue now. Even if the UN reforms the principle of sovereignty and the veto power in the near future, the lack of funding will limit the success of the organization. Deadbeat nations, countries that do not pay their UN dues despite having the ability, must replenish the UN's peacekeeping funds. The reasons why deadbeat nations fail to pay their dues vary. A brief look at the world's leading deadbeat nation, the United States, will clarify the definition.

Although the US has agreed to pay nearly $1 billion over the next three years, UN supporters cannot accept this partial payment because $600 million will go unpaid. Perhaps most Americans fail to realize the significance of their nation's debt. According to the author of an essay which appeared in a recent issue of *The Economist*, "Americans, with their minds on congressional and presidential primaries, assume that the UN should be extremely grateful for getting at least most of the money that was owed to it" ("Don't Ask"). This apathy explains the lack of public outcry for the US to repay the UN. Besides, even if Americans were very concerned, most would not strongly support repayment because they would really pay the check through higher taxes or less funding for government programs. Certainly, the money (of which one-third must be paid by the end of the year) will immediately impact countries that desperately need the UN's help. However, only a partial repayment will also hurt the UN, especially in the near future because more aggressive intervention will require more funding.

As a superpower and a permanent member of the Security Council, the US must assume a leading role in the peacekeeping efforts of the UN by accepting the responsibility that comes with possessing great power. But the deal to partially repay the UN does not enhance America's reputation as a world leader. Unfortunately, the majority of the articles published about this subject deal with the concern for international embarrassment for America over the possible loss of a General Assembly seat. The big concern for the international community is the precedent this American cancellation may set. The author of the same article in *The Economist* asks, "If the United States can walk away from its debts, why not others?" ("Don't Ask"). Indeed, the possibility exists that many nations will follow the lead of the US, the world's richest country. For example, a country with a poor economic year may spend their UN dues domestically rather than pay the organization; its justification will be the example set by the world's greatest superpower.

Perhaps more outrageous than the cancellation of debt to the UN are the conditions attached to this agreement. As Christopher S. Wren noted in his recent *New York Times* article, the nation that accounts for 30 percent of the world's GDP will soon have a smaller share of the UN budget. According to the terms of the agreement, the US will pay 22 percent of the UN budget, rather than the 25 percent the US has been obligated to pay in recent years. Furthermore, the US share of funding for peacekeeping missions will be trimmed to 25 percent, down from 31 percent. Also, to ensure that America's contribution will not increase, the UN budget cannot grow in spending, even if inflation occurs. Finally, every other member nation must accept the partial payment as payment in full (Wren A25). Thus, even when the US agrees to partially repay its debts, it must do so under the stipulation of having a lesser obligation in the future. Still, several supporters of the US policy point to the fact that the US is still the biggest contributor to the UN. However, considering that the US is also the UN's biggest debtor, this claim means little.

Contrary to many assumptions made in articles on this subject, the US seat in the Security Council lacks complete security. According to John Carey, the editor of the UN Law Reports, the US could lose its Security Council seat as well as the General Assembly seat if debts are not repaid in full. In a letter to the editor of *The Washington Post*, Carey says, "The day might come when the International Court of Justice in The Hague could rule that our failure to live up to our Charter obligations forfeits our special Charter Privileges" (Carey 24). Despite the fact that Carey's scenario could technically happen, the US will likely never lose its seat in the Security Council. Nations that depend on the US would hesitate to jeopardize their relations with the great superpower by voting it out of the Security Council.

If the founders of the UN could evaluate the world today, they would certainly admit that sovereignty, the veto power, and the lack of funding fail to resolve our problems. In fact, they would probably agree that these changeable charter laws have prevented the UN from achieving its goals in the 1990's. The new millennium is nearly here, and the greatest moral question of our time has yet to be answered. Should the international community reform the UN, the organization that ended the downward spiral of WWII? To end the downward spiral of today, the world must answer with a resounding "yes."

## Bibliography

Abitbol, William and Paul-Marie Couteaux. "Stirring Notions of Nations." *The Times* (London) 1 Oct. 1999.

Annan, Kofi. "Two Concepts of Sovereignty." *The Economist* 18 Sept. 1999: 49–50.

Berman, Louis A. *Proverb, Wit & Wisdom*. New York: Perigee, 1997.

Broderick, Bridget. "Can the UN Bring Peace?" *International Socialist Review* 1.7 (Spring 1999): 27–31.

Butler, Richard. "Bewitched, Bothered, and Bewildered." *Foreign Affairs* 78.5 (1999): 9–12.

Carey, John. "Jeopardized UN Status." *The New York Times* 18, Nov. 1999: A24.

Carroll, Joe. "Clinton Urges UN to Challenge Poverty, Mass Killings, Arms." *The Irish Times* 22 Sept. 1999: 9.

*Charter of the United Nations*. San Francisco: 26 June 1945. 11 Nov. 1999 <http://www.un.org/aboutun/charter>

Cobban, Helena. "A Deeper Redefining of Sovereignty." *Christian Science Monitor* 14 Oct. 1999: 11.

"Deploy UN's Will Rapidly." *The Straits Times* (Singapore) 4 Oct. 1999.

"Don't Ask for More, Mr. Annan." *The Economist* 20 Nov. 1999.

Falk, Richard and Andrew Strauss. "Globalization Needs a Dose of Democracy." *International Herald Tribune* 5 Oct. 1999: 8.

Fischer, Joschka. "Address/54th Session of the UN General Assembly." *Bangkok Post* 28 Sept. 1999.

Ford, Peter. "Few Sacred Borders to New UN." *Christian Science Monitor* 29 Sept. 1999: 1 +.

Glennon, Michael J. "The New Interventionism." *Foreign Affairs* 78.3 (1999): 21+.

Hoagland, Jim. "Murder in the Name of Sovereignty." *The Washington Post* 28 Oct. 1999: A33.

Joffe, Joseph. "The Many Meanings of Sovereignty." *Foreign Affairs* 78.5 (1999): 36+.

"Kosovo Resurgent." *The Economist* 25 Sept. 1999: 57.

Kouchner, Bernard. "Establish a Right to Intervene Against War, Oppression." *Los Angeles Times* 18 Oct. 1999: 7.

Leopold, Evelyn. "Limit UN Vetoes, Germany Urges." *The Toronto Star* 23 Sept. 1999.

Luck, Edward C. "A Road to Nowhere." *Foreign Affairs* 78.4 (1999): 118+.

Luttwak, Edward N. "Give War a Chance." *Foreign Affairs* 78.4 (1999): 36+.

Main, Victoria. "McKinnon Attacks UN Veto Power." *The Dominion* (Wellington) 1 Oct. 1999: 2.

Mufson, Steven and Colum Lynch. "E. Timor Failure Puts UN on Spot; Interventionist Ability in Doubt." *The Washington Post* 26 Sept. 1999: A1+.

"New Game, New Rules." *The Straits Times* (Singapore) 29 Sept. 1999: 34.

"Paying Our Dues." *The Times-Picayune* 19 Nov. 1999: B6.

"Saving the UN." *Foreign Report* 16 Sept. 1999.

Schmitt, Eric. "Deal on UN Dues Breaks an Impasse and Draws Critics" *The New York Times* 16 Nov. 1999: A1+.

Takdir, Muhammad and Sunu Soemarno. "Will UN Interventionism Work?" *The Jakarta Post* 30 Sept. 1999.

"The End of Sovereignty?" *The Detroit News* 4 Oct. 1999: A8.

Thoenes, Sander and Minh Vo. "In Indonesia, the UN Again Comes Too Late." *Christian Science Monitor* 13 Sep. 1999: 1+.

"Three-Phased Approach towards Charter Amendment." *UN Chronicle* 36.1 (1999): 64.

Whitelaw, Kevin. "Struggling to Deliver on Promises of Peace." *US News and World Report* 13 Sep. 1999: 32.

Williams, Ian. "Another UN Disaster." Salon.com. 11 Sep. 1999 <http://www.salon.com/news/feature/1999/09/11/un>.

Wren, Christopher S. "United States May Yet Lose its Vote in UN General Assembly." *The New York Times* 16 Nov. 1999: A25.

# IT'S TIME FOR EDUCATIONAL TELEVISION

Ryan Stimmel

*At a time when most arguments about television focus on its negative impact on society (see the articles in Unit Four, for example), Ryan Stimmel takes an unusual position: television can be used as an effective learning tool both at home and in the classroom. In his efforts to refute the commonly held perceptions about television, Stimmel draws the audience into his argument by asking them to imagine different situations. He then details specific ways in which teachers, especially, can use television in their classrooms.*

## Audience Analysis

Parents and teachers who are neutral on the issue of television and children's education.

What a thrill it was to see real live footage of Neil Armstrong taking a small step on the moon and a giant leap for all of mankind. And let's not forget when Michael Johnson won the gold for the United States at the 1996 Olympic Games in Atlanta. In less than a minute's time, he became the fastest man in the world, and his tears had others crying with him. Millions of people witnessed the reunification of friends, families, and a nation after the destruction of the Berlin Wall. The tremendous relief, when Baby Jessica was safely rescued from out of the well, put thousands of hearts at ease. Do you remember when Mark McGwire held his son in his arms, in front of millions of people, after he broke one of the greatest sports records of all time? Television allowed us to see these inspiring moments. It is one of the most influential forces in the nation, and it's time we used television's influence to improve and expand education for our children.

Educational television started off as a social experiment aimed specifically at lower income minority families. "In the mid-1960's, a consortium of educators, creative artists, and others launched an experiment using television to provide early childhood intervention that would reduce the risk of school failure" (Huston and Wright 10). Then something unexpected happened. This experimental program, otherwise known as Sesame Street, was a tremendous success. Today, broadcast stations are required, by the Children's Television Act of 1990, to provide programming that "meets the educational and informational needs of children and youths" (Huston and Wright 9). More recently, the Telecommunications Act of 1996 has required television set manufacturers to install the V-chip in every new set produced (Zoglin 64). Parents can use the V-chip to block out undesirable programming (Schorr 9A). Federal regulations have raised serious questions about television programs that broadcasters claim are both educational and informative.

Consider "learning" for a moment. Webster defines "learning" as the acquiring of knowledge or skill (Morehead 391). It is important to realize that a person's brain never stops acquiring knowledge, and therefore, never stops learning. Psychologists agree, even while we sleep, the brain constantly receives and processes information. Try to clear your mind for a second and think about absolutely nothing. It's hard not to think about anything without your brain starting to wander. The brain will always surpass any computer ever made because computers lack critical thinking skills. The brain, which is technically an organ, is so complex that it actually thinks about itself. Just imagine, something not even classified as a living organism, thinks about itself! Yet, critics of educational television claim the brain magically turns itself off when the TV is turned on.

Neil Murry, literacy education teacher, claims, "[Television] kills communication. Worse: it is the enemy of literacy" (Mace 162). He goes on to state that television "corrupts the masses," "stops people talking to each other," and "prevents children's education" (Mace 162). But on what evidence does he base his claim? A study conducted by the University of Kansas found that children who watched Sesame Street actually "spent more time reading than those who had watched more adult programming or noneducational cartoons" ("Thanks, Big Bird" 14). The research team based their findings on a three year study of 250 pre-schoolers across the United States ("Thanks, Big Bird" 14). The children were also found to have performed better on math and verbal tests than those who had not watched the program ("Thanks, Big Bird" 14). Educational television can increase learning rather than prohibit it.

Just imagine you're a small child growing up in a third world country. Poverty and farming are the only things you know. You don't even realize you're living in a third world country because you've never been outside the village. Then, with the flip of a button, everything changes. You're watching the only television in the whole village, and as you begin to flip through the channels, you are inspired by all the different people and places that you see. Suddenly, you no longer want to live a life of poverty, just trying to survive from day-to-day. You want to receive an education and become president, or perhaps a doctor, maybe even a teacher. Television has expanded your horizons and increased your imagination. This is going on right now. It's called the globalization of cultures and ideas, and children from all over the world who can't afford to travel or don't know how to read are being introduced to a diversity of information at the international scale because of satellite television and new technologies (Clark 135). However, critics of television education claim television is a passive device that destroys the imagination and retards intellectual growth.

"TV Doesn't Teach," at least that's Dr. Lyman Page's headline in his letter to the editor of the *New York Times*. Page, a professor of pediatrics at Brown University Medical School, specifies that "Sesame Street," or any program for that matter, "doesn't enhance children's learning skills" (Page 22). Page is not alone. Mark Bricklin, of *Prevention* magazine, claims television prevents the "development of healthy minds" because "the viewer is cut off from participation" (144). But have you ever seen a young child watch television? Most parents will agree that young children are very active, when viewing a program.

What does inactivity prove anyway? Writing and studying demonstrate a lack of interactivity, yet these activities are considered to be highly intellectual (Huston and Wright 13). Scholars like Aletha Huston and John Wright, from the American

Academy of Political and Social Science, have proven, children are constantly absorbing and reacting mentally to the content in television programs (14). Educational television is not a passive activity because children are getting something out of it.

What does educational television have to offer? Certain programs can enhance a child's social skills, and encourage behaviors such as "helping," "sharing," and "cooperation" (Huston and Wright 13). Informative programs can better prepare a child for school, resulting in a positive learning cycle (Huston and Wright 13). Educational television can "enhance children's self-esteem and their understanding of others' feelings and behavior" (Huston and Wright 14). It can reinforce a visual image for young children. It allows viewers to travel to different places in time and space. It transmits and communicates the thoughts and ideas of people from all over the world. The possibilities are endless. Television is a powerful resource that should be used to improve and expand education for our children.

Cable in the Classroom supports television education for schools nationwide. It provides over 540 hours of commercial-free educational programming every month for teachers, parents, and students to choose from ("Helping Working Parents..." S7). Program schedules and informative articles can be found in their monthly magazine, which is only available for their members (Witherup 10c). They also provide 24-hour support from the Internet that you will find easy to use ("Get Cable in the Classroom" 2). The resources will be available for you to make strategic and informed decisions over what programs to incorporate into the classroom. The best part is, because Cable in the Classroom is a nonprofit service of the cable industry, it provides programs absolutely free of charge (Cradler 43). Once Cable in the Classroom has been incorporated into your school, children will reap the benefits of educational television, while your school builds up a library of new resources. Three hundred schools in the Sacramento area have already been wired to Cable in the Classroom ("Get Cable in the Classroom" 2). Why shouldn't yours as well?

New technology has created further possibilities for educational television. Closed captioning is being used to teach children how to read, thanks to new computer technology. Terry Roso, a first grade teacher from Illinois, allows students to write captions for their own videos, tapping into their natural interest in television, while building their reading and vocabulary skills at the same time ("Illinois Teacher..." 48).

Another example of high technology is Asynchronous Transfer Mode, or ATM ("Learn at Warp Speed" 3). An advanced fiber optic network allows instructors to teach students several miles away, at several different locations ("Learn at Warp Speed" 3). In Georgia, PeachStar satellite network offers a full range of educational programming to elementary and middle school children ("PeachStar Accentuates..." 26). Two examples of the types of programs available are electronic field trips and Super Science with Molly & Bert, where kids go through a hands-on science theme once a month ("PeachStar Accentuates..." 26). This is only a small taste of the type of technology that is available to teachers right now.

It's your decision. Television's influence could be used to improve and expand your children's education. New technology will further increase television's role in the future. The first step is to join the Cable in the Classroom community and gain access to resources available right now. Educational television carries a vast number of powerful advantages in children's education. It is by no means the passive activity that critics would like you to think. Even the government agrees that television can and should be contributing to children's development. Children are already accustomed to watching TV, and let's face it, so are you and I. It's time to grasp educational television and demand it be brought to your school while it is still free.

## Bibliography

Baker, Kevin. "Programs Offer Ways to Guide Children as They Watch TV." *The Courier-Journal* 14 Mar. 1997: pg. O1C.

Bricklin, Mark. "Why Johnny Can't Learn." *Prevention* Nov. 1990: 144–5.

Clark, David. *Urban World/Global City*. New York: Routledge, 1996.

Cradler, John. "Ed Tech Resources." *Thrust for Educational Leadership* Apr. 1996: 43.

Fink, T. "Couch Potatoes." *Total Health* Apr. 1992: 38+.

"Get Cable in the Classroom." *Sacramento Business Journal* 20 Nov. 1995: 2.

Goldstein, Richard. "Grand Illusion." *Village Voice* 14 Jan. 1997: 44.

"Helping Working Parents Stay in Touch." *HR Focus* Aug. 1998: S7.

Huston, Aletha C., and John C. Wright. "Television and the Informational and Educational Needs of Children." *Annuals of the American Academy of Political & Social Science* 557 (1998): 9+.

"Illinois Teacher Applies Closed Captioning to Help Youngsters Learn Vocabulary." *Technological Horizons in Education Journal* 24.10(1997): 47+.

Johnson, Steve. "V-Chip may mean Victory for Parents and Ratings System." *Chicago Tribune* 18 Mar. 1998, sec. Tempo: 1.

Keeshan, Bob. "This Old Playhouse." *Entertainment Weekly* 22 Nov. 1996: 149.

"Learn at Warp Speed." *Business Journal Serving San Jose and Silicon Valley* 13.15(1995): 3.

Mace, Jane. "Television and Metaphors of Literacy." *Studies in the Education of Adults* Oct. 1992: 162+.

Morehead, Albert, and Loy Morehead, eds. *The New American Webster Handy College Dictionary*. New York: Penguin Group, 1995.

Page, Lyman A. M.D.. Letter. *The New York Times* 16 Apr. 1998: A22.

"PeachStar Accentuates Education in Georgia." *T H E Journal* 22.9 (1995): 26.

"Pediatricians Say TV Ratings Should Label Content, Not Viewers' Age." *Brown University Child & Adolescent Behavior Letter* Mar. 1997: 5.

Schorr, Daniel. "Violence on TV: So What's New?" *USA Today* 13 Feb. 1996: 9A.

Streisand, Betsy. "When Rivals Get Animated." *US News and World Report* 9 Dec. 1996: 76.

"Thanks, Big Bird." *Women's Day* 19 Sep. 1995: 14.

Trillin, Calvin, et al. "Child's Play." *Time* 30 Dec. 1996: 48.

Webster, Nancy. "Winnowed Kids' TV Field Still Drawing Big Bucks." *Advertising Age* 10 Feb. 1997: 28.

Witherup, Kathy. "Cable-to-Computer Service Brings the World to the Classroom." *Cincinnati Business Courier* 27 Dec. 1993: 10C+.

Zoglin, Richard, et al. "Prime-Time Summit." *Time* 11 Mar. 1996: 64+.

# DOUBLE STANDARD IN AMERICA'S "HUMANITARIAN" POLICIES

Yausamin Abediyeh

*In this essay, Yausamin Abediyeh marshals strong evidence to make the case that refugees of color from Haiti and Africa have not been given the same level of treatment as European refugees from Kosovo. She blames this partially on the disparate U.S. media coverage of the crises, and makes a plea for equal treatment. Note the wide range of sources she uses and how she develops her personal ethos as one who is sympathetic to Muslims.*

## *Audience Analysis*

My audience will consist of a group of key state department policy makers, Clinton foreign policy advisors at the White House and the National Security Agency. This group of white-collar professionals ranges in age from 25–55. Most of them would try to deny that there is a dichotomy in the United States foreign policy towards refugees with different ethnic backgrounds and will reiterate that there is no discrimination in the current U.S. foreign policy towards different refugees. My paper will originally be presented to this group of U.S. foreign policy analysts who have been invited to attend a conference/symposium entitled Double Standard in America's "Humanitarian" Policies? The political science department at the University of Maryland will sponsor this symposium. Papers presented in this symposium will be published in the *Diamondback* and in the Op Ed section of the *Washington Post*.

Throughout American history there has been evidence of inherent discrimination against minorities. Yet, it is hard to believe that such prejudices still exist today. Many are quick to dismiss any such comments. I must admit that even I, until recently, thought that narrow-mindedness and discrimination was a thing of the past. Yet, after researching about the refugees in Kosovo I realized that there were many other refugee groups in Africa and elsewhere that were largely forgotten and neglected. My research has shown that neither the United States humanitarian aid policy nor the mainstream network television coverage of the plight of refugees from different ethnic backgrounds has been fair or equitable.

There is ample evidence that the U.S. government has accommodated white European refugees generously, while other refugees of different ethnicities, such as the Haitians or Africans, have and still do receive little or no assistance. According to the United Nations, $1.60 a day has been spent on a Kosovar refugee, compared to the 11 cents a day per refugee in Africa (Shelby 23). These figures attest to the glaring fact that the United States government still continues to support biased causes. Now do not get me wrong: I am not saying that the U.S. government should stop helping the Kosovars, but they should definitely strive to be fair and equal in their assistance to refugees from different countries. For instance, a couple of years ago when the Haitians were fleeing their country by the boatloads and asking the United States for assistance, the U.S. did very little to help. Thousands drowned in the vast ocean while trying to make it to the U.S. in makeshift rafts.

According to an article in the *Los Angeles Times*, the refugee camps in Kosovo are much better staffed and equipped than refugee camps in African countries. The paper documents how the European refugees were accommodated much more generously than African refugees (Browne 2).

Although the daily food ration for both groups of refugees is the same in terms of calories, about 2,100, the types of food served differ tremendously. European refugees were often given ready-made meals with cheese, orange, milk, coffee, and fruit tarts, whereas ready-made meals do not even exist in African camps. In the African camps refugees get some wheat and sorghum grains in a bag. In countries such as Eritrea families as large as ten must share 3½ gallons of water to last them three days. In the Balkans, on the other hand, some camps even had mobile phones, soccer fields, basketball courts, and ping pong tables. One camp even had two movie theatres (Cathcart A7).

Medical attention was also much better in the European camps. The ratio in some camps was one doctor for every 700 refugees, whereas in Africa some refugee camps have one doctor for every 100,000 refugees (Curtis 6). NAACP President Kweisi Mfume commented, "Food, shelter, and supplies such as clean water and medical services should be dispensed to refugees based on need and not skin color" (Crisis 80). NAACP Chairman Julian Bond added:

> The disparities are a monumental disservice to mankind and discredit the humanitarian aid efforts across the globe. The fact that Yugoslavia rests in Europe's backyard should not obscure the basic fact that people are people and refugees in Africa want and deserve to be treated with dignity just as the Kosovar refugees. (Crisis 80)

During the Kosovo crisis many refugee aid workers in Africa were transferred to Kosovo. These workers were able to witness firsthand the disparities between the aid given to each group. One ex-Rwanda aid worker commented, "compared to the refugee camps in Africa, Strankovac (a Balkan refugee camp) is a five-star hotel" (Curtis 6).

Reading such accounts of the tremendous differences between refugee camps alone is disenchanting. In a country where we pride ourselves in being humanitarian and compassionate it is unbelievable to think that the United States could be capable of discriminating in such an uncivilized fashion. Yet, these accounts are true and many are not even aware of them. The media is also partly to blame.

The predominately white dominated network television companies such as ABC, CBS, and NBC have covered the Kosovar refugee's plight and black refugees such as the Haitian and African refugees in two totally different ways. It is interesting to note that America's major prime time network anchors of the evening nightly news broadcasts are all white. Mr. Peter Jennings anchors ABC's "World News Tonight," Mr. Dan Rather anchors CBS's "Evening News," and Mr. Tom Brokow anchors NBC's "Nightly News." During the plight of the Haitian refugees all major networks broadcasted similar news stories depicting the refugees as an uncivilized "herd" of people in desperation. There were also many stories about hundreds drowning at sea with U.S. television cameras just "rolling" but offering no help. And the media seems to want to ignore the problems in Africa. Hardly any stories have been covered on the dilemmas facing the hundreds of refugees in Africa.

On the other hand, these same networks portrayed refugees from Kosovo in a more civilized fashion. There were scenes of Kosovar families entering the U.S. from planes and being greeted by U.S. officials and representatives of humanitarian organizations such as the Red Cross. The media also went so far as to provide information on how the general public could sponsor Kosovar families. They also showed examples of some these families being sponsored and adopted by American families in different parts of the United States. There was hardly any similar coverage for the black Haitian refugees. These disparities have even been recognized by some U.S. officials such as Sen. David Patterson (D-Manhattan) who recently commented, "It is interesting that refugees from Kosovo have been portrayed as human beings and that their sufferings are what many in the U.S. connect with." The senator also noted, "if these refugees were from Haiti or Africa, the entire immigration machine would be standing by to challenge their rights to enter the country. And if they are admitted they would enter with a stigma" (Browne 3). New York City Councilman Bill Perkins also said, "there has never been a welcome mat for Haitians and other refugees of color to come to America." Yet, he also made it clear that, "this is not to say that refugees from Kosovo didn't deserve help" (Browne 2).

Now, I understand that the problems in Kosovo were big and tens of thousands of Muslims were being persecuted. Being a Muslim myself, I empathize with the Albanian refugees. I was also fortunate enough to become acquainted with a few during this past summer, and I was able to hear about the tremendous pain and suffering that they have undergone firsthand. No one should ever have to endure the hardships that they have gone through. I even commend the Clinton administration for taking the initiative to do something about the atrocities being committed towards them. However, this does not mean that we can ignore or forget about the millions of refugees in other parts of the world, namely Africa. Many African nations are in turmoil. They have experienced much hardship and are still suffering some of the same problems that the Albanians were facing just a few months ago before the United States intervened. Countries such as Ethiopia, Eritrea, Sudan, Rwanda, the Congo and many others are immersed in ethnic conflicts and political turmoil resulting in an overflow of homeless refugees with no one and no where to turn to (Curtis 6). Why are the U.S. and other so called "humanitarian" nations not doing anything to help?

It appears that the aid given to Kosovo was not entirely out of pure goodwill. Furthermore, one cannot help but feel that there were some underlying motives. For one thing, it seems to be the first time that the U.S. has shown any interest in the needs of a Muslim group. Generally speaking, Muslims have not been favored by U.S. foreign policy. Muslims have been stereotyped as ruthless terrorists who bomb buildings and wreak havoc everywhere. America has been quick to blame Muslim terrorists for numerous bombings such as in Israel and also in America. It should be pointed out that the Oklahoma City bombing was first blamed on Muslim terrorists. They were among the first suspects. Given these prior incidents of hostility and prejudices towards Muslims it is hard to believe that the U.S. genuinely cares for the Muslim refugees. Robert Mark from Harlem agrees, "I am not tricked by Clinton's claim that he's concerned about the Albanians and the bigotry they are suffering because they are Muslims. Clinton is the same guy who, under false pretenses, bombed the pharmaceutical factory in Muslim Sudan, the only such plant that manufactured medicine for the Sudanese" (Browne 2).

Many believe that the ethnic Albanians were in dire need of assistance. Others may contend that the problem in Africa is not as serious as it was in Kosovo. This may appear to be the case, however statistics show that Africa contains approximately 6.3 million refugees, which makes Africa the most affected area of the world (Baali 1). The problem is that most are unaware of the plight many African refugees undergo. Again, the media is partly to blame. For the past year the news has been filled with stories and reports on the Albanian refugees. Nevertheless, hardly anything has been reported on the problems in Africa. For instance, an ongoing border dispute between Ethiopia and Eritrea has been going on for about two years now and hardly anybody is aware. This same pointless war has already claimed more lives than the one in Kosovo ("Africa's" 42). The astonishing fact is that the two countries have agreed to accept a ruling resulting from international arbitration, however, hardly anyone has stepped in. The Organization for African Unity (OAU) was the only group that seemed to show any interest. Though, either intentionally or not the OAU gave the two governments different explanations of its own plan. Mr. Meles, Ethiopia's prime minister has publicly taken the position that Eritrean forces must withdraw from all occupied areas in Ethiopia, while, Mr. Issias, Eritrea's president, publicly contended that withdrawal of Eritrean forces only referred to a small area known as the Badme. The OAU has yet to take a clear public position on this matter ("Africa's" 43).

Ladies and Gentlemen, I understand I may have been quite harsh throughout the course of this speech. Please remember, I commend what you have done and accomplished for the Albanian refugees. "Witnessing human suffering and the denial of basic rights must always make us recoil in disgust, and eventually, respond with conviction" (Cathcart A7). However, as American citizens we should pride ourselves in being humanitarian to refugees regardless of their ethnicity or race. Today, we are learning more about the horrors that occurred in Kosovo. The brutal ethnic cleansing of the Serbian campaign to flush out the ethnic Albanians is covered daily by the media's coverage of the peacekeeping efforts in Kosovo. This information is vital if we are to prevent such atrocities in the future. But we must not forget the deplorable conditions of the refugees from countries such as Eritrea, Ethiopia, Rwanda, Angola, Afghanistan, and Chechnya that need immediate humanitarian assistance.

## Works Cited

"Africa's Forgotten War." *The Economist* 8 May 1999: 41–43.

"Atrocities Reported in Sierra Leone." *The Associated Press* 7 Dec.1999. 8 Dec. 1999 <http://www.softlineweb.com>.

Baali, Abdallah. "M2 Presswire." *M2 Communications Ltd* 17 Nov. 1999. Lexis-Nexis. 11 Dec. 1999. Keyword: African refugees.

Browne, J. Zamgba. "Do Kosovo Refugees Receive better treatment than those from Africa and the Caribbean?" *New York Amsterdam News* 23 June 1999: 2.

Brownstein, Ronald. "Americans Will Weigh Kosovo War Against Price of Good Intentions." *The Los Angeles Times* 19 Apr 1999. 11 Dec. 1999 <http://www.latimes.com>.

_____. "Effort to Stop Bleeding in Balkans is no Blueprint for Intervention." *The Los Angeles Times* 8 June 1999. 11 Dec. 1999 <http://latimes.com>.

Cathcart, Christopher D. "The Color of Humanity-Refugees in Black and White." *New Pittsburgh Courier* 29 Sep. 1999: A7+.

Curtis, Emory. "Another View: Refugee Skin Color Makes a Difference." *The Sun Reporter* 3 June 1999: 6.

Deck, Stewart. "Red Cross Uses Net To Help Refugees." *American Red Cross* (July 1999). MdUSA. Ebscohost. 19 Oct. 1999. Keyword: Kosovo Refugees.

Dennis, Mark. "The Road to Peace." *Newsweek* 21 June 1999: 6.

Duffy, Brian. "Heartbreak House." *U.S. News and World Report* 12 July 1999: 2.

Haney, Elissa. *Kosovo Fact Sheet.* 16 June 1999. 19 Oct. 1999 <http//infoplease.lycos.com/spot/kosvol.html>.

Hu, Winnie. "Kosovars Prepare to Leave U.S. for Homeland." *New York Times* 3 Aug. 1999: B1+.

MacLeod, Alexander. "Balkan Refugees Find Tense Welcome in Britain." *Christian Science Monitor* Vol.91 Iss.186, p7, (08/20/99). MdUSA. Ebscohost. 19 Oct. 1999. Keyword: Kosovo Refugees.

Mason, Elisa. "Against All Odds: Refugees Coping In A Strange Land." *American Libraries* Vol.30, Iss.7, p44, (Aug99). MdUSA. Ebscohost. 19 Oct. 1999. Keyword: Kosovo Refugees.

Rogers, David. "Kosovo Debate in Congress Turns More Partisan on Costs, Troops." *Wall Street Journal* 28 Apr. 1999: A16.

Shelby, Barry. "Double Standard." *World Press Review* MdUSA. Ebscohost. 19 Oct. 1999. Keyword: Kosovo Refugees.

Stanley, D. L. "Africa 'Forgotten and Ignored' By U.S., McKinney Charges." *Atlanta Inquirer* 31 July 1999: 1.

Ukshin. Personal interview. 25 Oct. 1999.

"U.S., African Forces Join in Exercise." *Christian Science Monitor* 22 June 1998: 10.

Usher, Rod. "Still High on Hatred." *Time* 16 Aug.1999 <http:// www.pathfinder.com>.

# A TIMELESS ATTACK

Justin Benoit

> *Justin Benoit, a student at the University of Maryland, wrote this paper
> in 1999. The paper has a dual audience because, aside from turning it
> in to fulfill an assignment, he also delivered it as a speech at the Uni-
> versity's Undergraduate Research Conference. Benoit argues that an
> earlier attack on Normandy during World War II would have been a
> mistake, and that, despite arguments to the contrary, the invasion was
> well-planned. Note the exigence he establishes by linking this historical
> attack to the more current Kosovo crisis.*

## *Audience Analysis*

This essay would be found in an issue of *The Washington Post Magazine*. This specific edition of the magazine would commemorate World War II, but would have
essays in it that were reevaluations of key battles and decisions in the war, instead of
just recapping history. This specific essay would be found in the section that discussed possible errors of the Allies in Europe. When the Allies should have opened
the second front in Europe is the topic being discussed. This essay supports the time
that D-Day took place in history. Many of these articles would be presenting radical
viewpoints along with standard ideas towards this topic in hopes to enlighten the
audience. Much of this edition's purpose would be to support the actions of America, since most of its readers and writers are citizens.

Although the actual audience of the essays would be people that have a subscription to
*The Washington Post*. Therefore, this audience would generally be well educated,
because they must enjoy reading *The Washington Post* every morning. Also, it is
assumed that this audience would overall be well off. However, they will not be
extremely well educated on World War II. This audience would not be a large group
of history enthusiasts but may contain war veterans. Overall it would be a group of
interested readers who would like to know about controversial strategic maneuvers
in the war. This entire issue would take a more basic look at the war so that readers
with little background information could come away with much knowledge. Almost
all age groups, war veterans to young adults, would be interested because of the similar curiosity in the strategy of war.

Other defining characteristics of this audience would be that most readers would
be male, with at least some interest in war. This is just because most females are not
very interested in battles of the past. Most readers would be American because it is
found in *The Washington Post*, but an American of any nationality would read this.
For obvious reasons, most readers would live in the DC area.

Bombs are falling right now in Kosovo. Is NATO doing the right thing? Are these
actions acceptable? President Clinton has set up a comparison between Kosovo
and World War II. He has argued that were allied leaders a little wiser, they would
have acted earlier and less lives would have been lost. In effect, President Clinton

has justified these actions by the consequences of a lack of action to start World War II. Will it make a difference now?

Clinton, just like the rest of us, has the urge to reevaluate past wars in hope for a better future. What was done right? What was not? These questions are raised often about World War II. It truly was a world war; the size of which has yet to be challenged. It is a great point of comparison, and one that President Clinton is using right now.

It seems easy to compare the pros and cons of entering World War II earlier; the number of Jews killed before America entered the war lies in the millions. So, what about something more complex such as the timing of D-Day; the pros and cons are not well defined. World War II and D-Day seem to sit side by side in the minds of most Americans, and rightfully so. D-Day, also known as Operation Overlord, has been called the greatest amphibious assault in the history of man because it signals the downfall of the Nazi party in Europe, a nation powerful enough to have taken over the entire world. Ultimately, this led to the end of World War II. So what if D-Day had taken place earlier? Would it too have been more successful like we assume an earlier entry into the war would have been? That isn't as simple to answer. There are political issues at hand that are only now becoming clear.

Yet, today this Normandy invasion has come under fire by historians, who, following a similar logic to Clinton's, claim that the attack should have occurred a year or two earlier. According to these individuals, D-Day occurred too late and as a result, many lives were lost unnecessarily. However, looking only at the soldiers killed in World War II is too narrow a view for a controversy the size of Operation Overlord. World War II is not the only event D-Day affected. It is a timeless attack that still affects us today.

Not all battles would have been better off if started earlier. It is not unrealistic to think that Kosovo could turn into a much larger war; many wars have started over less. Therefore, we must choose our course of action carefully. This decision has been made, but to justify Kosovo on an evaluation of World War II, one must pick one's battle carefully. D-Day is not one of those battles. Attacking any earlier than the dawn of June 6, 1944 not only could have cost lives then, but would still be costing lives now in terms of later wars. The British and American leaders understood the magnitude of Overlord, and reacted accordingly; the timing was perfect.

To look at this timeless attack, it is important to work chronologically to see all the reasons why an earlier attack would not have worked, as they unfolded in real life, before we get to the present.

America today is the number one superpower in the world, in terms of military might, even though it is a relatively new country. This status is a direct result of World War II where America won on two different fronts at the same time, while still having an extremely low casualty rate. Right after World War II, the year 1945, America contributed 49% of the world's produced goods (Olson). This is extremely high for a single country, and shows this country's power. However, many forget that before World War II, America's military was not as strong as countries like Great Britain, Germany and Russia. It is at this time where the events that led up to D-Day start. American troops were untrained and so America was not as strong then as it is now by any means.

Though the weak American army was sure of its own power, and wanted to attack Europe, the British convinced them that they needed a stepping stone towards an invasion of Germany. Dr. Walter Dunn, a major proponent that the attack on the Germans in Europe should have been in 1943, even admits in his book that "American troops lacked combat experience and therefore were not capable of facing the German Army" (198). What was needed back then was a place to train soldiers, and yet still hurt the Germans since time was of the essence. Africa was the perfect candidate so that a victory at D-Day would be possible. Africa, at the time, has been described as a place where the training of American soldiers could be prolonged so they would be ready for a more serious affair (Higgins 155). The more serious affair was D-Day. By attacking Africa the Allies were ensured that troops would get valuable training on weak troops and that German oil supplies would be threatened. Attacking Africa also opened the possibility of attacking the heart of Germany from the southern boarder. Germany had a weaker Italian ally in 1942 that was a great place to attack. Africa was the best of everything (Stoler 4).

Although this idea to invade Africa seemed perfect, it did not go over well with the soldiers of the United States and Great Britain. Dr. Olson of the University of Maryland history department says that one of the best reasons to have attacked earlier is because Americans thought that Africa was a side show. These soldiers wanted to fight the Germans on their territory. By attacking right away, there would have been great deal of morale harnessed for the advantage of the Allies. However, all the energy in the world won't save a division of troops if they don't know how to fight. Besides, the opposite proved to be true. Since American troops felt like they had not been fighting "real" German soldiers, when they finally got their chance at D-Day, their morale was higher than it was in '42 or '43. Soldiers that got to fight in this battle were actually considered lucky at the time. After D-Day, General Patton, the main American ground leader in Europe, and his troops swept though German territory faster than anyone had expected. According to the Eisenhower Foundation, Allied planners expected to reach the Rhine no sooner than 260 days after D-Day. Because of the soldiers' high morale, it only took a mere 19 (91).

After the African campaign, American troops were well trained and ready to attack, but one should not assume that America's allies were ready to fight the Germans before Africa, either. While the troops of Great Britain were more skilled in the early phases of the war, they also could not attack earlier than 1944, because of the risk. If an attack was to go forth earlier than the African mission, then the assault would have depended on Great Britian's willingness to use mostly their troops and their willingness to take the risk (Stoler 34). Although the opening of a second front was important to the war effort, a loss at this battle would severely weaken Britain which was already weak at the time (Bruce 51).

Just as it was unpopular that the Americans did not attack right away, so too was it unliked that Britain waited. Historian Trumbull Higgins argues that if the British had lost many men in France in 1942, then they should just try again in 1943 (143). However, Higgins fails to take into account that Hitler was planning an attack on Britain, code named Sea Lion. If Great Britain had attacked, and then been defeated in 1942, there would have been no time for an attack in 1943 because Hitler would have already counter attacked, and more than likely defeated Britain because Hitler's forces were still strong. This course of events would have left no hope for America and so Great Britain needed an Africa just as much as the Americans. The bottom line is that an earlier attack would have been devastating to the Allies; they just weren't ready until 1944.

So what if Allied soldiers had been ready earlier; they still wouldn't have gotten ashore. Throughout much of World War II, a new kind of weapon had been perfected until it was a lethal armament that could destroy and never be seen again. It was the submarine whose attributes had been improved. The depth at which they could safely travel increased, making them even harder to destroy, along with extended range on both the sub and torpedoes. The Germans were expecting that if an invasion of Europe was going to be attempted by the Allies, then the attack would come from Britain and attack somewhere on the north coast. As a result, Hitler ordered a constant patrol of this area by large numbers of submarines. The Germans knew right where to deploy this weapon and this threatened the Allies' plan for an invasion greatly. It was assumed that the subs would reduce the flow of the soldiers to the landing zone (Dunn 44). Had the attack come in 1943, fewer soldiers would have reached the beaches during a longer period of time. What was key to this invasion was a complete barrage of troops onto the beaches. A small group would have been destroyed by German machine guns. It wasn't until 1944, due to losses and a shortage of supplies, that the submarine problem was practically eliminated.

So far, everything that has been discussed, which has included the readiness of troops along with the feasibility of the journey across the English Channel, has taken one thing for granted, which is the ability to cross the sea with or without competition from the Nazis. Hundreds of thousands of troops can not just magically appear on Europe's beaches. D-Day's plan involved troops going across the water in landing craft specially designed for this mission. The problem was very simple; these landing craft were not available. Historians like Mark Stoler, an expert on international politics, said that because of political and economic reasons, still unclear today, American troops could not arrive in England fast enough to take place in an earlier D-Day (34). The tardiness is because of that lack of landing craft. Although this statement has been contested by others, it really doesn't matter either way. The problem still remained that the number of landing craft was not available like it was by 1944, when they had more time to build. In 1943, there was no time to build due to constant fighting.

There were many problems standing in the way of the Allies' plan to open up a second front. Many of these problems discussed previously were solved with time. However, one problem was solved unexpectedly by time; the problem of Hitler.

Make no mistake, Hitler was a great tactical leader. Next to Napoleon and Genghis Khan, no single leader has ever conquered so much territory in such a short period of time. In the early 1940's, he was a dangerous leader. However, by the time that 1944 came, Hitler had become more of a problem to the Nazis than to the Allies. His poor judgment on many key tactical decisions helped to seal the defeat of the

Germans (Overy 153). By waiting until 1944 for the attack, the Allies had the advantage that Hitler was no longer a great leader.

Hitler's lack of good leadership was very present when D-Day took place. Hitler knew that a direct attack on his empire would come at some point in the war, and so he prepared many defense mechanisms to throw the coming invasion back into the sea. Yet, when the Normandy invasion did occur, he was convinced that it was just a decoy and decided not to send reinforcements. Rommel, a main German General, wanted three panzer divisions dispatched directly behind the site where D-Day took place, a month before the invasion. The divisions were the 12th SS Panzer, Panzer Lehr, and 21st Panzer Divisions. However, only one of these divisions was deployed to this area and it was the weakest one. This suggests that D-Day was won just because Hitler refused to give a few commands in 1944. Had Hitler agreed with Rommel, which may have happened in 1943, the Allies could never had been successful.

So far we have dealt with the war in Europe and why an earlier attack on the heart of German territory would never have succeeded. Yet, there are still many who would disagree with the facts and look at the events leading up to D-Day in a different light. But that is the problem right there. People are only looking at the immediate consequences or benefits of the Normandy invasion, and specifically when it occurred. This invasion of Normandy in 1944 didn't just help the Allies win the war in Europe, it is affecting us now, because it occurred when it did. It is naive to think that an attack of this magnitude would not have repercussions in the future, and these repercussions are sometimes unrecognized.

In Dr. Dunn's book, *Second Front Now—1943*, he describes why the second front should have been opened in 1943. After reading his book it becomes evident that his main point is that "The true reasons for the course of action in World War II were political rather than military" (43). By this, he means that the American and British troops failed to attack not because they were untrained, or because they lacked supplies, but because the they did not want to support the Russians and instead they wanted to watch them suffer. While the American and British troops were planning D-Day, Russian troops were bearing the brunt of the Germans attacks, and were getting slaughtered. If they really regarded Russians as an important ally, they would have attacked in 1943. This puts the blame of many deaths on the Americans and British because of this political agenda which is the main point of many historians who think that the second front should have been opened up sooner.

I could not agree more with this statement. However, Dr. Dunn fails to look at anything past World War II; he fails to look at the usually unrecognized repercussions. The Americans and British did fail to attack because they had a political agenda, but this is not a critically incorrect action like Dr. Dunn would have you believe. Quite the contrary, this is the best decision that Roosevelt and Churchill made because no matter what you believe about D-Day, in the long run, it saved many more lives, maybe even your own, just because they waited.

The first effects of their waiting, that is outside of World War II, are in the Vietnam and Korean wars. These wars were not on the level of the Second World War.

They were about containing Communism. These wars were bound to happen because of conflicting governmental issues after World War II, and the leaders of that war knew it back then. The alliance between America and Britain with Russia was forced and based off of a common enemy, not on friendship.

Keeping in mind that these two wars were going to occur no matter what developed in World War II, suppose that the American and British soldiers did attack Germany in 1942 or 1943, and they were successful in their attempts. It is reasonable to assume that they would have then defeated Germany soon after, and would have actually defeated the Nazis sooner than they did in reality. This sounds like an ideal situation; it is anything but. The one thing that changes from this outcome is that the Russians no longer bear the brunt of the German army for so many years. I argue that the result would be a Russia that comes out of World War II much stronger than it really did. If we assume that history continues on its path the Korean war would soon start because of differing views between the Americans and Russians. This time, however, the Russians are strong and can support their communist allies. The Korean war becomes a huge battle because both sides are very strong.

The world came close to full nuclear war during the Cuban missile crisis. The Russians, however, ended up backing down. Realizing that in this new world the wars between the Americans and Russians are much larger, there would now be even more tension between the two countries. Also, the Russians are still stronger than they were in reality because they had not been destroyed by the years of attack from the Germans. Again, history repeats itself and the Cuban missile crisis occurs. In this new world, because of the wars between America and Russia, and because Russia is stronger, there is no way the Russians would have backed down. Nuclear war would have proceeded, and the cold hard consequence is that many would be dead.

The American and British leaders had a very strong political agenda, because they realized what was going to happened after the war. Number one is only large enough for one country, and if two are in competition for it, they will go all the way. It was crucial that the Russians come out of World War II weakened so that this nightmare of nuclear war would have less of a chance of happening. They came out weaker because the attack was late. History affects many things, not just what occurs right after the event.

This brings us back to Kosovo. To determine what to do, we must look to the past. In some cases, such as the beginning of World War II, it would appear that we acted too late, and an earlier attack would have been beneficial. However, this issue over D-Day is a case where the opposite is true. Waiting was the best plan for the allies. It is utterly important for the leaders of NATO to realize these kind of discrepancies in history. Many Albanian lives are now at stake, and the right choice needs to be made.

As for Operation Overlord, an attack as large as that, the size of which the world had never seen before, is going to affect much more than just that battle. The leaders of the free world knew of these destined repercussions and so they knew that June 6, 1944 was the best and only time for D-Day to take place. Thank you.

## Works Cited

Astor, Gerald. *June 6, 1944: The Voices of D-Day*. New York: St. Martin's Press, 1994.

Bradley, Omar N. Foreword. *D-Day: The Normandy Invasion in Retrospect*. By The Eisenhower Foundation. New York: The University Press of Kansas, 1971. vi.

Breuer, William B. *Unexplained Mysteries of World War II*. New York: John Wiley & Sons, Inc., 1997.

Bruce, George. *Second Front Now!: The Road to D-Day*. London: Macdonald and Jane's Publishers Limited, 1979.

Currey, Cecil B. *Follow Me And Die: The Destruction of an American Division in World War II*. New York: Stein and Day Publishers, 1984.

Dunn, Walter Scott, Jr. *Second Front Now—1943*. University, Alabama: The University of Alabama Press, 1980.

Eisenhower Foundation. *D-Day: The Normandy Invasion in Retrospect*. New York: The University Press of Kansas, 1971.

Higgins, Trumbull. *Winston Churchill and the Second Front 1940–1943*. New York, NY: Oxford University Press, 1957.

Hoyt, Edwin P. *The Invasion Before Normandy: The Secret Battle of Slapton Sands*. New York: Stein and Day Publishers, 1985.

Liddell-Hart, B. H. *The German Generals Talk*. New York: William Morrow and Co., 1948.

Miller, Russell. *Nothing Less Than Victory*. New York: William Morrow and Company, Inc., 1993.

Morison, Samuel Eliot. *Strategy and Compromise: Reappraisal of the Crucial Decisions Confronting the Allies in the Hazardous Years, 1940–1945*. Boston: Little, Brown and Company, 1958.

Nadeau, Remi A. *Stalin, Churchill, and Roosevelt Divide Europe*. New York: Praeger Publishers, 1990.

Olson, Keith. Personal Interview. 6 Nov. 1998.

Overy, Richard. *Why The Allies Won*. New York: W. W. Norton & Company, 1995.

Parker, R. A. C. *The Second World War*. Oxford: Oxford University Press, 1997.

Powers, Stephen T. "The Battle of Normandy: The Lingering Controversy." *The Journal of Military History* 56.3 (1992): 455–471.

Rooney, Andrew A. *The Fortunes of War*. Boston: Little Brown and Company, 1962.

Stoler, Mark A. *The Politics of the Second Front: American Military Planning and Diplomacy in Coalition Warfare, 1941–1943*. Westport, CT: Greenwood Press, 1977.

Tsouras, Peter. *Disaster At D-Day: The Germans Defeat the Allies, June 1944*. London: Greenhill Books, 1994.

# PORN AND WOMEN—WHERE TO GO FROM HERE

Roberta Cosentino

> *Roberta Cosentino's final position paper, written in August 2001, argues that the readers of* Ms. *magazine should consider how pornography shapes men and women's thinking about gender roles and sexuality so that these readers can determine how best to work towards gender equality. Notice how the second paragraph of the text works to partition and create exigence for this complex argument.*

## Audience Analysis

I will be writing for *Ms. Magazine*, a mainstream feminist publication. It will be mostly women who read the magazine, probably of all ages. Because *Ms. Magazine* also has a web page, the audience will be worldwide, but again, mostly women. I am a complete stranger to my audience, so I will have to use my intrinsic ethos to develop a relationship. My audience will most likely already have opinions formed about the issue of pornography. This means the audience is aware of and probably educated about the topic and will be looking for a good argument, including things they haven't thought of before. The magazine leans towards liberal feminism, so my audience will probably be hostile towards pornography.

After doing a search on the *Ms. Magazine* web page using "pornography" as a keyword, I was surprised to find no articles that discuss the issue of pornography directly. I assume that, because it was mentioned in a few articles, there is general knowledge about the issue.

Values I can capitalize on include gender equality and a general desire to improve the position of women in our country today. There are values that will be difficult to work against, though. First, many feminists are highly in favor of upholding the First Amendment and see any anti-porn discussion as going against that value. Also, many people may discount an anti-porn argument without hearing it out because of past experiences with one-sided arguments. Another value is freedom of expression of sexuality. Many people value porn as a gateway to that freedom. Last, the very fact that I am speaking to feminists can work against me because, if there are so many different groups of feminists, they are going to be varied in their beliefs. It will be hard to accommodate everyone.

Exigence should not be difficult to establish because I will tell them it is in women's favor to take this issue and use it to further their progress with feminist ideals. If we really want gender equality, we need to look at anything that may be inhibiting that goal, and my argument will be made with this in mind.

Four score and several years ago women were subject to living their lives in a prescribed and predetermined way. Today we are still waging a slow but progressive war on traditional gender roles with discrimination, subordination, and inequality in tow. These are the things that help to perpetuate violence in our culture and should be the concern of anyone who is interested in the goal of equality. This war will not end as long as pornography and the porn industry exist as they do today. Pornography is a major factor in helping to preserve the very gender ideals most feminists are working to redefine. We need to be concerned about all women, the victimization of them, and the future we seem to be destined for. Because victimization of women in the United States does not seem to be on the decline, we should reexamine pornography and the role it plays in the formation of sexuality and gender ideals in both men and women.

Religious groups, feminists, politicians, and so on have argued against porn. This is neither solely a religious debate nor a feminist issue and certainly should not be left in the hands of politicians. This is an issue that involves looking at factual evidence, probabilities, and first-hand accounts. As feminists, whatever your ideals and goals for the movement, we should have one common goal: to improve the conditions facing women. Looking at the effects of pornography on our culture needs to be part of that goal. My own purpose is not to censor porn or regulate it. I am not afraid of porn and I'm not afraid of sexual expression, as some porn advocates may have you believe the anti-porn crusaders are (Strossen 119). I am afraid of the possibility that information without education can lead to acts of ignorance. I'm afraid that not dissecting pornography and looking at the hold it has on our culture could be detrimental to any goal of the feminist movement. In order to look at this issue rationally and thoroughly I will first discuss the traditional gender ideals that lend a hand in perpetuating the acceptance of the victimization of women and how this is normalized in different facets of our culture. Next I will look at the violent acts committed towards women, which will lead to the discussion of violent pornography and whether there is a correlation between the two. I will also introduce similar concerns about pornography in one of our neighboring countries and how they have dealt with the issue. Finally, I will discuss one of the most important issues for pro-porn crusaders, which is the idea of sexual liberation, and how pornography plays a role in that.

Gender roles are ingrained into our socialization and help to normalize violence against women. Our gender roles are based in tradition and learned over the course of our lives, in every part of our lives. Women's roles have not and will not change overnight, or even over a few decades. To be clear, gender is a socially constructed phenomenon that differs from culture to culture. Femininity, in our culture, includes the ideals of sensitivity, being reserved, and being available as a sexual object. Masculinity, on the other hand, includes the ideals of aggressiveness, being the sole breadwinner, being physically strong, emotionally rational and ambitious. Though these ideals may strike us at first as out of date, they are still normalized through language, the media, and institutions today, thereby normalizing violence towards women (Wood 328–32). To be sure we can look at each individually and find examples of this normalization.

Language is something that is often overlooked as a means of normalizing violence towards women. It is more powerful than some are aware, as Julia T. Wood (a well-published researcher and professor in the fields of gender, communication, culture and communication in personal relationships) notes. Referring to Sharon Lamb, Wood says, "She asks why we use inappropriately gentle terms such as *domestic dispute* or *spousal conflict* to camouflage actions such as smashing women's faces with fists and hammers, slashing women with knives, and breaking bones by throwing or stomping on women" (332). Domestic violence, although more public today than ever before, is still accepted as something private and between intimates. As with most acts of violence, there is always an assumption in the language that we use that dismisses the man as fully responsible for his actions. Why didn't she leave him? Why was she walking alone at night? What was she wearing? The immediate assumption that a woman is responsible for her own victimization proves the traditional gender ideal of submissiveness. Because language such as this is used on such a regular basis and has been a part of our culture for as long as anyone can remember, it tends to be forgotten as a factor in affecting other cultural patterns. As feminists, we have a responsibility to be aware of the language we use because it is no trivial matter and helps to gloss over the victimization of women.

Another normalizing factor, much talked about, is the media. Violence of any kind is the norm in all facets of the media. Television, movies, video games and music all portray violence in not-so-unique ways. In conjunction with this is the portrayal of women as sex objects. MTV's music videos that show half-naked women and insinuations of sex, and FOX's "Ally McBeal" as a sexy-but-intelligent-young-lawyer who is overly preoccupied with love and relationships, suggest that, no matter what a woman does or who she is, she is still a sexual object. Although this is not a debate about the media and the responsibility they should have, it's important to note that these two portrayals of women and many portrayals of violence exist together in our mainstream culture.

The media alone is not to blame for normalization of violence. Institutions also play a big role. The family is a major socializing factor, and is also a place where the female and male gender ideals are encouraged. Girls play with their Barbie dolls quietly in the corner while boys build a fort outside to fight off intruders. Although this is not fully accurate for all families, there are hundreds of ways the traditional ideals find their way into the lives and upbringing of children. Parents, unless they consciously make continual efforts to avoid it, teach their children to behave in certain ways that adhere to the traditional gender ideals. The justice system lets domestic abuse go unprosecuted. When it is prosecuted, it often does not receive a harsh punishment. Many religious groups tell women to concentrate on being good wives and mothers and just live with the rest. The education system, it has been proven, is a place that continues to discriminate against women, both in and outside of the classroom (Stone and McKee 134). Whether the institution is family, the justice system, religion, or education, women are continually treated as the "other" gender. These are not new issues to anyone, but provide the context for how pornography plays into the issues we already are fighting.

Hopefully it is evident that through language, media, and institutions the traditional gender ideals we seem to be fighting against continue to be normalized thereby normalizing any violence that is associated with them. If men are portrayed as aggressive, it is okay for them to be aggressive in any way. If women are portrayed as submissive and sex objects, it's okay for them to be treated in that way. To continue along these same lines, it's important for us now to look at the different types of violence women face in the United States and to be reminded of the urgency of these problems.

Although we are all aware of the types of violence women are victims of, we sometimes forget, even as women, how prevalent it is. According to the U.S. Department of Justice, there were an average of 4.6 million violent incidents involving a female victim between 1992 and 1994. They also report that "in 1995 women were about two-thirds as likely as men to be victims of violence; 20 years ago they were half as likely. [...] For rape, robbery and assault in 1992–3, female victims experienced 7 times as many incidents of violence by an intimate as male victims" (Bureau of Justice Statistics). These numbers indicate that not only are there a large number of female victims of violent crime, but the numbers have risen from 20 years ago. How is it that in the midst of our women's rights revolution, violence has risen against us? It is essential to compare the statistical data with cultural fallacies. One of these fallacies is that pornography is not harmful.

To research pornography empirically, data is collected by organizing and cataloging scenes with explicitly stated acts of violence. This data is then used to show the prevalence of violence in pornography. In the discussion of their research, Elizabeth Monk-Turner and Christine Purcell conclude: "we find sexism and racism evident in the pornographic material analyzed. Women continue to be portrayed as sexual objects ever available to perform sexual acts. Women are often cast as the submissive part in these relationships." Although they establish that these scenes are widely seen in porn films, they make no determination about their effect on violence towards women in the general public. In similar research, Martin Barron and Michael Kimmel look at three pornographic media (magazines, video, and the Internet), and find

"changing levels of violence within a context of men's relations with each other, and in their constant and ceaseless efforts to prove their masculinity in the eyes of other men. The changes in violent content among media, then, has more to do with the definition of hegemonic masculinity than it does with technological proliferation and democratization, or with the psychological propensity to require greater and greater thrills before satiation".

Both of these conclusions point to the fact that men's desires are affected by pornography and women are portrayed as living out the traditional gender ideals which harm more than sexually enhance us. An example of this is the rape myth. "Rape myths—that is, scenarios that show women getting sexual pleasure from rape—are among the favourite fictions of pornographers. When they are presented to men in clinical settings, they have been shown to have an enormous influence on male attitudes towards sexuality. The more they see the more likely they are to believe that women really enjoy rape and prefer force in sex" (Cole 218–9). Obviously, this is only one of many ways that pornography reinforces myths about women, so as women we need to ask ourselves why we allow this portrayal.

Although there is no research that can prove that pornography directly causes violence towards women in the general public, there has been research to show a correlation between the two. As Leslie Friedman Goldstein, a professor and researcher of women's rights cases, points out, "sexual responses often are unthinking responses, and the association of sexual arousal with the subordination of women therefore may have a substantial effect" (294). Although porn advocates claims that using pornography is a method of enhancing sexual desire (Queen 144), for some people it has more of an effect. Porn allows people to enter the realm of fantasy, but at some point and for some people, it becomes harder to draw the line between what is fantasy and what is reality. Robert Jensen, a researcher of pornography and its relation to violence, interviewed several sexual offenders. The patterns Jensen found were that for the men he interviewed, "pornography was an important factor in shaping a male dominant view of sexuality, and in several cases the material contributed to the men's difficulty in separating fantasy and reality" (535). It is vital to realize that not all people are capable of using porn in a healthy manner. Of course everyone shouldn't have to pay for the mistakes of a few, but in the context of gender ideals and the impact of porn on women, it would be detrimental to ignore the fact that porn has negative consequences.

There is more than one way to look at the portrayal of women in porn. Women inside the porn industry have fallen victim also. During the Minneapolis Hearings on July 25, 1984 those victims got a chance to be heard. Even if we cannot specifically say porn causes anything in the larger culture; even if we cannot blame one person, or one thing; even if in the future porn continues to function as it does today, there is something to remember. During the Hearings, answering a question as a witness, Linda Marchiano (a.k.a. Linda Lovelace), talked about the film she is most famous for: *Deep Throat*. "Virtually every time someone watches that film, they are watching me being raped" (qtd. in MacKinnon and Dworkin 65). Allowing something like this to continue is literally a crime.

Obviously, the United States cannot be the only country facing the dilemma of pornography. In fact, we are not. Our neighboring country, Canada, made a move that was extremely significant to the issue of pornography in this country. As a country with similar norms, values, and obstacles facing gender equality, Canada took a very progressive step in 1992.

> "The Supreme Court of Canada on February 27th upheld the obscenity provision of the criminal code, ruling that although the anti-pornography law infringes on the freedom of expression, it is legitimate to suppress materials that harm women. [...] This makes Canada the first place in the world that says what is obscene is what harms women" ("Canada").

By trusting communities to bear the responsibility of deciding what pornographic material is obscene, Canada has shown that it realizes that this is not an issue that should be left solely to the courts. Instead, this is an issue that needs to be recognized by the community as a whole. Canada has sent a meaningful message to the porn industry that material that harms women will not be tolerated. On the other hand, the United States has proven that, close to ten years after the fact, we are still unwilling to face the possibility that pornography is not the innocent private indulgence we want to think it is.

Finally, it is essential that there is a discussion about the sexual liberation of women. Proponents of porn agree that pornography has helped women to realize sexual liberation and feel more comfortable with voicing their desires, either publicly or privately (Queen). As mentioned earlier, we must realize that socialization and normalization of ideals occurs through not only the media, but also through institutions, including family, and language. The sexual liberation of women will not occur through pornography alone, but through a change in socialized norms that allow women to accept their bodies and their sexuality. Pornography sustains the traditional gender ideals of submissiveness and subordination, thereby not allowing for the sexual liberation of all women. The privileged few that have been helped by pornography should be applauded for their willingness to open themselves up to the possibilities of sexuality, but they should not assume that this would be the case for everyone. Catherine MacKinnon says, "I define sexuality as whatever a given society eroticizes. That is, sexual is whatever sexual means in a particular society. Sexuality is what sexuality means. [. . .] Because sexuality arises in relations under male dominance, women are not the principal authors of its meanings" (53). To say that the sexual liberation of women will stem from pornography, therefore, only makes sense if we want our sexuality to be defined by men. Andrea Dworkin sees the issue this way: "the ways and means of pornography are the ways and means of male power" (24). However a woman feels about pornography, we should not let any part of our sexuality be defined by something that was started for and by men. We should not define our sexuality by something that harms women, both in and out of the industry.

You may agree that pornography is harmful to the future of sexuality and gender ideals for women. You may have the opinion that pornography and the consumers of pornography should be left alone. You may think that the anti-porn feminists are against sex and sexual desire. But you hopefully adhere to the fact that pornography has played a role in perpetuating traditional gender ideals that pervade our culture today. Pornography needs to be reexamined in the context of gender equality. We need to work on a method for seeing a decline in the victimization of women that results from the stagnant interpretation of gender roles in our male dominated world. Pornography may not be the enemy, but the more we continue to ignore it, the longer we will continue to live in the past.

## Works Consulted

Barron, Martin, and Michael Kimmel. "Sexual Violence in Three Pornographic Media: Toward a Sociological Explanation." *Journal of Sex Research* 37.2 (2000): 161–169. EBSCOhost. 3 Aug. 2001 <http://www.lib.umd.edu>.

Britton, Patti O., Jennifer Maguire, and Beth Nathanson. *Feminism and Free Speech: Pornography*, 1999. Feminists for Free Expression. 13 Aug. 2001 <http://www.well.com/user/freedom/porno.html>.

*Bureau of Justice Statistics.* "Female Victims of Violent Crime." 12 Aug. 1998. U.S. Department of Justice. 23 Aug. 2001 <http://www.ojp.usdoj.gov/bjs/abstract/fvvc/fwc.htm>.

"Canada: Supreme Court rules pornography harms women". *Women's International Network News* 18.2 (1992): 51–54. EBSCOhost. 13 Aug. 2001 <http://www.lib.umd.edu>.

Cole, Susan G. *Power Surge: Sex, Violence & Pornography*. Toronto: Second Story Press, 1995.

Diamond, Sara. "Pornography: Image and Reality." *Women Against Censorship*. Ed. Varda Burstyn. Vancouver: Douglas & McIntyre, 1985. 40–57.

Donnerstein, Edward, Daniel Linz, and Steven Penrod. *The Question of Pornography: Research Findings and Policy Implications.* New York: The Free Press, 1987.

Dworkin, Andrea. *Pornography: Men Possessing Women.* New York: F. P. Putnam's Sons, 1981.

Goldstein, Leslie Friedman. *Contemporary Cases in Women's Rights.* Wisconsin: University of Wisconsin Press, 1994.

Jensen, Robert. "Knowing Pornography." *Violence Against Women* 2.1 (1996): 82–102. EBSCOhost. 13 Aug. 2001 <http://www.lib.umd.edu>.

Kaminer, Wendy. "Courting Unsafe Speech." *The American Prospect* 18 July 2001: 31. EBSCOhost. 13 Aug. 2001 <http://www.lib.umd.edu>.

Lau, Leslie. "Don't Just Blame Pornography for Sex Crimes, Women Tell Government." *The Straits Times (Singapore)* 17 July 2001: A6. LEXIS-NEXIS. 13 Aug. 2001 <http://www.lib.umd.edu>.

MacKinnon, Catharine A. *Feminism Unmodified: Discourses on Life and Law.* Massachusetts: Harvard UP, 1987.

MacKinnon, Catharine A., and Andrea Dworkin, eds. *In Harm's Way: The Pornography Civil Rights Hearings.* Massachusetts: Harvard UP, 1997.

Monk-Turner, Elizabeth, and Christine H. Purcell. "Sexual Violence in Pornography: How Prevalent Is It?" *Gender Issues* 17.2 (1999): 58–68. EBSCOhost. 3 Aug. 2001 <http://www.lib.umd.edu>.

Pontifical Council For Social Communications. *Pornography and Violence in the Communications Media: A Pastoral Response.* 7 May 1989. Vatican City. 12 Aug. 2001 <http://www.vatican.va/roman_curia/pontifical_councils/pccs / documents/rc_pc_pccs_doc_07051989_pornography_e.html>.

Queen, Carol. "Pornography and the Sensitive New Age Guy." *Reconstructing Gender: A Multicultural Anthology.* 2nd ed. Pennsylvania: Cleis Press, 1997. 134–148.

Russell, Diana E.H., ed. *Making Violence Sexy: Feminist Views on Pornography.* New York: Teachers College Press, 1993.

Stone, Linda, and Nancy P. McKee. *Gender & Culture in America.* New Jersey: Prentice Hall, 1999.

Strossen, Nadine. Defending Pornography: *Free Speech, Sex, and the Fight for Women's Rights.* New York: Scribner, 1995.

Wood, Julia T. *Gendered Lives: Communication, Gender, and Culture.* 4th ed. California: Wadsworth, 2001.

# MISSILE DEFENSE UNDER A MICROSCOPE: A PLEA FOR PATIENT LEADERSHIP

Chris Wise

*Written in 2001 for an English 101 class, this final position paper by Chris Wise offers the history of U.S. plans for a ballistic missile defense program as part of an argument requesting George W. Bush to delay his administration's plan to implement such a program. This historical background, combined with the essay's use of facts and statistics, enables the author to make a logical appeal to his intended audience. Notice how the logic of the argument is strengthened by the author's deft use of ethos and pathos, as he encourages a hostile reader to reconsider his stance on national defense policy.*

## Audience Analysis

The audience that I have chosen for my paper is President Bush. Since, I oppose an aggressive national missile defense initiative and he is proposing it, the President can be considered a hostile audience. Some of the many values that I will have to work against are his willingness to develop the system, his inherent distrust of foreign nations, and the belief that a strong national defense is made up of armed guards at the border. Basically, I believe that the President is trying to become President Reagan. One of the factors that will heavily influence his position will be popular opinion on the subject. As an elected politician he is interested in getting re-elected. Ego will also play into this because as he decides many of these policy issues so will his mark be left on the history books. I have to make him feel that the American people will hate this system, that they will be worse off, and that history will not be kind to him for this kind of decision. I need to get him to simply slow down.

Dear Mr. President,

I was seven years old the only time I saw my grandfather cry. I was sitting down with him watching a television special about WWII. It was a day I will never forget. That was the day I learned what a prisoner of war was, and the day I learned of what had happened to my grandfather. That was the day I learned what sacrifice and patriotism mean. I learned that if my grandfather can suffer through a POW camp in Nazi Germany, then my responsibility to my country can never wane. I am the "umpteenth" generation of military service members in my family. I, like you, have served in the armed forces. My responsibility cannot stop there, however. Neither can that of the rest of the men and women who serve. Not only our vigilance in defense of this nation is required but also our intelligence and our voice as American citizens. There are clear problems facing this country and the dangers are immense.

Currently you and your administration are deciding what the force structure for this nation is going to look like. The primary focus has been put on a proposed missile defense initiative. I, on behalf of my family and my country, ask you to forego the advanced development of this system. This system if rushed through development will further embolden traditional adversaries, spark a new arms race, harm world opinion of the United States, detract from our current defense and domestic policy agendas, and fail to produce an effective and complete system. Simply, the United States must slow the development of the proposed ballistic missile defense package in order to avoid serious damage to both our foreign policy standing and our domestic security. I understand that you are inundated with advice and recommendations from senior level advisors, but I ask you to please take a minute to listen to my reasons and consider the alternatives.

The missile debate, as you know, began back in the 1960's. With the signing of the 1972 Anti-Ballistic Missile treaty by U.S. President Nixon and Soviet Premier Brezhnev, the United States and the Soviet Union created a system that would ensure the stability of both nuclear arsenals. This treaty limited the amount of interceptor missiles that each of the superpowers was allowed to build and held each nation to one deployment site inside their respective countries. This was accomplished in hopes of curbing the necessity to build more and more nuclear weapons. In the early 1980's President Reagan instituted a policy of research and potential deployment of a ballistic missile defense, calling it the Strategic Defense Initiative. The program, affectionately called Star Wars, was a very costly and ineffective program. The development of this program overshadowed all other peace processes with the Soviet Union. For example, in 1986 when then Soviet Premier Gorbachev offered a 50 percent cut in Soviet and U.S. nuclear arsenals in exchange for limiting SDI research, President Reagan rejected the proposal. The administration's main focus was not to deal at all with the government of the Soviet Union, even as the establishment of communism began to erode in this long-time adversary. This precedent seriously hampered the disarmament process. After President Reagan left office, the programs were limited to protect against forward deployed American forces.

The theater missile defense, TMD, has been the focus of national policy for the last ten years until North Korea was able to fire a three-stage ballistic missile over Japan in 1998. The successful test by north Korea marked a significant turning point in the national debate over missile defense. The strongest debates center around the development of a National Missile Defense (NMD), and the deployment to allies of TMD. Since 1998 the development of a missile defense system has been increased and the demand for deployment by Congress has risen. Currently your administration has decided to support an aggressive development policy by increasing funds to the Ballistic Missile Defense Organization, and to begin deployment as soon as possible. I urge you to slow down the development process and reassess the potential pitfalls of this program.

The proposed Ballistic Missile Defense program will seriously disrupt the United States and help to undermine our goals. The program at this juncture is flawed and needs to be readdressed. The negative impacts of this program are evident through the foreign policy effects of a paradigm shift in defense, the developmental difficulties, the costs, both financial and otherwise, of creating this system, and finally the fact that the threats the United States will face are not solved by this program.

National defense must be more than a fence around the United States, hiding the nation from its neighbors. Defense is a series of relations and treaties in which nations can find a balance of power and establish security with that balance. The fact that the United States is taking a unilateral approach to its dealings with the rest of the world has not been lost on foreign leaders. If the current deployment strategy were to persist, then I fear that the United States' position in world politics would be significantly damaged. While it is true that with an operable missile defense program we would still have the largest GDP and we would have a frighteningly powerful military, the potential for backlash from the other nations is tremendous. Both Russia and China have shown vehement opposition to the development of missile defense. While your visit to Genoa was productive, and I do not doubt your ability to work with President Putin, his public reversal on August 13th has created significant concerns. During Secretary Rumsfeld's trip to Russia this August, President Putin and his government withheld support of any missile defense initiative and rebuffed efforts to amend or abrogate the 1972 ABM treaty: "President Vladimir Putin and other Russian officials rebuffed Defense Secretary Donald H. Rumsfeld's efforts to secure a joint withdrawal from the 1972 Anti-Ballistic Missile Treaty today, telling him that treaty commitments on national missile defense and on reducing strategic nuclear arsenals are 'unconditionally linked'" (Loeb A09). It seems clear that Russia has begun to link disarmament of nuclear weapons under the "START I" and "START II" treaties with America's willingness to abrogate the 1972 ABM treaty. If the United States is to develop an ABM package, it will seriously harm relations with Russia and potentially end the progress that was started by your father. With President Putin's willingness to reverse his stance on cooperation with the United States and threatening former disarmament agreements, the development of this defense system currently would significantly damage the further relations with one of the most powerful and dangerous countries in the world.

While Russia has recently begun a strong campaign against missile defense, the People's Republic of China has long been a fervent adversary to the development of missile defense by the United States. With the current tensions between the United States and China, developing and deploying a system that would further threaten them could lead to another arms race. Whether or not the NMD or even TMD systems would actually counter a Chinese missile strike, the development of an ABM package would be seen as a threat to China. The Monterey Institute of International Studies found in a recent report on Chinese reactions to U.S. policy that "China's concern that current US missile defense programs are designed to entrench US military supremacy and achieve 'absolute security.' Chinese experts and officials bluntly state that NMD is directed against China"(3). If ballistic missile defense development is to continue, then a country as reactionary as the PRC will begin further development and deployment of weapons of mass destruction. "China would likely respond through a combination of increased ICBM deployments, use of penetration aids, and possible use of MRV or MIRV technology" (Monterey 2). China is showing a clear willingness to push the arms race if their strategic or tactical threat is reduced. These foreign implications should not be taken lightly. Unless we want to further exacerbate the weapons buildup dilemma throughout the world, we must focus on different strategies to defend ourselves from missile attack. The current plan, as it is being discussed, will only add to an already distrustful and strained relationship between China and the United States.

Our traditional adversaries and rogue nations are not the only opponents to the development of this system. Traditional partners in strategic defense have been outspoken opponents to this system. Europe has not supported the new foreign policy, and many of its citizens are opposed to ABM development. With the attempts that have been used to reach out to Europe in the past several months, the likelihood of any improvement is slim. In a recent Washington Post article, Keith Richburg reported that "The poll, conducted in association with the New York-based Council on Foreign Relations, found that Britons, French, Italians and Germans overwhelmingly opposed Bush's decisions to withdraw from the Kyoto Protocol on global warming and to develop a national missile defense system that might mean unilaterally abrogating the 1972 Anti-Ballistic Missile Treaty with Russia" (Richburg A1, 7). While I understand the United States is not bound by the whims of Europe, it does not bode well if our traditional counterparts in global defense are willing to abandon us on this issue. Many of the programs that are in development with your administration are in danger without a strong backing internationally. Already European nations have colluded to remove the United States delegation from three key councils at the United Nations, and further development might cause a serious backlash on many controversial topics. With the necessity to create and install a rational counterpart to the Kyoto treaty, and the growing threat of terrorism, the alienation of Europe over an ineffective and costly system would not be wise. Some proponents of missile defense erroneously claim that defense is simply the ability to physically repel attacks from outside aggressors, and ignore the utility of less militaristic tactics. The strategy for security must be worked through international negotiations to combat a wide variety of new challenges and threats. With strong leadership an international partnership could lead to a more prosperous world in which the United States is secure. The new risks of international terrorism and environmental regulation require much more focus, and we will need the rest of the world to assist us in combating these new challenges.

While other threats are raging in the world, an effective national missile defense system will take years to develop, if it is possible to develop it at all. I understand that recent tests have shown marked improvement; however, the system itself will fail to be fully operational for many years. The creation of a defense system is not a process that we should rush. If the goal is to create an effective defense against incoming missiles, then the development process should be careful and methodical to ensure that the system is a practical, credible, and complete deterrent. The challenges of the system' creation, and the countermeasures that will be invoked to avoid this type of system, make this development as difficult as creating the weapons that we are trying to stop. Although the latest test was a success, the U.S. is no closer to having a fully operating system. The test itself used criteria which invalidated the system's interception of the target missile. Theodore A. Postol, an analyst from MIT, said that the system had to be programed with the correct identifying information—information that the enemy would never know. Further he pointed out that at no time was an effective decoy system used (Loeb A05). The fact that the intercept missile was programmed to the exact specifications of its target counters the belief that the missile was actually able to detect its target. The missile cannot shoot down an incoming ballistic missile if it cannot decide which is the missile and which is the decoy. If the discrimination system for the missile's targeting computer does not work, then the entire program fails. The scientists in charge have admitted that money will not solve the problem of development and that the speed with which it is being sought is negatively affecting the process itself. Dr. Jack Gansler, former Under Secretary of Defense, Acquisition, Technology and Logistics, stated "We have always said, and they have said the same thing, that in terms of making the schedule it is a high risk program" (Gansler July 8, 2000). If the system will take time to develop and it is not considered reasonable at this time, then why would we attempt to create the missile defense system at the cost of international security and financial burdens? Philip Coyle, former Director of Operation Test and Evaluation in the Department of Defense has said that the government does not have to abrogate the ABM treaty just yet. He has said that the continual development questions that need to be answered can all be taken care of under the auspices of the treaty (Korb A11). The system cannot be created instantaneously no matter how much money we are willing to spend. If we pursue this system with the same ideologic fervor that we showed in the development of the atomic bomb then we will surely incur an incredible cost. Currently the technology simply needs time to develop so that we are able to ensure the best possible outcome.

While the system is far from being operational, the continuation of current development programs will cause the U.S. to divert its attention from more significant threats and substantially detract from other national programs. Conventional weapon defense and intelligence gathering is suffering. The BMDO's budget for last year was $4.6 billion, and this year it is expected to jump to above $8 billion (BMDO June 7, 2001). In the current debate over funding, military direction, and the shrinking surplus, the willingness to reduce the overall expenditure on a controversial program would help your administration in the long run. Ballistic missile defense has cost a lot of money and will cost substantially more. In a response to the findings of the Rumsfeld commission in 1998, Lisbeth Gronland and David Wright wrote that "estimates have run as high as $100 billion for the first 10 years" (11). Funding for the BMDO is taken directly from the Defense budget, and while BMDO's budget will almost double, the remaining defense budget will probably shrink from last years total (BMDO June 7, 2001). While the final budget analysis has not been completed, the Washington Times on August 22, 2001, speaks to the fact that our economy is producing less money than we expected. With the cutbacks in military spending, the last thing we need is to invest in a program that will not come to fruition until years down the road. Conversely, we could see the payoffs of a much stronger multilateral disarmament process sooner. In an issue brief in 1999, Physicians for Social Responsibility revealed some startling data about missile defense. The Congressional Research Service found that the Pentagon has spent $70.7 billion on missile defense from 1984–1994, without producing a valuable system (PSR). Even more astonishing is the fact that Air Force General Lester Lyles, who leads the missile defense research project, says that more money will not help develop the system any sooner (PSR). No matter how much money we are able to spend on the system the overall speed of development will not be increased. The reality of the situation is that missile defense spending does not have to proceed at such an alarming rate if it means cuts to other programs.

This is going to be a contentious topic during the next year with the elections, and the opposing party already smells blood in the water. Senator Majority Leader Tom Daschle was quoted in The Washington Post as saying that missile defense is "the most expensive possible response to the least likely threat we face" and that it would "cannibalize the personnel and force structure that deal with the threats we are far more likely to face"(Dewer A 01). The development would impact the defense structure and still would not reduce the sizable threat to U.S. security. Overall, the system would detract from an already taxed armed force, hurt the nation's ability to collect intelligence, and create more problems for our nation to deal with.

While the cost of the program to the U.S. is enormous, the threat of any nation attacking the United States with ballistic missiles is highly unlikely. A ballistic missile attack creates a unique situation for an opposing country. If a country were to fire a missile at the United States the traditional U.S. policy would be to respond to that nation with complete and utter nuclear devastation. Continually, the government has assumed that the strategic value placed on nuclear weapons would be utilized carelessly by the leaders of Iran, Iraq, and North Korea. The reality is that all of those leaders must protect a nation so that they can lead, however fanatical and ruthless their tactics are. The greatest mistake they would ever make would be to attempt to attack the United States with an overt weapon, such as a ballistic missile. The fact remains that in a world with such terrorists as Osama Bin Laden, the most likely threat is that of a suitcase bomb or a covert terrorist action, such as the World Trade Center bombing. The threat of a missile attack on the United States is not likely, and the necessity for a pervasive system of missile defense is minute. While I will grant that the National Intelligence Estimate conducted in 1995 was probably too optimistic in its predictions that "rogue nations" would not be able to develop ballistic missiles that could hit the United States for another fifteen years, the likelihood of being attacked by any nation with ballistic missiles is very small (Garwin). The Rumsfeld commission that was convened by Congress in 1998 examined the threats of a potentially accelerated budget priority in nations like Iran, North Korea, and Iraq. The commission did conclude that with a primary focus on development of a ballistic missile threat these nations could implement weapons of mass destruction into their force structure. While that may be true, the fact remains that the Rumsfeld commission never addressed the issue of whether or not these leaders would potentially fire upon the United States. Lisbeth Gronlund and David Wright found in their report on the commission that some of your own advisors find this attack highly unlikely. "The chair of the Joint Chiefs of Staff, Gen Henry Shelton, seconded this view: 'The [Rumsfeld] commission points out that through unconventional, high-risk development programs and foreign assistance, rogue nations could acquire an ICBM capability in a short time, and that the intelligence community may not detect it. We view this as an unlikely development'" (4). The actual risk involved in not developing the system is very small when you compare it to the other risks that the nation currently faces. With the potential cost ranging from a few billion to over $100 billion, the most prudent decision would be to slow down and focus on intelligence and foreign relations. The cost of this program, both financially and politically, would be an enormous price to pay for an unlikely threat.

The United States is at a crossroads. After several years of high economic growth, the bottom has seemingly dropped out. You were right when you declared that the challenges we will face as a nation will be tough. It takes strong leadership and a brave man to face them. The threats that face the United States are not as simple as the media would have us believe. The fact that a ballistic missile could potentially reach the United States in five years may not need to be the top priority. Why countries feel that they need or want missiles may be the primary concern. The missile system that is hastily being built right now at the expense of many other programs will hurt the United States. The system does not work, will not work for a long time, and may not be efficient to spend our resources on. I have shown you that even your own scientists say that throwing money at the problem will not solve the developmental issues that they face. The threats to the United States from weapons of mass destruction will not be solved by the development of this system, however, the need around the world for more missiles and more weapons will be increased. I am not opposed to a missile defense system entirely. The greatest legacies of all times are of those leaders who are resolute and patient. You showed both when you brought home one of my friends, serving on the EP-3 that landed in China. Please show it now. I looked into my grandfather's eyes that day when I was seven and I learned what the cost of war is. I am prepared to give my life and everything I have in defense of this country. I am asking that you do the same, sir.

Respectfully,

Chris Wise

## References

Bowen, Tom. "Missile Defense Test May Conflict with ABM Treaty in '02." *The Baltimore Sun.* 13 July 2001: page 3A.

Butcher, Martin, and Tarek Rizk. "NATO Allies, Russia Snub US on Missile Defense." 29 May 2001. Physicians for Social Responsibility. 11 Aug. 2001. <http://www.psr.org/natorebuke052901.html>.

Charles, Dan. "Strike back at the Empire." Editorial. *New Scientist.* 4 Aug. 2001: 40.

"China's Opposition to U.S. Missile Defense Programs." *CNS Programs: EANP Factsheets.* 22 Apr. 2001. Monterey Institute for International Studies. 22 Apr. 2001. <http://cns.miis.edu/cns/projects/eanp/fact/chinamd.htm>.

Cooper, Henry F. "Cooperative Defense, Collective Security." Editorial. *The San Diego Union-Tribune.* 13 May 2001. Opinion, sec. G: 1.

Dewar, Helen. "Democrats Step Up Foreign Policy Attack." *Washington Post.* 9 Aug. 2001. sec. A: 1.

"The Early Missile Defense Deployment Option: Ft Greely, Alaska in 2004." 23 July 2001. The Council for a Livable World. 09 Aug. 2001. <http://www.clw.org/nmd/fortgreely.html>.

Evans, Graham, and Jeffrey Newham. *The Penguin Dictionary of International Relations.* New York, NY: Penguin Books, 1998.

*FY 2002 President's Budget Summary.* 27 Jun. 2001. Ballistic Missile Defense Organization. 11 Aug. 2001. <http://www.acq.osd.mil/bmdo/bmdolink/html/bmdolink.html>.

*FY 2000 President's Budget Summary.* 4 Feb. 2000. Ballistic Missile Defense Organization. 11 Aug. 2001 <http://www.acq.osd.mil/bmdo/bmdolink/html/bmdolink.html>.

Garwin, Richard. "What we did." *The Bulletin of Atomic Scientists.* November/December 1998; Vol. 54, No. 6 <http://thebulletin.org/issues/1998/nd98/nd98Gronlund.html>.

Gronlund, Lisbeth and David Wright. "What they didn't do." *The Bulletin of Atomic Scientists.* November/December 1998; Vol. 54, No. 6 <http://thebulletin.org/issues/1998/nd98/nd98Garwin.html>.

Henry, Reg. "Face It: Missile Defense Is Coming." Editorial. *Pittsburgh Post-Gazette.* 22 Apr. 2001. sec. E: 1.

*Issue Brief: Ballistic Missile Defense.* 29 May 2001. Physicians for Social Responsibility. 09 Aug. 2001. <http://www.psr.org>.

Kadish, Ronald, Lt Gen. USAF and Dr. Jack Gansler. DoD News Briefing, Washington, D.C., 8 Jul. 2000.

Krannawitter, Thomas, and Brian Kennedy. "America is Worth Defending." Online posting. 23 Jul. 2001. The Claremont Institute. 11 Aug. 2001. <http://www.claremont.org/publications.krannkenn0120723.cfm>

Korb, Lawrence. "Reagan's Good Example on Missile Defense." Editorial. *The Boston Globe.* 13 Aug. 2001. Op-Ed, sec. A: 11.

Loeb, Vernon. "Pentagon Says Missile Killer Hit 'Sweet Spot.'" *Washington Post.* 10 Aug. 2001. sec. A: 5.

Loeb, Vernon. "Russians Resolute on ABM Pact." *Washington Post.* 14 Aug. 2001. sec. A: 09.

Owens, Mackubin Thomas. "Defense for an Uncertain World." *The Baltimore Sun.* 20 May 2001 final ed., sec. Perspective: 1C.

Richburg, Keith. "Europeans Object to Bush Approach on Foreign Policy." *Washington Post.* 16 Aug. 2001. Page A17.

Rumsfeld, Donald. Munich Conference on European Security Policy, Munich. 3 Feb. 2001.

Tenet, George J. "Worldwide Threat 2001: National Security in a Changing World." Senate Select Committee on Intelligence, Washington, D.C., 07 Feb. 2001.

Tenet George J. "Worldwide Threat 2000: Global Realities of Our National Security." Senate Select Committee on Intelligence, Washington, D.C., 21 Mar. 2000.

# RHETORICAL ANALYSIS OF TWO PERSUASIVE ARGUMENTS

Wendy Chou

## *Audience Analysis*

Robert Dole's "Nightmares of Depravity" is a 1995 speech delivered live in Los angeles, during the presidential election campaign (106). As Dole was the candidate for the Republican party, we can infer that his target audience is the older American citizens who constitute the majority of the Republican voting population. As mature Republicans, we know that they are most likely to be married with families and children. This, plus the fact that Republicans are pro-family, suggests that the audience will expect a presidential candidate to address what can be done for their families and to further improve the development of the society as a whole. Besides these potential voters, Dole's overhearers include the entertainment industry in Hollywood, who may feel that he is posing a threat to their lucrative business and freedom of speech. Unlike Dole's audience, Jeff Jacoby's main audience is the younger generation of adults who read the *Boston Globe* where his article, "A Desensitized Society Drenched in Sleaze," originally appeared. As young adults, their attitudes toward sex and violence are likely to be less judgmental than Dole's audience.

From the titles of Bob Dole's speech, "Nightmares of Depravity," and Jeff Jacoby's article, "A Desensitized Society Drenched in Sleaze," it is evident that they are both advocating the same argument that too much sex and violence in the media can cause serious long term damage to the moral standards of the society and its children. Addressing potential voters in Los Angeles, California, Dole wants to expose the negative influences that the profit-driven entertainment industry has on America's children, and urge the big corporations in Hollywood to take responsibility for their actions. Likewise, Jacoby blames the media for the desensitization of the American society, which results in the numbing of our sense of morality and decency. Despite their similar objectives, Dole and Jacoby direct their argument towards different audiences. Dole is clearly trying to get through to an older audience while Jacoby is focusing his argument on a younger generation of adults. Thus, they have to use different rhetorical skills and rely on different appeal methods to persuade their respective audiences. In the following rhetorical analysis, I will identify and compare their use of ethos, pathos and logos, including the four common topics, to determine the effectiveness of Dole and Jacoby's arguments for their respective audiences.

Dole has already established an air of authority and respect: not only has he run for the presidency in the past, he is also a former Republican Majority Leader and U. S. Senator for Kansas. Making use of his extrinsic ethos, Dole starts out his speech in a very assertive manner, commanding the attention of everyone present at his speech. His first words are, "I want to talk about . . ." and he repeats this in the third sentence, "I want to talk to you . . ." (106) to emphasize the urgency of the matter at hand. Once Dole has caught the attention of his audience, he shows his good intentions and sincerity to establish his intrinsic ethos and credibility with his audience. In order to achieve this, Dole says that he is concerned about the "future of America," and he wants to talk about "issues of moral importance, matters of social consequence" (106). Knowing that his audience is mainly parents, he constantly refers to American youths as "our children," saying that he wants leaders of the entertainment industry to "think about the influence they have on America's children" (106), thus letting his audience know that he is also interested in the welfare of their children.

Both Dole and Jacoby demonstrate fair-mindedness and logical thinking to their audiences by proclaiming that Hollywood is not entirely to blame for society's behaviors (107; 112). Asserting that violent movies and music do not automatically turn people into criminals but numb their morality and cloud their ethical judgments, these concessions serve as clear evidence that Dole and Jacoby possess sound reasoning and clear minds. In this way, both further establish their intrinsic ethos.

Unlike Dole, however, Jacoby does not have a particularly strong extrinsic ethos. Being a columnist for a newspaper, his credibility can only be established by his writing. Thus, Jacoby must offer a quick but accurate portrayal of his personality and background. He therefore cleverly begins his article with a recount of his personal, real-life experience: a regretful depiction of his encounter with pornography when he was seventeen. Based upon the shame and guilt he felt, his readers are now better convinced of his claims to a "parochial-school education," and "strict upbringing" (111). With his intrinsic ethos firmly established, Jacoby proceeds to work on his audience's emotions.

"Guilty," "dirty," "conscience-stricken," "ashamed," (111): these words all appeal strongly to our sense of morality and decency. Jacoby's use of such language is dramatic, his choice of words is forceful, and they combine to create pathos. With the audience's emotions all fired up, Jacoby easily manipulates his own unpleasant experience, and turns it into a case of victimization of the American public by the morally irresponsible entertainment industry. His emphasis on the fact that "I've become jaded" (111) and "nothing makes us blush" (112) anymore is clearly a means of eliciting anger out of his audience: anger towards Hollywood and big corporations alike, who have robbed the society of their innocence and virtue. In his article, he asks several rhetorical questions such as, "Was *this* the forbidden delight hinted at by those ads?" and "who *wouldn't* recoil from *Cry for Cindy* or feel repelled?" (111). By "asking" these questions, he is actually *telling* his readers that they should feel repelled by such things, and that glamorized sex and violence are far from being delightful. However, Jacoby's pathetic appeal to our guilty conscience may appear to be too emotional; he does not consider how his young readers may not actually regard sex and violence in the media as critically as he does. In fact, they may even think that it *is* a form of art and self-expression.

Dole, on the other hand, takes a rather different approach to establishing pathos. Making a public enemy out of the entertainment industry, Dole appeals to his audience's self-interests by saying "we must hold Hollywood and the entire entertainment industry accountable . . . [so that they will not] profit from our weaknesses . . . [and] play on our fears of life's dark corners" (106). On top of this, Dole also skillfully creates a sense of shared identity between himself and his audience, frequently using words like "we," "us," "our" to foster a sense of shared values and common goals. Again making use of the fact that a majority of his audience are parents, he takes special care in cultivating a common bond between himself and America's parents, assuring them that he is on their side. His sympathy for the parents is implied in many instances. For example, he says ". . . parents are growing afraid, and growing angry. There once was a time when parents felt the community of adults was on their side. Now they feel surrounded by forces assaulting their children and their code of values" (108). Judging from the numerous occasions that Dole adeptly establishes a shared identity with his audience and appeals to their self-interest, it appears that the primary appeal for his speech is pathos, an appeal that works perfectly on his audience.

Dole's speech, however, is not short on logical appeal and he manages to convince his audiences with greater ease than Jacoby. This is because Dole has established his ethos throughout the speech. Therefore, when Dole suggests a definition, such as submissiveness "is not tolerance but surrender," or when he makes a contrasting analogy between "the description of evil through art" and "the marketing of evil through commerce" (107), his audience is ready to believe his words. Knowing that a persuasive argument also requires outside testimony and authority to give his claims validity and truth, Dole quotes box office statistics, proving to his audience that the top five grossing films of the previous year were family-oriented movies (108). With this, he straightforwardly strikes down the defense of his overhearers, the entertainment industry, who claim "[they] are simply responding to the market" (107). But it is Dole's use of cause and consequence that is his most ingenious use of a common topic. If the industry doesn't make more 'PG'-rated films, Dole quotes Mark Canton, a film executive, as saying, "this decade will be noted in the history books as the embarrassing legacy of what began as a great art form [and] 'the decline of an empire'" (108). This is a particularly effective tactic because throughout his speech, Dole has taken special care in praising the American people, making them "feel proud" (107) of their country's achievements. With this patriotism instilled into his audience, how could they, as Americans, possibly allow their glorious days to be reduced to an "embarrassing legacy"?

Jacoby also provides his audience with logical appeals in the later half of his article, using the four common topics to back up his main claim. Jacoby uses the barbaric and crude lyrics of the Geto Boy's rap songs, and film director Clive Barker's selfish response to criticisms of the entertainment industry (112) as testimonies to vividly illustrate to us the horrifying outcome of a society that doesn't "blush." These testimonies also serve as cause and consequence arguments, such as when he asks his audience the rhetorical question "what happens to an unblushing society?" (112). The consequences he offers are the extreme cases of vicious real-life crimes such as when "sixth graders sleep around" and "boys blow off their parents' heads" (112). In addition, Jacoby also makes an argument of definition, noting that "debauchery is not art." Finally, he draws an analogy between Snoop Doggy Dogg's rap and "Sophocles's tragic drama, Chaucer's romantic poetry, or Solzhenitsyn's moral testimony" to show their dissimilarities (112). With these logical appeals in place, his argument becomes more substantial and objective.

All in all, Dole makes a better-rounded argument than Jacoby because Dole considers his audience, while Jacoby fails to show clear awareness of his. Attempting to win his audience over with only a one-sided argument that is based mostly on pathos,

Jacoby neglected the fact that his audience is mostly younger adults and they may not have the same moral principles that Dole's elder, Republican audience has. In contrast, Dole's eloquent speech and his use of pathos as his primary appeal worked perfectly because he has a clear sense of his audience; he appeals to their patriotism and love for the family as the primary values of a Republican voter. In addition, Dole also fully refutes any arguments that his overhearers may have, thus increasing his persuasiveness and credibility significantly. This, together with Dole's strong ethos, expertly wins his audience's support.

## Works Cited

Dole, Robert. "Nightmares of Depravity." *Perspectives*. College Park: Pearson Custom Publishing, 1999. 106–108.

Jacoby, Jeff. "A Desensitized Society Drenched in Sleaze." *Perspectives*. College Park: Pearson Custom Publishing, 1999. 111–112.

*The final essays in this chapter show the value of analyzing one's own writing. Jawad Muaddi, an English 101 student, gives a self-reflective analysis of his own Pro/Pro papers, which many of you will write later in the semester and is included here. What is noteworthy about the rhetorical analysis is the way the student assumes the persona of the editor of a real magazine,* The Economist. *In the guise of this persona, Muaddi is able to distance himself from his own writing and critically analyzes both the essays in terms of their rhetorical effectiveness. Noting both the strengths and weaknesses of both papers, Muaddi's analysis suggests that if he were to revise his work, he has a good idea of how to improve his already strong arguments.*

# A QUESTION THAT WE ALL MUST ANSWER

Jawad Muaddi

## *Audience Analysis*

The audience members for my paper are subscribers to *The Economist*. This group of informed followers of foreign affairs has read numerous articles about the UN, especially in recent months due to the extensive coverage of the Kosovo and East Timor crises.

For this paper, I shall adapt the persona of Dr. Mawad Juaddi, Professor of International Law at Princeton University. This will allow me to author two opposing, persuasive arguments to the same audience.

If we are to learn anything from the tragedies of this decade, then our chief concern as we enter the next millennium must be to secure and ensure human rights. The inhumane acts in Kosovo and East Timor have exposed a weakness in the international system, and these problems will continue unless world leaders reform the UN charter in three ways to allow intervention when necessary, even if such intervention violates state sovereignty. Kofi Annan, the first UN Secretary General to recognize these weaknesses, has shocked traditionalists who believe the thread of state sovereignty must remain intact. His idea to reform the UN has met with a tide of resistance, and he needs worldwide support to achieve his goals. Although most nations can control and contain hostile activities within their borders, other nations simply are unable, or unwilling, to maintain order.

Recent tragedies obviously illustrate a dire need for a change in the UN's attitudes toward resolving crisises. The most glaring example, the well publicized ethnic cleansing, of the Kosovars by the Serbians, resulted in a storm of criticism raining down on the UN for failing to intervene in this conflict. Of course the Security Council members and world leaders noticed both this horrific atrocity and the UN's inability to handle it. Even the US-centric George W. Bush might have read about Serbia's crimes against its own people. However, the almost helpless UN could not intervene because sovereign Serbia, as a member nation of the General Assembly, has the protection of the interventional shield when internal problems occur. In his *Washington Post* editorial, Jim Hoagland asserts that Serbia used this shield to, "[etch] in blood its sovereign right to kill as many of its own masses as it sees fit"(Hoagland A33).

In the future, the UN must not allow sovereign nations like Serbia to mask atrocities within their borders. In an interview with Hoagland, Annan states one of the best arguments for this necessary change when he says that, "Today what is internal doesn't remain internal for very long"(Hoagland A33). A similar, though less severe, example of the sovereignty problem occurred in East Timor, where the UN needed special permission from Indonesia to intervene. The delay allowed barbaric militias to murder and rape thousands of East Timorese citizens, in addition to annihilating their villages, which forced the survivors to flee to the mountains. Fortunately, these victims have started to return to their homes, or rather the land where their homes once stood. Nevertheless, the, victims of this tragedy would have suffered less had the UN acted more quickly.

In the debate over state sovereignty, all agree that the UN charter respects the independence of member nations. Also, nobody debates that the founders of the UN made this rule to end the international conflicts of WWII. For over fifty years, nobody questioned the sovereignty clause. In his address to the UN General Assembly, Annan opened the door to change when he said aggressive "intervention to protect citizens from wholesale slaughter is an evolution we should welcome"(Ford 1). The time has come for the international community to reconsider this principle because the world greatly differs from the WWII era.

While the problems 55 years ago resulted from conflicts between nations, the problems of our era result from conflicts within nations. Critics who fear that world leaders will eliminate a great international tool must realize that sovereignty has served its purpose in the last 55 years, but the time has come to envision a new UN that can keep pace with all the changes in the world. Other critics label aggressive intervention as human rights imperialism. Bernard Kouchner, the UN governor in Kosovo and recipient of the Nobel Peace Prize, strongly refuted such views when he said, "Everywhere, human rights are human rights. Freedom is freedom. Suffering is suffering. Oppression is oppression"(Kouchner 7). Indeed, Kouchner's simple statement makes sense in this time of senseless UN diplomacy.

If the founders of the UN could evaluate the world today, they would certainly admit that sovereignty fails to resolve our problems. In fact, they would agree that sovereignty has prevented the UN from achieving its goals in the 1990's. The new millennium is nearly here, and the greatest moral question of our time has yet to be answered. Should the UN intervene at the cost of state sovereignty, the tool that ended the downward spiral of WWII? To end the downward spiral of today, the world must answer yes.

# THE MORAL DILEMMA OF THE 21ST CENTURY

Jawad Muaddi

## *Audience Analysis*

The audience members for my paper are subscribers to *The Economist*. This group of informed followers of foreign affairs has read numerous articles about the UN, especially in recent months due to extensive coverage of the Kosovo and East Timor crises.

Inhumane atrocities have marred many of the great accomplishments of this century, and if UN Secretary General Kofi Annan has his way, we will witness the worst tragedies in next hundred years. Annan wants to take one step forward in the direction of anarchy by calling for the UN to possess the power to intervene in the affairs of any nation. Indeed, Annan has the best intentions of the international community at heart, but he lacks the vision to achieve his goal of a world without genocide and ethnic cleansing.

Unfortunately, Annan has a firm grip on the steering wheel of UN diplomacy, and his maneuvers influence his passengers, the world's leaders and their nations. He has gained tremendous support, but one must question the timeliness of his outcry for a new world order. Because it follows on the heels of Kosovo and East Timor, most interested people believe that aggressive intervention would have prevented these conflicts. The international community must learn from its mistakes, but people must also realize that all situations differ. Simply put, what may have prevented the mass murder and rape in East Timor will not prevent a future conflict in Africa. Edmund Burke best summed up this common diplomatic pitfall when he said "You can never plan the future by the past"(Berman 191). The world now faces a fork on the road to Utopia. William Abitbol and Paul Marie Couteaux, members of the European Parliament, best described the dilemma as, "sovereignty or barbarism: this is the choice now facing us"(Abitbol). To end worldwide atrocities, we must make the proper choice and bear to the right. The concept of state sovereignty, the thread that has kept all nations together, must not be cut.

The most important reason for upholding state sovereignty can be found in the UN charter, which clearly states. "nothing . . . shall authorize the United Nations to intervene in matters which are essentially within the domestic jurisdiction of any state"(1:2:7). The organization was partly founded on sovereignty because of the disaster known as World War II. A UN violation of state sovereignty would be as disastrous as the US government violating the Constitution; such a scenario simply cannot happen, therefore Kofi Annan must work with world leaders to find other ways to remedy the exposed UN problems of the 1990's.

At least it can be agreed that meeting the best interests of the international community is the primary goal of the UN. Unfortunately, no governing body has mastered the art of perfect diplomacy, and we have no reason to hope that a more interventional UN will always make proper decisions. Perhaps Kofi Annan unjustly assumes that a direct relationship exists between more funding and more successful missions. Many critics, such as Uri Ra'anen, director of Boston University's Institute for the Study of Conflict, Ideology, and Policy, assert that the success of a peacekeeping mission hinges on the implementation of the plan rather than the funding. He stresses the need for a "clear, coherent, and sensible system" to stop tragedies(Ford 1).

Furthermore, because more power carries more responsibility, the international microscope would focus on every facet of the UN, and the international community will expect the UN to halt inhumane acts. Imagine if the almighty UN entered a crisis and the campaign miserably failed. It would not be long before member nations took matters into their own hands as NATO did in Kosovo, which would lead to the rapid demise of the UN. For member nations, especially the US, the small humanitarian victory of such peacekeeping missions would not outweigh the economic burden on their economies. By overriding state sovereignty, the UN would place massive expectations on its leaders. With such high standards, the organization could crumble when faced with a diplomatic failure.

Instead of playing a more authoritative and powerful role in the world's affairs, the UN should try to succeed in its current role, the protection of human rights. Although difficult for Annan to admit, perhaps the UN can only go as far as placing a humanitarian band-aid on wounds brought about by crises. Rather than taking on a greater responsibility, the UN should work with regional defense organizations like NATO, groups that act as mini-sovereigns, with a focus on a specific area of the world. This effective strategy could work because these organizations have a greater stake in the problems of their respective regions, more so than a general world body.

The much larger and complex world of today greatly differs from the world in 1948, and of course, changes must happen. Such reform absolutely does not imply the assumption of greater responsibility by the UN through the elimination of the sovereign principle. Perhaps Algerian President Abdelaziz Boutefika best described the importance of sovereignty when he called it "our best protection from the rules of an unjust world"(Ford 1). World leaders cannot ignore this message, especially considering that President Boutefika spoke on behalf of the Organization for African Unity.

There may or may not exist alternative strategies for the UN to carry out its mission effectively, but the fact remains that one organization cannot blanket our large world. The true role of the UN, though valuable and important, has been rendered imperceptible and elusive by the recent outcry for more aggressive intervention. Despite this dense fog of ambiguity, one issue clearly stands out: the UN cannot and should not violate state sovereignty.

# COMPARISON OF TWO PERSUASIVE ARGUMENTS

Jawad Muaddi

As the editor of *The Economist*, I receive many articles from writers who hope to be published in my scholarly journal. Often, when I receive multiple essays about the same topic, I have to make a tough choice between them. Luckily, I have a very useful tool, an editor's checklist, to make such painstaking decisions less difficult. With this guide, I will analyze two articles and choose the most suitable for publication in my journal. The first essay, written by Professor Mawad Juaddi of Princeton University, calls for the United Nations to aggressively intervene in future crises at the cost of state sovereignty. The second, submitted by Jawad Muaddi, a student at the University of Maryland, argues from an opposing perspective. He asserts that the UN must find other ways to solve their problems. My editor's checklist requires me to compare these essays in technical areas, such as mechanics and grammar, as well as style, organization, and audience interaction.

Obviously, the audience members for both papers read *The Economist*, but, in particular, the essays target individuals with extensive background knowledge, such as subscribers to my journal. Both Juaddi and Muaddi use the educated and elevated language that my subscribers expect in an essay.

Unfortunately, I do not know much about Muaddi, but I can say that Juaddi, as a Professor of International Law, brings extrinsic ethos to his work. Any reader would have to acknowledge and respect his advanced knowledge of foreign policy. However, in general I only have one criticism of Juaddi's essay. I expect very advanced vocabulary from a university professor, but his vocabulary seems to belong to an intelligent college student. Some of my keenest readers may see a discrepancy between the vocabulary used in the essay and Juaddi's knowledge.

Although both introductory paragraphs catch my attention in terms of style, the college student beats the professor with a better opening. Juaddi's ten-line opening needs a final sentence to firmly stand behind Kofi Annan. At first, it seems as if the paragraph needs to be shortened, but after further analysis, I have determined that the length is adequate because Juaddi has much to say. Muaddi's beautiful six-line, three-sentence introduction states his view in addition to a brief rebuttal of the opposition's side. However, the professor strikes back with a fantastic closing, one that the overachieving college student cannot equal. His final metaphor, the "downward spiral" of the world, makes perfect sense and Juaddi poses a question to his audience that he answers. This strategy makes the audience work less and respond more. Muaddi's closing, although well done, does not compare to Juaddi's. His "dense fog of ambiguity" metaphor applies to the situation, but his final phrase merely restates his thesis. Such a standard textbook closing lacks the polish of Juaddi's conclusion.

Both essays lack clarity in some respects. In particular, Juaddi unintentionally loses the audience at some points because he possesses such superior knowledge of the subject. Had he thought more about his audience's knowledge, his arguments would make more sense. Muaddi's paper has similar clarity issues. For example, in the paragraph where he asserts that the UN may crumble under a great responsibility, Muaddi makes the argument briefly. He could have explained the reasons behind this prediction, for such deep subject matter deserves more detail. Although Muaddi may fully understand his arguments, the readers may not. Both authors effectively use figures of speech, especially metaphors. Juaddi's best metaphors, the interventional shield and the downward spiral, exemplify his great usage of figures of speech. Muaddi's best metaphors, the thread of state sovereignty and the humanitarian band-aid, demonstrate his creative flair. Although both papers have relatively fluid styles, they do not flow equally smoothly. Both authors present their arguments systematically, but the professor does a better job of transition between paragraphs. On the other hand, Muaddi jumps from one argument to another. For example, at the top of page two, he ends a paragraph by stating that the UN should find other ways to solve their problems. He starts the next paragraph laying the foundation for his next argument. As an editor, I can sense his direction, but this lack of clarity would temporarily confuse most readers. At the beginning of this paragraph he needs one sentence that briefly describes the main argument of the paragraph. Then he should lay the foundation for the argument. Muaddi probably never tried to rearrange the order of his arguments in the outline, and had he experimented the paper would have better transitions. Both papers contain no vague pronouns and neither paper uses passive voice.

Mechanically, both papers contain few grammatical errors. Muaddi and Juaddi have all the i's dotted and the t's crossed. However, both authors erred in the citation of quotations. In every instance, they failed to leave a space between the closing quotation mark and the parenthetical citation. They may have thought this mistake would go unnoticed, but my eyes, sharp as a hawk after thirty years of editing experience, hardly miss an error. Furthermore, the professor makes another mistake when he seems to drop a quote on page two. He quotes Annan, who says we should welcome aggressive intervention. Then, he states a similar idea without letting the reader know that the author took the microphone. He should have started the sentence with "I agree" or a similar phrase for better transition.

Now for the most important part of my editor's checklist: the quality of the argument. First, I will state that Juaddi has a much easier argument to make. He can use numerous examples of recent tragedies where the UN failed to stop genocide and ethnic cleansing, but he cites Kosovo and East Timor because these recent situations stand out in the readers' minds. This strategy allows Juaddi to appeal to pathos, the most effective rhetorical appeal, to create. Despite a great effort, Muaddi's essay does not appeal to pathos nearly as much as Juaddi's. Muaddi resorts to making predictions and stating facts, such as the article in the UN charter that respects state sovereignty. He relies on witnesses and he makes logical statements throughout the paper while sticking with his thesis. However, his essay does not construct solid arguments like Juaddi's paper. Both writers clearly argue in the stasis of evaluation. They agree with their audience in the fact stasis because the UN charter respects sovereignty. The cause stems from the international conflicts of WWII. Thus, the authors evaluate the article that protects sovereignty, and they try to persuade the audience to evaluate the article as they do.

Finally, the big question, which sums up all the others, lies at the end of my helpful editor's checklist: which paper would persuade my readers more effectively? The answer is Juaddi's. His essay, although a bit disappointing for the vocabulary level of a college professor, contains more fluid transitions and more effective quotations. He makes a stronger argument while using 157 fewer words. Despite a solid effort and an above-average writing style, Muaddi simply cannot equal the professor's superior talent for argumentation.

Therefore, after serious deliberation, I will publish Professor Juaddi's article in the next issue of The *Economist.* However, I believe that Muaddi has raw talent, and I want an article written by him to appear in a future issue. Therefore, I will return his paper and ask him to both build upon his argument and expand his thesis.